MANAGING YOUR MIND

MANAGE YOUR MIND

The Mental Fitness Guide

Gillian Butler, Ph.D.
Tony Hope, M.D.

New York   Oxford
OXFORD UNIVERSITY PRESS

Oxford University Press, Walton Street, Oxford OX2 6DP

Oxford   New York
Athens   Auckland   Bangkok   Bombay
Calcutta   Cape Town   Dar es Salaam   Delhi
Florence   Hong Kong   Istanbul   Karachi
Kuala Lumpur   Madras   Madrid   Melbourne
Mexico City   Nairobi   Paris   Singapore
Taipei   Tokyo   Toronto
and associated companies in
Berlin   Ibadan

Oxford is a trade mark of Oxford University Press

Published in the United States
by Oxford University Press, Inc., New York

A catalogue record for this book is available from the British Library

Library of Congress Cataloging in Publication Data
(Data available)
ISBN 0 19 262383 4

Printed in the United States of America

Preface

This book is a guide to help you in both your personal and your work life. It will show you how, through managing your mind, you can develop the relationships you want, enjoy your leisure, be more effective in your work, and deal with your moods. It is a keep-fit guide to the mind.

One of the false dichotomies of modern life is that between work and personal time. It is widely held that there is a set of skills that we need for the one and a quite different set that we need for the other. But this is not true. The skills of problem solving, for example, are of great value in our personal lives, and overcoming stress and anxiety is a key skill in our work. Being fair to yourself, and to others, helps both personal and work relationships. Low mood is a major cause of unhappiness and also reduces effectiveness at work.

In this book we show how you can make use of effective strategies, for example, giving yourself rewards (Chapter 7), or using the methods of cognitive therapy (Chapter 9), and simple techniques, for example, the salami rule (p. 348), to improve the management of your life.

It is impossible to acknowledge all the sources and influences that have contributed to the writing of this book. First and foremost is our experience in helping people with difficulties in their lives. Then there are our teachers and colleagues, from whom we have learned techniques and refined our use of them. We have also been helped by the writers of other books, many of which we have referenced in the section on further reading. It is the fact that we have found books so helpful, both for ourselves and for helping others, that gave us the impetus to write this book.

We thank the many colleagues who helped us develop our own methods and thoughts, including Julie Chalmers, Nigel Eastman, Chris Fairburn, Melanie Fennell, Maria Gilbert, Helen Kennerley, Joan Kirk, Catherine Oppenheimer, John Sadler, and Alan Stein and the members of the Oxford Adult Mental Health Department of Clinical Psychology.

We thank our agent, Caroline Dawnay at Peters Fraser and Dunlop, and Joan Bossert and the staff at both the New York and Oxford offices of Oxford University Press, not only for their hard work and skills in the production of the book but also for their support and encouragement throughout the process of its writing. Donna Dawson and Julie Hurn gave extremely useful feedback on the entire book. Kathleen Mooney not only gave detailed advice on the first draft but also invaluable help on the provision of further reading. We are most grateful to them both. We would also like to thank Marie-Anne Martin for her witty and imaginative index and Sandra Cooper for her accurate and speedy word processing.

The feedback on individual chapters has been most important. We would particularly like to mention Josephine Butler, Sophie Butler, Kathy Gedling, Chris Lake, Sheena Meredith, Ingrid Skeels, Rachel Turner, and Anne Yates.

Without the continual support and encouragement of our families, and in particular from Christopher Butler and Sally Hope, we could never have written this book.

This guide is intended to be practical. We hope that it achieves its aim of making available to the reader a wide variety of strategies and techniques for managing the mind.

Oxford, England G. B.
April 1995 T. H.

Contents

Introduction

1

◆ ◆ ◆

What to Expect from this Guide

"The past is a foreign country, they do things differently there."[1] The future, too, can be a different country. This book is both an invitation and a guide. It is an invitation to you to enjoy your life to the full, and it is a guide for achieving such enjoyment. It is based on our accumulated thirty years' experience of helping people through times of difficulty, and it is based on modern scientific research.

You can expect to find, in this guide, practical ways of improving many aspects of your life: your life as it affects your relationships, your mood, your health, and your work. These practical ways have been developed both through helping people with the stresses and strains of life and through helping to increase the effectiveness of managers we have worked with.

You can expect to find many ideas on how to improve your life by developing skills, understanding, and strategies to suit your circumstances and inclinations. Using this guide will help you to use your mind to its fullest potential: to improve your psychological fitness. Specific ideas are presented in a step-by-step manner. Psychological skills, skills of the mind, just like physical skills, are usually best learned by adopting a clear step-by-step approach. You would expect a keep-fit book to give some precise guidelines about specific exercises. You would expect a cookbook to give precise recipes so that you know what you should be doing at each stage. This book is intended to be used in just the same way to make practical improvements in your day-to-day life.

Psychology and Management: The Two Bookshelves

Look around your local bookstore. On one shelf there are books on psychology—for example, "How to treat your anxiety." On another there are books on management skills—for example, "Effective time management." These two types of book seem to inhabit different worlds. The first is the world of your personal life, your feelings, and your home. The second is the world of work: the world of action and the office. We believe that these two worlds are not so different and that we need to integrate feelings and action, work and play. The skills and attitudes which help you to be more effective in your work also help you to find fulfillment in your personal life. The attitudes and skills which help in personal life are relevant to improving your effectiveness in your work.

It is time that we gave up the habits which separate feelings and action, home and work. They originate in old-fashioned and unhelpful stereotypes. It is time for the techniques of psychology and of management to be integrated so that we can develop our own strategies for personal growth. One purpose of this book is to bring about such an integration.

A Keep-Fit Guide to the Mind

The relationship of physical fitness to health is now well known. Simple measures can improve physical health: for example, exercise and sensible diet. We no longer think about physical health only when we are ill; but do things regularly, as a matter of course, which will help us to keep fit and well. Such a keep-fit approach is also relevant to the mind. There are specific ways of improving mental as well as physical health, of stretching and strengthening the mind as well as the body, which will enable us to lead a fulfilling life and help to prevent us from becoming overwhelmed by the stresses and strains which none of us can entirely avoid. A second purpose, therefore, of this book is to provide you with specific methods and techniques needed for keeping the whole person, not just the body, in good working order.

The Inner Game of Life

In recent years there has been much interest in the idea of "inner games" of various sports: tennis, for example. The idea behind the concept of the "inner game" is that how one plays a sport depends on the mind as much as on the body. Indeed, it is first and foremost the mind that is important. For the mind is the seat of motivation: it determines how well and usefully and frequently we practice, and it determines whether we want to do it, and whether we enjoy playing the game. It is also the mind that determines whether, like true champions, we rise to the challenge at key moments, or let ourselves down on the points that really matter. In short, even with physical activities, inner factors—mental factors—are of critical importance

This book could be called the *inner game of life*. Whether you are concerned about managing your work or your personal life or your leisure, success and satisfaction will depend on your inner thoughts. Your inner thoughts will help to determine your outer life (just as the inner game of tennis determines how much and how well you practice); and your inner life will affect how you react to your experiences (just as the inner game determines whether you enjoy the tennis).

This book will help you with this "inner game" so that you can increase both enjoyment in life and success—however *you* would like to measure success. And this last point is important. This book is not designed to impose our way of living on you. How you want to live is up to you. What we want to show you is how you can develop your inner skills so that you can live life in the way that you wish.

Our Clinical Experience

The scientific assessment and development of ways of helping people have been of enormous importance both in our own work as therapists and researchers, and in selecting the techniques for this guide. But science does not have all the answers, and this book is the result of our extensive clinical experience. We believe that techniques and ideas that are useful come from a range of sources, as we have outlined in the next chapter on the *scientific background of the techniques presented here*. In our own work we make use of and synthesize this range in order to help each particular person as best we can.

In writing this book we have drawn extensively on our own experience. This experience has guided us in the choice of techniques, and we have tried to explain these using the methods that our clients have found helpful. We have thought for a long time that many of these techniques and ideas would be useful to everyone, because they can help in the process of keeping mentally fit; knowing about them will make it easier to take action quickly when you need to. Delay may perpetuate or worsen all sorts of difficulties. Another purpose of this book is, therefore, to make available to all the ideas and techniques which have been helpful to many, many others.

How to Use This Guide

This book is a practical guide to keeping fit—in your mind as opposed to your body. Its purpose is to help you to enjoy your life to the fullest. For most of us, joy in life is at times diminished by too much worry, by periods of depression, or by other disturbing moods. The demands of modern life keep up a pressure which constantly threatens our psychological well-being. Keeping psychologically fit will help you to withstand these demands and will give you the flexibility and stamina to make the most of yourself.

This book is a guide for you to use in whatever ways you find most helpful. We recommend that you read Parts 1 and 2 first. Select from Parts 3, 4, 5, and 6 as appropriate, reading them all if this is the way you like to read or browsing through them if you prefer.

- *Part 1* explains the two principles on which our ideas are based.
- *Part 2* describes, in practical terms, the seven basic strategies, or skills, that will enable you to take positive control of your life.
- *Part 3* focuses on three keys to help you develop fulfilling relationships.
- *Part 4* provides specific and practical guidance about ways of overcoming anxiety and depression: the two big killers of pleasure and confidence.
- *Part 5* gives guidelines on looking after those aspects of the body that most closely relate to the mind.
- *Part 6* is concerned with skills that will help you to develop your full potential in an effective and creative way.

This guide is to be kept close at hand. To benefit most, you will want to refer to it again and again. Changes take time and persistence. At first, you will easily revert to old habits: to old ways of thinking, feeling, and behaving. As this happens, re-read the relevant passages. Bear the following three points in mind:

1. Think of this book as a buffet table, and select those dishes which attract you. We present many ideas—those which we have found are helpful to the people we have worked with. Not all ideas are helpful for everyone. Pick and choose those which are relevant to you.

2. Learn the techniques which we describe so that you can apply them to your particular situation. Throughout the book we provide stories based on real people in order to show how the ideas presented can be used in real and specific situations. In some of these examples you will recognize a part of yourself; others will seem quite foreign to you. If the example does not seem to fit, do not dismiss the general method. For instance, in Chapter 8 we describe the technique of problem-solving using a specific example. The particular solutions this person used may not work for you; but it is the technique of problem-solving which is important and which you should think about using to solve your problems.

3. Do not dismiss ideas because they seem like common sense. Good psychology, once you know it, often seems like common sense, but it rarely seemed that way before you knew it. Common sense involves too many contradictions always to be right. Besides, in moments of uncertainty, when doubts set in, in the heat of the moment or in the depths of despair, most of us lose sight of common sense. It often deserts us in the hour of need. The ideas and techniques presented in this book have been chosen because they are helpful and effective when put to use. One value of this book is that it can nudge you into applying a technique you already know about but are not making proper use of. You may "know" the "Distant Elephants rule" (p. 41). It may be common sense, or you may have learned it before, perhaps in a management course. But you may not be using it. You may still be saying "yes" to things because they are so far in the future that you fail to work out just how large a commitment they will be. Think of this as a workbook that will help you to learn new techniques, and to apply techniques you already know but do not use.

The future is an exciting country. You need not be held back by the past. If this book can help you along the road, then it will have achieved its purpose.

2

◆ ◆ ◆

The Scientific Background

The methods and techniques we describe in this book are derived from research in many different branches of psychology. They are derived both from basic research itself and from the application of basic research to helping people in practical ways. We also draw on scientific knowledge about physiology and physical medicine, to relate what is known about the mind to what is known about the body.

Experimental Research in Psychology

Fundamental research in psychology tells us an enormous amount about how the mind works. The painstaking, experimental work of psychologists, which started just over 100 years ago, has mapped out some of the basic processes involved in learning, remembering, and thinking. It has revealed the part we ourselves play in constructing our perception and understanding of the world around us. It has helped to explain how we develop, and to unravel the stages that we go through on the road from childhood to old age. It has thrown light on the relationships between our thoughts, feelings, actions, and sensations, and how these interact with the outside world: with the context within which we find ourselves. Its findings help us to understand more about the relationship between the mind and the body, about what motivates us and how we acquire new skills.

Psychologists have, through their scientific work, contributed to our knowledge about which aspects of ourselves we can change and which are fixed, and their work has revealed much about the processes of personal change. Applications of psychology, therefore, help us to control these processes, to use them to our advantage, and to recognize their limitations, in the same way as applications of physiology help us to keep our bodies in good shape without overstraining them. You do not have to be a physiologist to keep physically fit. Nor, nowadays, do you have to be a psychologist to make use of the science of psychology, even though the work of experimental psychologists is not over: many questions remain unanswered and new puzzles constantly emerge.

Applications of Psychological Science to Therapy

Over the last forty years, therapists have developed new and effective ways of helping people with problems in living, most of which are relatively brief forms of psychotherapy. Following the decades after Freud, psychoanalysis was the main form of psychological treatment, but it typically required a long and intensive course of therapy, often extending over several years. In this book we focus predominantly on recent treatment methods, and we give most weight to those that have been scientifically evaluated and are based on scientific findings.

Psychodynamic therapies, including psychoanalysis, are based on extensive and sophisticated theories about human development, from infancy onwards. The infant's development is understood in the context of relationships with others. Psychodynamic therapists have developed methods for increasing awareness of their own and of other people's feelings, in order to use the therapeutic relationship to help people to continue to develop. The theories underpinning these therapies were developed while experimental psychology was young, and they have not been amenable to scientific confirmation. Nor has it been easy to assess the effectiveness of the therapies derived from them, both because they take so long and because their goals are so complex. They have, however, provided therapists with a rich and fruitful source of ideas about emotional development and about relationships. Debates about the extent to which early patterns of relationships determine later functioning continue, but now have to be understood in the context of the proven effectiveness of other forms of psychotherapy.

BEHAVIORAL THERAPIES

The theoretical background to behavior therapy, which developed in striking contrast to psychoanalysis, comes from experimental psychologists' work on learning. It is based on what is called learning theory, which now recognizes that there are many ways in which learning takes place. The first type of learning found to have major implications for therapy was classical conditioning, first explored by Pavlov.

Discovering the rules of the different types of learning has led to the development of behavior therapies, such as exposure treatment for phobias. To take phobias as an example, learning theory suggests that a person's phobia can be overcome by breaking the association between the feeling of anxiety and situations that are basically harmless, such as seeing a spider or going to a supermarket. We now know from research that the most efficient way to do this is in step-by-step stages, practicing frequently and regularly. A person who is afraid of heights, for example, might start by walking up a stairway and looking down from progressively higher points. The next step might be to look down from a third floor window; then a fourth floor window; and so on. Depending on the severity of the phobia, it might take days or even weeks to progress from stage to stage. This step-by-step method is simple but effective.

Behavioral therapies originated in learning theory but have since developed beyond these beginnings and now employ a large number of methods for dealing with a wide variety of conditions. What they have in common is a focus on changing behavior in very specific ways. Behavioral methods can be used, for example, to help change eating, smoking, or drinking habits, to build self-confidence, and to improve time management and personal organization. Changing behavior can lead to changes in thoughts, feelings, and sensations, and also to changes in relationships. People who have recovered from a phobia are likely to *feel* more confident, to *think* better of themselves, to suffer less from the *sensations* of anxiety, and to *relate* more easily to others.

One of the most important contributions of behavior therapies is their focused attention on effectiveness and practicality. This is because they are based on specific, clear-cut, and observable changes. A therapy with goals can be tested to see if it works, and moreover, the therapy can be improved. Each of the improvements can then be tested to discover which precise methods are the most effective. In this way better and better therapies have been developed. This scientific evaluation of therapies has also revealed more about the processes involved in change, and has led to the recognition that changing behavior is only one way of initiating the process of change.

COGNITIVE THERAPY

Cognitive therapy developed partly as a reaction against the exclusive focus which behavior therapy places on behavior, and partly as a reaction to the unscientific aspects of psychoanalysis. It is based on the recognition that thoughts and feelings are closely related. If you *think* something is going to go wrong, you will *feel* anxious; if you *think* everything will go fine, you will *feel* more confident. By focusing on our patterns of thinking and on our beliefs, cognitive therapists have found many methods for helping us to change both our feelings and our behavior.

Cognitive therapy was first tried and tested as a treatment for depression. It has since proved to be effective in helping with many other problems, such as anxiety, panic, disturbed eating patterns, and difficulties in relationships. Cognitive therapy shares with behavior therapy the advantages of being a clearly articulated therapy, and this has meant that it has been, and is still being extensively and rigorously studied and improved.

THERAPIES FOCUSING ON RELATIONSHIPS

Relationships play a key part in our lives, and contribute much to the ways in which we understand and feel about ourselves. They provide one of the main contexts for the things that we think, feel, and do. Many types of therapy focus on relationships, but unfortunately not many of them have been tested and evaluated. *Interpersonal therapy* has been evaluated and has proved to be effective, not only in improving relationships, but in overcoming depression and disturbed eating habits.

Applications of Psychological Science in Management

Many psychological findings are of particular value in the world of work, of action, and of management and have been put to practical daily use in a large number of settings. Most of these findings concern ways of using the mind effectively. Applying management techniques can help organize both your personal and business lives, make the best use of your time, communicate well, negotiate change, and make decisions. Research into logical thinking and into memory systems has been especially productive and applied most creatively in the field of management, but these skills are also of general use in managing ourselves and our lives outside work.

Research in Physiology and Physical Medicine

Mind and body interact. Perhaps, last night, you lay awake worrying. You think it is the worries which kept you awake; but it may have been the coffee you had after supper. In reducing alcohol intake or in coming off tranquilizers, you need to know about some facts of physiology in order to make use of the best strategies. And there are times when depression is helped by drugs. In this book we will show you how you can apply the results both of *psychological* and *medical* research in improving your life.

PART ONE

♦ ♦ ♦

Two Principles Underlying Mental Fitness

Two principles guide the development of mental fitness. Success, however you wish to define success, can be achieved if you understand how to make use of these principles. The first involves *valuing yourself.* When this is difficult to do many aspects of life suffer. For example, it becomes hard to manage yourself and your problems, your relationships seem less satisfactory, you may feel anxious or depressed or sleep badly or eat too much, or you may find it hard to concentrate and make decisions. This book provides many strategies for learning to value yourself more.

The second principle involves *recognizing that you can change.* The process of change is, in fact, inevitable. Like time, it cannot be stopped. The ideas in this book are designed to help you to direct or control the way that you change, and to learn how to react differently to changes beyond your control. The various ways in which each of us reacts to change have advantages and disadvantages. Learning new ways broadens our repertoire and gives us more options. It can also help us when we feel stuck. These two principles together provide the basis for mental fitness.

3

♦ ♦ ♦

Valuing Yourself

In that confident decade of the 1950s, Richard Hamilton titled one of his paintings: *Just what is it that makes today's homes so different, so appealing?* Sometimes we look around and everyone else seems to radiate the sense of success captured by Hamilton's title. We alone are haunted by the feeling that we are no good; by a sense of low self-worth. But we are wrong. Many of those who appear so confident from the outside are beset with doubts from within, just as most of us as we grow older still feel much younger than our looks reveal.

Why do so many of us believe we are of such little value—the belief that causes more misery than all others put together?

The Chef's Tale

Marc was a chef. He ran a successful restaurant but had one ambition: that he and his restaurant should be recommended in the *Good Food Guide.* He believed that he was not good enough for even a passing mention. Like so many people, he was riddled with self-doubt. Then, one day, the great honor came, and his excellence was recognized with a wonderful review. But he did not feel happy. He had wanted this honor all his working life and now when he attained it he felt wretched and miserable. Why? Because, instead of valuing himself more as a result of this achievement, he valued the opinion of the *Good Food Guide* less. His reasoning went something like this: there can't be much to being in the *Good Food Guide* if they include the likes of me!

- **If you do not value yourself independently of your achievements, you will not value your achievements.**

We remain so vulnerable to losing the sense of our own worth because we tend to value ourselves by our achievements. The lesson of *The chef's tale* is a profound one. Finding within yourself a sense of value that does not depend on your achievements will make you more resistant to crippling self-doubts.

Unconditional Positive Regard

This inner sense of value can perhaps be best explained by using the analogy of parental love. The child may do things of which the parent strongly disapproves; the parent may not even like the child at times, but the love remains—whatever the child does. Carl Rogers called this sense of love "*unconditional* positive regard." The positive regard is unconditional in the sense that your personal, unique value does not depend on your origins or on your talents any more than it depends on what you do. It cannot be lost by doing something "bad" any more than it can be gained by doing something "good." You do not have to strive in any way to deserve it, and you cannot forfeit it by any of your actions. Losing sight of it is painful, while keeping it clearly in mind provides you with a sure foundation. We must each try and hold onto this attitude of unconditional positive regard toward ourselves. It is not selfish, nor egoistic to do so. On the contrary, it provides the foundation for being generous and open with others. Feelings of guilt and a constant need for reassurance from others lead to egoism and selfishness—and to unhappiness.

This idea that each of us has an intrinsic value is one that forms a part of many religions. "Each of us is equal in the eyes of God" encompasses not only our intrinsic value but the idea, too, that at this fundamental level we all have the same value. The democratic principle— that each of us has one, and only one, vote— is the political embodiment of this idea; and we are all susceptible to the same feelings—of love, grief, fear, doubt, and so on.

Why Is It Important to Value Yourself?

Valuing yourself helps you to build your life on a secure foundation. This book is a guide to helping you become your own helper, advisor, friend, and therapist. You will gain most from it if you treat yourself with respect, as someone who has intrinsic value. Valuing yourself is different from liking yourself. We may respect, and even admire, someone whom we do not like. And we may accept that someone whom we do not like has intrinsic worth. Similarly, although it helps if you like yourself, it is not necessary to do so, and certainly you do not need to approve of all your actions. But you do need to value yourself, for unless you do, you will be taking away with one hand what you are giving yourself with the other. You will only undermine yourself, and dissipate your strength, if you allow yourself to believe that you are worthless or that your actions are pointless.

No Double Standards

If you tend to undervalue yourself, you are almost certainly applying double standards: underrating yourself just because you are you and not someone else. If you do value yourself less than you value other people, ask yourself "Why?" Is this fair? If you look at yourself from outside, as if you were someone else examining you as you are now, would you think differently? Are you downgrading your view of yourself just because it is you? Do you have one standard for others and a higher standard for yourself? If you do apply these double standards, you are constantly undermining yourself. It is like trying to build a house on top of a swamp. The house will not last, and its foundations will be constantly eroded.

Three Common Reasons for Undervaluing Yourself

1. I AM NOT A MOTHER TERESA

You say: "I am not valuable because I have not helped people in the way that Mother Teresa has helped people. Now *there* is someone who really is valuable, unlike me."

We reply: "What Mother Teresa has done is to help people. That can only be valuable because the people she has helped are of value. If those people are not of value, then what good has she done? Why do we admire a Mother Teresa? It is because she sacrifices herself for others. Would you admire her if she sacrificed herself for something worthless? Clearly not. Our admiration of Mother Teresa depends on our valuing the human beings she has helped. It is only in the belief that each of us is of value that we can argue that anyone is of value.

2. IT WOULD BE ARROGANT

Arrogance is valuing yourself, your own opinions, and character *more* than other people. It is being unfair to others. If you undervalue yourself, you are making exactly the same error as the arrogant person, except in reverse. You are not being fair to yourself. Many an apparently arrogant person is in fact driven to behave in an arrogant fashion because of a deep-seated lack of self-confidence. Being fair to yourself, valuing yourself, is not arrogant, and it will help to protect you from behaving in an arrogant fashion.

3. I HAVE BEEN BAD

Sometimes we undervalue ourselves not because we are disappointed in our achievements, but because we are disappointed in ourselves, in our moral character. We have not come up to our personal standards of behavior, and we whip ourselves for this mercilessly. We set standards for our children and tell them off when they fail to meet some of these standards because we love them. But it is in the nature of standards that they cannot be lived up to all the time: if they could, they would perhaps be too undemanding. Failing to meet a standard is, actually, a reason for valuing yourself, for recognizing that it is worth trying to make changes and starting to make them; it is not a reason for ceasing to value yourself.

Where Do You Go from Here?

You already have the basis on which to value yourself; otherwise, you would not be reading this book. But you can also gain from building on that basis and from recognizing that you are of equal value with others. A sense of low self-worth will eat away at your life, preventing you from enjoying life to the fullest. This book will help you to put the principle of valuing yourself into effect. It will show you ways in which you can increase your effectiveness in achieving your personal goals, and ways in which to gain control over your moods. In Part 2 we explain many of the basic skills you will need, and Chapter 10 deals specifically with self-esteem. But before we tackle the skills, we will turn to the second principle on which to build: recognizing that you can change.

Chapter Summary

Valuing yourself will help you to build your life on a secure foundation: this book provides many practical ways to help you increase your sense of self-worth.

4

◆ ◆ ◆

Recognizing That You Can Change

You have already embarked on an adventure. You are making a journey that has not yet ended, and peer as you will into the darkness you cannot discern what lies ahead. You did not choose to set out on this journey. You did not choose when to begin, or where, nor who some of your companions would be, nor the circumstances that surround your journey, nor the climate that alternately helps you to flourish or stunts your growth. It all happened without anyone consulting you—and indeed before you were able to make any sense or use of being consulted anyway.

The question is not whether to change or not, change is a part of all journeys. The question is whether the processes of change can be harnessed and mobilized to work for you rather than against you. Working with, rather than against, the inevitable process of change is easier if you know more about the way the mind works. This book will show you how you can use this knowledge to direct the ways you want to change. It draws on our knowledge of research, on our clinical experience, and on our understanding of our own culture and education. It is not that we can tell you how to change. That is something you will continue to decide, for yourself. We do not know all the answers, but we can provide useful guidelines that, in your hands, can be used to re-condition, strengthen, and update the rudder by which you steer. We believe that knowledge will give you the power to change in the ways that are right for you. As clinicians, engaged inevitably in the struggles and difficulties of others, we know this power is limited but is most effectively used when it is most clearly understood. Greater understanding, then, is what we are aiming for, so that greater confidence and control may replace feelings of helplessness in the face of the adventure on which we are all embarked.

The Climate and the Terrain

A guidebook to a new place is designed to provide information so that the reader can make choices. It starts with a summary of geology and geography, history, sociology and economics, and goes on to describe particular places to visit and how to visit them: how to travel, where to stay, whom you will meet, and what you might eat—if you know how to ask for it. It is designed to help you make your visit enjoyable, and it assumes your pleasure is determined both by external factors such as the scenery, the weather, people, and their doings, as well as by internal factors such as your interests (in history, good food, or sport), your need for rest or excitement, your language skills, your sense of humour, and your stamina and adaptability when plans are frustrated. However, this guidebook, unlike others, will help you to link up internal and external factors, both of which influence how much you enjoy the journey. A guidebook can only be an approximate tool because both internal and external factors change as the journey, inevitably, continues. Your constant movement provides you with an ever-changing perspective, so it is wrong to assume that things are static, that we are stuck and cannot change. We are changing all the time as we encounter new challenges, new information and new people. This book will help you make positive use of these changes.

INTERNAL FORCES FOR CHANGE

The mind as well as the body grows older daily, sweeping us along in the path of an inevitable process of change. There is some order in this change. As the dependence of childhood decreases, the turbulence of adolescence takes its place. Together with ever-increasing competence and independence, there comes the need to define an identity and to find one's way in the world. The middle years are often described as if they were static, as if once you had settled on a certain pattern of occupation and family and sexual relationships, you would stop changing. But knowing more about who you are and what you can do does not stop the process of change.

At times, you will feel on top of the world; at other times, out of your depth. You may alternate between being in the swim of things and being in a calm backwater. One day you may reach a peak, and the next plunge into the slough of despond. You may know that every cloud has a silver lining, and be able to look optimistically ahead, or you may lose sight of the light at the end of the tunnel. You may confidently stand your ground in stormy weather or nervously keep a wary eye out for thunder clouds looming on the horizon. The language we use to describe life's patterns and changes shows how naturally we think in terms of a journey through differing terrains, subject to varying climates.

EXTERNAL FORCES FOR CHANGE

The external world that provides the specific context for each of our lives is also constantly changing. We may play a part in influencing some of these changes, but many are beyond our control. We can all too easily come to think we are powerless: that, as there is little we can do about the external factors themselves, there is also little we can do about our reactions to them. This is a mistake. Changing our reactions to external events is one of the most effective ways we can change our experience of life.

Five Caricatures

We have written this book because we believe that change is possible. But, sometimes, all of us feel stuck in the situations we find ourselves in, not knowing how to bring about the changes we want. If that is how you feel, this book will help you find ways to move forward—it will help you to get unstuck.

You may, on the contrary, feel full of energy, full of the power to change and develop, but uncertain of the direction to take. Again, we hope that this guide will help by enabling you to find a path that leads you onward.

Different people respond differently to pressures for change. Here are five caricatures—you might recognize elements of yourself in one or more of these. They illustrate two points. First, most people learn to cope with change by developing a particular style of response. Second, each style has both advantages and disadvantages.

1. THE SAGE

The sage is the seeker after knowledge: the person who reads all about it.

Many people who use word processors only use a small percentage of the options open to them. When learning to use a new machine they quickly master the basic skills, and then they go straight to work. They put the skills into practice, usually pleased and impressed with the speed at which they can do things like sending circulars to their clients, or invitations to their friends, and then they cease to learn about other features of their computer. Such people do not make full use of their word processor since they have never read to the end of the instruction manual. The sage, on the other hand, knows that the more you know, the more options you have, and therefore peruses the instruction manual from cover to cover. Sages make full use of their word processors, but the down side of this is that they may waste time learning about functions they do not need.

Sarah discovered the advantages of becoming a "sage." She had recently been assigned *Hamlet* at school, but when she started reading the play, she found the language hard to understand and she became bored. Her parents took her to a local performance of the play. This helped her to understand more about what was happening, and she started to enjoy it. She read it again when she had to write an essay, and then the class went through the play scene by scene, analyzing the language, the construction of the play, and the development of the characters. They had discussions about whether Hamlet was depressed and about his relationships with women: his mother and Ophelia. They found themselves talking about issues such as whether revenge is ever justified, about the meaning of forgiveness, and about what sorts of things might drive people mad. Sarah felt that a new world was opening up for her. A book that had been closed was gradually opening. The more she learned, the more she thought she understood—both about Shakespeare's play and about people and their feelings for each other. She began to find knowledge in unexpected places—knowledge that helped her to change.

2. THE TRAVELER

Travelers extend the journey and behave as if there is a purpose in the journey. They assume that because we are constantly on the move, we must be going somewhere, as if perfection, or nirvana, or the end of the rainbow could someday be reached. The quest goes on because no stopping place ever satisfies them for long. Travelers continue to search for the golden fleece, overcoming mountainous obstacles as they go, constantly hoping that they will find a resting place or that the grass will be greener on the other side of the fence.

Some sports enthusiasts show this degree of dedication, striving constantly to improve on their last performance, treating each new record or personal best as the next hurdle to jump. Provided they do not go overboard, and still enjoy the sport, they may indeed reach unexpected heights. Other people may think of their most intimate relationships in this way, as if the knight in shining armor or the fairytale princess is still waiting to be found, if only they keep on searching. They believe that the ideal person will be instantly recognizable and immediately responsive, and that when the knot has been tied the relationship will continue happily ever after. No wonder the quest continues.

Many of the changes that form part of our experience are cyclical. We get hungry, search for food, eat until we are satisfied, and then forget about food until we are hungry again. Or we look for a challenge, choose a mountain to climb, struggle to the top, and then start looking for the next challenge. We might become curious, focus on a particular puzzle or problem, wrestle with it until it is solved, and then our curiosity re-emerges and we seek another puzzle. The process is never static, and the cycle may complete itself without any help from us. Our hunger, striving, or curiosity re-emerges seemingly of its own accord and keeps us traveling onwards.

David, to the outside, appeared a successful academic. He had progressed smoothly from doctoral student, to lecturer, to associate professor, and now to full professor. Ten years ago this would have been the peak of his ambition, for which he had strived hard, putting his career before personal relationships. But even now, as full professor, he could not enjoy his success: he thought only of being elected president by his professional association. His continual striving helped him achieve, but not to enjoy his achievements.

3. THE DRIFTER

Drifters retire from centerstage, give up the struggle, and allow themselves to be carried wherever the current takes them. They bend to the inevitable and "go with the flow." They can be made to sound either weak or strong depending on how they are described, and on how their actions and decisions are viewed within their social contexts.

Tracy tried for four years to combine her work as a dental hygienist with caring for her elderly mother who suffered from Alzheimer's disease. Eventually something had to give, and she decided to pack in her job. She devoted her energies to looking after her mother and hoped that in time she would take up her career again. Meanwhile, she would focus on keeping up contacts with friends. But many of Tracy's friends thought she had opted out and submitted to pressure against her better judgment. Tracy herself, however, accepted that for a while the direction of her life would be determined by someone else's circumstances.

4. THE OSTRICH

The ostrich has two characteristics: it hides its head in the sand and it has a powerful kick. Refusing to accept the inevitability of change can lead to both of these reactions.

At some level, Christopher feared that his relationship with Lisa was over. He hardly dared to think about it, but the signs were there. It scared him when he noticed how little she had to say to him and how often she was busy at times when they might have been doing things together. He behaved as if nothing was wrong, carried on as normal, and continued to make plans for the summer holiday they had talked about earlier. Hiding his head in the sand might help Christopher to cope with the hiccup in their relationship, but perhaps he is failing to read the writing on the wall.

Or take the example of Barbara, a laboratory technician. Barbara was accused by her boss of inefficiency, and she was furious. From her point of view she had been offered inadequate training. She had been left to her own devices to learn a set of complex procedures, and if she made a muddle, the fault lay more with her line manager than with her. She knew she did not have all the skills she needed, but thought that it was her boss's responsibility to help her acquire them. Barbara left the tasks she could not manage to others and was the only person in a busy office who regularly finished her work before the end of the day. From her point of view, this was efficiency. From her boss's point of view it was a failure to show the initiative needed to acquire new skills. She argued forcibly for what she wanted. She explained why she felt the accusations against her were false. Her boss was not convinced and warned her that unless she made the effort to learn from her more skilled colleagues, she would be sacked. He gave her a month in which to change.

5. THE CONDUCTOR OF THE ORCHESTRA

Conductors work at harnessing the action of many different musicians, who if left to their own devices would produce cacophony. They know what they want to achieve, and provide the leadership that makes the difference. They take control and set out to make things happen. A conductor who loses control no longer has an impact. The conductor's success depends partly on being able to recognize which things are fixed and which are changeable. Good conductors may be able to work with ongoing processes of change and bend them to their will. Bad ones will use their energies ineffectively. Parents are conductors in the home, just as managers are conductors outside it.

Mike was a highly successful businessman. He went into the shoe trade immediately after leaving school, worked his way through all aspects of the industry, until, at age 56, he owned a chain of children's shoestores. He kept a close eye on all aspects of the business, and no major decisions were made without consulting him first. In fact, his knowledge of the trade was encyclopedic. People at all levels relied on him to be able to answer questions, to solve problems, and to lead them in the right direction. Then he had a small stroke. He made an almost complete recovery but was dismayed to find himself having to search for the answers to people's questions. He stalled for time by keeping them talking until he remembered what he wanted to say. Shortly after returning to work, he forgot a couple of trivial things in quick succession: to return a phone call and to tell his secretary the time of an appointment. After catching a puzzled look on the face of a colleague and realizing that he must have told him the same thing twice, he asked his doctor to arrange a formal test of his memory. The results showed that the stroke had caused a slight, but nevertheless definite, impairment in his memory.

Mike's memory impairment interfered with his habit of being in complete control. He was a natural problem solver, however, and bought a book on memory improvement. With the help of his secretary, he devised some effective reminder systems. An unexpected consequence of his memory problem was that he also sought expert help in putting the information he held in his head onto the office computer, making it readily accessible to everyone. By recognizing the limitations placed on him by processes beyond his control, Mike discovered how to change himself.

Each of these caricatures shows a different cognitive style that people may adopt in the face of change. There is no one method that suits every person in every circumstance. We all tend to develop habitual ways of dealing with change. Use these caricatures to think about whether to enlarge your repertoire of styles for making changes.

Three Conditions for Fruitful Change

This guidebook will help you to direct the processes of change. Your journey is not yet complete; there is more to come, and none of us knows where it will take us next or what the weather will be like on the way. Circumstances constantly shift, demanding that we continue to adapt. On this journey we can use all that we know to give ourselves more options and better chances. No one way of dealing with change will fit all circumstances or all people, so the more you know about the various methods of helping yourself to change, and the better you understand yourself, the more you will be able to change in the ways you wish.

1. UNDERSTAND THE PRESENT

Choices about change can only be made in the present. That means that it is important above all to accept where you are now. The first condition, therefore, for fruitful change is that you see clearly where you are at the moment. Do not hide away from present reality. If there are aspects of the present you do not like, you can start to plan how to change: but if you pretend these aspects do not exist, you will never change them. Sometimes you will want to be energetic and active, and will need to know how to exert your will to direct or control the forces around you. At other times a quieter, more accepting form of change may provide what you need, and help you to steer away from turbulent waters into calmer ones. The potential for changing the future can lie only in the present.

2. DO NOT BE BURDENED BY THE PAST

"If only things had been different." "I wish I hadn't said that." It is understandable to feel dismayed by the mistakes and concerns of yesterday, but it is a mistake to allow the past to become a prison. The past can no longer be changed, so the second condition for fruitful change is to step lightly from the past. The past is an information bank from which you can learn. But it is not a web in which you are caught.

3. ACCEPT THE UNCERTAINTY OF THE FUTURE

We can only take one path and can never know what would have happened had we taken a different one. It is as if there were an endless branching of possibilities stretching out before us. The place we find ourselves in is determined by the past, but it tells us little about how things will turn out in the distant future. The path that appears to wind wearily uphill may provide unexpected rewards later on.

Thus, the third condition for fruitful change is to accept the uncertainty of the future. Many of the ideas in this book will help you to direct the changes you wish to make toward the goals you value. But we cannot foresee the future; much is outside our control and the unexpected is a continual possibility. In bringing about fruitful change, we need to leave room for uncertainty. An attitude of openness and confidence is needed for the future as well as the past.

It Is Better to Light One Candle Than Curse the Darkness

You can change, and we have written this guidebook because we have seen how people can benefit from trying out new directions. We hope this book will help you make the choices you wish to make, and increase your ability to enjoy the journey on the way. It contains many ideas so that you can choose those which are most relevant for you. You may be thinking that you want to make so many changes, you do not know where to begin. Do not try to do too much all at once. Decide which change to make first. Lighting one candle is enough for a start.

Chapter Summary

The future is a journey, and change is a part of all journeys. This guidebook will help you to direct the processes of change.

There are three conditions for fruitful change:

1. *Understand the present.* Do not hide from reality but see the present clearly.
2. *Do not be burdened by the past.* The past cannot be changed. Do not allow it to weigh you down.
3. *Accept the uncertainty of the future.* Much of the future is not under our control. We must accept uncertainty, and learn how to face the future with confidence.

PART TWO

◆ ◆ ◆

The Seven Basic Skills

To keep fit, mentally, you need seven basic skills. In this part, we show you how you can develop these skills. They will enable you to improve both your mood and your effectiveness.

As with all skills, you will improve with practice. Read and reread this section using it as your workbook for mental fitness.

The seven skills are:

- Managing yourself and your time
- Facing the problem
- Treating yourself right
- Problem-solving: a strategy for change
- Keeping things in perspective: help from cognitive therapy
- Building self-confidence and self-esteem
- Learning to relax

5

◆ ◆ ◆

Managing Yourself and Your Time

Time Management Is Personal Management

Donald's full beard was as dark as his mood. He had been miserable since taking early retirement nine months before. He hung around the house with little to do, feeling bored and useless. His wife was at the limits of her endurance. They both wanted the problem solved and hoped that there might be a medication that could cheer him up. He was taken aback when we started talking about the principles of time management. "Isn't time management what all those successful young business executives learn? That's for people who have too much to do. My problem is that I have too much time and not enough to do".

Hilary was just the kind of young businesswoman for whom time management courses are designed. From the outside she appeared happy and successful, but from the inside she felt anxious and out of control. That is why she had come to the clinic. Her work was an endless series of pressures, but she knew all about time management. She brought out her "Filofax" which was full of appointments and lists of projects which were color coded as urgent or important, or both. It was easy to see why she felt stressed: she had so many urgent projects, and so many appointments, she was never still. It was fortunate that her clinic appointment had been color coded as very important or she would never have had the chance to see where she was going wrong. She knew a great deal about some of the techniques of time management, but she did not understand the principles. At the end of the first meeting she said: "You are not talking about time management but about personal management." She was right. It is not time which needs to be managed; it is ourselves.

The Central Principle of Time Management

Enormous books and long courses are devoted to time management, but the central principle is simple and profound: *spend your time doing those things you value or those things that help you achieve your goals.* This is not an invitation to selfishness. The idea is not that you only do those things which are in your interests at the expense of others. Altruistic people want to spend time helping other people: this is what they value and this is one of their main goals.

Most of us would admit to spending a great deal of our time involved in activities which we neither value nor which help us to achieve our goals. Why is this? It is tempting to think that it is because of weakness of will, or laziness, or inefficiency. But although these can be contributing factors, they are rarely of major importance. The most important single reason is being unclear about our values and our goals. This was the case with Hilary. She was busy and she worked efficiently, but a great deal of the time she was doing things that did not contribute to her main goals. She did not choose which projects to take on and which to reject with reference to her values and goals, and this was because she did not have a clear idea what these values and goals were. The result was that she took on almost all the projects which were thrown her way; most of them worthy enough, but too many of them when considered together. She had no clear vision that could enable her to decide on her priorities. She ended up doing whichever tasks were the most urgent. The result: stress and dissatisfaction.

Clarify Your Values and Your Goals

To help clarify your values and long-term goals, carry out the following "thought experiment." Imagine your own funeral three years from today. What would you like people to say about you. What would you like a close friend, a member of your family, and a colleague at work to say about you? The point of this exercise is not to think about your death, but about the kind of person you want to be and the kinds of thing you wish to achieve. Three years from now is far enough away for you to do new things but near enough not to feel remote.

Do not try to guess what people would really say about you; the point of the exercise is to clarify what you would *like* them to say. Here is what Hilary wrote.

Results of Hilary's Thought Experiment

The family speaker He said that I was warm, fun, and stimulating; that I spent time with the family and gave them the highest priority. He added that I was thoroughly dependable.

The friend She confirmed that I was fun to be with and that I gave support when it was needed. She added that I was completely honest and sophisticated.

The colleague at work She spoke of my integrity and productivity: I got valuable things done. She added that I brought out the best in my colleagues at work so that they flourished.

The purpose of this exercise is to help you to realize what is important to you. When you have done this exercise you are in a position to write a statement, for your own personal use, about your values and goals. Such a statement provides you with a touchstone against which you choose your priorities and decide how to spend your time. It need not be written on tablets of stone; it may change gradually as you grow older, or change suddenly at certain points in your life. But at any one time this statement reflects your values and goals. It may be something you wish to keep private, or something to share with those you are close to. It may be short or long. But we do recommend that you write it down and keep it in a convenient place so that you can read and reread it until you know it in your bones. Only then can you ensure that it illuminates your important decisions. Hilary was typically terse in her statement but it served her purpose well. It is clear how the funeral exercise helped her in producing her personal statement.

Hilary's Personal Statement

Central value of integrity and honesty

Caring for my family

Not, however, rigid and rule bound

Forgiving

Creative and imaginative

High value on hobby of painting

Stimulating and fun

Enabling others (for example, at work) to flourish

Main work objective over next three years: to expand my division of the company by 20%

Donald had never thought about what he valued and what he wanted to achieve after his retirement. His life had revolved around his work, and when that stopped he just existed, bored and rudderless. He could not see the point of the funeral exercise but he agreed to do it anyway. He did not begin by thinking about what he would like his wife to say; he thought instead about what she was probably thinking now. "I wish he would go back to work so that he wasn't around me all the time getting in the way. He's so miserable it would be better if he were dead." He suddenly saw what he was like from her perspective, and he did not like what he saw. What would he like her to say in three years time?

"That's simple. I would like her to think that my retirement years were good ones for both of us. That the time which it gave us together was time we enjoyed and took advantage of. That I was helpful to her, but also that I was interesting to be with." Donald thought about what he would like his son to say, and his four-year-old granddaughter. By the end of the week he had not only written out a detailed statement of his values and goals, he had also planned how he wanted to spend his week.

Be Led by Your Goals and Values

Making a personal statement of your values and goals helps you to center your life around what you believe in. But knowing your values and goals is not by itself enough. You need also to *act* in accordance with them. The problem is that we often act as though we were being directed by someone else rather than by ourselves.

"But What If I Have No Control over My Life?"

You might be thinking that this is all very well for someone like Donald, who is retired and can do pretty much what he likes. But what about those who do not have much control over their lives? Perhaps you are clear about what you value, and you know exactly how you would like to spend your time; but you have to earn your living, and in order to do this, you must spend a lot of your time doing things you do not really value.

It is a sad reflection on our society that there is much truth in this objection. We certainly all have to spend time doing things we neither enjoy nor find valuable. The central principle of time management tells us, however, that the only reason for spending time in this way is if it is necessary for achieving one of our long-term goals. If the only way of earning a living at the moment is by doing a job which we neither value nor enjoy, then it may be necessary to do this, at least for the time being. However, we need to look carefully at whether there are other ways of achieving our goals.

Anne worked as a secretary. Her father had always wanted her to be a secretary, but she hated the job. When asked why she did it, she said that she needed the money. We asked her what job she would prefer. She was quite clear about that: she would like to work in a travel agency. She had found out, however, that to do this she would have to work for a year at much lower pay, and even after a year, she was not likely to be earning as much as she was now. We discussed her values and goals. One of the things she really wanted to do was to travel. If she worked for the travel agent, she would be able to travel more cheaply, but she had not costed out the value of this to her. It turned out that if she traveled a lot—and this is what she wanted to do—the cheap fares available to her went a long way to making up the difference in income between the two jobs. It did not make up all the difference. So what could the extra income in her present job help her to do that she would not do if she worked in the travel agency? For the first year, she would not be able to maintain a car. After that, the difference would have little effect on her day to day life.

Anne had thought that the ideas behind time management had little value for her because she had no control over how to spend her time. It turned out that by getting clear for herself what her values were she did have some choices. What it boiled down to was that she could continue in her present job, which she neither enjoyed nor valued, or she could do what she really wanted and sacrifice her car for a year. When put in these terms, she was certain that she would rather change jobs. It was only through applying the central principle of time management that she had become clear about what it was she wanted.

A Piece of Pie

Donald discovered a technique that he found useful and that may be of help to you. He drew a pie chart of how he wanted to spend his time. In writing his statement of values and goals, he identified a number of different aspects of his life that he wanted to develop, and decided roughly how much time he wanted to spend on each. His pie chart looked like the one in Figure 5.1.

The Designer Week

Donald used his pie chart to design his week so that it had the elements that he wanted, in the proportion that he had chosen. He wanted to help his son and daughter-in-law. He looked at the pie chart and then

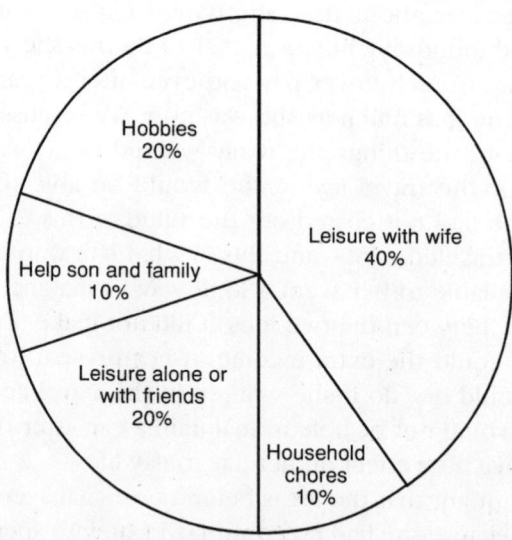

Figure 5.1   Donald's time-management plan.

he asked them: "If you could have four hours of my time, how would it be most helpful to you?" Their answer was simple: an evening of babysitting. So Donald wrote this evening into his weekly timetable.

He had wanted to learn French properly for years but with his work schedule he had never had the time. He went to his local library and found out about adult study programs. There was a local French class one afternoon a week, so he put this in his diary and also scheduled some time for homework. He talked with his wife. If he did the cleaning, she would do the cooking and washing. So she taught him how to clean the house, and this gave her more leisure time. They both enjoyed looking at antiques so they decided to plan outings to antique fairs and house sales, with a light lunch out. Donald put this on his weekly timetable.

His timetable did not provide a rigid list of musts, but was a helpful guide to make sure that, by and large, he spent his time following the pursuits he wanted. Having felt aimless and miserable with nothing to do, he started to think of his retirement as a purposeful rather than as an empty time of life, and began to feel more fulfilled.

The pie chart and the designer week are as useful for the busy person whose work seems to take up the whole of life as they are for those whose life seems filled with empty space. Often the busy person has lost touch with what is really important. So if you are very busy, take time to produce your statement of values and goals and then draw a pie diagram showing how much time you would like to spend on each of the main areas in your life: your family, your work, your friends, your hobbies and interests. How does the distribution of time shown in your ideal pie compare with how you are actually spending your time? One of the problems the busy person faces is that work can take up an increasing and excessive amount of time at the expense of family and friends. Of course, economic factors often force people to work more than they would ideally like to. If your ideal pie and your actual pie show any marked discrepancies, think carefully about how you could bring them more into line. Do you really have to do as much as you are doing at work?

Classify Your Activities

Many books and courses on time management display a diagram much like the one in Figure 5.2. The idea is that each of the activities that occupy your week can be classified in two ways: in terms of how *important* they are and how *urgent* they are. Some authors devise

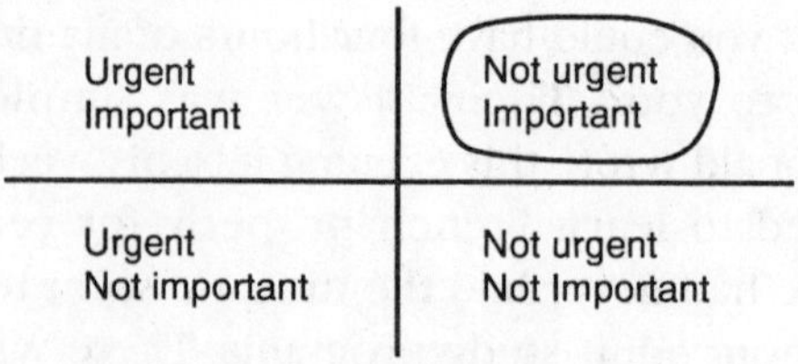

Urgent Important	Not urgent Important
Urgent Not important	Not urgent Not Important

Figure 5.2 Weighing the importance of various tasks as a part of time management.

elaborate rating systems, but for most purposes, it is enough to place each activity in one of the four quadrants.

The importance of an activity is determined by your values and goals. Urgent tasks, like returning phone calls or doing the household chores, pop up of their own accord until you find yourself snowed under by them. The nonurgent important activities, like developing new markets or keeping up with friends, never get done unless they become urgent. Because it is so tiring living constantly with urgent tasks, we sneak into the "comfortable" quadrant of activities that are neither urgent nor important, like flicking through a magazine with no great enjoyment, whenever we can, just, as it were, to get some rest.

The central principle of time management is: *spend your time doing those things you value or that help you achieve your goals.* In other words, spend your time doing those activities that are important to you. The aim, therefore, is to spend no time on activities described as *not important*—whether urgent or not. Furthermore, it is desirable to spend as much time as possible on nonurgent activities, because not only is it more stressful to be working on urgent tasks, many of the most important activities never become urgent. If you spend most of your time doing the urgent things, these very important but nonurgent activities get continually put off. Such activities include spending time with family and friends, developing your interests and hobbies, and planning the long-term aspects of work. As you increase the time spent on nonurgent activities, gradually you will reduce the amount of time you need for the urgent tasks, because you will be carrying them out before they become urgent.

What about My Leisure?

You may be thinking that this sounds far too much like hard work—spending all your time doing important activities. What about time to stand and stare? What about time to be frivolous? What about time relaxing with friends? It is vital to understand what is meant by *important*. An important task might include lying on the beach in the sun, or having a drink with some friends, or putting your feet up to take in a football game on TV. In other words, relaxing and pleasurable activities are indeed important. In spending your time doing those things which are important to you, we are not advocating constant work and lifelong grind. Quite the contrary. Paradoxically, good time management often means spending less time on what is considered work. If the work is drudgery and not relevant to key goals, then it should be abandoned. This will leave you more time for doing those things you enjoy and value.

Important but Not Urgent in Two Steps

In order to shift to spending as much time as possible on important, nonurgent activities, you need to take two steps.

Step 1 Refuse to commit yourself to unimportant activities in the first place; and this means that you need to have clearly in mind what your values and goals are. Time management comes back, again and again, to this fundamental notion. Do not expect to ditch all the unimportant tasks that you have taken on overnight. You may need to carry them out simply because you have already committed yourself. But, from now on, do not agree to any unimportant activities.

Step 2 Use the time created by cutting out unimportant activities in order to engage in important, nonurgent activities. Do not fill this time with urgent tasks.

By applying this two-step process, over a period of a few months, you can ensure that most of your time is spent on important but not urgent activities.

Nine Tools and Rules of the Time-Management Trade

Once you are clear about your values and goals, you can use whichever tools you find helpful in order to get organized.

1. Use Your Starter Motor

An old Renault car ran as smoothly as cream once it was going, but was a devil to get started, particularly in the wet weather. Most of us are like that car. A survey of students showed that the main difference between good students and average students was in the ability to get down to work quickly. The first tool of time management is to get to the task at hand. Do not spend time in that limbo of neither getting down to the work nor enjoying your leisure. For ideas about how to make it easier to get started, see Chapter 28.

2. Make Routine Your Servant

Routine can be your servant or your master. Mindless routine may become a prison and may curb your creativity. But routine, when used well, can release time and energy. Donald decided to learn French. He chose to devote half an hour each day, in addition to his weekly class, working on his French. He found that it was easy to skip a daily session, and if he skipped one, it was even easier to skip a second session. Two weeks went by, and he had only done his half hour of work on two days. We discussed ways to help him get down to work. He chose to make it a routine. After breakfast each day, he would work for half an hour. He established a routine. In fact, he had previously spent half an hour successfully delaying doing the work. Now he found that he had done his work before he had time to think about not doing it. He established the habit that, after breakfast, he would take his coffee into the sitting room and work for half an hour. It worked.

3. Every Yes Is a No to Something Else

Many of the best things in life arise by chance, and saying *yes* to an opportunity can lead to unexpected treasures. But the mistake most of us make is to say *yes* to too many things, so that we live according to the priorities of others rather than according to our own. We fail to recognize that doing one thing means that we are not doing something else. Every time you agree to do something, another thing you might have done will not get done. When someone asks you to do something, think to yourself: "If I say *yes* to this, from what other activity will I take away the time?" The problem is that almost all of us find it difficult to say *no* to other people's demands. The skills of *assertiveness* are necessary for the good management of time. These are described in Chapter 13.

4. Distant Elephants

From far away, even elephants look small; but when you come up close, they are as large as they always are. Peter received a letter asking him to give a lecture in Edinburgh. He knew it would take two days of preparation and a couple of days to travel to Edinburgh and back. It was not a lecture he particularly wanted to give, and if he had been asked to give it within two months, he would have had no hesitation in saying no. But he was being asked to give the lecture in a year's time. It was so far away he almost said yes without thinking, but then he remembered about distant elephants. In a year's time it would still be four days' work, and he would still have other priorities. This lecture was never going to be a top priority, and he would always have more important things to do with four days. *Do not commit yourself to unimportant activities no matter how far ahead they are.*

5. Salami

Large tasks can be so daunting that you either never start them, or having started them, you become dispirited and give up. The principle of *salami* is that large tasks should be broken up into a series of small tasks: like eating a whole salami over weeks, slice by slice. This principle is explained in detail on page 348.

6. The Curse of Perfectionism

Louise was a good scientist and was devastated when she failed to get the promotion she thought she deserved. The problem was that hardly anyone knew much about her work because she had published so little. Several of her colleagues had found it difficult to work with her because, when they came to write up their results for the professional journals, she was so slow. The reason for her slowness was her perfectionism. She thought so carefully about every word, and worried so much about every sentence, that her results remained lost to the world in half finished, unpublished manuscripts.

There is a place for perfectionism. The great Dutch painter Vermeer worked with painstaking care and has left us a number of masterpieces. But for most activities, there comes a stage when there is not much to be gained from putting in a great deal more effort. It is usually possible to spot when this stage has been reached. This is the time to call a halt and focus on something else.

7. Once Past the Desk

Slightly unpleasant or tricky things, like letters we do not want to answer, seem to turn up again and again. What typically happens is that the letter arrives, we read it, and put it aside. Later we read it again, start to think about it, but put it aside again. We can even repeat the whole process and end up wasting yet more time. We could have dealt with it once and for all in the time we have spent putting off dealing with it. To prevent this waste of time, apply the rule of *once past the desk:* either deal with the task straight away, or decide when to deal with it and put it aside until that time. The successful application of this technique requires a certain discipline. The discipline is made up of four steps, all of which should be taken with deliberation, at least until they become a habit. The first step is a quick assessment of what you will need to do in order to deal with the matter: for example, to reply to the letter. This assessment should be brief. And in making this assessment, use your values as a yardstick: do not undertake tasks that are not important to you. The second step is to decide when to tackle what you need to do. One good reason for delaying completion of the task is that you need time to mull it over. Again, this decision should be made rapidly. The third step is to put the matter aside until the allotted time. The fourth step is to carry out the action at the allotted time. These four steps may often be carried out in quick succession—when you decide to deal with the matter right away. But do not keep revisiting the task without carrying it out. Deal with what is on your desk, whether literally or metaphorically, just the once.

8. Appointments Need to End as Well as Start

Be as aware of when appointments are due to end as you are of when they begin. For example, suppose that you are making a date to meet with a colleague to discuss an issue at work, or a date to have coffee with a friend. When arranging the time to meet, arrange also the time to finish. You will need to make some estimate of how long you need together, but the ability to make such estimates improves with practice. There are two reasons for scheduling the ends of appointments. The first is so that you know when you will be free for other activities and appointments. The second is that, if everyone knows when the meeting will end, you will all make better use of the time you have together.

9. Make Time to Plan

The final tool of time management is to schedule a regular time to plan your activities. Some people find it helpful to plan the day first thing in the morning. For others, it may be better to plan in terms of a week. The minutes spent in planning will be saved many times over. It is also useful to review your priorities from time to time. Holidays are a good time for this because you are away from the demands of everyday life.

Nine Tools and Rules

1. Use your starter motor
2. Make routine your servant
3. Every *yes* is a *no* to something else
4. Distant elephants
5. Salami
6. The curse of perfectionism
7. Once past the desk
8. Appointments need to end as well as start
9. Make time to plan

Chapter Summary

1. The central principle of time management is: *spend your time doing those things you value or that help you to achieve your goals.*
2. It is therefore important to know what your values and goals are.
3. You could clarify these by imagining what you would like a close relative, a close friend, and a work colleague to say about you.

4. Write down your personal statement of values and goals so that you can refer to it often.
5. Having clarified *your* values and goals, make sure that you are led by them. Do not be led by someone else's goals.
6. Classify the activities which fill your week in terms of their *importance* and *urgency.* Many leisure activities and time with family and friends will be classified as important.
7. Aim to spend as much time as possible doing those things that are important but not urgent. This is a two-step process:

   Step 1: From now on, do not commit yourself to doing things which are not important.

   Step 2: Use the extra time this gives you to do the *nonurgent* things. Gradually, fewer and fewer things will be urgent because you will have done them before they become urgent.

8. Make use of whichever of the *nine tools and rules of the time-management trade* are useful to you.

6

◆ ◆ ◆

Facing the Problem

It is tempting to pretend that our fears and problems are not always with us. It is tempting to close our eyes to them, half hoping that they will, of their own accord, go away. But the problem with problems is that they rarely go away in silence. They usually need to be tackled and solved. If we pretend the problems do not exist, if we ignore their presence, then they will grow in the dark of our neglect. The longer the neglect, the larger, and more entrenched, those problems are likely to be. The earlier you recognize the problem, therefore, the better.

Much of this book is about the methods and ideas that have been developed for tackling the problems of everyday life. These methods can only help if the problems are brought out into the light.

If this sounds hard, it is important to take hold of the encouraging fact that most problems, when seen clearly, are a fraction of the size they seem when glanced sideways in a fearful or gloomy mood. Most problems shrink still further when confronted.

Crumbs under the Skin

Paul had a demanding job as a junior member of the Parks Department, responsible for supplying both plants and equipment to the town gardeners. Paul was also learning a new computer system for the control of these supplies. He had been doing this work for only two years and his responsibilities were growing. He had saved nearly enough to own a car, and he knew that his prospects were good—but he was not happy. He dragged himself out of bed to go to work, kept forgetting details of the new computer program, and was never satisfied with himself. It was becoming harder and harder to concentrate on the job, and he had to make ever-increasing efforts to keep going. His girlfriend noticed that he seemed depressed and asked him how he was feeling, but he simply said that everyone was overloaded by the changes in the office, and suggested that they go for a walk, hoping it would make him feel better.

Mandy had always been ambitious. She worked as a personnel manager, was married to a teacher, and had come back to work soon after having her first child, Lizzie, who was now two years old. She had excellent day-care arrangements for Lizzie, and liked to think that she could cope with whatever was thrown at her, both at home and at work. But she still felt troubled. She had started to worry about "silly" things, like whether Lizzie would make friends at school, and whether Lizzie was really as happy and contented as she seemed. Although she knew that Lizzie was fine, the worries continued, and she became increasingly bad tempered, both at home and at work. She resented it when people asked her what was the matter since it only made her feel worse. She was angry that they could not see how many demands were being made on her, and did not make allowances for her moods.

Storing Up Trouble

Both Paul and Mandy knew that they felt bad, but neither of them found it easy to face their difficulties. Like most of us, they found that avoidance was tempting. In the short term, avoidance felt like a solution because it made them feel better and because they could not face talking about the difficulties to someone else. But by facing their problems, they were storing up trouble for the future for three reasons:

1. Avoidance can make the problem worse. The more Paul and Mandy avoided their difficulties, the more insurmountable the problems seemed and the more depressed and irritable they felt.

2. Avoidance creates new problems. Mandy's resentment and irritability were making her working relationships difficult, and Paul's self-confidence was being gradually eroded. He had convinced himself that he would be no good at anything else, that he would be given a bad reference despite his obviously good work record, and that no one would understand how he could dislike a job that he obviously did well.

3. Avoidance interferes with your life. Neither Paul nor Mandy felt they could do what they wanted to do, nor enjoy the things that they were doing. The problems they did not face did not go away, but stayed to contribute to the storehouse of trouble.

Facing the Difficulties Instead

RECOGNIZE THERE IS A DIFFICULTY

For these reasons, it is best to face difficulties instead of avoiding them: to acknowledge the difficulty instead of denying it is there; to accept what is happening instead of trying to reject it; to recognize the facts for what they are without twisting or distorting them. These different ways of expressing the idea have slightly different shades of meaning but are tied together with a common thread: facing difficulties is helpful even though it may be alarming. To do this, you first need to recognize that the difficulties are there, or to recognize that you are avoiding them, and this is not always easy.

Paul's girlfriend did not give up when he suggested that they go for a walk. She helped him to talk more about his job, and eventually he explained to her how much he hated it. He had applied for the job because he was interested in gardens but now he had to spend the day confined indoors, pushing pieces of paper across a desk and fighting with a computer. There were many reasons why he avoided facing up to the difficulty: he feared a change would disappoint his parents or lead to a drop in salary, and he was not confident that he would find another job or, at any rate, one that he would like better. Besides, he was terrified of interviews, although he had hardly even admitted this to himself.

Mandy's situation was a little different. She was confused by her feelings and embarrassed when she let her irritability show in the office. She welcomed each weekend with relief, absorbed herself in family life, enjoying the pleasures of her days off, until Sunday evening, when she would "suddenly" realize that she had a briefcase full of work which she could not face opening. At first, she thought this was just a temporary phase, but one Sunday when her husband offered to put Lizzie to bed so that she could catch up with the work, she lost her temper. She was shocked and upset by the strength of her feelings. It took her a long time to calm down, and when she did, she said to herself, "I've got to do something about this." That evening when everyone else was in bed she started, for the first time, to think about what was going on.

CLARIFY WHAT THE AVOIDANCE IS REALLY ABOUT

Sometimes when we are avoiding difficulties, it is obvious what these are, but sometimes it is not. Paul avoided talking to his girlfriend about his predicament, and Mandy avoided thinking about the problem altogether. When Paul began to talk about how he felt, he realized that he was also avoiding many other things: upsetting his parents, admitting his unhappiness, making a change, taking a risk, and possibly going for an interview.

Mandy found it easier to begin facing her fears by herself. Once she had admitted to herself that the bad feelings were not just going to go away of their own accord, she started to wonder what was making her so tense and irritable. Gradually, her thoughts became clearer about what was happening. She had been surprised to find that her ambitions had dissipated since Lizzie was born. As a committed career woman she had returned to work as soon as possible, and now she was both confused and embarrassed to admit, even to herself, that she wanted to stop work to look after Lizzie. She had vaguely hoped that this was just a temporary phase, and when people asked what was bothering her, she felt criticized and angry with them. Deep down she was dreading what her friends would think of her change of heart, and she had not dared even to begin to contemplate how the family would manage if she no longer earned a good salary.

THE UNWRITTEN MESSAGE

There is an unwritten message we give ourselves whenever we avoid something. The message is: "This is alarming and scary." Our attitude builds up an expectation that cannot easily be disconfirmed, because avoidance prevents us from finding out whether our fears are real. Imagine, for example, that you are feeling stressed at work to the degree that makes you think you will have to do something about it. You do not know what to do, and avoid talking to anyone about how you feel for fear of what they will think of you. Indeed, you try to work harder and harder so no one will notice that anything is wrong. Your avoidance prevents your finding solutions to the problem yourself, since you never have time to stop and think, nor does it allow you to draw on the wisdom of others or to turn to them for support.

It is crucial therefore, in facing our difficulties, to pay attention to the bad feelings and use them as a prompt to look more closely at what is happening, to clarify exactly what those difficulties are. This might be done, as in the case of Paul, by talking to a trusted friend, or it might be done, as in the case of Mandy, by thinking carefully on one's own. But unless the difficulties are clarified, they cannot be effectively tackled.

ARE YOU AVOIDING DIFFICULTIES?

Sometimes it is hard to know whether or not you really are avoiding something. It is helpful, therefore, to be alert for signs of avoidance. These three guidelines may be helpful.

1. Consult your feelings. Your avoidance may show itself in subtle ways. If the reason you do not do something is because it makes you anxious or worried, then it is likely that you are avoiding it. If you persist in doing something you find difficult but feel no better for it, then you are probably avoiding some subtle aspects of the situation. Ask yourself this: "What would I have to do in order to feel more confident?"

2. Observe your behavior. If you find yourself stuck, or wavering, between two courses of action, then think about whether you are avoiding something, and if so, see if you can work out how to approach it instead.

3. Tune in to your thoughts. Are you expecting the worst? Or predicting a disaster? Do you think something will go wrong, or that you will not be able to cope in some way? Such exaggerated, fearful thoughts can prevent you from even beginning to face the problem.

CATCH THE PROBLEMS EARLY

Avoidance not only keeps problems from being solved, it can also make them worse and increase the difficulty of facing them. The sooner that the problem is identified, the sooner you can start to tackle it and the more effective this is likely to be. The problems that make you feel bad are not like clouds that appear out of the blue and blow away of their own accord; they are more like crumbs under the skin that irritate until they are removed.

ADOPT AN ATTITUDE OF APPROACH

Konrad Lorenz tells a story about a neighbor's dog which barked aggressively when safe behind its fence.[1] It seemed to be a terrifying and dangerous beast until one day part of the fence was removed for repair. As Lorenz and his own dog walked along the path beside the fence, the beast, as usual, barked furiously from the safety of the other side. But then they came to the place where the fence had been removed. The beast found itself bristling at Lorenz and his dog with no barrier between them. Its aggression disappeared.

The avoidance of our problems is like the fence. From the safety of our neglect, the problems can bark at us with all their might. But if we take down the fence and meet them face to face, their ferocity will usually disappear. Ideas about how to overcome avoidance are described in more detail in Chapters 16 and 17.

Tackling the Difficulties

Facing difficulties and problems is the necessary prelude to tackling them. It is the first—and often the most difficult—step. Once the difficulty is clearly seen, a strategy for making you feel better is needed. The purpose of much of this book is to explain the variety of techniques available to you so that you can choose those which suit you best.

Related Chapters in This Book

Chapter 8 Problem-Solving: A Strategy for Change

Chapter 16 Getting the Better of Anxiety and Worry

Chapter 17 Overcoming Fears and Phobias

Chapter Summary

Facing difficulties is rarely as alarming in practice as it is in our imaginations, and avoiding them only perpetuates the difficulties.

Avoidance is unproductive for at least three reasons:

- It can make the problem worse.
- It creates new problems.
- It interferes with your life.

Facing difficulties involves recognizing that they are *there*. Only then can you work out what the difficulty is and think about what to do next. Catching problems early means that they have less chance of growing into imaginary monsters. Most problems shrink in size when they are looked at directly.

7

♦ ♦ ♦

Treating Yourself Right

Most children are able to throw themselves into the smallest delights, abandoning themselves to the joy of the moment in a way that is, alas, all too easily hidden away and kept securely out of sight and out of mind as we grow to adulthood. We behave as if pleasures are so precious that they have to be kept for special occasions, as if they were in danger of being destroyed with use.

Two Reasons for Rewarding Yourself

Should we put away childish things as we grow older? Some things, perhaps, but not the readiness to enjoy simple pleasures or the ability to immerse ourselves in them. The ability to give yourself treats and rewards is one of the basic strategies for improving mental fitness, and this is true for at least two reasons. In the first place, they provide enjoyment and pleasure, which contribute to feeling good and confident. In the second place, treats and rewards create the very best environment for helping you to change in the directions you wish to change. A joyless time filled only with tasks done out of duty or guilt cramps your ability to develop, and feels more like a preparation for life than living life itself. It runs the risk of turning effort into drudgery—purpose into pointlessness.

For most of us, there are relatively simple things which can give us a great deal of pleasure—things which need not be expensive. A senior nurse in a psychiatric hospital went to her hairdresser once a week. She found that having her hair washed and styled was immensely relaxing and provided a much needed indulgence. She would forget all the stresses of work as she allowed her whole being to become immersed in the sensual pleasure of having her hair washed. She knew and liked her hairdresser, and having listened so often to the troubles of others, she thoroughly enjoyed being asked about herself. The time and money spent on her appearance gave her pleasure and confidence for the rest of the week.

Treats: An Effective Way of Adding Pleasure to Your Life

PERMISSION TO TREAT YOURSELF

The wonderful thing about treats is that they can give pleasure well beyond what would seem possible. The secret is to choose the right treats for *you*. Once we are grown-up, life can become so full of chores, both at home and at work, that it is easy to get bogged down in routine and forget pleasure. We can even come to feel that it would be frivolous to give ourselves treats when there is always so much to do. Or if the problems in life seem large, then the small things in life, which could give us pleasure, may seem unimportant, and so we fail to give ourselves any pleasure. It is when life's problems are getting on top of you that it becomes particularly important to reward yourself.

Adding treats to your life can be very difficult if you are not used to it, and you may have to start slowly. For example, you may need to start by ensuring that you give yourself a treat once a week, and work up to having a treat every day.

Giving yourself treats is a skill that needs to be developed. The first step is *to give yourself permission to have treats*. Treats bring pleasure, and pleasure is worth having purely because it makes you feel good. But treating yourself will also enable you to accomplish more, and enable you to change in ways that are right for you. *Giving yourself treats is the right way to treat yourself.*

THE WRONG KINDS OF TREATS

We have offered help to many people, from many walks of life, and it is amazing how few offer themselves the small rewards we call treats. Are there wrong kinds of treats? Yes, those which either damage important relationships, or which fuel a problem. An example of the first kind might be if the treat is going out to the pub with friends when this behavior is already causing marriage problems. An example of the second is when the treat is eating a box of chocolates when there is already a problem with binge eating. In choosing treats for yourself, do not exacerbate any problems you might have. Choose treats that give harmless pleasure.

OCCASIONAL BIG TREATS

Lucy and Jeff have two sons, aged seven and three. Jeff works full-time and Lucy part-time, mainly from home. With two young children they find themselves weighed down with endless chores. The one thing they always enjoy is holidays, but although they have the time for two short vacations a year, they only take one. Why, given that holidays can provide them with so much pleasure? The reason they give is the cost.

Jeff's father is a widower living four hundred miles from Lucy and Jeff, and they take him with them when they go on holiday. This arrangement works well since it gives them all a chance to be together; Jeff's father can spend time with his only grandchildren, and Lucy and Jeff can go out together knowing that their children are well looked after. But it does make the holiday expensive because they pay for Jeff's father.

In fact, Jeff's father could afford to pay for himself, but he is saving the money to pass it on to his grandchildren. Jeff and Lucy therefore pay for him in order to leave their children's inheritance intact. Is this the best arrangement? Jeff and Lucy had never asked themselves this question because, at the back of their minds, they felt it would be self-indulgent to have two holidays. It was not until they realized what they were doing that they could begin to think about what was best.

There is a great danger in our culture that we unconsciously block out possibilities for fun because, at some level, we think that we ought not to be enjoying ourselves. We are apt to think that other things are more important, or that planning for pleasure is too self-indulgent; but the reverse is likely to be true. Having fun, giving ourselves treats, makes it more likely that we will do those other worthwhile and important tasks because we will have more energy, strength, and resilience.

Lucy and Jeff thought anew about the situation. They decided that holidays gave them the refreshment needed to tackle their demanding lives. They worked out that they could afford two holidays if Jeff's father paid for himself. All three of them discussed the situation and agreed that it would be best all round if they had two holidays a year together, and that Jeff's father paid his share. This second holiday was a big treat and it was expensive, but it added an enormous amount of pleasure not only to Jeff and Lucy's lives, but for Jeff's father, and to the lives of the grandchildren, for whose sake, it once appeared, this second holiday was being denied.

USING TREATS TO SOFTEN UNPLEASANT TASKS

Few of us are lucky enough to avoid unpleasant tasks completely—either in our jobs or our personal lives. Unpleasant tasks, however, can be softened. For Jonathan, a general practitioner, the part of the job which he found most unpleasant was the nights "on-call." On such nights he might be woken at any time and have to deal effectively and compassionately with a medical emergency. When the phone rang, in the small hours of the morning, he would wake from deep sleep and immediately feel miserable having to drag his mind from the comfort of sleep to think about the medical problem, and more often than not to get up and drive to the patient's home. The problem he set himself was this: How could he soften that miserable feeling when the phone rang on his on-call nights? One of his great pleasures in life is listening to music, and he had just recently indulged himself and bought a new CD player. He hit on the idea of "giving" himself a CD token for every night visit. For every three tokens, he would allow himself to buy a CD of his choice. This system did not, of course, make night visits a total pleasure, but now, when the phone rings, a voice inside him says "another CD token—good." Getting up is still a strain, but he can think, as he drives to the patient's house, about which CD he will buy with the token he has earned.

Such a system, adapted to suit your own pleasures, can be used in many ways to soften the impact of unpleasant tasks. If there is something you have to do but are dreading, or if you find yourself dragging your feet, plan a treat for yourself for having accomplished the dreaded deed. Link the two: see the treat as being a result of having had the courage to face the unpleasant task.

USING TREATS TO OVERCOME BARRIERS

Planning a treat helps to knock down the barrier which gets in the way of getting the job done. It is much easier to get down to a difficult task if we promise ourselves a tea break in a couple of hours. Treats should work as rewards and not as punishments. We are not saying that unless we spend a certain amount of time doing the dreaded task we cannot have the treat. The problem with making agreements with ourselves in that spirit is that they are so easily broken; we allow ourselves the treat even when we have not done what we agreed with ourselves to do. The treat is not therefore, strictly speaking, a *reward;* instead the treat helps us to look over the barrier to the pleasure that lies beyond. Treats planned in this way are all the more enjoyable because they come after the dreaded, dull, or difficult task has been done, just as the lager is all the more tasty after a game of tennis.

Creating the Right Conditions for Change: The Carrot Not the Stick

It is by no means as hard to change as it often seems; what gets in the way is the "Dotheboys Hall attitude." This is the wrongheaded but deeply ingrained belief that the best way to bring about change is through punishment. Dotheboys Hall was the school, owned by Squeers, where the young Nicholas Nickleby took up his first teaching post. To quote from Dickens,

> "Bolder," said Squeers, tucking up his wristbands, and moistening the palm of his right hand to get a good grip of the cane, "you are an incorrigible young scoundrel, and as the last thrashing did you no good, we must see what another will do towards beating it out of you."[1]

Although we would no longer dream of behaving like Squeers to our children, we can still behave like Squeers to ourselves. Listen to your internal voice when you are trying to change or trying to learn something new. Do you hear yourself saying things like: "That's idiotic"; "Don't be so stupid"; "You should know this by now"; "Are you never going to improve?" It is curious how good we are at punishing ourselves—maybe because we know exactly how to hit where it hurts. Self-criticism and self-blame are two powerful and most discouraging forms of punishment which may be intended to goad us into action but which, more often than not, make it harder to change and to learn. The result of all these barbed and sarcastic comments is that you end up feeling disgusted with yourself, miserable, dejected and disillusioned having ignored the principle that *being kind to yourself makes it easier to change.*

One of our patients said: "I wouldn't treat a worm as badly as I treat myself." This insight was the beginning of an important change in attitude. But it was one thing for her to realize that she punished herself and another for her to do anything about it. Cultural attitudes, including religious ones, seem to make rewarding oneself seem bad, as if doing something for oneself or acknowledging one's good points is conceited, boastful, or dangerously self-indulgent. It seems that we are conditioned to put ourselves down. We cannot put the years of conditioning behind us all at once. But by *developing the habit of rewarding ourselves* we can gradually replace the automatic reflex of self-abasement with one of valuing ourselves.

Constructing a Personal Reward System

An effective system of rewarding yourself has three components: pick the treats that work for you; make your system work to your advantage; and avoid the punishment trap.

PICK THE TREATS THAT WORK FOR YOU

Think about the things that you enjoy, that give you pleasure, that make you laugh, or help you to relax. Think of small things like spending an extra few minutes over breakfast, and big things like taking a holiday. Think of things you could buy now or save up for and get later; things that you could do for yourself and things you could say to yourself; things involving others and things for yourself alone. Try and make a list of 20 things. The longer the list the better. The box on the following page makes some suggestions for the categories you could adopt and offers some examples of possible treats.

MAKE YOUR TREAT SYSTEM WORK TO YOUR ADVANTAGE

1. Get the timing right. Treats work best when they come quickly after the specific goal. Immediately after forcing yourself to sort out the unpaid bills, give yourself a treat. If you treat yourself first, the bills will be even harder to face, and if you delay the treat when you have paid the bills, the connection between the two will be lost.

Some Ideas for Treats and Rewards

Things to eat or drink, for example:
Having a chocolate biscuit, a glass of wine, your favorite meal, a cup of tea

Activities, for example:
Taking a walk, watching TV or a video, planning an outing, enjoying a hobby, doing a puzzle or the crossword, playing bridge, poker, or your favorite game of cards with friends, gardening, going to a restaurant for dinner

Relaxations, for example:
listening to music, taking a long bath, calling a friend, reading a novel or magazine, sitting by the fire

Treats, for example:
Buying a bunch of flowers or a bar of scented soap, planning a trip to the theater, buying a new piece of clothing, getting up late

Time, for example:
10 minutes on your own, a mid-morning break, a proper lunch hour, time to think, a weekend break, a holiday

Exercise, for example:
Joining the local gym, taking an exercise class, going for a swim, walking the dog

Self-talk, for example:
"I'm doing fine," "I'm really pleased with . . . ," "well done," "you can make it," "you deserve a break"

Setting limits, for example:
Number of chores, bedtime, a time to stop work, demands made by others

Other people, for example:
Chatting by phone with or visiting a friend or relative, having a long lunch with an old friend

---

2. Treat yourself often. Everyone would benefit from a daily treat: small pleasures make life easier and more pleasurable. But make sure that you do not use treats which fail to satisfy. If rewards like shopping or having another cigarette, drink, or doughnut only perpetuate the search for pleasure, or make you feel better or less lonely only briefly, they may be the wrong kinds of treat for you.

3. Saving up and cashing in. You may want to save up for a big treat like a new piece of sports equipment, or an item of clothing, or a day's outing. If so, give yourself tokens toward what you want. Decide how many it is worth (for example, you could go out for a meal when you have earned 20 "tokens") and use a tick in your diary as the marker of when you have earned a token. As you collect more ticks, you can see how well you are doing.

4. Give yourself variety. You might get bored with the same treat just as with anything else, and then it loses its power to encourage. Like a diet of pure chocolate, it could lose its appeal entirely. So update your treat system from time to time, remembering that different things feel like treats at different times. Going for a long walk may be your idea of fun in the summer, but in the winter you might prefer to watch TV. You may not value peace and quiet as much at 25 (when being on your own might feel more like a punishment than a reward) as you do at 35, when the thought of a few moments to yourself can feel like pure luxury. Or the challenge that you might enjoy at 50 (traveling on your own) may feel overwhelming at 19.

5. Give yourself a break. Not doing one of the chores when you are worn out can feel good even though you know you will have to do it later. Allow yourself such breaks, and remember that a change can be as good as a rest if you need one badly. It might feel better to swap chores with someone else from time to time.

6. Turn routine pleasures into effective rewards. Leaving all the things you hate doing to the last is like creating a quagmire to struggle through later—probably when your energy and enthusiasm are at a low ebb. For example, if you have a coffee break every morning, this will feel more enjoyable, and work better as a reward if you do one hateful task before it rather than after.

AVOID THE PUNISHMENT TRAP

Do not make a virtue out of being a martyr. Do not fall into the trap of serving other people's needs so much at the expense of your own that you carry the sacrifice too far. Overburdening yourself "for the sake of others," treating yourself unfairly, makes others feel guilty and can become an undeclared way of punishing them. Saying "don't worry, I can manage" when you really mean quite the opposite punishes both you and others. In the long run everyone is worse off, and you may be building up resentment within yourself that will eventually burst out in anger, or push in on you as depression. Beating your head against a brick wall, is another version of the same thing. It feels good when you stop beating yourself, but if this is your only reward for tackling the brick wall then persisting in punishing yourself is pointless.

Parting Thoughts

In our society, people have tended to choose self-punishment over self-satisfaction, with the result that they often fail to provide for themselves the kind of encouraging environment that makes for constructive change and development. Perhaps it is because of our "puritan" inheritance that we can so easily think it wrong to indulge ourselves. Rewards and treats work better than self-criticism. They provide an important source of pleasure, and help in solving problems and overcoming difficulties. They also make it easier to learn new skills.

Chapter Summary

1. Give yourself permission to enjoy treats: they add pleasure to life and help you make the changes you want to make.
2. Replace habits of self-criticism with the habit of rewarding yourself.
3. An effective system of rewards has three components:
    *   Pick those treats that work for you.
    *   Make your system work for you.
    *   Avoid the punishment trap.

8

♦ ♦ ♦

Problem-Solving:
A Strategy for Change

SUSAN

Susan was distraught when she came to the clinic, unable to cope any longer. Looking from the outside, she seemed a highly successful professional who combined work and home life with enviable skill; but this was not how she felt inside.

Susan worked half time as a lawyer. She was married, had two young children, and her husband worked full-time as an engineer. When Susan was at work, her children were looked after by a trustworthy childsitter. So what was the problem? The problem was that she felt that she was not doing anything properly. "I don't have time to read the law journals to keep myself up to date in my job; and the house is always a mess. I've had enough." Susan was feeling bad about her life and bad about herself. "The trouble is that I've never been a tidy person, but the house is getting me down. I feel quite hopeless about it."

Susan had got herself into a downward spiral and was focusing on her weaknesses. She felt bad about herself and so hopeless about the possibility of change that she was failing to tackle the problems.

MOST STRENGTHS ARE WEAKNESSES
AND MOST WEAKNESSES ARE STRENGTHS

We tend to see things in black and white and from one perspective only. Forty years ago, adventure films were often about Cowboys and Indians: the Cowboys were the good guys and the Indians were the trouble makers. Then came James Bond; the West was good and the USSR was bad. The same simplistic pattern has been used for adventure stories throughout the ages. That is fine for adventure stories, but it is a poor model for ourselves. *Whether a characteristic is good or bad depends on the situation, and on the way we view the situation.* Take Susan's "weakness" of untidiness. If she had been a very tidy person she may not have been able to go out to work at all because she would have needed to spend so long keeping the house clean. Tolerating some degree of untidiness enabled her to devote her energies to her profession. It is too simplistic to label her habits as good or bad, and doing so means seeing them from only one point of view. The categories of good and bad are too exclusive; life is messy.

Before teaching Susan the technique of problem-solving, we talked about how she hated the mess at home and wished she were a neater person. Perhaps tidiness seems like a trivial problem, but it is often the comparatively trivial things which get us down, and which lead to stress out of all proportion to the problem. She decided that she did not want to be the kind of person for whom tidiness was of great importance—she did not want to change her *personality,* but she did want to make some changes. The question was what changes to make, and how to make them. This is where the *technique of problem-solving* came in.

The Technique of Problem-Solving

Problem-solving is such a simple and effective technique that it is easy to dismiss it as just too simple. The fact is that most people hardly make any use of it, although it can be used to resolve many different kinds of problems. It is as though we tried to tighten and loosen screws using our fingernails when we could be using a screwdriver. Once you have mastered the technique, you will wonder how you managed without it. The key to success is to go through the various stages in a methodical manner, step by step.

STAGE 1: IDENTIFY THE PROBLEM

The most important stage of all is the first stage. The problem must be clearly identified, and even named. A vague feeling of unease, of anxiety, or of depression is hard to tackle. A particular problem is much easier. At first Susan could not name her problems. She just felt that it was all too much. "Life's getting on top of me, and I'm no good at anything," was what she said.

"You said that you didn't have enough time to keep up with the law journals. Is that the most frustrating thing in your work right now?"

Susan thought for a moment. "Yes."

"If you did have time to do this and were able to keep up-to-date, would you feel better about your work, or are there other things that frustrate you?"

"In my work, you mean?"

"Yes. In your work."

"Its mainly not keeping up-to-date. Other things can be frustrating but mostly I can cope with those. I think I could be good at my job but I won't be if I don't keep on reading and learning."

"Good. So you've identified the main problem at work. What shall we call it?"

"A name, you mean?"

"A name or a phrase to describe it."

"Let's call it simply: *inability to keep up-to-date.*"

"*Inability* sounds as though the problem can't be solved. What about calling it *how to keep up-to-date?* Now what about the problems at home. What is getting to you most?"

"Undoubtedly the mess."

"What is this mess?"

"Lots of things. There are toys and half-sorted piles of clothes everywhere. The kitchen seems to be bursting at the seams and there's no place to put anything down without moving a heap of other things, so things keep getting lost..."

"Do you have help with the cleaning and tidying up?"

"Yes. Someone comes in two mornings a week to clean the house. But she can't do the tidying up because she wouldn't know where things go."

"Could you show her?"

Susan thought for a moment. Then she replied: "The problem is that we don't have enough space. Take the kitchen, for example. I buy things like kitchen towels and cereals in bulk and have to store these wherever I can find room, like on top of the kitchen cupboards, and this makes everything seem a mess..." She stopped and fell silent.

"What name would you give to this problem?"

"The problem about the mess?"

"Yes."

"The main thing is that we don't have room for everything. If we could put things away then we wouldn't leave everything lying around in a mess."

"Okay. So what do you want to call that problem?"

"I suppose it is about *lack of storage space.*"

We have given the dialogue between Susan and the therapist in some detail to show you the thought process that led to identifying some of the problems. Do not be satisfied until you have done this. Talk the problems over with someone else if you can, and ask them to help you pinpoint exactly what the problem is. Then write out a list of the problems you want to tackle.

If you find it difficult to specify what your problems are This first stage sounds simple and sometimes it is, but often it is hard to clarify exactly what the problems are. The following tips might help.

Tip 1 Talk to someone you trust and who knows you well.

Tip 2 Take a break—a short one if that is all you can manage, or a relaxing vacation if you can afford one. Think about the problems from time to time while you are away from them. Difficulties can often be more clearly seen from a distance, and when you are not in the thick of them.

Tip 3 Trust your intuition. Think about what irritates you most— where the trouble spots are. This is particularly useful if you feel generally dissatisfied but cannot put your finger on where in your life the main problems are. Is it at work or at home? Is it the weekends or the week-days that are the problem? If you are having great difficulty pinpointing the problem, *it may be because you are too frightened to admit it to yourself.* Do not be frightened. Acknowledging the problem puts you two-thirds of the way along the road to solving it. Running away from it means it will stalk you in the years to come. (See also Chapter 6.)

STAGE 2: THINK OF AS MANY SOLUTIONS AS POSSIBLE

Choose one of the problems that you have already specified clearly in Stage 1, and do a brainstorming exercise (see box opposite) to think

---

Brainstorming

Brainstorming is a useful method for generating possible solutions to a problem. It is best to brainstorm with a friend, but you can do it alone.

1. Write down a brief description of the problem you want to solve.
2. Use this description to get clear in your mind what the problem is.
3. Suggest a solution to the problem—any solution, whatever comes to mind.
4. Do not "censor" the solution—no matter how silly it sounds.
5. Make a quick note of the solution.
6. Suggest another solution, and repeat Steps 4 and 5.

Do not "censor" any solutions even if they are similar to previous solutions. If there are two or more of you, allow your ideas to be stimulated by the suggestions of the other(s).

In brainstorming you allow your mind to take off in any direction—but always with the problem in sight.

---

of as many solutions as you can. Ask a friend to help you if you can, and write down each of the possible solutions. The important point is: *Do not reject a solution at this stage however preposterous it sounds; just write it down and go on thinking about other possible solutions.*

This is how Susan tackled her second problem: the lack of storage space at home.

"Well, I suppose I could buy fewer things, but the problem with that ..."

"Stop there. At this stage the idea is to generate as many solutions as possible without evaluating them. Write down: Solution 1: Buy fewer things. Now think about other solutions."

"Okay. We could increase the storage space in the house, but I'm not sure ..."

"Stop! Write down: Increase storage space in house. Go on."

"We could, I suppose, move to a larger house, but. Sorry. I'll write down: Move to a larger house."

"We could go on as we are and stop fussing about it."

"We could build a hut in the garden and just throw everything in there! Or we could build a cellar. We could leave the car on the street outside the house and use the garage for storage."

By the end of our brainstorming session, Susan's list looked like this:

PROBLEM: THE LACK OF STORAGE SPACE AT HOME

Possible solutions
1. Buy fewer things.
2. Increase storage space in house.
3. Move to larger house.
4. Stack things all over.
5. Build storage hut in garden.
6. Build storage cellar.
7. Use garage for storage and put car on street.

STAGE 3: TAKING S.T.E.P.s

Select a solution. *Try* it out. *Evaluate* what happens. *Persist* until you feel better.

Select a solution Look through your list of solutions and decide which one looks the most promising. It may help to discuss this with someone you trust.

Susan quickly rejected solution 3. She enjoyed her garden and did not want to reduce its size by building a storage hut. The price of a storage cellar was prohibitive, and she was not keen on parking her car on the street since there had been a considerable number of car thefts in her neighborhood. Although she had lived in a messy house for several years, she was sure that she could no longer ignore the problem. This left her with two solutions to try. She thought that she could buy fewer things, and indeed get rid of a number of things she already had. Although this would help, she did not think that by itself it would be enough. She would still need more storage space. The solution she chose to focus on was solution 2: increasing the storage space in her house. There was one obvious part of the house which could be used for more storage: the loft. Susan decided that she would have the loft boarded over and a ladder put in the trap door for easy access. The cost was reasonable and the amount of extra accessible storage space would be considerable.

Try it out Having selected your preferred solution, try it out. Work out exactly what it would involve, and take the necessary steps.

Evaluate what happens The solution you have selected may be exactly the thing, or it may not be effective. If it works, you need to know this so that you can do it again if you need to, or persist if it looks as if it has put you on the right track. If it does not work, it is even more important that you know so that you can go back to your list of solutions and try something else. Many solutions are helpful but do not provide the complete answer. Again, you need to know so that you can work out whether to persist with the chosen solution or to look for further solutions to supplement it. Whatever the outcome, you need to evaluate it.

Two months after Susan had the loft space built, she evaluated the effect. She had decided to put all the things for which there didn't seem room in the loft. This had been easy and effective. She had managed to get rid of a lot of the piles which had previously cluttered up the house: her large suitcases, the children's sleeping bags, the Christmas decorations. The extra space available in the main parts of the house meant that she could start to make a place for other things. Her evaluation showed that there was still one part of the house which irritated her: the kitchen. This was still a mess. She needed to learn the last step of problem- solving.

Persist until you feel better The evaluation may show that you are on the right track, but have not gone far enough. Problems are not often solved over night. Some persistence is usually necessary. Susan's evaluation had made her feel good because she had made a great deal of progress. But the kitchen was still a problem and she needed to persist. She took another look at what the problem really was. Her kitchen was not large, but there was enough room for the things she used every day. She and her husband stood in the kitchen, glanced around, and discussed how much space was occupied by things they rarely used. Together they decided to put a large number of items up in the loft: gifts that had never been used, the barbecue grill, the cake decorating set, to make room for the things that they used every day.

The process of evaluating, and then persisting until the problem is solved, is ongoing. After another two months, Susan felt she was coping somewhat better and the therapist asked her to think again about the problem of the "mess" and the lack of storage space in the kitchen. This problem she had successfully solved, but how about the rest of the mess? Was the house now normally tidy? Did the mess still get her down? Her answer was that she had only partially solved the problem. She felt less overwhelmed and the kitchen was less cramped, but the house *was* still messy. There were toys lying around all over the place and most surfaces—for example, the tops of drawers and window sills—were cluttered with odds and ends. There definitely were still problems.

Susan was then encouraged to use the whole problem-solving method again, right from Stage 1, and she identified two new problems: the fact that many of the things lying around had no place where they belonged, and the fact that no one in the family had the habit of putting things away. These two problems were related: the fact that so many things had no "home" meant that no one saw any point in tidying up.

Susan started generating solutions to the new problems, and two months later, although the house was still not as tidy as she would ideally like it, it was significantly better than it had been. Meanwhile, she was also tackling her other problem—her inability to keep up-to-date. Her list of possible solutions looked like this.

PROBLEM: HOW TO KEEP UP-TO-DATE

Possible solutions

1. Read journals every Saturday morning while her husband looks after the children.
2. Negotiate with childsitter to look after children for extra two hours and use the time for reading.
3. Arrange a child-sitting "swap" with a friend—so that she looks after the friend's children one afternoon, and the friend looks after her children on another afternoon (giving her extra time for reading).
4. Negotiate three hours less work with her partnership and use the extra time to keep up-to-date.
5. Plan one evening a week to meet with one of her partners at work for an "update session" in which they each spend an hour and a half reading different journals and half an hour summarizing their reading to each other.

She first chose solution 3, but on evaluation, it had not proved very successful. In practice the extra time was filled with work related to her clients rather than keeping up-to-date. She went back to her problem list and selected solution 5. This proved far more successful. Sharing an "update session" with a colleague was more fun and she and her partner encouraged, or perhaps shamed each other into doing the work.

The Uses of Problem-Solving

We have explained the method of problem-solving using a relatively straightforward case for the sake of clarity. The key thing to learn is the technique, not Susan's particular problems, or her solutions, neither of which may be appropriate for you. The technique can be helpful when the problems are more complicated: when they involve your relationships with other people; or when they are more emotional in nature. If, for example, you are feeling irritated by someone with whom you live, the problem-solving method may help to clarify the problem and initiate some useful solutions.

Four Guidelines for Problem-Solving

Four Guidelines for Problem-Solving: Summary

1. Do not waste time on problems that cannot be solved: shift your focus.
2. Tackle one problem at a time.
3. Work on changing yourself, not on changing others.
4. Consider doing nothing, at least for the time being.

---

1. Do not beat your head against a brick wall. There is no point in trying to solve a problem for which there is no solution. One of our clients was finding it difficult to cope with looking after her mother who had Alzheimer's disease. We suggested using the technique of problem-solving. There was no point in trying to find ways of curing the disease; that was not possible. Instead, we helped her to focus on the aspects of caring that she was finding most difficult, such as the fact that she never had time off in the evenings for her own social life.

2. Tackle one problem at a time, and tackle that in earnest. If you try and tackle too much, you end up not solving any problem effectively. If your problems seem so numerous and so overwhelming that you need the rest of eternity to solve them all, do not lose heart. Remember the *80:20 rule: 80% of difficulties are due to 20% of problems.* If you tackle, one by one, the few most important problems, you will be overcoming a disproportionately large number of difficulties. *It is always worth tackling a problem no matter how many more problems there seem to be.*

3. Work on changing yourself. If the solutions you select force changes on other people, they are likely to fail. The person you *can* change is yourself: take responsibility for your part of the problem. It may be important to work on changing attitudes (see Chapter 9), or on learning how to be fair to yourself and others (Chapter 13), or at improving your negotiating skills (Chapter 15).

4. You could consider doing nothing for the time being. It is sometimes enough to accept a problem and decide that you can cope. For example, Susan could have decided to live with the mess in her house until her children were older, though this is not how she would ideally like it. The time and energy needed to solve a problem is sometimes not worth it.

When to Seek Help

The problem-solving technique is powerful yet simple. But there are times when you may need more help from others—for example, if you are so depressed that you cannot solve problems effectively. If this seems to be the case, read the chapters on *depression* (Chapters 20 to 22). Another signal that you may need more help is when your problems are causing serious troubles for you or those around you. *Addictive drugs,* and especially *alcohol,* can be like this (see Chapters 23, 26, and 27). If addiction is an issue, you may need some professional help before you can solve your problems alone. Sometimes anxiety and phobias can be difficult to tackle without help. Read the chapters on *anxiety* (Chapters 16 to 19) if this applies to you. *Disturbed eating* (anorexia and bulimia) may also be best tackled with some professional help (Chapter 25).

Chapter Summary

Do not be put off by the simplicity of the technique of problem- solving. Be pleased that it is so simple and yet so effective. First, specify the problems clearly. Next, choose the problem you want to start on. Then brainstorm for solutions and start to take STEPs: *Select* a solution; *Try* it out; *Evaluate* how it went; and *Persist* until you feel better.

Problem-solving is a simple but powerful technique. Use the following box as a summary and reminder.

Three Stages of Problem-Solving

1. Identify the problem clearly.
2. Generate as many solutions as possible: do not reject a solution at this stage, however preposterous it sounds.
3. Take STEPs toward solving the problem:
   • *Select* a solution.
   • *Try* it out.
   • *Evaluate* what happens.
   • *Persist* until you feel better.

9

♦ ♦ ♦

Keeping Things in Perspective:
Help from Cognitive Therapy

Men are disturbed not by things but by the views which they take of them.

Epictetus, A.D. 55–135

About 1900 years ago, Epictetus stated a profound truth. But only in the last 25 years has Epictetus's insight been developed into a type of therapy, called *cognitive therapy*—one of the most important recent advances in practical psychology. This therapy was originally developed by Albert Ellis and Aaron Beck.[1] This chapter explains how you can make use of the methods of cognitive therapy to change perspectives that have a negative effect on your feelings and actions. These methods will help you to tackle a whole range of problems and difficulties: those that affect your mood, such as feeling depressed, anxious, or angry; and those that affect your behavior, such as continually striving for success, eating too much or too little, or avoiding social situations. It is one of the most important tools available to psychotherapists and to you.

The Three Fundamentals of Cognitive Therapy

Cognitive therapy is built on three key principles. The first is understanding that the viewpoint you "choose" is vital to your mood. We use the word "choose" because your viewpoint is, to a large extent, a matter of choice. This is Epictetus's point. The second principle involves understanding how mood and thought are linked: change the one and you also change the other. The third principle consists of learning how to work on your thoughts and beliefs. The methods of cognitive therapy improve mood, but they do this not by working directly on your mood—they work directly on your *thoughts*. By changing your thinking, you can improve your mood. The first question to ask yourself is this: *Is there another way of seeing things?*

The Vital Importance of Viewpoint

If you visit a new place, or take a journey through a new country, you quickly accumulate impressions of what you see and develop your own point of view. You draw conclusions: "The people here are really friendly." And form opinions: "Life here is much less stressful than it is at home." Indeed, developing your own personal picture of the place and comparing it with the pictures others have developed contribute to the pleasures of travel. Each of us develops our own point of view, shaped by our particular, limited experience, and this experience is filtered and interpreted in our own particular way. We all use our own point of view, our own perspective, as a basis for our conclusions and our opinions.

Once on home ground again, however, it is easy to lose sight of this point. Our own ways of seeing things become habitual and compelling so that we easily forget that they are only one point of view. Imagine that you return from a vacation refreshed and throw yourself back into everyday life, maybe with one or two groans, but certainly with every intention of doing your best. Things go well for you. You get a lot more done and are given a pay rise and more responsibilities. You are pleased with your success, and the good mood that it brings pervades your life generally. You know you are a success.

Now imagine a different chain of events. You throw yourself back into the fray with energy and enthusiasm, but events beyond your control mean that things go wrong. Maybe someone gets ill, or jobs have to be cut and you are made redundant. There was nothing you could have done to prevent these things happening, but all the same you blame yourself, feel helpless, and think of yourself as a failure. A mixture of feelings—sadness, anger, frustration, resentment, among other emotions pervade your life.

In one case you see yourself as a success, in the other as a failure. In both, the point of view seems to be the one and only truth. But this is not so. When you visit somewhere new, there is not just one possible point of view, there are many. Some perspectives may fit the facts better than others, or be more or less helpful to you, but each person's perspective has its own limitations and obscurities. The person who succeeds at work may do so at the expense of relationships. The person who lost a job may be a successful parent, friend, or musician. Neither of them is anything so one-dimensional as a "success" or a "failure," and both of them might see things differently looking from a different perspective. The point is this: *There is always more than one way of seeing things.* Not just sometimes, but always. You may feel at times as if you have no choice, but this is an illusion. So when the good mood evades you, learn to ask: How else could I think about this? How would someone else see it? What other points of view are there? Answering these questions is a mental exercise you should try from time to time. It flexes your emotional muscles, challenging you to expand your perspective, to think flexibly, and to search for a viewpoint that helps you feel better.

KEEPING AN OPEN MIND

If it is true that *there is always more than one way of seeing things*, then the difficulty is to find other points of view to choose between. One's own perspective is bound to feel most convincing, especially in the heat of the moment. The methods described in the rest of this chapter help you step back from your viewpoint and to see the facts clearly, to give yourself a choice of perspectives. As you shift your perspective, you will find that your mood also shifts. Looking for new, and wider, perspectives prevents you from getting trapped in a one-sided view and gives you more control over the way you feel. The spectacles through which you see the world are so familiar that you hardly notice that you are wearing them. By taking them off and trying out others, you can discover which things were out of focus and whether you have been looking through distorted or colored glass.

We are not recommending a kind of "cock-eyed optimism." We are not suggesting that whatever your circumstances you should look on the bright side. Our point is captured by Viktor Frankl, in his most moving book about life as a prisoner in a concentration camp when he describes "the last of human freedoms"—"the ability to choose one's attitude in any given set of circumstances."[2] Developing the habit, in the course of our more mundane lives, of searching for different and wider perspectives helps you to cope realistically and flexibly with difficulties as they arise. It gives you more options.

The methods of cognitive therapy are relatively new but the ideas behind them are old and familiar. Mr Thornton, a successful industrialist described by Mrs. Gaskell in her novel *North and South* written in 1855, decided not to talk to his mother about an interview she had with the woman he loved because "he felt pretty sure that . . . his mother's account of what passed at it would only annoy . . . him, though he would all the time be aware of the coloring which it received by passing through her mind."

The Links between Feelings and Thoughts

Feelings influence how you think, and thoughts affect how you feel. These interrelations are quite dramatic. In one experiment different kinds of music were played to different people.[3] Some people listened to bright, happy music (an extract from *Coppélia,* by Delibes) to put them in a good mood. Other people listened to some very miserable music. In fact, it was an extract from the music for the film *Alexander Nevsky,* called *Russia under the Mongolian Yoke* by Prokofiev, and it was played at half speed to make it even more lugubrious. It sounded like Eeyore on a bad day. The people who listened to the bright music felt happy. The people who listened to the sad music felt miserable. That is not surprising. What was interesting was that those who felt miserable after listening to the sad music had different *thoughts* from those who had listened to the happy music. They remembered more bad things that had happened in their lives and thought that they were less likely to do a relatively simple task successfully.

Other research has confirmed these results and has shown *how* thoughts affect feelings. One of the most dramatic illustrations of this connection involved merely reading a list of words arranged in pairs.[4] This research was done in a therapist's consulting room during treatment for panic. When the subjects of the study were quite calm and at ease, people who experienced panic attacks read out loud a list of word-pairs. If their list of words contained pairs such as "breathless–choking" or "palpitations–dying," they experienced sudden and intense waves of anxiety, and started to panic. This reaction demonstrated that episodes of intense anxiety can be precipitated entirely by thoughts.

These links between feelings and thoughts are being made all the time in our daily lives. For example, you feel miserable, and you think about the things that have gone wrong in your life, or you feel apprehensive and think you will make a mess of something. You think somebody you are fond of might be ill and you feel worried, or you think somebody is insulting you and you feel angry. Feelings and thoughts influence each other all the time—and there is a close match between them. If you think you have failed, you will feel disappointed, or sad, but you will not feel envious, since this emotion does not fit this stream of thought. If you did feel envious then you would have different thoughts, for instance about the good fortune of people who had been more successful than you.

Our very process of thinking—what we readily remember, what we think about, how we see things—is altered by our mood. The problem is that the bad mood in turn brings about more bad thoughts, so that the feelings get worse in a vicious cycle:

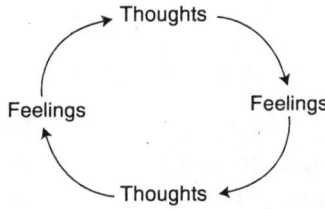

Here are examples of two common cycles, a "depressed" and an "anxious" one. In both of them you can see how the thoughts influence the feelings, and how the feelings trigger more thoughts.

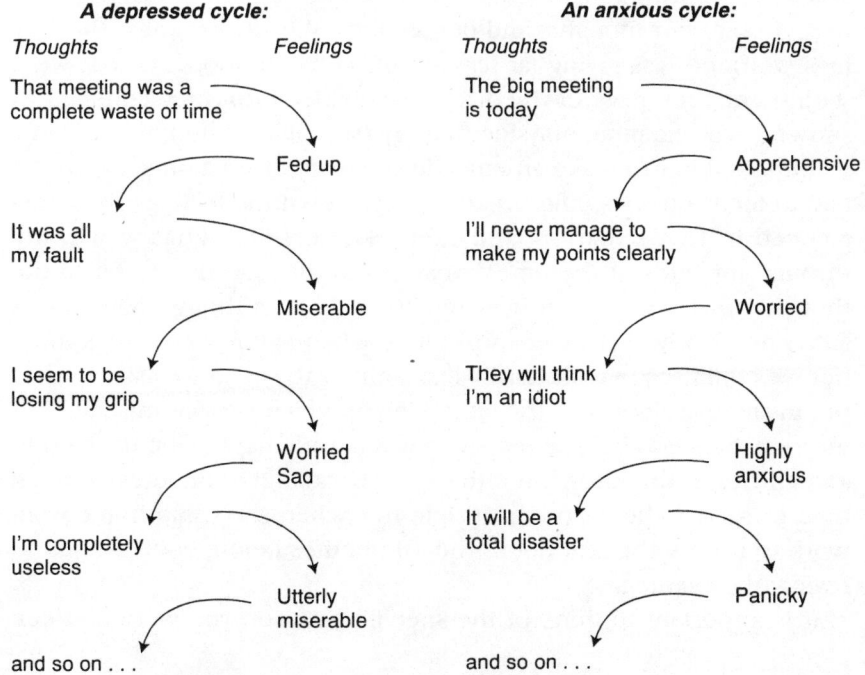

Working on Your Thoughts and Beliefs

If you were able to *think* differently, or to adopt another point of view, you would also *feel* differently. This is the key to cognitive therapy. Cognitive therapy tackles thoughts as a way of tackling mood. If instead of thinking you have failed, you recognize that everyone makes mistakes, the error you have just made will feel less like a sign of failure and more like a triviality. The skill lies in looking for ways of thinking differently, and the first step is to recognize your present viewpoint. First, you need to identify the specific thoughts that trouble you in the specific situations that make you feel bad.

STEP 1: HOW TO IDENTIFY PROBLEMATIC THOUGHTS— THE THOUGHT RECORD

Ashley came to us for help because she was often miserable and worried. She had accepted the offer of a new job, moved to a new place, leaving her boyfriend, Ben, behind, and she felt lonely and depressed. Over the last few weeks her feelings had been getting worse, until she felt utterly at their mercy. The vicious cycle had spiraled down until all she could think about was how bad she felt. At our first meeting we explained the relationship between thoughts and feelings, and asked her to keep a "Thought Record": a special kind of diary to help her pinpoint her thoughts and her feelings. She already knew the feelings well, and was giving far less attention to the thoughts that went with them. Each page of the diary was divided into three columns, as shown in the example of Ashley's diary (see facing page).

We asked her to make an entry in the diary at least once a day. She had to focus on a specific situation, note down the feelings she experienced in that situation, and then ask herself, "What was going through my mind at the time?" Answers to this question revealed the thoughts that linked with her specific feelings. Although Ashley was suffering greatly, there were still times when she felt relatively good, but we could see that she easily lost sight of these. So we asked her to put in the diary not only the situations in which she felt miserable or worried, but also those when she felt relatively happy. She decided to add entries in the diary three times a day: taking 10 minutes at lunch time to review the morning, 10 minutes when she came home from work to review the afternoon, and 10 minutes before going to bed to review the evening.

It is important to think of the specific situation you were in when you noticed feeling bad, and not just to dwell on the feelings themselves. This makes the task of identifying specific thoughts easier, because it tells you where in your memory to start searching for them. Doing this exercise is like becoming an expert mechanic who can listen to the sound of the engine, watch how the car performs, and then tune in to possible sources of trouble. Some of the entries from Ashley's diary are shown below.

Thought Record

Situation	Feelings	Thoughts
• Be specific.	• There may be more than one.	• Keep the different thoughts separate.
Traveling to work	Sad	1. I've made the wrong decision about accepting this job. 2. There's nothing I can do to change it.
Sitting at home after work	Depressed Lonely	1. I'm all on my own. 2. I don't have any friends.
After getting flustered talking to my boss	Miserable Anxious	1. I should be able to cope better than this. 2. I'm useless and feeble.
Ben telephoned when I was out	Worried Tense Upset Confused	1. I'm losing touch with him. 2. I'm not sure I want to stay with him.
Shopping	Cheerful	1. Ben is coming for the weekend. 2. No lines in the supermarket. 3. Things might be okay after all.
Waking up	Wretched	No thoughts—but I know it's Monday morning.

It is often difficult to tune in to what is in one's mind. Sometimes the thoughts are not easily put into words. Or they can be so familiar that they "go without saying," like assuming others think you are stupid, or that they are too busy to be bothered with you. When cognitive therapists talk about "thoughts" they are using a kind of shorthand to refer to thoughts, beliefs, attitudes, ideas, images, and all the other contents of your mind—even including your dreams. So your thoughts may not have been put into words before, and they may not easily be expressed in proper sentences. Here are some key questions that can help you to identify your thoughts:

Key questions for Step 1: Identifying Problematic Thoughts

What went through my mind at the time?

How am I seeing things now?

What is it about this that matters to me?

What does this event or situation mean to me?

Or what does it mean about me?

Look for thoughts that fit with the way you feel. Sometimes it is easy to make this fit: if you think you have done something wrong, or you remember doing something foolish, those things obviously fit with the way you feel—ashamed or embarrassed. Sometimes it is much harder: you feel discouraged even though nothing particular seems to have provoked that feeling today. Using the Thought Record can help you to solve this problem. Keep asking yourself the key questions, and try to stand back from the problem far enough to identify your personal perspective. Maybe feeling discouraged reflects a more pervasive attitude—lacking self-confidence or harboring dissatisfaction, for example. The links may seem obvious once you have identified them, but they are hard to recognize at first because it is so easy to become blinded by your own personal viewpoints. The more often you use the Thought Record, the easier this will become.

THIRTEEN KINDS OF CROOKED THINKING

Like looking through a prism, or a pair of distorting eyeglasses, some ways of thinking add a particular bias to your view of the world and are especially likely to be associated with feeling bad. Getting rid of the bias and getting your thoughts back into perspective will make you feel better, but first you need to recognize that the bias is there. These are the thirteen most common types of biased thinking which lead to feeling bad. *Which of these is contributing to your problems?* Most people have favorites, and readily fall into habitual patterns of thinking. Once you have identified, and named, the biases in your thinking, you are halfway to defeating your bad mood.

1. *Catastrophizing* Predicting the worst outcome. If something goes wrong, it will be a disaster. Every twinge is a sign of serious illness, every frown a sign of rejection. "If I make a mistake, I will lose

my job." "I'll lose control completely." "My heart is beating so fast I could die."

2. *Overgeneralizing* Assuming that because something happened once, this means it will always happen. "You always forget to do the things I ask." "I never seem to say the right thing." "Politicians always tell lies." "We always do things your way." "I'm such a fool. I always blow it at the last minute."

3. *Exaggerating* Giving negative events more importance than they really deserve, and positive events less importance. "I'll never get over it." "Any fool should be able to pass a driving test." "I can't bear it." "The way I look, nobody could take me seriously." "People never enjoy being with me because I'm too shy." "Landing this contract doesn't really mean anything at all."

4. *Discounting the positive* Rejecting good things as if they did not count (or using a negative filter). "She only said that to make me feel better." "I could never have done that on my own." "It's just that I was lucky." "I happened to be in the right place at the right time." "What, this old thing? I bought it at a garage sale."

5. *Mind reading* Believing that you know what others are thinking. "She knows I've made a mess of this," "They all thought I was stupid." "He doesn't like me." "You only say that because you want to get at me." "They only asked me because they couldn't find anyone else."

6. *Predicting the future, or fortune telling* "Everything is bound to go wrong." "I won't be able to cope on my own." "I couldn't face it if something dreadful happened." "The interview went so badly I know they won't give me the job." "It's no use, I'll never get it right." "I'll never be able to do that sort of thing."

7. *Black and white thinking* Switching from one extreme to another. "If I can't get this right, I might as well give up altogether." "If you can say that, then our relationship means nothing at all." "One mistake ruined the whole thing." "One false move, and the business will crumble."

8. *Taking things personally* "They didn't ask me because they don't like me." "You're criticizing me" (when someone asks you to do something differently). "That waiter just ignores me." "If they don't get here it's because I gave them such bad directions."

9. *Taking the blame* Taking responsibility when it is not yours. "It's all my fault." "Sorry." "They'd be happier if I'd been a better mother." "If only I'd done more for . . . " "He failed the test because I was so nasty to him last night."

10. *Emotional reasoning* Mistaking feelings for facts. "I'm so worried, I know something is going to go wrong." "I'm sure they've had an

accident." "I love her so much she's bound to respond." "I don't care what you say, I just feel the way I do."

11. *Name calling* "I'm an idiot." "You're completely heartless." "Anybody who could do that must be brain dead." "I'm stupid." "I'm bad."

12. *Scare mongering* "Maybe she's really ill." "What if the car breaks down?" "Suppose they can't do anything about it?" "People do suddenly drop dead—you read about it in the papers." "Perhaps I'll fail." "I couldn't cope ..."

13. *Wishful thinking* Supposing things would be better if they were different. "If only I were ... younger ... thinner ... smarter ... not the way I am."

Pressurizing words to watch out for. These words are often used when people want to motivate themselves to do better or try harder, but instead they tend to make them feel pressured and resentful so that motivation drains away.

- *Should:* "I *should* have done better." "You *should* have let me know."
- *Must:* "I *must* get this right." "I *must* not make a mistake."
- *Have to:* "I *have to* get there on time." "I *have to* keep this relationship going."
- *Ought:* "I *ought* never to lose my temper." "I *ought* to be on time."

Extremist words to watch out for. Extremist statements are (by definition) only very rarely true. Like meeting someone who is 7 foot tall, it might happen, but it would be worth writing home about if it did.

- *Always:* "You *always* leave me to sort things out." "I *always* have to clear up after you."
- *Never:* "I can *never* do what I really want to do". "I'll *never* get what I want." "I'll *never* change." "You *never* listen to what I say."
- *Nobody:* "*Nobody* ever notices how much I do for them." "*Nobody* ever laughs at my jokes."

STEP 2: HOW TO LOOK FOR OTHER PERSPECTIVES—
THE ALTERNATIVE DIARY

However compelling your thoughts and beliefs seem, there are other points of view as well: other angles from which one can look at the facts. After a couple of weeks of hard work with the Thought Record, Ashley was much better at identifying her thoughts. We then introduced her to the "Alternative Diary." Taking one thought at a time, she started the search for alternative points of view: the search for other ways of thinking that would make her feel better.

The Alternative Diary has only two columns: one for the thoughts and the other for alternative points of view. We asked Ashley to take one thought at a time, to write it down in the first column, and then to pose the following question: *"Is there another way of seeing things?"* She wrote down, in the second column, any alternatives she could think of, regardless of whether they seemed credible. An example of Ashley's *Alternative Diary* is given on the following page.

It is best to do this exercise on paper first. When you are good at it, you will be able to do it in your head. If you only do it in your head, and never write it down, you may forget how it went later. When the bad feelings sweep over you, it is only too easy to lose sight of the whole landscape and get lost in the mist.

The skill of looking for other perspectives lies in asking yourself some more key questions:

Key Questions for Step 2: Looking for Other Perspectives

Questions about thoughts   What other points of view are there? How would someone else think about this? How else could I think about it? How would I think about this if I were feeling better?

Questions about reality   What are the facts of the case? How can I find out which way of thinking fits the facts best? What is the evidence?

Questions about crooked thinking   Could I be making a mistake in the way I am thinking? Am I thinking straight? Am I using one of the thirteen kinds of crooked thinking? Am I pressurizing myself? or using the language of the extremist?

Questions about coping   What is the worst that could happen? How bad is this going to get? What can I do when that happens? How can I get help?

Look for answers that fit the facts and that make you feel better. If the answers do not fit with the facts they will not help because you will not believe them. *A note of caution:* You are not looking for "the right" answers. You are looking for a way of seeing things that makes you feel better. There is no one right way, but there are many options (or perspectives). The problem is getting stuck with the option that makes you feel bad and forgetting that it is worth looking for others.

Alternative Diary

- *Reminder:* Look for alternatives that make you feel better.

Thoughts: Take one at a time.	*Alternative points of view:* There may be more than one.

---

1. I've made the wrong decision.	It seemed the right one at the time. It's too soon to tell. I probably think that because I feel so bad.
2. There's nothing I can do to change it.	Extremist words creeping in! Things I could do: Stick with the job and think how to make a go of it. Chuck it! Talk it over with Sandra (friend) and Alvin (brother). Get out and about more. Find somewhere to play squash.
3. I'm all on my own.	That's true. I *am* sitting here alone right now. But I'm not all alone in the world. There's Ben, even if I'm not sure about us. There are people at work even if I don't know them yet, friends as well. I've made friends before, so I can probably make new ones too—it's ridiculous to think I always will be alone, and exaggerated to think it means no one cares.
4. I should be able to cope better than this.	The "should" really puts the pressure on. Maybe anyone would feel unsettled right now. Perhaps it's just a settling down stage. Anyway I *am* coping in some ways. The facts: Found somewhere to live; working things out with Ben; learning new things at work.
5. I'm useless and feeble.	If someone else said that about me, I'd think it was a complete exaggeration—and a real putdown. I know it's not true, and saying it only makes me feel worse.

How Does It Work in Practice?

Looking for the evidence. Mary was helped by cognitive therapy. She was a junior hospital administrator working in the accounts department and thought that she was being given too many of the rotten jobs at work. She felt she was being used as a dogsbody. She had recently been asked to take on three major projects: to update the package of introductory material for people joining the department;

to sort out the communal filing system; and to coordinate with other departments over joint projects. She felt she was providing the framework for other people to do the work rather than doing it herself. She tried to put a brave face on the situation, but nevertheless assumed that she was not considered very able. She dreamed about moving to somewhere where she would be better appreciated.

These were all Mary's assumptions, and she had not checked whether they were fact or fantasy. Her therapist asked her, "How could you find out whether these assumptions are right?" Together they discussed the possibilities, and Mary decided that she would talk first to one of her colleagues and then to her immediate boss. She found this difficult to do, but having thought about it carefully, decided that it was important enough to try. She was surprised to hear that no one realized either how she felt, or that she minded being landed with these tasks. From their perspective, they thought well of her skills and were exploiting her good nature. Everyone found these tasks boring and all of them were glad that they were in the hands of someone as efficient as Mary. Contrary to what she had thought, the evidence suggested that Mary's colleagues admired her abilities. After she talked about how she felt, her boss gave her more interesting work.

In Mary's case tackling the thoughts resulted in a plan of action which she carried out. As a result she felt much better. Sometimes the facts will be painful to hear, and not as reassuring as they were for Mary. This point will be taken up below. Nevertheless, getting the facts straight is crucial, although it often takes courage to find them out.

Looking for other points of view. After they had a fight, Nancy walked out of the house leaving Jerry fuming inside. He thought; "Right. That's it. She's done with me for good. I might as well leave now." He was both angry and miserable. He did not want to lose the relationship.

What other views are there? Here are some of the possibilities from Nancy's point of view:

> Its her way of cooling down. She does not realize how Jerry will interpret her behavior. She had to go out anyway, and did not explain because she was angry. She regrets the things she said and is blaming herself. She has difficulty controlling her temper and was taught to walk away from it as a child. She is ashamed. She thinks he really means the unpleasant things he said about her during the fight. She wants to get back at him.

You can probably think of others—and the situation is very likely to be complex as well as explosive. The point is that, especially in the heat of the moment, one's own perspective has a blindingly obvious quality, while that of others becomes almost invisible.

Asking "What is the worst that could happen?" What if Mary and Jerry were both right, and their worst fears came true? So Mary finds out that no one thinks she is any good at the job, and Jerry discovers that he is going to lose Nancy.

If this happens Mary and Jerry will, almost certainly, be upset. But it is important that they do not turn their difficulties into catastrophes. If Mary thinks she will *never* be good at *any* job and Jerry predicts he will *never* find another relationship, then their thoughts will rub salt into the wounds, and the worse they feel the harder it will be to cope with the real difficulties they are in. If it seems to you likely that the worst really will, or has, happened, then the next step is to ask yourself how to cope: how to deal with this particular, difficult situation.

When problems seem insurmountable, or when they really are insoluble, it is tempting to give up—or to give in. Neither Mary nor Jerry may be able to find what they want in terms of "the right" job or a new relationship. Do they then *have* to go on feeling bad? Is this inevitable? What are their choices?

It would not be helpful to pretend that the difficulties did not matter. But Mary, and Jerry, may also have the resources to help keep the distress within acceptable limits. They each have personal assets and skills that could help: a sense of humor, an ability to accept what cannot be changed, persistence, flexibility, and so on. They have each coped with difficulties in the past and could think about what they did then—like looking to friends or relatives for help, advice, or support. They may need information, about openings for further training or where to meet people with similar interests. There may be more ways of looking for new jobs and different relationships than they have yet tried.

The point is that resources come in many shapes and sizes: personal qualities, skills and abilities, other people, general knowledge and information. Using them helps to keep the problems you encounter in perspective. If you do not use them when you feel bad, you will tend to feel helpless and be prone to self-blame, with thoughts in your head such as "I'm useless," "there's nothing I can do," "I should be able to cope better than this," which only make you feel worse, and make it harder to accept the reality for what it is: often not nearly as comfortable as one wishes it could be, but with smooth patches as well as rough ones along the way.

THE MEANING OF THE SITUATION

In Nancy's family, arguments were often violent: people got hurt physically as well as psychologically. She "knows" that it is better to get out while you can if you are involved in an emotional argument, and she ran away from Jerry in fear even though, in her right mind, she was confident that he would not resort to violence. She just thought, "I have to get out of here," and acted on this thought quickly, as she would have done as a child. This is an example of how one can be misled by one's thoughts. Nancy's thoughts made sense in terms of her past, but other ways of thinking would fit the facts far better in the present.

Many situations carry with them a load of meaning from the past what is often called "emotional baggage." For example, when someone is angry with us, or critical, or when we are unable to get our own way, many of us behave and feel rather like we did as children. If we felt rejected by such things then, and wanted to run away and hide, then we may feel the same way now and want to do the same things. The old reaction is understandable but out of date. Present meanings may differ from old ones, and what felt like rejection in the past may be no worse than bad temper or a temporary reaction to a mistake in the present. This is another reason why it is so important to keep in touch with present facts and not assume that each new country you visit is just like the last one.

All sorts of activities carry with them meanings that trigger patterns of thinking that are associated with strong, and often disproportionate, feelings. When small children refuse to eat a meal that has been specially prepared, parents often feel surprisingly concerned and upset, as if the well-being of the child depended on this particular meal, or as if the refusal to eat was a personal rejection. Losing a game of cards, or a competition for someone's business, can feel like a humiliating defeat rather than a temporary setback. Perhaps "winning" has become a way of gaining something important, like approval from others, or greater self-esteem. Or "losing" may have been associated with the kind of teasing from brothers and sisters that felt cruelly rejecting as a child. When relatively small events provoke much more strong feeling than you think they should, then it is likely that these events have some critical meaning for you. *This is when it is useful to go back to the beginning and ask yourself the key questions about meaning: "What does this mean to me? Or what does it mean about me?"* It is as if the meaning of these events has given them a disproportionate significance. Cognitive therapy helps you to feel better by getting your problems into perspective, and by testing your beliefs and assumptions against the facts.

Some Rules of Perspective

Having a problem can dominate your life. Whichever way you turn, the mountain or the cliff edge looms ahead, providing a dispiriting or alarming perspective. The following rules may be helpful when trying to find the most useful perspective.

1. *The 100-year rule* (p. 177). Will it matter in 100 years? Will anyone even remember what the problem was? Of course, this is something of an exaggeration, since none of us will be here in 100 years. It is meant as a reminder that those things that seem hugely important today may matter little when seen from a great distance. When you stand beside an elephant, it is extremely hard to see anything else. When you step back from it, the rest of the animal kingdom, the other visitors to the zoo and their surroundings, all come back into view.

2. *The measuring rod rule* (p. 177) Is the thing that is bothering you really the most important thing in your life at the moment? Imagine you have an important job to do today. You feel tense and worried about it, and the traffic jam on the way to work is enough to send you into a tirade of anger against all the bad drivers on the road. Of course, the traffic jam is important to you, but only as an impediment. Only as something that gets in the way of doing something that is of far greater importance in the long run.

3. *The middle of the night rule.* In the early hours of the morning, when you are lying awake, problems and worries assume insurmountable proportions. In the cool light of day, they can be more truly seen for what they are—molehills rather than mountains. The rule is: Think about them in the morning or during the day. It is always hard to keep things in perspective when lying awake worrying at night. Tell yourself "This is not the time." (See also Chapters 16 and 24.)

4. *The water-under-the-bridge rule, or the statute of limitations.*

You feel bad about things that you did, or things you did not do. They continue to trouble you long past the time when they should. Let them flow by you instead, and look back on them as if they were someone else's mistakes or troubles. You may be carrying an unnecessary load, weighing yourself down with bothers that are well past their sell-by date. There comes a time when you have punished yourself enough.

Chapter Summary and Reminder

- **There is always more than one way of seeing things.**

This means that although you may not be able to choose the facts you may be able to choose how you react to them, and help yourself feel better and act more effectively by looking at them differently. The methods explained here reveal how your feelings and thoughts are linked, and how these thoughts and feelings color your mood. If you practice using them, you will discover the kind of thinking that helps you to feel good. When practicing them, it is useful to ask yourself questions. The first one is this: "Is there another way of seeing things?"

- *Step 1:* Recognize your thoughts and the way your thoughts and moods link together.

Key questions for Step 1:

What went through my mind at the time?

How am I seeing things now?

What is it about this that matters to me?

What does this event or situation mean to me?

Or what does it mean about me?

- *Step 2:* Reexamine your thoughts. You will find that there are many perspectives from which you can look at a situation. Finding new perspectives gives you more options and helps you feel better.

Key questions for Step 2:

Questions about thoughts: What other points of view are there? How would someone else think about this? How else could I think about it? How would I think about this if I were feeling better?

Questions about reality: What are the facts of the case? How can I find out which way of thinking fits the facts best? What is the evidence?

Questions about crooked thinking: Could I be making a mistake in the way I am thinking? Am I thinking straight? Am I using one of the thirteen kinds of crooked thinking? Am I pressurizing myself? Or using the language of the extremist?

Questions about coping: What is the worst that could happen? How bad is this going to get? What can I do when that happens? How can I get help?

10

◆ ◆ ◆

Building Self-Confidence and Self-Esteem

Lacking Self-Confidence

Rachel believed she could never be confident. She was convinced that confident people had something that she just did not have, like blond hair or long legs. She was not sure how the differences between her and them allowed their confidence to remain strong in the face of adversity while hers remained fragile and elusive, even in good times. She suspected that confidence was unchangeable because it was written in the stars, or determined by chance. Confidence to her meant having a strong personality, which was either built in from the start or built up from encouragement at home and at school. Now that she was an adult of 32 it seemed to her that opportunities for becoming confident had gone for good. Lacking self-confidence was a cross she had to bear—whatever she did it was likely to remain with her and to let her down, in the same way as her unmanageably frizzy hair. She could wait for the lucky break (the perfect hair lotion, or a fashion for corkscrew curls), but in her heart of hearts she believed she had no other option but to remain forever unconfident.

In the box on the following page, you can see how low self- confidence can affect the four aspects of life: your thinking, your feelings, your behavior, and your body. Being unconfident has surprisingly pervasive effects—it sneaks its way into hidden nooks and crannies and interferes with the things you want to do even when you least expect it. Look at the box and think about your own level of confidence. Adapt the list, if necessary, to fit your own experience.

Some of the Effects of Low Self-Confidence

Thinking

I can't.
That's too difficult.
I don't know how.
Maybe I won't be able to handle this.
It won't be good enough; someone else would do better.
I just can't decide what to do.

Feelings

Apprehension
Anticipatory anxiety
Worry, especially about forthcoming difficulties
Frustration and anger with yourself
Fear of the unknown, or of new situations
Resentment—it seems so easy for others
Discouragement and feeling demoralized

Behavior

More passive than active; keeping yourself in the background
Finding it hard to make suggestions, or put yourself forward
Prevaricating; being a slow starter
Avoiding taking on anything new or making changes in your life
Seeking help and advice even when you know the answer
Hesitating—and repeatedly needing encouragement
Taking a back seat
Asking for reassurance

Bodily signs of low confidence

Posture: tending to stoop, or retreating into yourself
Not looking people in the eye
Fumbling or fidgeting
Feelings of tension and nervousness
Sluggishness and lethargy

Becoming More Confident: Four Basic Insights

Rachel started to work on her confidence from the moment we first met her. Since confidence comes from *inside,* there was little point in giving her answers she might not believe, or could easily discount. She was ready with her favorite objection: "It's easy for you, but I'm just not like that." Instead, she took on the following assignment: to find out more about confidence from the point of view of others. This assignment made sense to Rachel because it could tell her more about the nature of this elusive concept, and carrying it out involved nothing more difficult than talking to people she already knew. She spoke to her brother; to someone who was starting her training as a nurse; to an aunt; to a colleague; and to various friends. She was surprised, once she developed ways of dropping the topic into the conversation, how many people had something to say about it, and how easy it was for her to sit and listen. Here are some of the things she asked: "What do you think confidence is?" "Where does confidence come from?" "Can you think of someone who is completely confident?" "How can you tell if someone is confident or not?" "How do you feel when you are talking to someone who is not at all confident?" "Does a confident person always feel confident?"

Rachel made both mental and written notes about her findings so that we could talk about them later. She found the following four points the most helpful—and they fit with what we know about confidence.

1. CONFIDENCE IS NOT JUST ONE THING

Confidence is not just one thing, it is many. Rachel was not confident when discussing a video she had watched with some friends, but she had no problem finding her way across country to visit her aunt. She had stopped to ask the way when she got lost, and did not berate herself for getting lost along the way. Most of the people she spoke to said similar things. One of them thought she would never be able to make sense of her tax form, and had found learning to spell so difficult that she treated it as a lost cause, but she still led her daily exercise classes with energy and enthusiasm. The most confident person Rachel spoke to was her cousin, a buyer for a clothes store—but even he admitted that he lacked self-confidence from time to time, especially when training his junior staff, despite his acknowledged success. He knew he was good at his job, but he had learned it the hard way, by being thrown in at the deep end and having to get on with it. New recruits to his department now arrived with college-polished theories, talking a language that he told himself was "jargon," but that he feared, deep down, was too clever for him. He felt particularly at sea when the "common sense" he hardly needed to put into words was given textbook names that distanced him from the reality he knew. Rachel concluded that whether or not you feel confident depends on what you are doing. Labeling yourself as irredeemably unconfident is like failing to distinguish between all the different ways in which you can be confident or unconfident.

2. APPEARANCES CAN BE MISLEADING

Many people appear confident even when they are not. It is as if they know they might make a mistake, get things wrong, or put their foot in their mouth, but still behave as if everything will be all right in the end. When learning to give injections for the first time, Rachel's friend, the trainee nurse, said she thought about what she had been taught and about the more experienced people to whom she could turn in a crisis. She hid her uncertainties for the sake of her patients. When she concentrated fully on what she was doing, she found there was little room left for doubts to creep in. Everyone Rachel spoke to could think of something that made them feel doubtful or shaky. Rachel learned that most people felt less confident than they looked.

3. CONFIDENCE COMES FROM DOING THINGS

Everyone Rachel spoke to agreed that confidence comes from doing things. Before you can ride a bicycle or drive a car, you have to learn how—confidence comes with practice, which makes it easier to recognize and accept that you really can do those things. Mistakes are inevitable when you are a novice. In fact, they are an important part of the learning process. Everyone makes mistakes, and they only get in the way if you let them undermine your confidence. Learn to shrug them off, or laugh about them with others who have found themselves in the same tangle (the video recorder that always misses the start of the program, the pasta that turns into a glutinous blob of sticky seaweed). If you try to avoid all mistakes, you run the risk of ceasing to learn.

4. PEOPLE TAKE YOU AT YOUR OWN ESTIMATION

When Rachel was using a friend's lawnmower, something went wrong. She was mortified. "I'm so sorry," she said. "I can't think what I could have done to it." She assumed the breakdown was her fault, and her friend went along with the assumption, hardly noticing that he had done so. Later it turned out that the clutch cable had snapped, and might have done so at any time. Her apologies, and her instant estimate of her own incompetence, led both of them astray: she convicted herself before she had committed a crime. He assumed a crime had been committed without even thinking about the cause of the breakdown. Rachel started to think again about her habit of apologizing—of assuming she was responsible for every mess she came across.

These four insights, coupled with the six guiding strategies which follow, provide the basis on which to start to build self-confidence.

Six Strategies for Building Confidence

1. PRACTICE

The first time you toss the pancakes they may fall apart—or onto the floor. But in the end, you will flip them over easily. Make building your confidence a habit—and that means practicing the other five strategies whenever you can. Do not think about building your confidence only when you are particularly vulnerable. Think about it when you are feeling buoyant, too. The more it becomes a habit, a practiced skill, the more secure your inner confidence will be when you really need it.

2. BEHAVE "AS IF"

When Cathy was sixteen years old, she flew with her family to Kuala Lumpur. A few minutes before landing they became engulfed in a severe tropical storm. There was insufficient fuel to fly to another airport. The pilot was forced to land after the runway had been flooded and closed to other aircraft. Sheet lightening surrounded the plane and fire trucks lined the airstrip. The lights went out. Someone screamed as the plane suddenly lost height. Cathy grabbed the arms of her seat. Her father, meanwhile, sat calmly reading his book. He turned the pages when he could see to do so; he kept his eyes on the print. The aura of confidence which exuded from him was almost palpable. It spread to those around and helped others besides his family to cope with the fear of the moment. It also helped him. He, too, was anxious, but by behaving as if he felt confident, he helped himself, and others, to become confident.

Ask yourself, at an unconfident moment (preparing for an interview or a presentation to your boss), "How would I behave if I really felt confident?" "How would so-and-so handle this?" where so-and-so is a confident person that you know. Adopting the behavior of confidence—the posture, the actions, and the thoughts—starts you on the upward spiral of increasing self-confidence.

3. TAKE THE ZIG-ZAG PATH

Confident behavior, especially when it is a newfound acquisition, can sometimes go to your head. This happened with Maggie who had read about assertiveness and confidence building. She spent three weeks pushing herself to make new strides, making sure that others noticed her. In three weeks, however, she had become insensitive to how others felt. Concentrating exclusively on herself, she had no attention left over for them. Her colleagues withdrew from her—when they saw her coming, they thought: "Oh no, Maggie again!" And Maggie knew that this was how they felt. Not surprisingly, she was upset and confused about what to do next. She felt at risk of doing herself more harm than good.

It is important, therefore, to pay attention to what works, and watch out for the clues that come from others. Flexibility and confidence go hand in hand. Rigidity, even if it feels safer, gets in the way as no two situations are exactly the same. Don't worry if you need to take a zigzag path to your goal. People lacking in self-confidence often feel as if they have to steer a careful, well-planned travel route, to avoid alarming pitfalls. But the pitfalls are largely imaginary, and the fear of taking a wrong step is inhibiting and becomes counterproductive.

4. MAKE THE MOST OF YOUR MISTAKES
AND THEN IGNORE THEM

The mistake made by unconfident people is to think that mistakes matter. If you tried every day for the next year to make a mistake that nobody had ever made before, you would most probably fail. What matters is not doing something "wrong," nor doing something "badly," but whether you can recognize the mistake and use it to try to set yourself on a better path next time. Samuel Beckett said it for us: "No matter. Try again. Fail again. Fail better."

Errors are for learning. Only those who have ceased to develop never take a wrong step. Mistakes are a source of information. The newspapers were only too ready to tell us all about it when a U.S. President confused the Balkans with the Baltic. They made hay with the political implications of the error. But the furor blew over within a couple of days and hardly seemed to interrupt the President's flow of normally confident speeches, decisions, and actions. He learned from his mistake and then ignored it, getting on with the business at hand. Would any mistake you might make be more embarrassing?

5. LIMIT THE SELF-BLAME

Apply the "water-under-the-bridge" rule, and operate a statute of limitations (pp. 86–87). Kicking yourself for past inadequacies, confusions, or failures gives fuel to your internal wavering voice—cut off its supply of oxygen and use an encouraging voice instead. Imagine you had a champion whose job it was to bring out the best in you. What encouraging things would this person be whispering in your ear? Amplify those messages, so you can hear them loud and clear.

6. BE KIND TO YOURSELF

Being kind to yourself is such an important strategy, and in our society such an underrated one that we have devoted a whole chapter to it (Chapter 7). It is a key strategy for building self- confidence. Problems with self-confidence are often rooted in a bad habit of punishing ourselves and of failing to seek out rewards and pleasures. If the habit of self-punishment is reversed, and you learn to treat yourself right, your confidence will be able to grow.

Six Strategies for Building Confidence
Use these six strategies often to build your self-confidence:
1. Practice
2. Behave "as if."
3. Take the zig-zag path.
4. Make the most of your mistakes and then ignore them.
5. Limit the self-blame.
6. Be kind to yourself.

Self-Confidence and Self-Esteem

Rachel knew her self-confidence had taken a turn for the better when she booked a water-sports holiday with her friends. She was not a good swimmer, and only learned to put her head under water when she was

14, shamed into it at the time by school friends. But she was prepared to give it a try. She was even prepared to do only what she could manage and watch the rest. She no longer felt as if it mattered much how good or bad she turned out to be at the new venture. She had begun to believe in her ability to cope with success or failure as each came her way.

So she discovered that confidence spreads—from things you can do to the general feeling that you can learn to do things. This is why a good school provides such a variety of opportunities. The trip to explore an underground cave system provides important lessons in competence as well as in geography. Helping to look after new members of the school, to make the stage scenery, or play the trombone in the school orchestra gives children a chance to make mistakes with all the rest, and to learn how to correct them. Those who fall flat on their faces learn two important lessons: first, how to pick themselves up again; and second, that falling flat is not a *real* disaster. Protecting children from making their own mistakes does *not* help them to build their self-confidence: providing a safe environment within which they can make mistakes—and within which they can learn—is far more effective. It is sometimes harder for people who have sailed through early life with very little struggle and strife to cope with the difficulties and setbacks that eventually come their way, since they have had much less practice earlier on.

Self-confidence is concerned with how we feel about our abilities. But even the most confident people can feel that they are no good, or not good enough, or that they don't matter. Being good at something, believing that you can handle most of the problems that come your way, may still not make you feel worthwhile. So building up confidence is only part of the story. Self-esteem needs separate consideration. Self-esteem is about your values, and whether you live up to them; it is about your sense that other people value and accept you irrespective of your achievements; and it is about whether you value yourself.

Alice Walker, when she wrote *The Color Purple,*[1] started the book with a vivid and moving image of low self-esteem. Celie knew what others thought of her: "She ugly." "She ain't smart." Her feelings counted with nobody. Her children were taken away. She was abused and forced into a relationship of subservience and disregard, not even recognized as sufficiently real to count as a marriage. She is reduced to saying "I don't know how to fight. All I know how to do is stay alive." "I don't fight, I stay where I'm told." The book tells the story of how Celie discovers (or rediscovers) herself and her ability to value herself. This is what self-esteem is about.

THE VALUE OF SELF-ESTEEM

Self-esteem is a difficult concept. If it is high we feel good about ourselves, and if it is low we feel bad about ourselves. This much is straightforward. The higher our self-esteem the more likely we are to achieve our potential, and the lower our self-esteem the more inhibited we will be. There is nothing so disabling as a sense of worthlessness. People who feel they are "worthless" or "do not count" also feel they have nothing to contribute. They hold themselves back and the prophecy becomes self-fulfilling.

Research has shown that children with low self-esteem don't try as hard and have lower expectations of success than others. A strong, positive self-esteem in adults is associated with being more assertive, with better physical health, with more satisfying relationships, and with an increased ability to tolerate and accept differences in others. People with lower self-esteem may denigrate others, including their companions, and thus get stuck in the "inferiority complex": "Anybody I like wouldn't like me; therefore, anyone who likes me isn't worth liking."

Sources of self-esteem. William James, writing in the 1890s, recognized that self-esteem depends on value-judgments made about the self, and not simply on a list of qualities or achievements—being a good friend, mathematician, or swimmer. This was the truth which Marc, the chef, discovered (p. 15). William James realized that value judgments about oneself are closely associated with judgments made about us by others, and value judgments are associated with corresponding feelings. They make you feel good or bad.

What makes self-esteem such an elusive idea is that it is so central to our feelings. It is as though it provides the medium through which everything else is experienced, like seeing the world through a colored, or self-doubting, filter. It is perhaps not surprising therefore that the origins of our level of self-esteem go back to our childhood. Warm, intimate and continuous attachments during childhood provide the kind of "emotional baggage" that helps to build self-esteem. This can be provided by *adequate* (not *perfect*) adults, parents as well as others. But it is not only our childhood which is important. Experiences in adult life, especially those involving warm relationships with others, are also important sources of self-esteem. Those who reach adulthood with low self-esteem are not, therefore, stuck in a deadend, but can take many steps toward feeling better about themselves—as did Celie in *The Color Purple*.

Five Strategies for Building Self-Esteem

You cannot change your childhood, but you can tackle those automatic thoughts—the legacy of your childhood—which work to undermine your self-esteem. Here are five strategies for counteracting these automatic thoughts. These make use of the skills of cognitive therapy described in Chapter 9.

1. ATTACK THE PREJUDICE

"Most women have no characters at all," according to Alexander Pope, putting into words a prejudice against which modern women have fought hard. Like all prejudices, it reflects the bias of the speaker far more than the qualities of the people spoken about. Once armed with this prejudice, the world seems to conform with it just as if the prejudice produced a biased way of seeing things. Women of character can be explained away as exceptions to the rule or by suggesting that they must have been provoked by exceptional circumstances. Or they might just be glossed over altogether— ignored to the point of invisibility. The information that fits with any other point of view has a hard time breaking through the barriers put up by a firmly held prejudice: instead, it is *discounted, deflected,* or *distorted.*

Low self-esteem is like a prejudice about oneself—seeing oneself as unworthy, or unacceptable. The self-perception is biased, or flawed, but the person with the prejudice has a hard time seeing it any other way. Learning to fight the bias involves acknowledging your qualities and talents rather than *discounting* them: "I like drawing. I was good at it even at school," "I've always been a good listener"; accepting compliments and signs of acceptability rather than *deflecting* them: "Thanks, I'm glad you liked my work/cooking/friends"; recognizing that you matter rather than *distorting* the evidence: "He really did seem interested in what I said."

Prejudices can be changed, but they are apt to reemerge at times of stress. Old habits die hard, but if you know them well and recognize their corrosive effects on the way you think and feel about yourself, you will have a better chance of fighting back when they start to reassert themselves.

2. STIFLE THE CRITIC

You were tired and shouted at the children—not just shouted, but yelled. They were storming about the house when you wanted peace and quiet. Then the internal critic started getting at you: "Nobody should treat a child like that. You're a hopeless parent. They'll never learn to behave. No wonder their grandparents don't want to come here much . . . it's all my fault."

The critic within you is remarkably resourceful; so beat it at its own game. Think about what really happened, and clarify the facts. Accept what went wrong, but talk back to the critic to keep the "badness" in perspective. Explain that you were tired. Maybe you had good reason to be so! Ask how children learn to consider the needs of others. Can they do this without knowing what those needs are? Remind the critic of your good moments as a parent, of the times when you help your children in other ways to learn about consideration. Apologize, and put the critic, the exaggerator, back in the box with the lid shut.

3. BURY THE JUDGE

The judge is the person inside you who says: "I'm not wanted," "I'm in the way," "I don't matter," "compared to everyone else I'm a mere crumb—a grain of sand, a worm," "I'm not important." When you bury the judge, you learn how to replace the judgments with facts.

It may be true that you were always the last to be chosen when children were dividing each other up for a game or a contest of some sort. That fact has nothing to do with your chances of being chosen for the job you are going for now. In the new situation examine the facts carefully. You may, or you may not, have a good chance of getting the job. Try to weigh the chances for yourself. That way you can learn how to make realistic judgments and how to trust your own judgment.

The judge is also that part of you which says to a friend "You did really well getting that job," but when you get a job says to you "Getting that job was just lucky. You'll have to watch it, or they'll get rid of you as soon as they find out how useless you really are." The judge is flagrantly unfair by applying different standards to different people. Your judge needs to learn to apply the standard used for others to yourself as well.

The judge is unfair in other ways. It makes negative predictions, it biases your expectations, it makes snap judgments on the basis of superficial information. Your judge may lead you to expect to fail. It stops you trying and casts you down. It makes you impervious to success, which is attributed to chance, and susceptible to failure, which is only to be expected. It is always finding "more successful" people with whom to compare you. Think of the child who rushes proudly home from school: "I came in second in class." "Who came first?" asks the parent, and the child retires crushed. The "judge of low self-esteem" is like that parent. Such judges could live happily in the same box as the critic, provided the lid was kept tight shut on them both.

4. DO THE BEST YOU CAN

Ray used to say that he "had to do his best in every possible way." Then his therapist asked him what his aim was when he made that rule. He answered that it was to do his best. To do as well as he could. To get the best out of himself. Together they examined his rule to find out whether it did, in fact, help him to achieve his goal—which seems reasonable enough. The disadvantage was that it put him constantly under pressure. He set his goals so high that he almost always failed to reach them. It felt good when he did, but those moments were rare. The bottom line was that he knew he was no good. He just could not live up to his rule.

There is an important difference between having an ideal and making a rule to live by. The ideal may be perfect, unflawed, without blemish, a standard one would be proud to attain. Such an ideal provides you with a guide, but it should not be a daily standard. Making the ideal into a rule is digging oneself an elephant trap. If you constantly fall into the trap, you feel so bad about yourself that it becomes increasingly hard to keep going. The rule needs to be clear, and to direct you toward the ideal if that is what you want, but it also needs to be realistic, if it is not to undermine your self-esteem. That is why it makes more sense to *do the best you can*—rather than aim for perfection. Aiming for perfection in this life is a recipe for disaster. Aiming for better self-esteem helps you to do better, and also to feel better.

Some of the rules often adopted (half unawares) by people with low-self-esteem are shown in the box opposite. You can see how they might be counterproductive. Revise or reject such rules so that they work for you rather than against you.

5. DEVELOP FRIENDSHIPS THAT MAKE YOU FEEL GOOD

Other people play an important part in one's feelings about oneself. If low self-esteem is a problem for you, think about your current relationships. Who helps you to feel good about yourself? Who undermines your self-confidence? Make a list and estimate how much time you spend with people in each group. What ways are there of increasing the time you spend with those who make you feel good; and of

---

The Rules that Perpetuate Low Self-Esteem

- A human being must be perfect.
- People should always help each other.
- Others are always right.
- I'm not good enough (or skilled enough, or wise enough . . . and so on).
- A woman should be helpful.
- Men should never cry.
- If I don't do excellently well, I'm no good at all.
- If I make a mistake, I shall never forgive myself.
- When they see how bad I am, they will only reject me.
- One should never burden others with one's problems.
- You can't help yourself—it's the way you are.

---

decreasing the time with those who make you feel bad? Making changes in your relationships may be one of the most effective ways of increasing your self-esteem—but making changes in relationships is rarely straightforward. In Part Three we describe a number of skills to help you to develop fruitful relationships.

A Logical Fallacy, or a Legacy from the Past

Self-esteem is not a constant. It is not something that is impervious to knocks and never varies. Even people with the toughest systems feel better about themselves some days than others. But there is one particular fallacy that is especially hard to uproot. For most people, when they were young they were sometimes punished in one way or another, at home or at school, and they learned the lesson well. If you do something wrong, you deserve to be punished. If you do something wrong, it means you have been bad, or that you are bad.

For some people, especially for those with memories of painful experiences in the past, for people who suffer from depression, and for those whose concerns about their weight and shape have led to disordered patterns of eating, it can be hard to break the link between being treated badly and believing that you are bad. If life is bad to you, you may be tempted to think that you are bad—that you have deserved "punishment." This is not so. Life is not a courtroom. Our experiences are not the just deserts for our characters. If you have been badly treated by others, or have suffered from bad luck, do not compound your problems by taking the blame—by seeing your suffering as a proof of your unworthiness. Value yourself, and this will give you the strength to face your suffering.

Related Chapters in This Book

Our sense of self-esteem and self-confidence have a great impact on our enjoyment and success. This is why valuing yourself is one of the two fundamental principles explained in Part One (Chapter 3). There are few chapters in this book which will not help you to increase your self-esteem and confidence. Five chapters are, perhaps, of particular relevance:

Chapter *3*   Value Yourself

Chapter *7*   Treating Yourself Right

Chapter 21   Digging Yourself Out of Depression

Chapter 13   Being Fair to Yourself and Others

Chapter 25   Good Eating Habits

Chapter Summary

You can build up your self-confidence, even if you have lacked confidence since childhood.

The *four* basic insights are:

1. Confidence is not just one thing. Each of us lacks confidence in some areas of our life, and has confidence in other areas.
2. Apparently confident people around you are not as confident as you think.
3. We gain confidence from doing things.
4. If you tell people you're no good, they might believe it!

These *six* guiding strategies will help you to build up your self-confidence:

1. Practice.
2. Behave as if you are more confident than you feel.
3. Be flexible in your behavior.
4. Learn from your mistakes. The only way of avoiding mistakes is to become stagnant.

5. Silence the voice of self-blame, and speak encouragingly to yourself.
6. Be kind to yourself.

Self-confidence is concerned with how we feel about our abilities. Self-esteem is subtly different: it reflects the degree to which you value yourself.

These *five* strategies will help you to build your self- esteem:

1. Attack those prejudices which lead you to undervalue yourself.
2. Stifle the inner critic.
3. Bury the judge within you that applies double standards: an unfairly strict standard to you, and a generous standard to others.
4. Do the best you can, but don't berate yourself for not being perfect.
5. Spend time with people who make you feel good.

11

♦ ♦ ♦

Learning How to Relax

The last thing Jess wanted to be told when she was feeling wound up was to calm down. The very demand was counterproductive, and ran the risk of winding her up further. At the time it seemed to her both impossible to do and the wrong thing to do. She admitted that she usually got tense and on edge when she felt under pressure, and worried that she was not going to be able to get things done, or that she would forget to do something important. What she really wanted to do was to keep going as fast as she could. In the heat of the moment she swept aside any helpful suggestions from others, dismissing them as insensitive intrusions into her personal affairs, or reacting as if they were fundamental criticisms of her as a person. But in the end she usually had to admit that the suggestion was right. She needed to calm down, and to do so sooner. If she went on too long, she became overtired, even more tense and strained, found it hard to sleep, and wondered if, having managed long ago to turn herself on so as to function on all cylinders at once, she had now lost the "off button." She found it extremely hard to switch off—but learning how to relax was a great help.

Learning how to relax is not one thing, it is many. It is an *attitude:* taking things calmly and in your stride, or keeping cool. It is a *physical skill:* learning how to recognize and release tension, both physical and mental. It is a *habit:* developing routines that work for you rather than against you. It is a *restorative:* a way of giving yourself rest and recreation, and refilling the systems that are otherwise constantly being depleted. We will touch on all these aspects of relaxation in this chapter. If you would like to learn how to take things more easily in your stride, read this chapter carefully, but look also through the rest of the book for chapters relevant to those things that make it especially hard for you to relax.

Relaxation is one of the most general ways of making you feel better. When you have learned to do it, you will find that it makes a noticeable and extremely worthwhile contribution to your mood and to your energy, not just when you are feeling tense or agitated, but at other times as well. Developing relaxed attitudes and habits also has a preventive, or protective, effect, so relaxation provides one of the main building blocks of psychological fitness.

Why Bother with Learning How to Relax?

TENSION IS PAINFUL AND UNPLEASANT

You should learn to relax because tension, the opposite of relaxation, has so many painful effects. It produces aches and pains, perhaps most commonly in the neck and back. The shoulder muscles for many people provide a kind of internal thermometer of their tension level. Learn, during relaxation exercises, to relax your shoulders and you will be surprised to find, if you tell yourself regularly to "drop your shoulders," just how often there is something to drop. Having aches and pains adds to your troubles and give you something extra to worry about.

Being tense also makes people irritable and is tiring. Everything that you do while feeling tense takes more energy than it would if you were feeling relaxed, and of course this is energy wasted. Tension tends to speed people up, like a clockwork toy: the tighter the spring is wound, the faster the machine will run. Learning to relax slows you down again, and helps you to cope more comfortably with the demands of daily living. So learning to relax soothes both the mind and the body.

RELAXATION IS A SKILL

You should also learn to relax because, for many people, this is not something that comes naturally. It is no use just telling yourself, or someone else, to "calm down" and to "relax" because relaxation is a skill that has to be learned before it can be applied. It's unlikely you will be able to do it effectively unless you first spend some time learning the skill, and then practice applying it in easy situations first. These principles are the same for learning all physical skills, such as riding a bicycle.

How to Relax

Did you ever lie awake at night feeling tired, tense, and worried, making every possible effort to switch off and relax only to find that the harder you tried the more elusive such a peaceful state of mind seemed to be? There is certainly something paradoxical about learning to relax: it is like making an effort not to make an effort; working hard at not working or taking control in order to let go. Maybe this is why, for many people, the state is so elusive: the harder one tries to do it, the more frustrated one becomes when it seems not to work.

The first thing to remember is that you can rely on both your mind and your body to do the job for you. If you can deal with those physical and mental tensions that interfere with your ability to relax, then the process will take care of itself. Your job is to deal with those things that, for you, get in the way of letting go. The four steps to go through are described next, followed by an example showing how these steps fit together.

STEP 1: PREPARATION

Preparing to Relax
• Choose the method which attracts you, and stick with it. • Schedule a time each day when you can practice, undisturbed, for half an hour. • Find a comfortable place for your daily practice.

There are many methods of relaxation and very little research on which ones work best. Research does show that learning to relax helps people become calmer, less tense and less anxious, so it may not matter which method you choose. What does matter is that you *choose one method and stick with it until you have learned it properly.* If you want to try out other methods, then do so later. Some of the main options include deep muscle relaxation, yoga, various types of meditation, and the Alexander technique. You may be able to find classes, videos or cassette tapes that teach these methods. Here we describe how to learn deep muscle relaxation.

Learning to relax takes time—at least half an hour a day for the first few weeks. But if you feel tense, learning how to relax should become a priority. *Decide first which time of day suits you best.* You need to find a time when you can make yourself warm and comfortable, and when you will not be disturbed, either by other people or by the telephone. If it is difficult for you to see how you can fit a relaxation practice time into your day, then ask yourself what you could give up in order to make time, or how others could help you protect the space and time that you need. Making relaxation into a routine, and practicing it at the same time, every day, can relieve you of the task of deciding each day when you will do it, and make it easier to remember to practice. It is usually best not to do it last thing at night, when it may send you to sleep. This is because you need to use the practice to learn how to recognize your personal signs of tension, to learn how to let them go, and therefore you need to remain aware of what you are doing. Also, should you fall asleep doing the exercise you will have to disturb yourself afterward in order to go to bed. Once you know how to relax, then you can, if you wish, use the method to help you sleep better.

Learn to relax at your own pace. Just as with anything else, some people can learn a method more quickly than others. But when learning to relax, trying to hurry is counterproductive. The more you rush, the harder it will be.

Deep muscle relaxation uses the pendulum method—if you want the pendulum to swing in the opposite direction, you first have to pull it back. So practice involves tightening up muscle groups and then letting them go. The aim is to work systematically through the body, and it is usual to start with the hands, work up to the shoulders, then back to the feet and up to the shoulders again, leaving the face and neck to last. We have no reason to suppose that it matters if you go through the body in another order, but it may be difficult to start with the areas in which physical and emotional tension seem to concentrate, such as the shoulders, neck, and face, and it may also be helpful at the end to repeat the exercise for any parts of the body that are especially difficult for you to let go.

Settle down in your warm and comfortable place. Undo any clothing that feels tight, especially round your waist or neck. We recommend that you lie down on your back and close your eyes. If you find this hard, then do whatever feels most comfortable, such as sitting in an armchair and starting with your eyes open. Give yourself a moment or two to subside, and then tune in to your breathing. When you are breathing in a relaxed way, your stomach will move gently up and down as you breathe in and out. If all the movement comes from your chest, then your breathing is less relaxed. To relax your breathing, tell yourself to "let go," as you breathe out, as this emphasizes the natural body rhythm. Telling yourself to "let go" as you breathe in is going against the grain, and therefore harder to do. You can find out how you are doing by putting one hand on your chest and the other on your stomach and feeling them move. Aim for the relaxed, diaphragmatic, type of breathing during which the hand on your stomach moves most, but accept calmly whatever is happening at the time. As you become more relaxed, your breathing will take care of itself.

When you are settled, start to work through the muscles one by one. You can work out ahead of time which order to go in, or you can make yourself a tape recording of the instructions which follow.

STEP 2: PRACTICE

The basic exercise. Turn your attention to your hands. When you are ready, tighten up all the muscles in both your hands. Clench your fists, and hold the tension while you count slowly up to three (pulling the pendulum back), then let the tension go. Feel the tension drain out of your fingers, and let them come naturally to rest. Each time you breathe out allow your hands to become heavier. Let the blood circulate freely right to your fingertips, as you feel more and more deeply relaxed. Give yourself as much time as you like to focus on your hands before you repeat the exercise with the next muscle group.

The muscle groups. This is the order we suggest, together with some ideas to help you tighten the right muscles. Work up to your shoulders from your hands, and then all the way from bottom to top. It does not matter if you make a mistake, or miss out on a muscle. It is more important to learn how to recognize tension and how to let that go, in order to achieve a state of deep muscular relaxation.

Finally, tune into your breathing once more. On every exhale, imagine you can reach an even deeper state of relaxation. Enjoy feeling more relaxed for a moment or two before you move about again, and then rouse yourself slowly. If you leap up quickly after the exercise you may feel slightly dizzy, and you will also undo some of the beneficial effects. The whole exercise should take about 20 to 30 minutes. Later in the chapter we will show you how you can shorten the time needed.

Deep Muscular Relaxation

Here is an order that we find easy to remember which will help you not to forget any muscle group. Remember, after tensing each muscle group, let go slowly, feeling the tension drain away and the blood flowing freely. Don't forget to breathe.

- *Hands:* Clench the fists. Now, let go.
- *Arms:* Tighten biceps and lower arms together, without the hands.
- *Shoulders:* Raise your shoulders as if they could touch your ears.
- *Feet:* Screw up your toes.
- *Front of legs:* Point your foot away from you so that it is almost parallel with your leg.
- *Back of legs:* Flex your feet upwards, stretching your heels down.
- *Thighs:* Tighten them while pressing your knees down into the floor.
- *Bottom:* Clench your buttocks together.
- *Stomach:* Hold your stomach muscles in tight.
- *Lower back:* Press the small of your back into the floor.
- *Chest:* Breathe in, hold your breath, and tighten all your chest muscles.
- *Shoulders:* Breathe in, hold your breath and raise your shoulders as if they could touch your ears.
- *Neck:* 1. Stretch your head up, as if your chin could touch the ceiling.
       2. Bend your head forward until your chin reaches your chest.
- *Mouth and Jaw:* Press your lips together and clench your teeth.
- *Eyes:* Close them up tight.
- *Forehead and scalp:* Raise your eyebrows as if they could disappear.
- *Face:* Screw all the muscles up together.

Relaxing mentally as well as physically. Some people find they can relax more easily physically than mentally. They keep thinking about worrying or upsetting things, even after all their muscles are deeply relaxed. This is when making use of relaxing imagery may be helpful (see also Chapter 24, pp. 296-299). Make a list of places or situations that you find calming or relaxing, and as you relax after doing your exercises, imagine that you really are in one of them. Do not worry if the images keep changing—imagery is rarely static. Just guide the images into calm waters, and away from sources of trouble. For example, you may be imagining a calm spot on the banks of a river where you once fell asleep in the sun. But your concentration might waver so that you find yourself thinking about tomorrow's problems. Gently bring your attention back to the river bank.

Making your own relaxation tape. Write yourself a basic script, or prompt sheet, using the preceding instructions, before you record it. Start by reminding yourself how to settle down. Then talk yourself through the whole thing, including all the instructions about how to tune in to your breathing. Tell yourself which muscles to tense up, remind yourself how, then tell yourself to let go. As you are letting go, talk to yourself about what you are trying to achieve. Give yourself reminders like this: "Let all the tension drain away. Allow the muscles to feel warm and heavy, as your relaxation becomes deeper and deeper. Each time you breathe out, let go a little further. Imagine that your limbs have become too heavy to move, and that you are completely, and comfortably supported" . . . and so on. You should talk to yourself slowly, in a quiet and calming voice, and of course you can add your own variations, like repeating exercises you find difficult, or some music you find relaxing to listen to before you begin or after you have finished.

Occasional problems with physical relaxation. People who suffer from pains in their joints, such as those caused by arthritis, may not be able to use the pendulum method as it may hurt to tense up before letting go. If this is a problem for you, you can learn to relax just by focusing on each muscle group in turn, or by using one of the forms of relaxation more closely related to meditation.

Some other people find the sensations they experience when starting to relax rather alarming, as if they were about to lose control, rather than sink into a state of restfulness and calmness. Usually it does not take long to realize that nothing alarming happens when you relax, especially if you proceed at your own pace, and follow these exercises with those described in Step 4 below.

STEP 3: APPLICATION

Once you are able to achieve deep muscle relaxation using the whole exercise, you need to learn how to use this new skill in ways that make you feel better. It is not possible to remain in a deeply relaxed state as you go about your daily life, so you may gain little benefit from Steps 1 and 2 alone. How can you drive a car, talk to people, or put the children to bed if you are deeply relaxed? The next stage involves learning how to recognize small degrees of tension early and how to let them go before they build up. This is achieved by shortening the exercise, so you can relax quickly, and by practicing in increasingly difficult situations, as described below.

Shortening the relaxation exercise. Shorten the exercise gradually, over the next 3 to 6 weeks. For example, you could try collapsing some of the muscle groups until you only work on your arms, legs, abdomen, chest, and face. Or you could settle down and see how relaxed you can get just by tuning in to your breathing, then work on any muscle groups that still feel tense. You could work through the first half of the exercises and then see if you can do the rest just by becoming aware of all the different parts of the body one by one. You could leave out the tension, and work only on the relaxation. Eventually, you want to be able to relax quickly and when needed— the thing that seemed impossible to start with. Use your imagination to find any way of shortening the exercise that works for you. You can see why first you need to use the whole body exercise to learn to recognize the signs of tension and let them go, however small they are.

Continue to practice daily, but as the practice times become shorter, look for opportunities to practice more frequently.

Practice in increasingly difficult situations. Once you are reasonably good at basic relaxation, try doing the exercises in different positions, such as sitting instead of lying down. Try to relax sitting in an armchair, and then try it sitting at a table, or walking round the garden. Try it when you are reading, watching TV, or washing up. Think about only using the muscles that are necessary for the job at hand. If there is tension elsewhere, for instance, in your stomach when driving the car, or in your shoulders when listening to music, then try to let it go. Tense the muscle up more to begin with, to make use of the pendulum effect, then allow the tension to drain away.

Once you can relax while engaged in normal daily activities, try to relax in the situations that make you tense—in those situations that trouble you. You will not be able to apply the relaxation successfully in the most difficult situations without a great deal of practice, so do not expect this to work the first time you try. Work up to the hardest situations by relaxing in the easier ones first, and remember it is always easier to relax if you catch the tension early. Check your tension levels regularly to begin with, and tell yourself to relax every time you check. You will be surprised to find how often there is unnecessary tension to let go.

A Quick Relaxation Routine—The Quick Fix

1. Tune in to your breathing. Take one deep breath in, hold it, then tell yourself to let go as you breathe out. Breathe naturally for a while, repeating the instruction to let go with every outward breath. Choose an instruction that fits for you: "Keep calm," "Hang in there," "Take it slow," "Let it go," etc.
2. Tense up and then relax a single muscle group such as your hand, foot, or stomach. When you let go, try to let all the unnecessary tension slip away.
3. Drop your shoulders.

If you start with the full relaxation exercise, shorten it to a quick routine, and then apply your relaxation skills in increasingly testing situations; you will soon begin to feel the benefit. Occasionally, go back to the whole exercise just as a reminder.

STEP 4: THE EXTENSION COURSE: SIX WAYS OF DEVELOPING A RELAXED ATTITUDE

Relaxation is an attitude, a habit, and a restorative as well as a skill. Make it part of your life in every way.

1. **Adopt a relaxed posture.** Do you catch yourself sitting on the edge of your chair? Fidgeting and fiddling with things? Tension can waste so much energy, so allow your body to rest when you get the chance.
2. **Stop rushing about.** It only winds you up. Most people find that they get just as much done when they go slowly as when they rush, and they can also keep going longer. Doing things calmly is much less tiring.
3. **Make a habit of doing the things you find relaxing.** Whether they are peaceful and calm things (like reading or doing nothing much of anything) or strenuous things (like playing squash or going to parties), do the things that relax you.
4. **Seek out pleasures and treats.** The more you are enjoying yourself, the more relaxed you will feel.
5. **Spread the risks.** If you put all your eggs in one basket, you will feel extremely tense and on edge if that basket is threatened.
6. **Give yourself breaks.** Take short breaks, like half an hour talking to a friend, as well as long ones, like regular holidays.

Many of these ideas are expanded in the example below as well as in the other chapters listed at the end of this one.

How Relaxation Can Work in Practice

Graham was the salesman for a small light-engineering company. His salary was paid on a commission basis, which meant that the more he sold the more he earned. He was always at the mercy of economic trends: if business was good he did well, and when it became scarcer his salary dropped. He came to the clinic after he had recently married and had taken on his first mortgage. As the recession had developed, he had felt increasingly tense and pressured. By the time we met he sounded frantic. He had been working extremely long hours, traveling to see potential customers, leaving little time for paperwork in the office, and an old rugby injury to his neck was causing him considerable pain after he had twisted it lifting his briefcase out of the car. There seemed to be many sides to Graham's problems. However, his tension was visible, and he was no longer able to relax on the rare days when he was not working. He wanted to learn how to relax, so this is how we started. These are the stages he went through.

1. Preparation He started by wrestling with his timetable, and talking to his wife, trying to find a regular time to practice. On working days he chose to do it as soon as he came home from work, regardless of whether he had eaten, and on other days, immediately after breakfast. He wanted to use the relaxation exercise to help him mark the difference between "time on" and "time off." Then he asked his wife to help him make his own relaxation tape. He knew he might forget to practice, or try and argue himself out of it when he felt rushed, so he stuck a small card on his shaving mirror with the days of the week written down the side, and ticked off the days when he practiced (5 out of 7 in the first week; every day in the second).

At first, he gained little benefit, since the more he relaxed the rest of his body, the more he noticed the pain and tension in his neck. He found himself struggling against the pain, frustrated at not being able to let the tension go. He had forgotten how important it is to accept feelings for what they are, and work at removing the blocks that get in the way of allowing the body to take care of itself. We suggested that he take special care to make his head and neck comfortable before practicing, using extra support, and also that he should do an experiment to find out which method of relaxation was most helpful: doubling the neck exercises to give himself more practice, or working on his neck without the pendulum—relaxing his neck by becoming aware of the tension already present and allowing that tension to drain away without first tensing up.

By the end of the next week, Graham had started to make noticeable progress. Doubling the neck exercises had given him the most help, and he was surprised to find out how much his general level of tension had been adding to the discomfort caused by his original injury. He also discovered that he needed to allow about double the average amount of time to let the tension in his neck drain away when he was letting go. Knowing that the next step involved shortening the exercises and using them in more testing situations, he repeated the tension and release exercise for his neck at other times during the day when he noticed the tension building up.

2. Practice Shortening the exercises posed little problem for Graham since he was so busy; he was glad to cut down on extra commitments, including this one. There was a danger that he would try to run before he could walk, and easily fall back into old habits. He needed to make the relaxation part of his daily life as quickly as possible. By the time he had learned to let the tension go while sitting at his desk, he agreed that it was worth devoting half an hour a day to relaxing, but he decided to break the time up over the course of the day. He worked out his own "quick fix" routine, then he put this into effect every time he sat down. Sitting down became a cue to practice, whether he sat down to eat, to work, or to drive the car. Even sitting in a pub or in front of the television, he ran through his quick routine (which was totally invisible to those around him) the moment he got the weight off his feet. Altogether, he probably practiced far more than half an hour a day at this stage.

3. Application For the first four weeks Graham had been working predominantly on the preparation and practice steps. He then moved on to applying his developing skills in more difficult situations related to work. We reminded him how important it was to catch the tension as early as possible, and together we devised a monitoring system. Graham needed to remind himself to check his tension levels very frequently during the day, but he was so pressured that he kept forgetting. He bought a sheet of colored sticky dots to use as reminders. He stuck them wherever he would see them: on his watch face, his diary, the telephone, the driving mirror, his bedside lamp, the kitchen window, and so on—about 30 of them altogether. These were his messages to himself: "Whenever I see a dot, check my tension level, and let the tension go." He found the dot on the telephone at work was the most useful, and realized that he was often so tense by the time he reached the office that he avoided using the telephone for fear of discovering more problems and adding further to his difficulties. By feeling relaxed when he used the telephone he was able to bring more of his work under control.

4. The Extension Course. By now, Graham had developed the habit of checking his tension level frequently and relaxing quickly when he needed to. If he put off doing his relaxation exercises for too long, he found it harder to let go, so we encouraged him to keep practicing. At this point he started extending the relaxation in other ways. By the middle of the working day, he was usually pushing himself along at full speed. We persuaded him to take a proper lunch break away from work—to find a way of leaving the problems behind even for a short time. So he decided to try, literally, walking away from them. Wherever he was, rain or shine, he went for a brief walk. If a meeting got in the way, he took the walk earlier or later. He gave himself a breathing space away from the pressure. And he did similar things at home and on Sundays. He started to do some work on the house. This does not sound relaxing, but he enjoyed the physical and relatively undemanding activity, it stopped him thinking about other things, and felt more constructive to his wife as well as to him. Together they decided that it would be a good idea to fit in more exercise, and so they planned some long country walks. The exercise felt good, but they soon discovered that this was not their kind of thing. They enjoyed more social activities, like bicycling with friends or dancing at a club in town. The more they engaged in relaxing activities, even tiring and strenuous ones, the more Graham shed the load of tension, and—to his surprise—the better he found himself coping at work. Even the pain in his neck disappeared. He had spread his interests wider again, and doing so helped him to develop a more relaxed attitude to the pressures at work.

RELAXING OUT OF PAIN

It is well known that prolonged physical tension is painful, even if the tension is as mild as that caused by sitting all day at a word processor. It is also well known that tension exacerbates pain. If you are in physical pain, then the more tense you are the worse this pain feels. This information has been of great value to women during childbirth, many of whom benefit from relaxation classes during their pregnancies.

It is less well known that relaxation can also be helpful to people with other sorts of pain, such as the pain of arthritis or persistent headaches. The exercises described here, including the ways they can be applied and extended, can be used in these circumstances too.

Other Chapters to Turn to If You Feel Tense

Chapter 18   Stress and How to Live with the Right Amount of It

Chapter 24   Overcoming Sleep Problems

Chapter 16   Getting the Better of Anxiety and Worry

Chapter 7   Treating Yourself Right

Chapter 9   Keeping Things in Perspective

Chapter Summary

1. The techniques of relaxation can be learned.
2. Practicing relaxation will give you more energy; decrease anxiety and irritability; and reduce pains due to tense muscles, such as neckache, backache, and headache.
3. Learning to relax is: an *attitude;* a *physical skill;* a *habit;* and a *restorative.*
4. Learning to relax involves *four steps:*
   • *Preparation* A regular time and place for daily practice is needed until you become competent.
   • *Practice* The basic method involves first tensing each muscle group and then letting go.
   • *Application* Once you are skilled in the basic method, you can shorten the daily relaxation period; and carry out mini-relaxations throughout the day.
   • *Extension* Make relaxation a part of your way of life by extending it to include relaxing and recreational activities.

PART THREE

◆ ◆ ◆

How to Improve Your Relationships

Satisfying relationships are a major source of happiness, but they can be difficult to achieve. When relationships go wrong, our whole life can feel as if it is in shreds, and one response to problematic past relationships is to avoid becoming close to anyone again.

We relate to others in almost all aspects of our lives. Close personal relationships can be a source of strength and of continuous renewal. But it is not only these close relationships which are important. Both in our work, and in our everyday pursuits, we are constantly relating to other people. How we do this will determine our effectiveness as well as our pleasure.

Part Three will help you develop skills that lead to good relationships. We have found that the following three keys are central in developing satisfying relationships:

1. Develop the skill of *assertiveness* so that you can *be fair to yourself and to others.*
2. Learn to recognize and understand the *voices from your past* so that you can use them constructively.
3. Understand that *relationships are systems* so that you can make changes in the way that you and others interrelate using *negotiation skills.*

12

◆ ◆ ◆

The Importance of Relationships

We are, to a great extent, social animals. Our happiness, our self-esteem, our moods, our capacity to flourish, all are influenced enormously by our relationships. Relationships are so central to our functioning that one form of psychological therapy— interpersonal psychotherapy—focuses entirely on ways of relating to others. It is tempting to think that, in order to improve our relationships, we need to change other people. It usually seems only too clear that the problem lies with the other person. But this is exactly where many people go wrong. In order to improve relationships we can only work on ourselves, and then others will change the ways in which they relate to us. So this part of the book, although about relationships, is just as much about ways of changing yourself as is the rest of the book. It is about changing yourself in the ways you relate to others.

We start this section with a story chosen to illustrate the following points:

1. Your relationships will work best if you are able to be yourself within them. Relationships in which you can be yourself are likely to feel more comfortable and to make you happier. This is not to say that you should throw tantrums when you feel like it, and be as rude to people as you wish. Nor is it to suggest that all relationships should be comfortable. Some very good ones can be provocative and challeng-

ing. It is rather that relationships tend to become unstable and to be less satisfying when you are not yourself. It follows that it is helpful to be curious about your relationships and to try to understand them.

2. Bringing about change in a relationship can be seen as a four-step process:

Step 1: Look for the patterns.

Step 2: Focus on specific areas of difficulty.

Step 3: Learn to pilot your own ship.

Step 4: Notice how others change in response.

The story which follows shows how to use these steps to bring about changes in your relationships. The steps are the threads that run through the other three chapters in this part of the book.

The Story of Debbie

DEBBIE'S DIFFICULTIES

Debbie had been given a black eye. She was 22 years old and worked as a receptionist and typist with a small firm of lawyers. She lived with her parents and younger sister, who thought of her as a rather quiet, uncommunicative person. Much of the time she was miserable. She felt that she was disgustingly overweight, and she hid herself in swathes of baggy, dark-colored clothes, always in the process of starting new diets only to give them up a few days later. She resolved to go to the gym after work and berated herself whenever she failed. She felt stuck, hopeless about being able to change, and convinced that nothing would get better unless she could change the way she looked. Her self-esteem and self-confidence seemed to have reached rock bottom, and over the past few months she had started to drink far more than was sensible. She drank nearly two bottles of wine when out with her boyfriend Nigel and then had an argument with him. They had arranged to meet on Saturday night, but instead he had gone out with some male friends to a football game and on to a party where they had all got drunk. When she did see him the next evening, she hit him on the head with a glass ashtray. He punched her in the eye. The shock of the fight with Nigel forced Debbie to stop and think. Her doctor referred her to a therapist who used interpersonal therapy, and together they worked through the following steps.

STEP 1: LOOKING FOR PATTERNS

Debbie recognized that her attempts to diet and to exercise were getting her nowhere so she concentrated instead on trying to understand what was happening. She blamed herself and felt guilty every time she failed to live up to her good intentions, but realized deep down that this was not the whole story. She needed to take a wider, and a longer, look, and she asked herself questions like these: *"When do I feel at my worst? What is happening then?"* and *"When do I feel at my best?"* She asked, *"do the same kinds of things keep happening to me? do I seem to keep going round and round in a circle?"* The first pattern she noticed was this: she felt especially bad when left out, ignored by her friends, and when anyone at home or at work said something critical about her, but she felt worst of all about herself after an argument or fight. These were the things that seemed to be happening when the diets went out of the window.

She felt better about herself, regardless of her weight, when other people were kinder to her and more friendly. The main pattern seemed to be that her relationships were calling the tune, and she suspected that all the important knobs and buttons controlling the mechanism of her relationships were in the hands of other people. However, she was now curious about how this worked. Instead of concentrating on her size and how much she ate or exercised, she started to think closely about the patterns of her relationships.

STEP 2: FOCUSING ON SPECIFIC AREAS OF DIFFICULTY

Interpersonal therapy recognizes three different types of relationship problems. It is useful to know about them because it helps to separate one problem from another so that you can think about them one at a time. Start by focusing on specific areas of difficulty and then label each as a problem of a particular type. The three types are:

1. **Disputes**—for example, frequent arguments between husband and wife, or parent and teenager
2. **Role changes**—for example, growing up and leaving home, or retirement
3. **Loneliness**—or a lack of close friends

Debbie focused on three particular areas of difficulty.

1. A problem of loneliness. Debbie noticed that her friendships, with both men and women, tended not to last (another pattern). She would spend a lot of time with new acquaintances for a short period and then fall out with them, often after a series of arguments and fights, and she did not have any long-standing close relationships. It was as if she was standing still in the midst of a constantly moving crowd of people who all knew where they were going and only stopped briefly within reach of her before moving on again. She had not noticed this loneliness before because she often went out, but not with people she was close to. The problem was so long-standing that she anticipated falling out with people almost as soon as she had got to know them. She had become passive, and tended to agree with whatever other people wanted so she would not precipitate a fall out.

2. A dispute problem. Debbie's relationships were undeniably stormy; the black eye was only a visible reminder of this—and it was easy to see how her tendency to have arguments led to her loneliness.

3. A problem of changing roles. Debbie's third area of difficulty concerned differences in her relationships with men and with women. She felt unable to get the balance right, as if this part of the mechanism was completely out of her control. If she met a new boyfriend, she went out with him every night and completely stopped seeing her girlfriends (another pattern). But when the relationship broke up, she found her girlfriends had not hung around waiting, but had gone their own way without her, leaving her feeling inadequate and lonely.

Focusing on specific areas of difficulty showed Debbie that there were even more patterns at work than she had at first realized. For example, she recognized that, even though she was always having fights, she also felt helpless to do anything about them, and was constantly trying to please other people. The fights only served to make her feel worse about herself—more evidence that she had failed, but this time in her relationships instead of with her diets and exercise plans.

She tried to please people by agreeing to do whatever they wanted, as if what she wanted did not count, or as if she did not really matter. This meant that if someone asked her out she agreed to go, and did whatever they suggested, behaving in exactly the same way, regardless of whether or not she liked them. She passively followed anyone who asked because she felt so unattractive and shapeless, and thought so little of herself, that it never occurred to her that she might have any choice. She assumed that people would eventually reject her. Trying to please people was a way of staving off the inevitable loneliness and isolation. Fights erupted when she felt trapped, or when others became fed up with her passivity and provoked a confrontation. She even wondered whether she engineered some of the fights with men, to escape from a situation that alarmed her, or to make sure she rejected them before they had a chance to reject her. Debbie discovered a truth about herself which is almost universal: suppressing our own desires for too long will lead to an explosion.

STEP 3: LEARNING TO PILOT YOUR OWN SHIP

The idea that Debbie could have some control over what happened in her relationships was not easy for her to accept. She felt as if other people had all the choices. She felt that socially she would have to be content with whatever came her way, and be thankful for small pleasures. But as Debbie thought more about her specific difficulties, she came to realize that her passivity, her tendency to go along with what others wanted without thinking of herself, might be affecting what happened in her relationships. Part of the responsibility for what was happening might lie with her.

For the first time, Debbie asked herself what she wanted from relationships. Instead of focusing on her outward appearance, she started to think about the inner person—about the Debbie she thought she would like to be. Instead of blowing with the wind, she began, in small ways, to take control. For example, she arranged to go out with a group of girlfriends and joined them in a regular, weekly outing. Instead of worrying about displeasing someone when she went out on a date, she thought about what she wanted to do, and began to speak up for herself. When she found herself in a relationship that she did not like, she had the courage to end it. She learned how to keep a better balance between her friendships with men and with women.

STEP 4: NOTICING HOW OTHERS CHANGE IN RESPONSE

One of Debbie's big fears was that if she disagreed with someone it would end in an argument. What she noticed, however, was that the more she took control and allowed herself to be herself, the more others respected her and the fewer fights she had. She started to meet girlfriends for lunch, and to her surprise found that they spontaneously kept in touch, and showed that they wanted to see her. At home it was a little harder to pilot her own ship because her mother was worried that Debbie was setting a bad example for her younger sister. After the episode with the black eye, she demanded that Debbie tell her where she was going in the evenings and tried to make her stay in for fear that she would get drunk again, or get hurt. Debbie was in a conflict: she wanted to please her mother, but she also wanted to live her own life. She had another *role change* problem on her hands. But this time she understood herself and her relationships better. She continued to go out as much as she liked, but she talked to her mother more about whom she was with and what she did. She continued to develop her independence, but this time opened herself up instead of hiding herself away. As her mother learned she could trust her, she too started to relax the effort to restrain her.

THE CHANGES DEBBIE MADE

Although Debbie had focused on the four steps to change her relationships, the benefits she felt were far wider than this. The better she became at playing her full part in relationships, the better she felt about herself. The better she felt about herself, the less she wanted to hide away behind layers of shapeless clothes. Others seemed pleased to see her, and she made new friends, so she stopped worrying so much about her weight. The changes Debbie made in her relationships set off a chain reaction, helping her to make many other changes. Once she accepted herself, others also found it easier to accept her.

Solitude

In emphasizing the value of good relationships, we do not wish to underrate the importance of solitude—the ability to enjoy, and to find creative strength, in our own company. To be at ease with yourself, alone, can be a source of refreshment and energy. It is a necessary component of many creative activities that require us to draw from our own inner depths. Solitude is not the opposite of good relationships. Indeed, if we are continually seeking company because we are uncomfortable with ourselves, this is likely to tarnish our relationships. If we are at ease with ourselves, we will be at ease with others.

Three Guidelines for Improving Your Relationships

We tend to be at our most unrealistic when looking at what went wrong in our relationships. This is probably because they are so important to us and we have so much invested in them. If you want to change, or to develop new ways in which to relate to others, then you will have to start with a good dose of reality. Three guidelines will help you focus on what is realistic.

1. WORK ON CHANGING YOURSELF, NOT ON CHANGING OTHERS

The temptation, particularly if a relationship is stormy, is to insist to yourself, and to others, that it is not you that needs to change but the other person. Now it may well be true that the other person should change, but since you can't change other people, it is not worth trying. Or perhaps it would be more accurate to say that the only way you can change another person is to change yourself—to change the way in which you relate to them. Working to change yourself is always difficult. Working to change your relationships is doubly difficult because it is so tempting to think that other people are at fault, and that they rather than you should make the effort. Do not be distracted by trying to change others: change yourself, and change the way you relate to others. The changes you make will precipitate changes in others. Leave these changes up to them, and the relationship will feel better to you both.

2. CHANGES TAKE TIME

When you change the way in which you relate to others, they may resist that change and do things to make you change back. So making changes in relationships can take longer than making changes in yourself alone, and it certainly requires persistence.

3. WORK WITH PEOPLE AS THEY ARE

When you find yourself saying "If only he would tell me what he's thinking," or "If only she didn't criticize so much," stop yourself and remind yourself to be realistic. If you want to bring about some changes in those relationships, you should put away these "if only's" and accept people as they are. Once you start to make changes in yourself, the other person is likely to begin to change. Then you will be able to find out if you can accommodate to each other and get on. If after you have tried to change you still find the relationship is no better, and you still keep wishing the other person were different, then it might be better to end the relationship.

The Three Keys to Good Relationships

Scores of books and articles have looked at ways of improving relationships. If you were to comb through all these works, you would find three recurrent themes, or keys.

The first key is: *be fair to yourself, and to others.* The core skill in ensuring that you are fair within your relationships is the skill of *assertiveness.* The second key is: *understand the voices from the past.* A central insight from psychoanalysis is that our past is always with us. When we recognize the presence of these voices from our past, and learn how to think about them, we can choose to ignore them or choose to listen to other voices instead. When we fail to recognize them, they can cause havoc within our relationships. The third key is: *understand that relationships are systems.* We have already seen that when we make changes in the ways we relate to others, those others will tend to respond to, and resist, the changes. In a system, one change leads to another and the skills of *communication* and *negotiation* help to ensure that the changes we want and the changes others want match—so that the relationship system can adjust and adapt. The following three chapters explore each of these three keys in turn.

Chapter Summary

Our happiness, self-esteem, and capacity to flourish are influenced enormously by our relationships.
In order to improve your relationships:

1. Work on changing yourself, not on changing others.
2. Expect changes to take time.
3. Accept other people as they are.

The three keys to good relationships are:

1. Be fair to yourself, and to others.
2. Understand the voices from the past.
3. Understand that relationships are systems.

The following three chapters deal with each of these keys in turn.

13

♦ ♦ ♦

The First Key to Good Relationships: Be Fair to Yourself and to Others

Being Fair Requires Being Assertive

Rita was 48 when she first became a grandmother. She was desperate to see the new baby and had been planning for months to take the necessary time away from her busy schedule. She was a governor of the local school, and involved in helping to raise funds for a kidney machine. Her husband, Daniel, buried himself in his work.

Rita telephoned her daughter-in-law, Karen, hoping to be asked to visit. Karen chatted happily about the baby's antics, sleepless nights, and feeding schedules. Rita started to worry that the invitation she wanted was never going to come. She listened, waiting to be asked. Then she said, "You must be frantic," and "I know there's no time to think of anything else with a new baby around." She talked about her husband's busy life, saying "He sometimes says he can't do without me." The message she wanted to get across was how useful she could be. The message Karen heard was that Rita had no time to spare. So Karen said questioningly, "I suppose you couldn't leave Daniel on his own?" Rita answered, "I sometimes think he hardly notices I'm here." Both Rita and Karen wanted the same thing—and they did not get it because they both beat around the bush. Neither was able to state what she wanted in clear language. Neither was fair to herself.

Rita's husband, Daniel, was very different. He was a hospital consultant. He told others exactly what he wanted without bothering to find out anything about their perspective. He had working for him a junior doctor, Richard, of whom he thought very highly. Daniel was quite often away at conferences and he would tell Richard to look after those of his patients he was most concerned about. Daniel would burst into Richard's office, without knocking, holding a pile of patients' records. "You will see these patients at the clinic next Thursday" and dumping the files on Richard's desk, he would turn on his heels and walk out. Richard felt he was being treated like a servant, not like the competent doctor he was. Things came to a head when Richard booked his skiing holiday for February. He had negotiated the timing with his colleagues—the other junior doctors—so that his holiday did not clash with theirs, following the normal procedure. When Daniel heard of Richard's holiday times, he was furious. They coincided with his own holiday and he had come to rely on Richard to cover his difficult patients. He marched into Richard's office and told him point blank that he could not take his holiday in February. He brooked no discussion. Richard felt he had little choice, and he changed his holiday times. Six months later he had found a different job, and Daniel lost the junior doctor he most respected.

Most of us will recognize aspects of ourselves in either Rita or Daniel—even in both. Their stories illustrate how different kinds of unfairness prevented them from building up the kinds of relationships that are rewarding for all concerned. It is easy to be unfair either to oneself or to others, and surprisingly difficult to find the middle ground on which we can stand up for ourselves without putting others down. We tend to be better at this in some situations than in others: we may be decisive, openminded, and assertive at work but passive at home. Being fair depends on being able to be assertive.

What Is Assertiveness?

Assertiveness is a skill based on the idea that your needs, wants, and feelings are neither more nor less important than those of other people: they are equally important. You should, therefore, make claims for yourself appropriately, honestly, and clearly. Learning how to do this helps ensure that you do not come away from situations feeling bad about yourself, or leaving others feeling bad.

The alternatives to assertiveness are either passivity or aggression. If you adopt the passive approach, you will either fail to get what is your due or become manipulative: "I'm useless at anything mechanical, I'll only make a mess of it," "I'm sure you'd do this better than me,"

"I just can't go on—I've got such a headache." Out of frustration, passive people may cajole, sulk, or cry to get their way. The aggressive approach becomes overbearing: "Get this done right away," "Like it or not, my parents are coming to supper," "That's your concern. It's nothing to do with me." Aggressive people may fail to listen to what others say, or dismiss the views of others as irrelevant. Neither passivity nor aggression are ultimately satisfactory, both because of the bad feelings they engender and because they are unfair: and in the long term, they usually fail to get you what you want. Michelle who went along with the crowd to an Indian restaurant, though she hates curry, ended up feeling resentful and inadequate. Brian who demanded angrily that a project should be scrapped and started again from scratch ended up feeling stressed and alienated. It is not that Michelle needs to learn about assertiveness and Brian needs something else, but rather that assertiveness provides a more effective solution to both kinds of problems. Assertiveness is about being fair both to yourself and to others.

ASSERTIVENESS INVOLVES CLAIMING YOUR RIGHTS

You are entitled to your own feelings and opinions. Other people may want you to feel and think differently, but this is their problem, not yours. If you value yourself and trust your own feelings you will express yourself to others effectively. The strange thing is that other people will then value and trust you more than if you bend over backward to try to please them. Passive people, and a surprising number of aggressive people, want to be liked by everyone. This is rarely possible and it is usually counterproductive to try to be liked by all the people you meet. *Instead of focusing on being liked, focus on being fair.*

Study the "Assertive Rights" given in the following box. They express the freedom you have to be yourself. Do you agree with them?

Assertive Rights

I have the right:

- To say "I don't know."
- To say "no."
- To have an opinion, and to express it.
- To have feelings, and to express them.
- To make my own decisions, and deal with the consequences.
- To change my mind.
- To choose how to spend my time.
- To make mistakes.

ASSERTIVENESS AS A BALANCING ACT

Assertiveness skills can be seen as providing three important kinds of balance:

1. The balance between aggression and passivity
2. The balance between yourself and others
3. The balance between reflecting and reacting

The balance between aggression and passivity. Aggression and passivity reflect two extremes, neither of which makes for good relationships. Assertiveness provides a better way because it helps people to make their own point of view known while recognizing and accepting the views of others. It is essential to understand the differences between passivity, aggression, and assertiveness. The following three stereotypes crystallize the main differences.

Roger was a passive person. He tried to please others and avoid conflict; he found it difficult to make decisions, and constantly criticized and blamed himself. He never accepted compliments and tended to foster guilt and frustration in others, who saw him as a bit of a pushover. He was liked but not much respected because people knew he could be pushed around, and he seemed not to respect himself. He did what those around him wanted and put his own interests last. When talking to others he cast his eyes down, and there was a note of pleading in his voice. His conversation was filled with such phrases as: "Would you mind if . . . ," and "Maybe you could . . . ," and "Sorry, sorry."

Bruce was an aggressive and extremely competitive person. He readily confronted others, talking loudly and forcibly, and tended to belittle others by picking on their thoughts, actions, or personal qualities. He often offended people and they tended to avoid him. Few people liked him because he was too aggressive, always out to win and minimizing the contributions made by others as if he deserved to take all the credit. His conversation was peppered with such phrases as: "You'd better . . . ," "That's stupid . . . ," "Typical!" and "or else . . . ."

Caroline was assertive. She said clearly what she wanted, and made the claims she wished to make while listening to others and recognizing their claims too. She could express her feelings strongly when she wanted to, and she could also cope calmly with disagreements. Caroline was easy to get along with whether you liked her or not. People felt they could trust her, and communicate with her well even when feeling confused or angry. It was easy to laugh with Caroline. In her conversation she used phrases like: "I think . . . ," "I believe . . . ," "What do you think?" and "How could we work that out?" *The assertive person uses the word "I." The others focus on "you."* The focus on "you" is damaging because it rarely changes anything—we do not have much control over others—and because it usually builds up resentment. The focus on "you" lays the blame at the other person's door, and one way or another, the other person is likely to strike back. By focusing on "I" you are taking responsibility for yourself, and leaving others to take responsibility for themselves.

No one behaves in exactly the same way all the time. Aggression comes more naturally when one is angry or after being frightened—for example, by someone stepping carelessly into the road in front of your car. Feeling low and unconfident makes people withdrawn and passive. No one can behave assertively all the time, but we can increase the frequency of doing so. Assertiveness is a skill, or set of skills. But underlying these skills is an attitude about yourself.

Low self-esteem, thinking badly about yourself, makes it extremely difficult to be fair. How can you be fair if you believe that you "don't count" or "don't matter," or if you fear that your weaknesses will become glaringly obvious unless you keep on trying to win? Or if you believe that failure is always just round the corner? The ability to stand up for yourself appropriately—and to make sure that your relationships, however unequal in social or other ways, reflect your assertive rights, depends on having a healthy, well-functioning basis for your self-esteem. Chapter 10 concentrates on ways of building self-confidence and self-esteem. This chapter is about fairness and assertiveness. The two fit well together.

The balance between yourself and others. When it comes to your right to have feelings and opinions, you are just as important as other people. This is one of the central lessons of this book (Chapter 3). The interesting point is that there are two sides to this lesson. One side is that you are not less important than other people; the other side is that other people are not less important than you. Passive people usually value themselves less than others, and this often shows in what they say: "I'm sure you're right"; "I'll leave that up to you"; and so on. With aggressive people it is often not so simple. Some are aggressive because they undervalue others. They ride roughshod over the opinions of others and treat them as if they did not matter. They say things like: "That's completely irrelevant"; "Stop complaining and get on with it"; or "You can take it or leave it." But aggressive behavior can also come from feeling inferior oneself, especially for people who have learned to "hit before they get hit." Those who have been bullied, or repeatedly treated badly, may feel vulnerable and readily hit out, verbally or physically, in order to protect themselves. Assertiveness is about recognizing the symmetry between yourself and others, and valuing all people—even when you disagree with them and have completely different feelings. It is not about *liking* everyone (we all have likes and dislikes), but about how to negotiate with them fairly. Assertiveness makes it unnecessary to resort to subterfuge or to adopt unnecessary armor in order to protect yourself. It helps both you and others to recognize and respect your mutual rights.

The balance between reflecting and reacting. Assertiveness may sound like a thoughtful, laborious, and rather unnatural kind of activity. It is not so much about reflecting *instead of* reacting, but about finding the balance between the two. If someone makes you angry— for example by borrowing something precious to you and damaging it—you might explode with a tirade of expletives, and end up saying many things that have little bearing on the present incident: "You are *such* a careless idiot. I don't want anything more to do with you— ever." The opposite extreme might involve thinking about how upset they must feel, avoiding making a scene, and hiding your feelings of anger under a veneer of friendly smiles. You might even accept part of the blame: "I should never have lent it to you." The balanced, assertive response would involve expressing your anger clearly and appropriately, focusing your anger on the behavior rather than the person: "That was a really careless thing to do" rather than "You're completely irresponsible." Then you can follow up by finding out how the other person feels (embarrassed? remorseful? unconcerned?) in order to decide how to resolve the difficulty, taking into account how you wish the relationship to continue after this hiccup.

ASSERTIVENESS BUILDS STRENGTH

The skills of assertiveness help you to build the stamina and strength to stand up for yourself, and so they also strengthen your relationships by placing them on an equal and robust footing. Linda was a high-school teacher, with her own teenage children at home, who found that as soon as she left work and set foot in her home, her family would begin to make demands on her. Because she was tired, she often snapped back and was irritable, and then the tensions would quickly escalate. She decided to make use of assertiveness skills. She explained that she was tired when she came home and needed a few minutes peace and quiet. She said she would make herself a cup of tea and take it into the sitting room, where she would drink it slowly by herself before joining the fray once more. At first her family continued to make the usual demands and interruptions, assuming that she would soon return to her old familiar, and irritable, self. But she persisted, chasing them out of the sitting room if necessary, until the new ways became second nature, both for her and for her family.

Risking even small changes takes courage—for an aggressive person as much as for a passive one. "Giving way to feelings," and "allowing your heart to rule your head" are only too readily labeled as signs of weakness. But taking the risk helps people to build confidence and self-esteem, and to take pleasure in feeling stronger. Being fair to yourself in this way also demonstrates your worth—to yourself and to others. It shows that you are worth considering and caring for in the same way as others. If you make your own needs clear, you are less likely to be irritable and more likely to have the strength to respond to the demands others make on you. If you fail to make your needs clear, but instead bottle them up or sit on them, or hide them under a self-deprecating smile, they will not go away but will gnaw at you inside, and make you feel resentful toward others. This resentment may eventually burst out as aggression. Indeed, many unassertive people fail to speak up for themselves precisely because they fear that, if they were to do so, the floodgates of their anger would open. Expressing yourself assertively defuses and bypasses the resentment and the anger, which quickly dissipate in the light of fair play.

ASSERTIVENESS LEADS TO FLEXIBILITY

The rigidity of both passive and aggressive responses means that they encourage only one type of behavior in other people and only one kind of solution to problems. Both tyrants and doormats are dominated by control: they either need to be in control or to be controlled. Assertiveness produces flexibility. It helps people to understand each other and to think about how they can both get what they want. It helps people adapt to each other and prevents them from getting stuck in fixed positions. Initial conflict followed by assertiveness leads to creative resolution. Aggressiveness and passivity both invite the opposite response, and close down other options. Assertiveness opens more possible paths and leads to a more satisfactory kind of adaptation. Assertiveness provides the secure foundation for effective negotiation (see Chapter 15).

Steps Toward Fairness

Treating yourself and others fairly involves combining the *attitude* of fairness with the *skills* of assertiveness. The attitudes provide the framework for the skills which, as with all skills, need to be practiced. The analogy with sports is a useful one here. In order to perform well in sports, you need both to train on a regular basis and to prepare for a specific important event. So it is with assertiveness. Three steps for building the framework are described first, followed by six specific skills. We also suggest some exercises that you can do at any time and can repeat in order to become highly skilled. Pick and choose those exercises that appeal to you, and combine them in the ways you find useful.

Nine Ways to Become Fair to Yourself

Building the framework

1. Build up your confidence and self-esteem.
2. Clarify what you want.
3. Lay claim to your rights.

Learning six specific skills

1. Listen to others.
2. Use the "unselfish I."
3. Stick to the important points.
4. Manage criticisms and complaints.
5. Use your body to back you up.
6. Say "no" with assurance.

Three Steps for Building the Framework

STEP 1: BUILD UP YOUR CONFIDENCE AND SELF-ESTEEM

If your self-esteem is low it tends to undermine you at every turn, as if your inner voice produced a stream of unfair comments, determined to cut you down to size: "I'm weak—stupid—a failure— making a fool of myself—upsetting the applecart." "People will— think I'm no good—dislike me—ignore me," and so on. A whole chapter is devoted to this important subject (Chapter 10), and three exercises are provided here.

Exercise 1. Make a list of your good points. Include things about your appearance, a skill that you have developed, something about your personality, and at least one achievement that you are proud of. Remember only you can know just how hard these were for you to achieve, so give credit where it is due, as well as where you think others might give it.

Exercise 2. Keep a diary for a week in which you write down only positive things—your achievements; struggles overcome; people who were friendly, helpful, or kind to you; things you enjoyed. Look back over the diary. Add to it when you feel good; read it when you feel bad.

Exercise 3. Practice saying clearly what you truthfully think by paying someone a compliment every day. Make sure your compliments are honest and appropriate: you are not learning how to use flattery, or false praise, but to give fairly and to receive what is your due. Notice the different ways in which compliments are received. When it comes to your turn to receive one, do not dismiss it, or laugh, or say "Oh, I was just lucky." Accept it as a genuine expression of someone else's feelings—as being perfectly fair and not a reason for feeling embarrassed or uncomfortable.

STEP 2: CLARIFY WHAT YOU WANT

Assertiveness is about stating clearly what you want, without either retreating into your shell or bullying others. Passive people may know what they want but be unable to ask for it. Aggressive people often bluster about aggressively because they do not really know what they want, like those customers who complain loudly about the poor service they think they are getting. They get angry with an inappropriate person, and are then so rude that everyone is upset and nobody feels satisfied. The problem arises from failing to think beyond the anger to what they really want: to cancel the transaction? a price reduction? a replacement? an apology? Assertiveness involves tuning in to what you want (this comes more quickly with practice), and then making requests without bringing unnecessary emotional baggage. This is much more effective than unfocused anger. *Keep asking yourself: What is it I really want?*

STEP 3: LAY CLAIM TO YOUR RIGHTS

Assertiveness requires that you truly believe that you have the same rights as others to have your interests and views respected.

Exercise 1. Reread the table of Assertive Rights (p. 129) and think about whether you believe in them or not. Remove any that you think should not be there, and add any that you think should be there. Relevant areas to think about might concern your independence; your needs; asking for help; time to rest, relax, or be by yourself; your right to enjoy yourself; or your right to change. Think about these questions: What rights do you have in an argument? Or if you want to end a relationship? Or start a new one? Your rights and those of others should be the same.

Exercise 2. Talk to others about whether they have the same rights as you; ask them what rights they think are important. If you think others have rights which you do not have, then you are probably not being fair to yourself. If you would find it difficult to allow others the rights you claim for yourself, then you may not be being fair to others.

Six Specific Skills

Attitudes and skills go hand in hand. Sometimes working on skills helps to develop attitudes, but sometimes it works the other way round and building attitudes makes it easier to develop skills. Liking the French encourages you to learn their language, just as learning the language helps you to get to know, and to like, French people. Assertiveness is, in fact, much like a language, or a tool, that facilitates communication and understanding. Like a language, it has many different facets and uses, and involves many different skills. Here are six skills that can build assertiveness.

1. LISTEN TO OTHERS

Think again about the behavior of aggressive people who make blustering demands without having any idea what others think. Instead of succeeding in the attempt to dominate others, these people often put themselves in a weaker, more vulnerable position and fail to listen. Listening carefully to what someone else is saying means giving them your undivided attention. A good listener will understand the words said, but will also be able to pick up on how the person is feeling. You may need to verify whether your guess is right: "You seem really worried about that," or "That sounds extremely irritating to me."

Guides to Good Listening

- Show that you are listening by looking at the person who is speaking, or nodding, or saying "Uh-huh."
- Reflect, or repeat, a few words: "You were tired," "You didn't?"
- Summarize what you have understood: "They asked you to join them."
- When you agree, say so. Especially when discussions get heated, it is very easy to concentrate on what you want to say in your turn and to assume other people know you agree with what they said. Then they feel that they have failed to get the point across, and repeat themselves or become irritated.
- Listen for what people mean by what they say, or to what is not voiced, and verify whether you are right. "You're late" could be an accusation or a sigh of relief; a monosyllabic answer could be a sign of being distracted, depressed, uninterested, bored, or in full agreement.
- Listen to the end. There may be a twist in the tail of the message.
- Take off your blinders: the assumptions that tempt you to jump to the wrong conclusions, like supposing when someone says "please help" that they want you to solve the problem for them rather than provide support and encouragement. Or supposing, when someone says they have had a dreadful day that they want to unload the agony on you, or that they are feeling overwhelmed or depressed. Maybe they just want to be heard and understood. Maybe saying it helps them to leave it behind.

---

2. USE THE "UNSELFISH I"

Saying "I want to go home at five tonight" is being fair to yourself if that is what you want; it is not being selfish. It is only fair to express yourself clearly, especially when you want something. There is no need to beat about the bush, nor to be vague, coy, or embarrassed. If others have the right to speak up for themselves, to express themselves, and to expect their viewpoint to be respected, then so do you.

Imagine you want to talk to someone about something that is troubling you. You may be able to get the help you want quite easily, but it is often far more difficult than it appears unless you explain what you need: "I need help in making this decision," "I need to let off steam," "I need a hug," "I need—space to breathe—to talk about the weekend—advice—to complain."

Accept your feelings for what they are and not as if taking account of them makes you selfish. If you feel angry, then that is what you feel. There is little point in telling yourself you *should* not be angry. Acknowledge the feeling, so that you can express it or manage it appropriately. The same goes for others. They have the feelings they have, and the right to have those feelings, to acknowledge and accept them—but they do not have the right to bombard you with them against your will. So, a feeling needs to be acknowledged. But do not confuse the feeling with the belief that may accompany it. If you feel stupid, that feeling is *real,* but it does not follow that you *are* stupid. You will find more about the relationship between thoughts and feelings in Chapter 9.

3. STICK TO THE IMPORTANT POINTS

Anthony Flew, the philosopher, used to talk about "the ten leaky buckets argument." This is putting forward many weak arguments in the hope that together they will add up to one good one—which of course they never will. What you want is one watertight bucket, not ten leaky ones. In reality, many leaky arguments actually weaken a good case. Leaky arguments turn your whole case into excuses rather than arguments.

Imagine that someone invites you to a party this coming weekend. Suppose you are off on holiday for two weeks starting tomorrow. You simply say that you cannot accept their invitation because you will be away. This is one, utterly convincing, reason for not being able to go to the party.

Now imagine that you are invited to a party but do not want to go because you have too much else on that weekend. You are actually free to go, but would rather not. You start to make excuses: you are not quite sure what you will be doing; you have to go out earlier in the day and are not certain whether you will be back in time; you have to get up early the next day and don't want a late night; you feel you might be developing a cold and would not like to give it to anyone. None of these excuses is entirely convincing and all could be challenged. If you are not sure what you will be doing, why not make yourself sure by accepting the invitation? You could turn up late, or leave early.

The most convincing reply is the straightforward and simple one: "Thanks, but I've got too much else going on." There is no comeback on that. You have stated your decision and have given a single clear reason. If your answer is not accepted, then repeat the message, either using just the same words or slightly different ones to say the same thing. "No, I'm afraid I can't," "I'm sorry, but I am too busy," "I would have liked to, but I can't." This is an extremely useful strategy that can be adapted for many different situations.

Learning to stick to your guns, to stay on track, and to use watertight arguments takes practice. The exercise in the following box describes three steps to take and provides examples of situations in which you could practice taking them.

Exercise for Sticking to Important Points

Step 1: Decide what you want.

Step 2: Express this clearly.

Step 3: Think of as many other ways of expressing your decision as you can.

Practice situations

1. Refuse to look after someone else's cat while they are away.
2. Ask for your money back.
3. Change some theatre tickets.
4. Turn down an invitation or date.
5. Get your children to pick up their clothes.

You could write your ideas down, or talk them through with a friend, or ask someone to help you with a dress rehearsal. This might be useful for particularly difficult events, such as telling someone their work is not good enough, or insisting that your request for a pay review be dealt with.

4. MANAGE CRITICISMS AND COMPLAINTS

Criticisms and complaints make feelings run high whether they burst out aggressively—"That's typical of people like you," "You're useless . . .," "You've never been any good at . . ."—or run more passively through underground channels of resentment, anger, and blame. Exploding with fireworks or seething with unexpressed emotion are two destructive extremes, the Scylla and Charybdis, that being fair to yourself and to others helps you to steer between.

First, it is essential to make a distinction between criticism and character assassination. Everyone does things wrong at times, makes mistakes, gives offense, behaves thoughtlessly or rudely, but these are all particular types of behavior, provoked by particular situations. It makes no more sense to draw general conclusions from them (and to label the person who does them as "bad") than it does to draw equally general conclusions when someone does something helpful or considerate. Counteracting false accusations is easier if you can admit to weaknesses *accurately*, without exaggerating their importance and without dismissing them as irrelevant. Three different strategies that help in responding to criticism are explained here.

Refuse to be labeled. Your critic says "You're always so illogical. You can't keep an idea straight in your head for more than 10 seconds," and you reply "Sometimes I say illogical things. Mostly I make perfectly good sense."

Agree with the critic and apologize appropriately. The critic says "You're late again," and you reply "Yes, I'm sorry—I've been running late all day."

Ask for clarification. The critic says "You're muddled and disorganized," and you reply "What makes you say that?" or "Is something in your way" or "What would you like me to sort out?"

When the shoe is on the other foot and you want to make a complaint, a three-step process is helpful.

Step 1: Name the problem. "Your music kept me awake last night"; "I have not had a pay increase this year"; "This order is incomplete"; "You have sent me the wrong tickets."
General rules: Be brief, specific, and clear, and do not make guesses about the other person's attitudes or motives. Stick to the facts.

Step 2: State your feelings or opinions. "It was really irritating"; "I am very disappointed"; "I think there must be a mistake somewhere".
General rules: Only state your own feelings and opinions, and take care not to exaggerate them. Keep it low key, without blaming or shaming others. Remember to focus on "I" not "you."

Step 3: Specify what you want. "Please could you turn it down after midnight?"; "Can you tell me why that is?"; "I need replacements by Wednesday."
General rules: Ask for clearly specified changes, one at a time, that others can reasonably be expected to manage.

On both the giving end and the receiving end of complaints and criticisms, it helps to remain calm. When feelings run high, they obscure our vision of other people, and distort our ideas of fairness. Shooting from the hip, saying things that you will later regret, tends to escalate conflicts. If your requests have been ignored, or someone is gratuitously unpleasant or critical, and you feel frustrated or undermined or angry about someone else's behavior, you may need to calm down before you can reflect as well as react. Ideas about dealing with conflicts and disputes can be found in Chapter 15.

5. USE YOUR BODY TO BACK YOU UP

There is a physical aspect to assertive behavior. How assertive you feel shows in your posture, eye contact, tone of voice, gestures and movements, facial expression, and the distance you place between you and others. The following exercises help to increase awareness of these factors. There is no one right way of being assertive. The exercises are meant to help you think about the signals you observe in others and those you send out. In general, more assertive behavior involves holding yourself straight, looking at people openly, and neither giving them a wide berth nor crowding them out.

Exercise 1. Think of someone you know who behaves assertively (not aggressively!). Get up and walk across the room in the way that they would walk. When you have the chance, observe what assertive behavior looks like. What do you notice?

Exercise 2. Repeat these exercises, thinking instead of aggressive and of passive behavior. Exaggerate the differences between them. For instance, when feeling passive, people tend to avoid eye contact; when feeling aggressive, they tend to stare. Try out each type of behavior in a conversation with those you know well, and observe the reaction. Ask them whether they notice the differences. Then see if you can find an "assertive compromise"— the right balance for you. Can you recognize your own body language? Is there anything you would like to change in the way you use your body? If there is, specify clearly what, and practice the new behavior as often as possible.

6. SAY "NO" WITH ASSURANCE

When others ask us to do things, we usually feel under pressure to say *yes*—a pressure which we often yield to against our better judgment.

Why is this? There are probably three main reasons. The first is not being clear about our priorities. The second is fearing the other person will be displeased or think badly of us if we say no. And the third, if the other person is a friend, is to make them happy.

Clarifying priorities. Every time you say "yes" to one thing, you will have to say "no" to something else. This is true even if you are not leading a busy life. So be sure that you say "yes" to those things that you want to say "yes" to. Do not say "yes" for the wrong reasons: just to please the person who asked you; or to get them off your back; or because it appeals to your sense of self-importance. When you say "yes," you should be agreeing to something which, given all your priorities, you truly want to agree to. What you agree to should be more important to you than what you have to give up (see Chapter 5). You might refuse to take on something extra because you are not prepared to drop other commitments that are more important to you— or that you would prefer to do. You might say no to helping a neighbor on Sunday because you want to relax with the Sunday papers.

Be fair to yourself, balance your own needs and wishes with those of others. Saying "no" is not being callous and uncaring, but treating your needs and wishes as equally important as those of others.

Saying no nicely. If someone asks you to do something that you do not wish to do, then all you need to do is to say no. You are under no obligation to explain yourself. You have as much right to say no and leave it at that as the next person. However, many people find it easier to say no if they know how to do so without provoking pressure, persuasion, confrontation, or dismay. Some people make it hard for us by refusing to take no for an answer. Strategies for saying no nicely can, therefore, contribute to your sense of fair play.

Here are a few ways of making a refusal easier on you and easier for someone else to accept.

- Make it clear that you appreciate being asked: "Thank you for asking me"; "That's nice of you"; "I'm really pleased to be asked."
- Acknowledge the other person's priorities and wishes: "I know that it is important"; "I understand the difficulty, but . . ."
- Give a clear reason for your refusal: "I am already committed to doing . . ."; "It would take more time than I've got"; "I don't know how."
- Help the other person to resolve their difficulty. One way of doing this is to make a suggestion—for example, suggesting

someone else they can ask instead. The aim is to find the balance between saying (or thinking) "This is not my problem" and taking on other people's problems as if they were your own.

The sleep on it rule Make it a rule not to commit yourself to anything important until the next day at the earliest. This gives time to think through whether, taking all your priorities into account, you really do want to say yes or no. This one rule saves many later regrets. A night's sleep is a powerful way of getting things into perspective.

Chapter Summary

Assertiveness is the core skill to being fair to yourself, and to others.
Assertiveness is different from aggressiveness.
Assertiveness provides a balance between:

1. Aggression and passivity
2. Yourself and others
3. Reflecting and reacting

Here are three steps for building the framework of assertiveness:

1. Build up your confidence and self-esteem.
2. Clarify what it is that you want.
3. Lay claim to your rights.

And here are six specific assertiveness skills:

1. Listen to others.
2. Use the unselfish "I"—express your wishes clearly and simply.
3. Stick to the important points.
4. When criticizing others, criticize their actions, not their character.
5. Use body language to reinforce your message.
6. Say no with assurance. Never commit yourself to something important or time consuming without first "sleeping on it."

14

♦ ♦ ♦

The Second Key to Good Relationships: Recognizing Voices from the Past

The past is always with us. It provides the base from which we start and the framework through which we see the world. It can be a source of creativity, but also a source of confusion and pain, particularly when we do not understand how it is affecting us and how to free ourselves from its limitations. In our current relationships, or in our lack of relationships, there will be voices from our past. These voices can be the source of problems, and the problems may only be effectively tackled when we learn to recognize—to hear—the voices from the past.

Our past is laid down in layers. We are like the earth whose layers can be revealed by looking at a cliff face. Looking back through time at the layers of rock, we can see the layer that was once the floor of a lake, where small creatures drifted to the bottom; the layer where the forest grew, now crushed by the weight of rock to a thin black line; and in places, because of the crush of the land, older layers are pushed through to the surface.

We too have layers, and as with the earth, past layers can rise gently to the surface or they can burst through unexpectedly, visiting us with disturbing images and feelings. The things that happen, or do not happen, in our relationships readily activate and reveal this movement between the present and the past.

Our past layers are of course complex, but simplified models can help us understand more about them, and also help us in our relationships. One method, transactional analysis, provides a model of ourselves, designed to be of practical value in understanding the voices from the past.

Help from Transactional Analysis

Our complex, layered personality can be thought of as having three *voices: Parent, Adult,* and *Child* voices, as if you were made up of three parts: a parent, an adult, and a child. The parent is not you as a parent of your children, but consists of the voices of your own parents or parent-like figures from the past. When you relate to others, all three parts might come into the picture. All three are important and none should be blocked out. But, in some situations, these "voices from the past" can cause trouble.

For our present purposes, we want to help you to focus on listening to, and understanding, these voices from your past. Listen to yourself. When can you hear the child's voice? When you're throwing a tantrum, for example? ("I'm not going to do what you say!") When are you listening to the voice of your parent? ("Pull yourself together and stop whining!") When relationships are problematic, it helps to replace the voices and behavior of the child and parent with those of the adult. This is not to say that there is no room for the child and the parent; the child within us is often the source of fun and of creativity and often good at warning us when we are in danger. The parent may provide us with useful discipline, or with goals and ideals to work toward. But the parent and the child will be more useful to us, and less troublesome in our relationships, if they are under the control of the adult. If the child or the parent takes over, problems arise, causing major difficulties in relationships.

The Adult's Voice

The adult voices the mature part of your personality—the part that has developed as a result of your own explorations of the world. It is the part of you that can think and reason about your experience and can learn to make predictions about how things will be in the future. It can make decisions based on reality. When the adult is in control, it can put the voices of the parent and the child to constructive use.

There is no need to stifle the voices of the child and parent; but you can prevent them from making themselves heard in destructive and unwanted ways by becoming more aware of what they are saying. The voice of the adult can help you to stand aside from them, or to use them constructively rather than to be swept along by them.

The Child's Voice

The child voices those feelings and responses that were mainly laid down during the first years of our lives. The child's voice can express the whole range of feelings, as children can experience intense and complex feelings long before they can talk about them. It can also express many childish, positive aspects of our personality, such as our curiosity, the ability to throw ourselves wholeheartedly into things, and the capacity for sheer fun. People who no longer experience much of this kind of fun may have repressed the child within themselves. But childish voices can also be the source of problems, particularly problems in our relationships.

When you listen to children, you will hear certain patterns of speech which are common: "Leave me alone"; "You never let me do what I want"; "I'm not going to do what you say." We may think that these complaints have gone from within us now that we are adult. However, this is unlikely to be true. The voices, and the behavior, of this child can still be heard, but in less obvious ways.

COMMON VOICES OF THE CHILD

Mine's better than yours. Children often compare their belongings with those of other children, insisting that they come off best—"I've got the biggest one"—and exaggerating its advantages "it takes 10 minutes to walk round my Dad's car." This voice can be heard when, as adults, we compare ourselves with others and emphasize how much better we are doing or insist on our superior equipment. Such comparisons often conceal underlying fears, and serve, as they do with children, as a rather ineffective type of reassurance: "At least my desk isn't such a mess as hers." The fears seem to reflect the assumption that if I am not the top dog then you will be, leaving me in danger of being trampled on, or of not being able to control what happens. The fear also breeds insensitivity to others: "I can rely totally on Dan in a difficulty. It must be dreadful for you not having someone like him to turn to."

This voice, when dominant, leaves us with an underlying bad feeling, which is why it is not so very different from jealousy.

I want yours. Children are often jealous of the better possessions of other children and become rapidly dissatisfied. One of the tasks of parenthood is to help children to learn to be satisfied with what they have rather than demanding the possessions of others. It is a difficult task, and few of us grow to be adults without this childish voice still making itself heard.

You hear of a friend's success, and instead of feeling happy for them it "gets to you." Is this your inner child playing: "I want yours"? Perhaps you have observed in yourself, or seen in the behavior of others, the desire to have *everything* that others have, ranging from a newfangled potato peeler or bottle opener to a new car; from gadgets to status symbols of all kinds. Just as when we take our children to toy stores almost everything seems eminently desirable.

Here is yet another variant.

It's not fair. This is seen in particularly powerful form between siblings. "You gave her a new drawing book, but you didn't give me anything." We can think, as we grow older, that this kind of rivalry with our brothers and sisters disappears, but it can come out in subtle and unrecognized ways. "It's my turn to throw the party, chair the meeting, get on the housing committee." "It's your turn to sort out the wash, pay for the drinks, come out with my friends."

The feeling of unfairness can be even more powerful when it is about *time* rather than *belongings*.

What about me? This can seem a particularly unfair accusation to parents with two or more children! You spend an hour reading to one child ignoring the others; then you spend a few minutes drawing with another and the first says, "What about me?." All children need attention, but not all to the same degree, and all children can at times have an almost insatiable desire for the attention of their parents. This desire can break through the surface when we are adults, especially in relationships with key people such as partners. In most close adult relationships, there are times when the voices of the child within us demand attention, and appeal to the adult or parent part of our partner for time or consideration. This is no bad thing as long as it does not dominate the relationship, but it can be a source of jealousy and friction when it is not recognized for what it is, and especially if there is a very unequal balance between the partners in the parts they play.

Voices of complaint: Temper tantrums and deep sulks. Few children do not respond to frustration, from time to time, either by throwing a temper tantrum or by going into a deep sulk—inviting parents to cajole them out of it but simultaneously determined not to be appeased.

The temper tantrum can be seen in adults in the form of almost uncontrollable rage, or the kind of angry shouting that seems to combine anger with pleading. The deep sulk may persist with some couples for days and be precipitated by apparent trivialities, such as finishing up the last of the bread or forgetting to give someone a message. The unrecognized meaning of these events is often the important factor: "You didn't consider me"; "I'm not important to you." The atmosphere created by this deep-seated response can be almost palpable: "You could have cut the atmosphere with a knife."

Some Common Voices of Childhood

A childish version	*An adult version*
I'll tell my teacher about . . .	I shall have to speak to the authorities.
If you don't, I'll . . .	Unless . . . I may have to . . .
I'll scream and scream and scream until I'm sick.	I'll continue making a fuss even if it kills me.
Everyone else has . . . running shoes	Our competitors are using . . .
Cry baby!	Softie! Moaner! Wimp!
I'm bigger than you are	Of course, speaking as someone who knows, . . .
I'm king of the castle . . .	I'm in charge here . . .

Some Useful Questions to Ask Yourself

- What am I feeling in these difficult situations?
  (For example, just before a fight.)
- When have I felt like this before?
- When was the very first time I felt like this?
- What was happening at the time?
- What is it I want in this situation?
- Who else in my childhood behaved like this (am I copying my sister . . .)?

The Parent's Voice

The voices of the parent reflect the voices we internalized as children, on the basis of the messages we received from our own parents, from the other adults who surrounded us as children, and even from television and radio. These are the voices of authority that we derive from internalizing some of the views we heard expressed. Most of what these adults said, if we were lucky, was sensible and helpful. But there will also be unhelpful, outmoded, or painful messages coming to us through the voice of the parent within us. Amy and Thomas Harris, who have made the ideas of transactional analysis generally available, wrote:

> One of the most powerful ways in which the Parent enters our lives in the present is the internal dialogue in which we hear the same applause, warnings, accusations, and punishments we heard when we were toddlers. The person in us who is at the other end of the dialogue is the Child, the preschooler in our heads. We can feel as bad today as we did then, when negative recordings in either Parent or Child are activated, and we hear the internal, unceasing voices of regret or accusation.[1]

COMMON VOICES OF THE PARENT

You can do better than that. Even though this is meant as encouragement, the message the child often receives is "That's not good enough." When no performance or achievement seems to satisfy, the parental voice may be acting as a goad and a reminder. If you are very distressed when something small goes wrong, or when someone points out that you have made a mistake, you may be listening to this voice from your past.

Stop making a fuss. Parents usually want to help their children develop self-control and the resilience to withstand knocks and setbacks in life. They may also have little time or energy to give to their children when things go wrong and they are distressed. Or they may be too troubled and preoccupied to attend to their children. They may even not care much about them. For some or all of these reasons, they may discourage children from showing their distress.

The voice of your parent telling you not to make a fuss may reveal itself in various ways—for example, if you feel guilty or embarrassed whenever you make a claim for yourself, or if you are tempted to apologize and hide your feelings when someone forgets to keep an appointment.

Don't be angry. This message is often backed up by actions or threats, such as banishing children from the room when they are angry, or refusing to speak to them until they have calmed down. Children brought up hearing this voice may later be frightened or alarmed by strong feelings of anger, and come to believe it is wrong to feel anger and to express it. They may find it hard to develop adult ways of expressing anger that allow them to acknowledge the feelings without damaging relationships that are important to them.

We can recognize our parents' voices within us particularly when we come out with inflexible rules and clichéd statements, and when we put others or ourselves down in a peremptory fashion. If you are vulnerable to being hurt by a particular person, or inexplicably go to great lengths to please someone else, it is probably because that person speaks to the child within you with the authority of your parent. Becoming aware of what the messages from these voices are telling you helps you to mobilize your adult voice, and either adapt or reject them as, on consideration, you wish.

How Voices from the Past Can Interfere with Current Relationships

ARGUMENTS WITH A PARENT

Arthur was 36 years old, married, with two sons. His parents lived far away, in the same village as their other son, Arthur's older brother. Arthur was only able to visit his parents about twice a year, and although Arthur was very fond of his parents and would normally get on well with them, at some stage during these visits he would have an argument with his mother. The topic of the argument would vary, but the quality was the same each time. It was as though he and his mother could not help having this argument, and it left them both unhappy. Arthur saw so little of his parents that he greatly regretted having these arguments since they spoiled what little time he had with them.

Arthur used the ideas of transactional analysis and this gave him the understanding he needed.

He realized that the main voice to be heard during his arguments with his mother came from the child within him. What underlay all these arguments, whatever their ostensible subject matter, was that powerful child voice of *sibling rivalry:* he was jealous that his brother was getting more attention from his parents than he was. His

---

Some Parental Voices That Can Be Unhelpful to Adults
(These Can Be Spoken by Friends, Teachers, and Others, Too)

- Stop moaning and groaning and get on with it.
- Hurry up, or you'll get left behind.
- Be careful. Make sure you get back safely.
- Don't interrupt.
- You can't just have whatever you want.
- Don't be selfish.
- Don't answer back.
- You're on your own now.
- Wait for your turn.
- Never an idle moment.
- If you've started it, finish it.
- You're clumsy, silly, a crybaby, irresponsible, bad.
- You're in the way.

There Are Just as Many Helpful Parental Voices as Unhelpful Ones

- You'll be okay.
- I'm sure you can manage.
- You can do it if you want to.
- Keep trying—I'll help if you get stuck.
- Nobody can do more than their best.
- You're wonderful, important, lovable, funny, etc.

Can You Recognize the Voices That Speak to You?

1. Think of the adult people in your life when you were a child: parents, relatives, friends, teachers
2. What are the main messages you picked up from them? If they could say one thing to you, what would it be?

---

brother saw his parents daily and had help with babysitting, taking the children to school, gardening, and much else besides. Arthur felt left out, just like the child crying out "What about me?" "Why are you spending all this time with my brother and ignoring *me*?" He was quite upset to realize that he still felt like a five-year-old. The fact that he did not need help from his parents now was irrelevant. The fact that these arguments were spoiling some of the precious time he spent with his parents was irrelevant. The child within him was simply jealous of his brother ("He's getting more than I am"), and it pushed him into the arguments with his mother.

Once he understood what was happening, he was able to cease arguing. The adult part of him could take over, recognizing, as it did, the jealous child within. The adult part could understand that the child's jealousy was misplaced, and he could then relate to his mother as adult to adult rather than child to parent.

A TEMPER TANTRUM

Sandra was normally a well-tempered and patient person. But just occasionally she would lose her temper. It was usually when she was particularly tired. To her it felt as though she suddenly "snapped," and when she lost her temper, she would shout, almost scream, at her partner. It seemed quite out of character, and it troubled her because she did not like it and it felt out of control. It was as though someone else took possession of her during these temper tantrums.

A friend gave her a clue about what was going on when he told her that she sounded just like her elder sister during these temper tantrums. Sandra asked herself how she felt at the times when she lost her temper. Did how she feel seem like any times in her childhood? She considered this. When she lost her temper she felt utterly help- less inside, just as she used to feel when her sister lost her temper with her. As a child this made Sandra feel both frightened and power- less—helpless. The feeling of helplessness was very similar to how she now felt, occasionally, when her partner insisted on having his own way regardless of what *she* wanted. She felt so helpless that she wanted to scream, just as her sister had screamed at her.

Recognizing this voice, which had seemed so alien to her, as the voice of her sister, and understanding the similarity in feeling between how she had sometimes felt with her sister and how she now sometimes felt with her partner, reassured her and helped her to manage her uncontrollable tempers. Understanding their origin had a profound effect because it enabled her to make use of her adult voice to free herself from the old pattern. These are some of the things she said to herself: "I know where this comes from"; "There's no need to stay the same way now." "When I feel helpless or powerless I can think of how to pilot my own ship" (p. 123). Her temper tantrums quickly became less dramatic, and less frequent.

A MARITAL DIFFICULTY

Andrea had a good relationship with her husband, Rick, but whenever they visited Rick's parents, irritation with him seemed to expand out of nowhere until hardly a civil word passed between them. He retreated into himself while she worried about what her mother-in-law was thinking. She could not put her finger on what the problem was. They did not have open arguments, and she could not honestly say that he did anything to upset her. On the contrary, he seemed to treat her just as he usually did. The problem seemed to be her fault, but what was it? Why did she feel so uncomfortable and irritable whenever she visited her in-laws?

Then she noticed something interesting. When Rick visited his parents, his behavior seemed to change. He reverted to childhood patterns and his behavior became dominated by the child within him. His adult part became submerged. That is what Andrea found so difficult. When at her parents-in-law her husband sat in the sitting room and waited to be looked after. He allowed his mother to serve him hand and foot. She pampered him and he just let her do it. Indeed, she even repeated some of the parental messages that he must have heard in his childhood "You're in the way dear. Keep out of my kitchen. You wait there and I'll bring you a cup of tea." It was this childish behavior in him that Andrea found so irritating, and until she talked to him about it, Rick had been completely unaware of what was happening. He had just fallen back into old habits automatically. Their problem was easily resolved once they noticed the pattern.

RECOGNIZING THE PATTERNS IN RELATIONSHIPS

Do the voices and messages from your past reveal patterns? And are these patterns helping or hindering your relationships? At the simplest level, if you grow up believing you are likable, your friendships are likely to reflect a more satisfactory pattern than if you grow up believing you are not likable (see Chapter 10). Learning how to free yourself from destructive voices from the past involves learning how to recognize these patterns. If your brothers and sisters always ridiculed your opinions, you may develop a pattern of keeping them to yourself, and not even notice this pattern until you find yourself in a conflict of opinions that really matters to you. But most situations are more complex than this.

When Steven and Denise started a relationship, they had a great deal to say to each other, and also went out a lot with their friends. Then Steven moved into Denise's flat, and their relationship came under a strain. Denise thought Steven no longer cared for her. He stayed home most evenings, they cooked together, and they shared the bills, but he hardly ever started a conversation. He seemed to her to have run out of things to say about himself and to have lost interest in asking about her.

But Denise was wrong. In his way, Steven *was* showing that he cared about her. Doing things together and sharing responsibilities were, for Steven, signs of caring. Signs of caring, for Denise, were different. She wanted to know how Steven felt and to be able to talk to him about her own feelings. For her, communication—talking—was a sign of caring. These differences reflected the different messages they had received as children. Parents can show that they care in many different ways: for example, by talking, paying attention, hugging, doing things together, paying for camping trips and music lessons, allowing a child its freedom, and just by being there. Children also pick up patterns of relationships from their friends, and the differences between Steven and Denise are common reflections of the different ways men and women behave in our society generally. It is a common pattern for women to talk more about their feelings than men do. The point is that, unless Denise and Steven learn to notice and understand their own patterns, their relationship will continue to produce emotional strain. Denise will continue to think that Steven does not care when really he does.

Recognizing the patterns provides the understanding that can start to take away some of the strain. Once Denise understood how Steven showed that he cared, she felt less rejected by his silences and would ask him directly for what she needed.

Some Common Patterns

Someone is angry with you. → You feel rejected.

You are criticized. → You think you are no good, or unacceptable.

Someone ignores you. → you feel no one cares about you.

You receive a complaint. → You feel incompetent or blame yourself.

Someone asks you to change. → You feel insecure or frightened.

Someone tells you they feel bad. → You feel responsible for making them better.

Someone notices your mistake. → You feel like a failure or give up trying.

Note: These are only a few of the many patterns that can interfere with relationships. To some degree, they are present in all of us. It is only when they become dominant—when present in extreme forms—that they cause major difficulties.

Changing the Patterns

Changing the patterns of thinking and behaving which originate from the child or parent within you may be quite easy and straightforward. You may be able to free yourself from their problematic aspects simply by recognizing that they are there, and realizing that they are an unnecessary piece of baggage that can be dumped. Their power may dissipate in the light of your new understanding. However, old habits sometimes die hard.

Patterns can be broken, but this sometimes requires strategic planning and constructive work. A wide variety of skills that can help you to do this work are described in this book. It is unlikely that you will need all of them, so pick and choose, and use the index to give you some good ideas. The main steps are as follows:

Step 1. Understanding is the first step. Use the ideas provided in the boxes in this chapter to help with this. If you can understand how the problems and difficulties make sense, in terms of the framework of your past, in terms of the messages it gave you and the voices that continue to speak to you, then the adult part of your personality can start to adjust and to deal with the problem.

Step 2. If you want something to change in your relationships, then think about what *you* can change, not about what you would like someone else to change. Being able to change, to become more flexible for example in the way you show affection, places your relationships on a broader, and firmer, footing.

Step 3. Accept that other people will have heard other messages in their past. There is no more point in blaming them for what they were told than there is for blaming yourself for what you were told.

Step 4. Learn about your "trigger points." Imagine that some small event triggers off some unexpectedly strong feelings: someone asks you to do something again and you feel deeply criticized; your friends go out for a drink without you and you feel completely rejected; someone fails to do what you ask and you feel wildly angry. These triggers are useful cues. They may make others accuse you of overreacting, but they may help you figure out what is going on. The idea is that the strong feelings you have in these situations arise because of what the situations *mean* to you. Some questions you might ask yourself include the following:

Questions for Unraveling Meaning

What does this mean about me?

What does this mean about how others see me?

What can this tell me about myself?

What does this mean to me?

How might this link with the past?

Who has said that sort of thing to me before?

What is important to me about this?

Note: You will find more useful questions in Chapter 9.

Not all the situations to which people overreact are ones that make them feel bad. Some people feel quite ridiculously pleased with certain kinds of compliments—and often that is because of what the compliment means to them. "You did really well to manage that so quickly"—you glow with pleasure knowing that you are efficient and competent. "I am so grateful for your help"—the feeling of being needed stays with you all day. "You look wonderful"—and you spend the rest of the day behaving as if everyone loved you. Someone you respect says, "Well done," and you bask in the pleasure of knowing you are an okay person. There is nothing wrong with any of these reactions. But you can use them as clues as well. They can tell you which are the important issues, which are the themes and patterns likely to weigh most with you. These are also the ones that will make you feel the worst when something threatens them.

Related Chapters in This Book

You will need to reflect on and think about what concerns you, so you can identify the patterns. Another way of doing this is described in Chapter 12, The Importance of Relationships.

It helps to be fair both to yourself and to others. Skills for helping with this are described in the previous chapter.

When caught up in the web of the past it is easy for you to lose perspective. Chapter 9, Keeping Things in Perspective: Help from Cognitive Therapy, explains how to look at things in new ways.

Communication skills of all kinds (listening skills, p. 137; the skills of assertiveness, pp. 134–143; negotiating skills, pp. 162–166) will be some of your main tools.

Problem-solving skills, which are discussed in Chapter 8, Problem-Solving: A Strategy for Change, may be helpful if you feel stuck.

Chapter Summary

The past is always with us.

It can be helpful to think of ourselves as consisting of three parts:

- Parent
- Adult
- Child

The "voices" of the "parent" within us reflect the messages we internalized as children from our parents, and other figures of authority.

The "child" voices those feelings and responses that we had as young children.

The "adult" voices the mature part of our personality.

The "voices from the past"—those of the "parent" and the "child"—can be a source of strength and creativity. But if they are not recognized for what they are, they can also be a source of problems in our current relationships.

By recognizing these voices from the past, we can prevent, or limit, the damage they can do and make use of their constructive possibilities.

- **The main message is this: although there is nothing you can do to change the past, you *can* change the way you look at it, and you can take control of the way it affects you in your relationships with others in the present.**

15

◆ ◆ ◆

The Third Key to Good Relationships: Relationships as Systems

Marjorie had married at the age of 18, and by the age of 34, she had three children between the ages of 14 and 11. She had not worked since her first child was born because she was busy and because her husband neither expected nor wanted her to work. He was an electrician employed by a small firm of builders. Marjorie kept the household running well and was the center around which her family revolved. She provided clean clothes, meals, a safe base to which everyone else returned each day, friendship, and most of the organizational energy needed for the family's functioning.

Marjorie loved her husband and her children and they loved her, but now that the children were getting older, she felt in need of a change. Indeed, she felt she had put off making changes for far too long, mainly because her husband said *no*. He was earning good money and told her she was needed at home. He thought she should put the family first, at least until the children had left school. The children joined in the chorus, saying "What about us?" and "Who will be here when I get home?" She found she could not raise the question, nor even talk to them about what she might do instead of housework, since the topic was slapped down as soon as it was brought up. She felt helpless, frustrated, and depressed; stuck and feeling as if everyone was conspiring against her.

Marjorie was caught in a system: the system of relationships within her family. And it was a system that, clearly, did not want a change.

What Is Meant by Seeing Relationships as Systems?

The idea is that what we are, how we relate, how we behave is partly determined by the role we fulfill in a system. Taking us out of the system changes our shape, so that putting us back in the system means that we no longer fit the old slot. The slot in the system which used to be our old shape changes, too, so it no longer provides the comfortable fit that it used to. When one part of a system changes, the other parts cannot help but change with it.

There are three practical consequences of understanding relationships as systems.

1. THE PRINCIPLE OF JOINT RESPONSIBILITY

Problems within a system of relationships are not the sole responsibility of one person: responsibility for relationships is shared. This is recognized in the language of our proverbs—It takes two to tango; It takes two to fight—and it is also recognized in modern methods of family therapy. The following brief sketches provide a glimpse of this principle at work.

At the age of 16 Ned was noisy, messy, and gregarious. He played loud music late at night; stayed out with his friends until the early hours of the morning without permission; slept much of the day on weekends; and his parents feared he would never get to school at all if they did not forcibly shake him awake. The rest of the family were fed up with being bombarded by uncivilized music and falling over the junk he left lying around. Exactly who has responsibility for what depends on the particular people involved and their actual situation. What is clear is that they share the responsibility for their interactions. Each of them plays a part in creating, and in changing, this situation: solving the problem depends on whether they can adjust to each others' ways. We will show how to manage such change later on.

Ruth was devastated when Jake lost his job. There seemed little possibility of his finding another. His early optimism soon evaporated and he wandered around at home with nothing to do, feeling depressed, unwanted, and miserable. The usual patterns of their relationship seemed to have been swept away at a blow. Ruth became the main wage earner and Jake ran the house, but they fought and argued as each one thought the other was making a bad job of something the other could do better.

Wayne, age 12, was brought to the clinic by his parents because his behavior was out of control. He scribbled over wallpaper at home, damaged the furniture, and had started to wet his bed seven years after he first learned to be dry. He was brought to the clinic because he had a problem that his parents wanted solved. With careful work, other problems emerged: difficulties caused by his father's night shifts; disagreements between his parents over the money his father spent on old cars; other children in the family demanding the lion's share of attention, and other problems too. Wayne's problems resolved as other members of the family worked on these problems, and the tension in the house decreased.

Alex lived in a house shared with three others. When one person left, she asked a friend to join them, but this friend failed to pay her share of the bills. She had a reasonably good job, but she spent her money on new clothes and holidays with apparently no thought to her responsibilities. Everyone else was angry, and blamed Alex for the problem. Although Alex was embarrassed, she did not think it was her fault.

Relationships of all kinds can be seen as systems, because one person's behavior impinges on that of others. All relationships within a system may be affected by changes that have started outside the system (e.g., losing a job), or by the behavior of one person (e.g., Alex's friend who failed to pay up). And one person's behavior (e.g., Wayne's behavior) may be the result of many interacting features of the system.

The first practical point is, therefore, that *it is essential to avoid "scapegoating"*—seeing either yourself or others as the sole cause of problems in relationships. The implications, when you have a problem, are:

1. You are probably under pressure from some quarter to change—to be different.
   - Where could this be coming from?
2. To solve the problem you will have to play your part in adapting to new solutions.
   - How can you adapt?
3. If you can change, the system around you will inevitably change, too.
   - What changes would you like to bring about?
   - Which changes can you initiate?
   - How will others react?

2. THE PRINCIPLE OF HOMEOSTASIS

Our bodies have a remarkably efficient way of keeping the inside temperature constant—within quite small limits. Whether we lie in the sun or roll in the snow, whether we go to an exercise class or sit watching a video, our internal body temperature stays pretty much the same. The system makes constant adjustments, sweating or shivering as necessary, to keep the temperature right.

A system of relationships works in a similar way. When one person within the system changes, the others will react by resisting the change in order to keep the system functioning as before. They say things like "That's not like you to do . . ." and "It's nice to see you back to your old self." Of course the system, just like the central heating, also has limits— it is possible to freeze someone out, or for someone or something to be too hot to handle within a particular system. But, generally, unilateral changes provide the impetus for corresponding changes of the opposite kind—so that the system returns to its previous state.

This principle has two important implications. It forewarns you that unilateral changes in your relationships will be resisted by others, and it emphasizes the value of making mutual and compatible changes, so that the changes you make are complemented by changes others make. In this way your changes "fit" with those of the others, so that the system continues to function, but in a new way. This is why learning how to negotiate will help the system both to keep functioning and to change.

3. THE PRINCIPLES OF NEGOTIATION

The term *negotiation* is usually applied to business and management. But we are carrying out negotiations all the time in our personal lives. We may use the word *discussion,* or *argument,* but often what we are talking about is negotiation, carried out more or less skillfully. Good negotiation is often thought of as if it were about getting the better of someone else, and as if it were about making (more or less unwelcome) compromises. The image that comes to mind is of dividing a cake—if one person gets more, the other gets correspondingly less.

Good negotiation, however, is not about dividing the cake, but about baking a new one. The principles of negotiation are based on the idea of abundance, on the idea that in relationships the size of the cake is not fixed at the start. One option, therefore, when faced with the fact that what you want may be very different from what I want, is to do some baking. Dividing up the spoils, so to speak, or competing for relative gain, ends up being counterproductive because it focuses attention on the costs and not the benefits, on what everyone may lose, or have to give up, instead of on what, by putting their heads creatively together, everyone stands to gain.

The implication is that negotiation is not about getting the better of someone else, or of thinking about what all parties to the negotiation are in danger of losing. Using the language of competition, the aim is for both of you to come out of the negotiation having won. This is not as daft as it might sound. Indeed, it is the attitude taught in management studies at Harvard Business School and at many other progressive schools of management. This attitude provides a firm basis for long-term relationships, especially when skillfully put into practice.

Negotiation Skills

Being able to negotiate skillfully is one of the most valuable assets you have when developing relationships. It is relevant to all kinds of relationships, in all kinds of settings. We are carrying out negotiations all the time—whenever two of us disagree about which film to go to, or which TV program to watch, or who left the mess in the kitchen. Children are born negotiators: "Only one more sweet, then you must put the package away." "No, two more" comes the immediate riposte.

Relationships are rarely static, so that those involved in them always need to know how to negotiate change. Negotiating skills help relationships to change smoothly and they help to steer them round the hairpin bends. They provide us with an approach to difficulties in relationships that is fair to all because they focus on helping everyone to get what he or she wants.

THE COOPERATION GAME

Here is a game that is played with two sides. The main aim is to end up with positive points; a secondary aim is to end up with more points than the other side. Both sides make their moves at the same time by playing either a round or a square coin. For each turn, each side places one coin in its bag. After each round, the two bags are opened and points awarded as follows:

- If both coins are round, both sides score –2.
- If both coins are square, both sides score +2.

- If the two coins are different, the values of the coins are reversed and doubled. This means that the side that played a round coin scores +4 and the side that played a square coin scores -4. Both sides know this scoring system from the beginning.
- After the first few rounds, the two sides *negotiate* their next moves.

The interesting aspect of this game is that both sides can win if they both play square, but this requires cooperation. Focusing on beating the other side results in both sides losing, since they both go for the highest possible score (a single round coin scoring +4), and both play round all the time, which means they both score -2. The point is that *lack of trust* and the *desire to do better* lead to mutual destruction. Play it and find out. Only groups that are prepared to trust others, and are prepared from the outset not to do as well as the other side (to risk playing a square coin when the others play a round one), can end up with positive points.

This game illustrates in stark form one of the ways in which we destroy valuable relationships. If we go into relationships to compete—to get more out of the relationship than we put in, or to win so that the other person loses—then we will develop a set of relationships in which everybody loses. Successful relationships are built on the idea that everyone in them will gain, and they require the skills of cooperation.

Some Pointers on How to Cooperate

- *Try looking at the situation from the other person's point of view.* Use your imagination to step into the other person's shoes.
- *Build up trust.* Risk saying how you feel and talking about what you want. Show you believe what other people say. Leave them the space they need to be their own person.
- *Keep in contact.* Do not allow yourself to slip into the habit of not being able to talk. Do not avoid thorny issues.
- *Recognize that people vary in their needs.* Realize people need different amounts of closeness, silence to express their feelings or let off steam, sharing, independence, and different forms of physical contact and sex.
- *Provide what you know you want.* Acknowledge another point of view; take what someone else says seriously; respond with warmth and encouragement.
- *Cut out the blame.* "You make me so angry/nervous/upset . . ." Ask instead, "What is it in me that makes me so angry?"

FOUR RELATIONSHIP PATTERNS

1. There is plenty for all. Everyone in a relationship has something to gain, and this attitude of abundance is, in the long run, the most satisfactory way of relating. It is based on the realization that working together with other people can make things happen that could not otherwise happen. Thinking about ways in which everyone gains engages two heads rather than one, and generates more options and more solutions to problems. It ends up being more *creative* than the other patterns, and this provides more potential for satisfaction.

2. I win: you lose. This is not only intrinsically unfair, it is also not to your long-term advantage. Either the people who lose when you win will draw away from you, or the ones who remain close are the ones who complement you by showing you a third pattern.

3. You win: I lose. This attitude builds up resentment and anger, and is therefore satisfactory to neither party: "If you act like a doormat, don't be surprised if people walk on you."

4. Lose: lose. This is a totally destructive pattern, and not likely to result in lasting relationships.

THERE IS ALWAYS THE POSSIBILITY OF NO DEAL

The bottom line in all negotiations is that you are free to make no deal and walk away. The bottom line in all relationships must be that if you cannot both make the changes needed for the relationship to give you both what you want, then the relationship is off. It takes courage to end relationships, but it must always be a possibility. The alternative is that you make unwise deals, or deals that maintain relationships which are destructive.

PREPARATION FOR SKILLFUL NEGOTIATION: MAPPING THE TERRITORY

Step 1: Find out what everyone wants. Relationships are systems, which means that if you think only about what you want, you obscure half your vision. You need to think both about your own perspective and that of others. If you are very specific about your wants, it may be harder to negotiate. For example, if you want help clearing up and others are not bothered about being messy, your negotiations may quickly get bogged down. What is it about the mess that bothers you? Would you feel satisfied if it was kept to certain places? Or removed only on special occasions? Or do you want most of all to feel that your burden of chores is shared? The three main ways to answer these questions are to *think*, to *ask*, and to *listen*. You need to do all three of these things, not just one of them.

Step 2: Look for common ground. Common ground is useful in establishing what you are *not* negotiating about—we both want to go out, but we cannot agree where to go; we both want to live here, but disagree about who makes the rules.

Step 3: Broaden the basis of the negotiation. A negotiation often founders because it all hinges on one thing, such as who is responsible for servicing the car, or whether one person's necessity is another person's extravagance. But often there are many negotiable aspects of a situation. In the commercial world, for example, a negotiation may center entirely on fixing the price, but there are many other aspects to the deal, such as delivery time, payment time, after-sales service, further orders, and promotion of products. This is often true of relationships, too. A narrow negotiation about heating bills might focus on closing the door when you leave the room. A broader one, leaving more room for considering what everyone wants, might also focus on resetting the time clock or thermostat; sharing the bills a different way; fixing the drafts in the house; or buying a warm sweater.

Step 4: Look for opportunities to trade. Identify the important issues for both of you. It is rare for two people to place exactly the same importance on particular issues, which means that you might be able to gain what is most important to you by giving way on what is most important to someone else. "I'll turn the music down after 11 P.M. if you agree not to fuss about the mess in my room." The broader the basis for the negotiation the more opportunities for trade.

FIVE STRATEGIES FOR PUTTING THE SKILLS INTO PRACTICE

1. Clarify. Be sure to clarify what the other person means and what you mean. "Are you cross with me, or has something else upset you?" Make your points clearly: "I'm angry that you didn't telephone me." Not "I'm fed up with you. You never bother to let me know where you are."

2. Build on what the other person says. Instead of reacting to what you do not like about it and instantly saying "no," look for what you can accept and start with a "yes." This takes you out of conflict and straight into negotiation.

3. Cut out the blame. Think of there being different points of view rather than one wrong one and one right one. Instead of thinking in terms of "fault," think in terms of shared responsibility. This might sound overoptimistic: sometimes one person is wrong. But a flurry of accusations, derogatory name-calling, or insults only raises the temperature, and makes this harder to admit. Cut out the blame, and look for ways of mutual change. Remember that there is always the possibility of *no deal*, but *no deal* is taking your share of the responsibility, not heaping all the blame on the other person.

4. Watch out for escalation. Anger easily spirals upward, especially when people are hurt by the angry things others have just said to them. Anger generates the sort of vicious cycle that stops all reasoned discussion and prohibits agreement. It usually leads to the "lose: lose" pattern.

It can sometimes be useful to tell the other person that what they say makes you feel angry, and it is also helpful to look behind the anger. Often people behave angrily when they are hurt (feel wounded by the angry things said to them) or frightened (by the implications for the relationship, or by threats of being hurt). It may be the hurt and the fear that need addressing rather than the anger.

Some Rules for Fair Fighting

1. *Stick to the concern of the moment.* Don't chuck in the kitchen sink and any old "unfinished business."
2. *Don't overgeneralize.* "You *always* complain . . . or *never* listen to what I say."
3. *No name-calling.* "You're stupid . . . completely heartless . . . domineering . . . childish . . ."
4. *Use the cooler.* Take a break from a fight. Count to ten before you answer back. Go somewhere you can calm down. Explain what you are doing— do not just storm out.
5. *Ask: What's my part in this?* Start your sentences with "I": "I'm furious," not "You make me wild."
6. *Avoid going for the jugular.* Hitting where it hurts mostly just adds to the pain, hurt, and anger. It makes it harder to forgive and forget.
7. *Do not use threats, verbal or physical.* They lead to escalation not resolution.

5. Bottle up the insults. Offensive comments impede negotiation until feelings subside. Examples of such comments are: "I can't talk to anyone as illogical as you," "You're so arrogant/pigheaded/clumsy," "You're as bad as your mother/father/sister," or putdowns such as "Everyone knows that ...," "I think you will find ...," "Any sensible person would realize ...," "I'll be generous, and leave that out of consideration/give you the benefit of the doubt." It is best to avoid making these offensive or irritating comments, and to try to ignore them when they are thrown at you.

When Others Ask for Your Opinion

Most people at times talk to others about their relationships, and they are especially likely to do so when they are stormy or difficult. In the following box we offer some guidelines for the times when others want to talk about their relationships.

Avoid taking sides because this can end up with one person feeling more isolated, rejected, and hurt, which will only perpetuate high levels of distress. Instead, your role is to help the other person to clarify and solve his or her problems. Trying to impose your solution on someone else's personal problem rarely works, and can end in disaster. If you strongly support one person rather than another, it may help to say so, but it rarely helps to add your barbs of criticism to theirs. There always are two sides to a story, and responsibility is always shared to some degree.

Talking to Others about Their Relationships

- Listen.
- Ask questions.
- Clarify what is going on.
- Do not judge, but show that you understand.
- Remember you can only change yourself: they can only change themselves.
- Ask how the person you are talking to feels.
- Ask how the other people involved feel.
- Think of yourself as offering support, not taking sides.
- Help them to mobilize their resources for coping.
- Help them to start the process of problem solving.
- Avoid giving advice.

Sometimes the problems of another person are too much for us. Remember that if you do not want to get involved, you have a perfect right to say "no." If you find this difficult, see pages 141 to 143.

Two Common False Beliefs about Relationships

There are two common false beliefs that can prevent people from adopting a constructive approach to developing relationships.

- "A relationship that needs working at is not worth having."

"I shouldn't have to work at it" is a reservation that gets in the way of solving relationship problems. The reservation takes many forms: the belief that working at a relationship removes the spontaneity from it, and makes it false, artificial, or contrived; or that if you have to work at it, it cannot have been much of a relationship to begin with; or that working at it is treating it like a kind of pathology, suggesting that the people in the relationship are suitable cases for treatment; or that a single sign of discontent is enough to show that the relationship is doomed anyway.

All these versions of the truth are false. Quite the contrary, relationships need work; satisfying relationships are unlikely to develop unless all concerned are prepared to be committed and to make an effort. The problem is perhaps in the terminology: in the use of the word "work." If relationships are systems, and systems of joint responsibility, then instead of work we can just think of adaptation. It is important to realize that such adaptation takes an effort, but the effort is likely to be amply rewarded.

- "You should know how I feel."

This reservation comes from supposing that feelings between people who are close to each other are readily observable, and that being close means that one should understand, as if by telepathy, how each other feels. Indeed, relationships often take off precisely because two people do easily understand each other, and later on a sense of disappointment and sadness arises because the understanding seems to get lost. Nevertheless, we cannot see into each others' minds, and however close you are to others, they will never be able to know exactly how you feel unless you let them know. It is easy to make mistakes, and also to take things personally: to confuse depression with irritability, preoccupation with indifference, frustration with the outside world with hostility, and so on. An important feature of close relationships is not telepathy, but the ability to say to each other, honestly, how you feel.

Chapter Summary

Relationships are systems. This has three implications:

1. The principle of joint responsibility
   - Within a system, the responsibility for the relationships is shared by everyone.
2. The principle of homeostasis
   - If you try to change the way you relate to others, your changes will be resisted.
3. The principles of negotiation
   - The best way of making changes within a system of relationships is through negotiation.

Good negotiation is not about dividing the cake; it is about baking a new one.

Preparing for skillful negotiation involves *four* steps:

Step 1. Find out what everyone wants.

Step 2. Look for common ground.

Step 3. Broaden the basis of the negotiation.

Step 4. Look for opportunities to trade.

The five strategies for skillful negotiation are:

1. Clarify.
2. Build on what the other person says.
3. Cut out the blame.
4. Watch out for escalation.
5. Bottle up the insults.

P A R T   F O U R

◆ ◆ ◆

The Twin Enemies of Good Mood

Anxiety and Depression

Anxiety and depression are the two most common enemies of feeling happy and fulfilled. They affect us all, but to different degrees. It is a mistake to assume that because they are a part of the human condition, there is nothing which can be done about them. This part provides information about anxiety and depression, and describes many ways of dealing with them. It shows how you can help yourself, and how you can support someone else. It is for those for whom anxiety, or depression, is an occasional problem as well as for those who suffer greatly.

The normal course of progress, as with most things, is not a smooth one but goes through ups and downs. Do not be discouraged if there are times when things seem to be getting worse rather than better.

Overcoming anxiety or depression involves taking steps:

S: Select an idea, and work out how it applies to you.

T: Try it out.

E: Evaluate how it went (keep a notebook).

P: Persist until you feel better.

The chapters about anxiety have been divided up to deal separately with tension and worrying (Chapter 16), fears and phobias (Chapter 17), stress (Chapter 18), and panic (Chapter 19). For clarity, we have devoted a separate chapter to each of these aspects of anxiety, even though they sometimes overlap. We suggest reading all four chapters, starting with the one that seems most relevant to you.

Depression is so common and so distressing that we have devoted a whole chapter to understanding the problem (Chapter 20). Strategies for dealing with it have been divided into those that can be immediately useful (Chapter 21) and those that can prevent a recurrence of the problem (Chapter 22). You will gain most from reading all three chapters.

16

♦ ♦ ♦

Getting the Better of Anxiety and Worry, Or Defeating the Alarmist

The wind was against them now, and Piglet's ears streamed behind him like banners as he fought his way along, and it seemed hours before he got them into the shelter of the Hundred Acre Wood and they stood up straight again, to listen, a little nervously, to the roaring of the gale among the tree-tops.

"Supposing a tree fell down, Pooh, when we were underneath it?"
"Supposing it didn't," said Pooh after careful thought. [1]

Anxiety and Worry

Many of us have more of Piglet in our makeup than of Pooh. Our minds, apparently spontaneously, come up with a string of alarming possibilities, one worry feeding upon another until, as for Piglet, it becomes impossible to think of anything other than the risks and threats that could lie ahead. The more we worry, the worse we feel; and the worse we feel, the more we think in an anxious and worried way. No wonder Dale Carnegie called his classic book: *How to stop worrying and start living.* Worry is one of the greatest enemies of a good mood, even though the vast majority of the time worrying turns out to be unnecessary. We cramp our existence worrying about things that never happen, or that turn out not to be as bad as we had imagined, or things that were never that important to begin with. Even on those few occasions when our fears were justified, the worry seldom helped. As Montaigne, the French philosopher put it: "My life has been full of terrible misfortunes, most of which never happened."

WORRY IS BAD FOR YOU

Worry is not only bad for you, but it also wastes time and energy. In the following box, we list some of the ways in which worry can affect your *thinking*, your *behavior*, your *feelings*, and your *body*. Think about how worry affects you personally and make additions to the list if necessary. This will help you to identify the bad effects that worry has on you and to focus on the aspects of it that you find most disruptive. Not everyone will be affected in all of these ways.

Some of the Ways That Worry Can Affect You

How worry affects your thinking: What is on your mind

- Keeps you on the lookout for problems, difficulties, or disasters (hypervigilance).
- Interferes with concentration and with your ability to give something your full attention.
- Focuses your attention onto yourself and your own concerns.
- Makes it hard to make decisions.
- Increases your ability to notice things and to worry about these more than other sorts of things (selective attention).
- Makes you more pessimistic, so you tend to predict the worst.
- Makes you problem-focused, so your mind leaps from one worry to the next.

How worry affects your behavior: The things you do

- Makes you less efficient (either over-careful, or unwittingly careless).
- Interferes with your performance.
- Makes you rely more on others and less on yourself.
- Leads you to do things less confidently.

How worry affects your feelings: Your emotions

- Makes you feel muddled or confused.
- Makes you feel apprehensive and fearful.
- Makes you feel out of control.
- Makes you feel overwhelmed, or that you can't cope.

How worry affects your body

- Reduces your ability to relax and to sleep well.
- Makes you weary and tired.
- Makes you tense.
- Gives you headaches.

WHAT'S THE USE OF WORRYING?

Worry is so common that it is tempting to ask whether it serves a useful function. One reason why it is so difficult to stop worrying is because one has a sneaking suspicion that some good may come of it, and this sneaking suspicion is hard to ignore. Even though we might say to ourselves and to others—"Stop worrying. It's pointless. It won't do any good." Or "Worrying will get you nowhere"—there is still something compelling about the process that makes it hard to give up.

Worry: The danger signal. Worry could alert you to the possibility that something is wrong: "That cough of yours has gone on much too long." "The steering on this car feels odd." Ignoring these things could be unwise. Worry is useful if it makes you sit up and take notice. It is not useful to be paralyzed with fear, as you might be if you got carried away by your imagination. It is useful to have a red light that flashes—but only if you do something to turn it off.

Worry: The action trigger. Worry can goad you into action. It makes you feel bad until you do something about it, like starting to study before an exam, or getting the cough or the steering checked. You feel better when these things are done. Once again, worry is useful, provided it is turned into a strategy for action.

Worry: The coping rehearsal. Worry can oil the coping machinery. It can provoke you into thinking about "What you could do if. . . .," or "What would happen if," and so it can prepare you for appropriate action or adjustment. Prompted by feeling worried, you may be more likely to develop better studying skills, stop smoking, or make arrangements to get your car regularly serviced.

Worry: The lesser of two evils. Worrying about something is often rather a vague and unfocused process compared with having vivid and alarming images. It is like asking yourself, "What if they have had an accident," when someone is late rather than imagining the horrors of the accident you fear. The things one can see with ones mind's eye can literally make one shudder and quake. But worrying can prevent the images coming, so doing it may be the preferred option, even though it keeps the worst terrors at bay at the cost of continued anxiety.

Worry is therefore *sometimes* helpful; *sometimes* it makes you feel better or *starts* you thinking about how to cope. This may be what lies behind the superstitious aspects of worry: the feeling that "unless

I worry something bad will happen," or that "worrying will prevent things going wrong." The grain of truth behind the superstitions lies in the potential value, or helpfulness, of a *certain degree* of worry in provoking strategies for action. *Useful worry prompts action. All other worry is pointless.*

WORRY: THE SELF-PERPETUATING PROCESS

Angela described herself as a "born worrier." She had worried about exams when she was at school, about what other people thought of her, and about starting her career in a small publishing business. She was sure that others could see how anxious or nervous she was and that none of them had similar worries. Even when she realized that everyone worries from time to time, this was of no help to her. Her own worries tended to dominate her life to such an extent that she was never free from worry. She worried about whether she was doing her job right, whether she would be promoted, whether others would recognize her abilities or ignore them, whether she would sleep well, and whether she would be too tired to work properly the next day. She worried about aches and pains, about her health, and whether she might be doing herself serious damage by her worrying. She worried about whether her partner Andrew was fed up with her, whether she might one day have to move to a new place, and whether someone in her family might get ill. No sooner was one worry laid to rest than another rose to fill its place, and just occasionally—for example, if she woke up in the middle of the night—all her worries crowded in on her at once. Angela was exhausted by her worries.

What was keeping the worry going? Was Angela just born that way? Research evidence suggests that there is a genetic component that affects our vulnerability to worry. It is also widely believed, by experts in the field, that experiences in childhood affect our tendency to worry, although firm evidence for this is lacking. We know that many people to whom alarming or frightening things happened in their childhoods cope extremely well as adults, but of course we hear less about these people than about those who remain troubled later on, and so we do not yet know exactly how many of them there are. So Angela may to some extent be a "born worrier," but this does not mean that she cannot change. On the contrary, Angela was able to change even though, for her, worry was a major problem. If you recognize yourself in even some of her worries, then you too can benefit from the methods that she found helpful.

How to Get Rid of 90% of Your Worries

There are three things which are not worth worrying about but which account for the majority of all worries: *the unimportant, the unlikely,* and *the unresolved.* Ban these from your life, and you will waste little time in worrying.

THE UNIMPORTANT

It is easy to fill one's life with worries about completely trivial things, and even when a worry is not trivial it is often essentially unimportant. When you catch yourself worrying, start to question yourself instead. Ask immediately: *"How important is the thing that I am worrying about?"* Here are three strategies to help you to answer this question.

1. The 100-year rule. Ask yourself, as Samuel Johnson asked his biographer James Boswell, "Will this matter in 100 years from now?" This is a way of putting your worry into a long-term perspective. Perhaps 100 years seems too long a perspective—very little is worth worrying about when looked at from a distance of 100 years. But this is partly the point. We tend to adopt such short-term perspectives that molehills appear to us like mountains. One hundred years gives us a distance on life from which most of our worries become trivial. There is, of course, nothing special about 100 years. View your worries from various perspectives: a week, a year, a decade. Ask yourself just how important is your worry—and how long from now will it cease to matter.

Angela found that asking herself "Will this matter at all in 5 years' time?" was particularly helpful when she was at work worrying about how much she had to do in a short time. It helped her to work more calmly as well as to disentangle the important from the unimportant things on her list.

2. The measuring rod. Ask yourself: Where, on the spectrum of bad experiences, is the outcome I'm worried about? In 1926, Philip Wakeham was a fledgling seaman onboard the *Snapdragon*.[2] Forty years later he gave a graphic account of one terrifying night. During naval exercises after World War I, the *Snapdragon* towed the practice target for the big battleships' night firing exercise. The target was "just a floating base upon which, at close intervals, masts or poles thirty feet high were stepped. Running across these poles for the whole length of the target were wooden slats, the whole making a huge lattice framework. This lattice-work carried two strips of canvas each ten feet wide. Before the firing was to begin, the canvas strips had to be set out like sails, a task which was carried out by seamen from the *Snapdragon*, including Philip Wakeham. He was the last to finish. He walked along the target's deck hanging on to the stays and slats. Suddenly, he stopped dead in his tracks. The small boat which had brought him and the other seamen to the target had gone. It was pitch dark; he was stranded, alone, on the target, and four British battleships were set, ready for their nocturnal target practice.

> Out there in the blackness four grey shapes were even then moving slowly towards me, the men in them preparing to come suddenly upon the target to blast it out of the water. . . . Any moment now . . . the order to fire would be given and a mass of metal would come screaming towards me. My arms were numb with cold, but I took off my black silk handkerchief and my lanyard and tied them together. Then I passed them round my waist and one of the battens—at least I would not fall into the sea by failing to hang on . . . I must not panic. . . . Thoughts of my mother came to me . . . I felt sick, empty, and very very cold. . . . Fear had taken possession of my whole body . . . I have very little recollection of what followed. A large orange flame that seemed so close that I imagined it to be warm; more star shells overhead; and the noise . . . four one-ton shells passed overhead with the shriek of a thousand furies and dropped into the sea beyond.

Shortly afterward, Philip Wakeham lost consciousness, not from an exploding shell but from sheer terror. It was fortunate that the British Navy needed the practice. Not one shell hit the target that night, and in the morning, Philip Wakeham was discovered, alive and unhurt.

This terrifying experience provides another perspective on daily worries. Beside such an experience, their significance pales. Fortunately, it is not necessary to have an experience like Philip Wakeham's in order to learn the important lesson. Using his experience as a yardstick, or a terrifying experience of your own, ask, of any worry that you have: How does it compare? *How dreadful, really, is the thing that you are worrying about?* When Angela had a disagreement with Andrew, she immediately jumped to the conclusion that they would split up, and predicted that she would soon have a major catastrophe to deal with. Of course, she might well have felt devastated to lose her relationship, but it would not have been catastrophic in the life-threatening sense. Looking at the problem more coolly she realized that the disagreement that made her worry about losing it was more like a molehill than a mountain.

3. The calculator. Ask yourself: "Just how much worry is this worth?" Our resources are limited. We only have so much time, so much energy, so much life. But it is very easy to put too many of these limited resources into the wrong things. William had a car crash. In fact, he had been stationary and a car had backed into his front end. It was a minor crash and resulted in a relatively small amount of damage to his car. The driver of the other car was profusely apologetic, and said she would pay, but there were no witnesses, and her insurance refused to pay for the damage. William was furious. He sought legal advice. He was in a black humor for weeks and decided to take the other driver to court. The whole process threatened to go on for months and months and become increasingly expensive. There is no doubt that William had been wronged; the other driver ought to have paid. But the way he was behaving was going to cost more than the original damage to the car, the results were uncertain, and he was making himself ill with anger and worry.

Whenever you find yourself worrying, ask yourself; *"Just how much worry is this worth?"*—and make sure that you do not spend more worry on it than it is worth. You need your energy for more important things.

THE UNLIKELY

Piglet was suffering from the very essence of worry. His mind was filled with all manner of possible horrors and disasters. "Supposing that . . .," "What if . . .," and their variants are the hallmark of worry and anxiety. "Supposing a tree fell down, Pooh, when we were underneath it?" Of course it is possible. All kinds of dreadful things could happen today, or tomorrow. But most of them are very unlikely. Once you allow yourself to worry about the unlikely, there is no end to worrying. Imagine looking back on a life of worry about the unlikely. It would be a life spoiled by anxiety about things, the vast majority of which never happened. Whenever you catch yourself worrying that something dreadful might happen, answer the Piglet in yourself with Pooh's reply: *"Supposing it didn't."* Tackling existing problems is quite enough; do not waste energy and happiness on problems which do not exist.

THE UNRESOLVED

Madame de Sévigné, in one of her letters describing seventeenth-century life around the French Court,[3] relates the sad story of Vatel, chief cook to the Prince. One day the Prince and his large retinue entertained the King. Vatel laid on a splendid feast in the evening, and then had to turn his attention to the morning's meal.

> By four in the morning Vatel was rushing round everywhere and finding everything wrapped in slumber. He found a small supplier who only had two loads of fish. "Is that all?" he asked. "Yes, Sir." The supplier did not know that Vatel had sent round to all the seaports. Vatel waited a short time, the other suppliers did not turn up, he lost his head and thought that there would be no more fish. He went and found Gourville (the Prince's Chamberlain) and said, "Sir, I shall never survive this disgrace, my honor and my reputation are at stake." Gourville laughed at him. Vatel went to his room, put his sword up against the door and ran it through his heart . . . . Meanwhile the fish was coming in from all quarters. They looked for Vatel to allocate it, went to his room, broke in the door and found him lying in his own blood . . . . Gourville tried to make up for the loss of Vatel. He did so and there was a very good dinner, light refreshments later, and then supper, a walk, cards, hunting, everything scented with daffodils, everything magical."

This tragic story emphasizes, in somewhat graphic form, the dangers of premature worrying. Even if the outcome that you are worried about is quite likely, like Angela's worry that someone close to her might get ill, there is no point in worrying prematurely.

Dealing with Persistent Worries

If you were able to rid yourself of worries about the unimportant, the unlikely, and the unresolved, 90% of your worries would disappear. But of course this is easier said than done. Some worries are remarkably resistant to reasoning, and continue to weigh on your mind despite your efforts to keep them in their place. And a few worries really are significant and realistic. There are two kinds of strategies for dealing with persistent and significant worries: strategies for letting them go and strategies for examining them.

1. STRATEGIES FOR LETTING WORRIES GO

Turn worries into actions. *There are two types of things not worth worrying about: those that you can do something about; and those that you can't.* This summarizes a simple but very powerful way of approaching persistent worries. Worry is useful when it pushes you to tackle and solve problems which need solving. But you can tackle and solve problems without the unpleasant effect of worry. So the first step is to turn your worries into problems and then develop strategies for solving them (see also Chapter 8). If nothing can be done, then, in the words of Dale Carnegie: *cooperate with the inevitable.*

The worry decision tree. The worry decision tree is a structured way of solving the worry problem. It is a way of asking yourself a branching series of questions that help to let the worry drop, and it is summarized in Figure 16.1. There are three questions to ask yourself. The first one—*"What am I worrying about?"*— helps you to pinpoint your

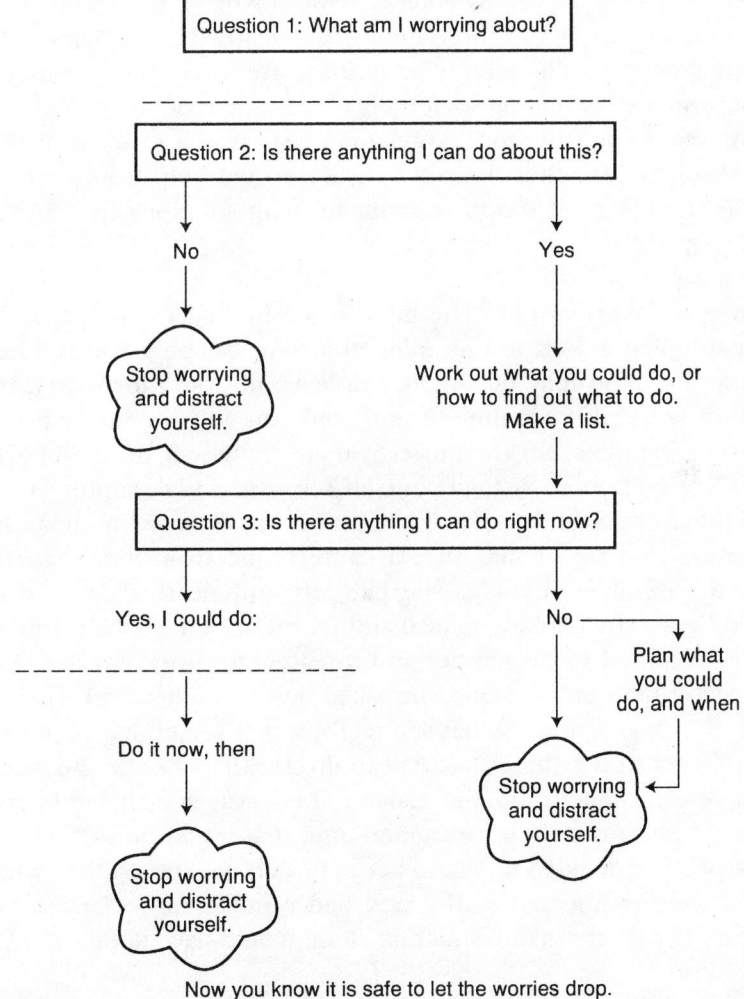

Now you know it is safe to let the worries drop.

Figure 16.1   Worry decision tree.

worry clearly. When you have clearly identified your worry, ask the second question—"*Is there anything I can do about this?*" The honest answer may be "No." If it is, you can be certain that you will gain nothing from continuing to worry. Cooperate with the inevitable. Distract yourself by finding something absorbing to do instead. If there is something you can do about the worry, however, think about the possibilities. Make a list if necessary. Then ask yourself the third question—"*Is there anything I can do right now?*" If there is something you can do straight away, then do it before occupying yourself with an absorbing activity to prevent further worry. If there is nothing you can do now, then plan a time to take appropriate action, write yourself a reminder if that would help, and allow yourself to stop worrying—it cannot possibly serve any useful purpose. Finding out clearly that further worry is unproductive makes it easier to let it drop. After each step is complete, distract yourself by finding something absorbing to do instead.

Sometimes you can work down a decision tree in your head, without extra help. At other times it is useful to get help from friends—help in clarifying the worry, in brainstorming solutions (p. 65), or in simple support.

Crowd your worries out. The mind has a limited capacity: you can only pay full attention to one thing at a time. Keeping yourself busy, keeping the mind fully occupied, will leave no room for worry. Your attention will drift from time to time, and you will need to redirect it when this happens, but the busier you are the easier this will be. For more ideas on how to distract yourself, see page 252 (Chapter 21).

Do not, however, misuse distraction as a way of avoiding the task of thinking about problems. Angela came home from work worried about the number of things she had left undone that day. She distracted herself by cooking a meal and felt better for a while, until the worries returned to plague her and threatened to prevent her sleeping. So later the same evening, she asked herself: "What am I worrying about?" She was worrying that she might forget something important. So she listed all the things she had to do. As the list grew she started to feel overwhelmed, and she realized there was a "real" problem to be solved, and not just an "imagined" one that could be swept under the carpet. She decided to talk to her manager, and started the process of problem-solving that in the end had a much more far-reaching effect on her worry than distraction alone would have done.

Ban night-time worrying. Worries tend to attack when you are at your most defenseless, especially in the middle of the night. If there is one time not to worry, it is at night when worries get out of all proportion, and it is not possible to tackle them effectively. As soon as a worry pops into your head at night, say *"This is not the time"* (see p. 297 for more on this). Worries like to crawl into bed with you and pinch and squirm so that you cannot sleep. Don't let them in. They can be trained to stay out of your bedroom, but as when training a dog to keep out of the kitchen, you need to be firm and consistent. You may find it helpful to imagine a pleasant image—a place perhaps where you felt particularly happy—in order to crowd your worries out of your mind. The technique of mental relaxation is described on pages 109 and 298.

Boxing your worries. Imagine putting all your worries, one by one, in a box and closing the lid; or hang them on a tree and allow the wind to blow them away. Cast them in handfuls into a river and watch them float away, or put them on the bonfire and send them up in smoke. If you are worried you might forget something important, write the worry down. Get it out of your head and onto paper, where it cannot get lost and can be properly dealt with later. It can be tempting to go on worrying because in the back of one's mind it feels as if some good may come of it, and of course, from time to time, a good idea does come to mind when worrying. But this is not because the process of worrying is useful, except as a trigger toward more effective problem-solving. The occasional solution found by worrying is a side effect that is unlikely to happen often enough to be worth the bad feelings that go with it.

Build a wall around your worries. If you are beset by worries, set aside a regular half an hour every day to worry. If you start to worry at other times, postpone the worry to the "worry time" and focus on what you are doing, or what is happening around you instead. When the "worry time" comes around, tackle each worry as a problem to solve. This strategy hits the worry in two ways: it builds a wall around the process, which stops it from spreading, and it turns the worry into something more constructive. Some people even find that they are unable to worry to order, so the worry time turns out to be trouble free. Then worry has found its own level, and you need not worry that it will sink too low: the alarm bells will ring automatically when you need them.

2. STRATEGIES FOR EXAMINING NEBULOUS FEARS

When fears and worries remain nameless, it seems impossible to work out how to deal with them. At an almost unconscious level, we may be too frightened to face the worry directly. In the end this will cause more problems than it solves. Our deep fear will keep returning as intractable worry. When faced directly, the underlying fear can be tackled; when hidden it can grow to grotesque proportions and undermine the foundations of our happiness.

Unpacking the fear. A child who was frightened there was a bogey man under his bed took a running jump to the safety of the stuffed menagerie he kept by his pillow, and then settled down to listen to a story and fell asleep perfectly calmly. Helped by others, he was able to overcome the fear.

An elderly woman who lived alone kept an orange by her bed. Every night before she climbed in, she rolled the orange underneath the bed, and when it came out the other side, she was able to settle down feeling safe.

Sometimes fears are nameless, and we like to be reassured by others, or by doing quite irrational things. The trouble is that if you *always* take a running jump over the fear, or find something irrelevant to do that makes you feel better, the worries cannot be laid to rest, and the bad feelings become overwhelming when comfort is not available.

Angela had two worries that she found particularly hard to face: worries about headaches, which she tried to ignore, declaring roundly that a headache was nothing to complain about; and worries about the times when Andrew seemed fed up with hearing about her problems, when she went into a paroxysm of apologies. Either of these things set off a bad bout of worry that spread from one thing to another and kept her awake for nights on end. The underlying fears, which she found hard to face, concerned the possibility that the headaches were a sign of serious illness, and that her worrying would interfere with her relationship with Andrew. She learned to face her fears by answering three sets of questions:

1. When did the worry start? What triggered it this time?
2. What's so bad about that? What does it mean to me?
3. What's the worst that could possibly happen?

Angela had learned to take out the fears from under the bed and look them full in the face. When she did so, she discovered two things: that the catastrophes she feared were unlikely to happen; but if they did, she had resources that would help her cope. Excessive worry did not help her develop such resources: on the contrary, it stopped her from even acknowledging what her fears were about.

What is the worst that can happen? Imagine a child, playing on the beach below a cliff. He finds a cave, and full of excitement, goes in. Suddenly fear seizes him. In the deep dark of the cave, he cannot see the way ahead. What is frightening is the sense of the unknown stretching into the black distance. Worries can be like this. Our anxiety is not about something specific, but more of a sense that unknown and uncertain possibilities may be out of sight far ahead. We can place a limit on these worries. A powerful torch or flashlight could have shown the child the limits of the cave. We can place limits on our worries by asking: "What is the worst that can happen?" More often than not, the worst that we fear is much less terrible than our vague, unarticulated fear. Once we know the worst, we can face it directly and work out more sensibly what to do.

CLARIFY YOUR UNCERTAINTIES ABOUT THE FUTURE

Worry and anxiety are about the future—about things that have not yet happened, so there is bound to be something unknowable and uncertain about them. It is not possible to walk around the mountain and discover it is only a molehill before you have reached it. Worries may seem to be about the past, but this is largely an illusion.

Although people say "I'm worried about what I might have said," or "I'm bothered about having lost my passport"—their worry is about the future effects of past events. If I have said something offensive, then I *will* be rejected or disliked. If I have lost my passport, then I *will* have to go through a lot of hassle to get another one. Worry refers in this way to some "unfinished business"; otherwise, the matter would either be forgotten or be a cause for feelings associated with the past, such as regret or sadness, rather than the future, such as worry and anxiety.

It follows that worry conceals hidden predictions: for example, about the awful things that might happen, or about one's own inability to cope with them, or both. It is therefore useful to identify and think about the predictions being made, which are often exaggerated or concern hidden guesses of the mind-reading variety about what others are thinking (Chapter 9 has more to say about this).

Ask yourself some questions:

- What am I predicting? Or expecting? Or supposing will happen?
- How can I find out whether my prediction is right?

Angela was anxious about preparing a report in time for a deadline at work. She predicted she would not be able to get it done in time, and also that she would not be able to handle the argument that would ensue. It turned out that her first prediction was right. Facing it helped her to think seriously about what to do. She drafted most of the report, indicating parts that would need to be filled in later. She took her notes about these along to the meeting. She explained why there was a delay. She estimated, as realistically as she could, when the final report would be available. She was surprised to find how many things she could do to alleviate the difficulty she was in, and her second prediction, that she would not be able to handle an argument, was shown to be completely irrelevant, as no such thing occurred. Having made the specific predictions beforehand, when in the throes of the anxiety and worry, Angela was finally able to reassess her worries with the facts at her fingertips. She had to conclude that she was more resourceful than she had feared.

If you write your predictions down, then you will be able to check out later whether you were right, and to think more clearly about problems you may have to deal with. The next time you will be able to challenge your predictions more effectively. Worry and anxiety die away as your confidence builds.

Question your assumptions. Sometimes it seems impossible to put your finger on exactly what you are anxious or worried about. The worry seems to come in vague terms: "What did they think of me?" "What if I get in a muddle?" "Suppose something goes wrong?" "Something dreadful might happen." The root of the problem in this case may be in underlying beliefs or meanings that are rather hard to put into words. Angela expressed her sense of vulnerability by saying that she was not sure she was "any good at managing by herself." Deep down she believed that being bad at managing on her own meant that she would never be confident. Her sense of inadequacy made her feel especially at risk and vulnerable. In her case this was a longstanding attitude. She made the assumption, without even realizing it, that she would not be able to cope, accepting the anxiety and worry that ensued as familiar and inevitable. What she discovered, as she learned to deal with her anxiety and worry more effectively, was that her assumption had prevented her from building up self-reliance and from using the resources, which she certainly had, more effectively.

Living with Uncertainty

Uncertainty about something important is a major cause of anxiety and worry. Many different situations create uncertainty: the threat of being fired, finding a lump in your groin, being told that someone close to you might have a serious illness, waiting for a mortgage to come through, selling your house, and so on. Uncertainty is especially difficult to handle when:

- The situation is *uncontrollable*
- You cannot *predict* what might happen

It is like being faced with an insoluble problem.

FIRST, DO WHAT YOU CAN

Try not to let uncertainty paralyze you. If there is something you can usefully do, then do it. Once you have done what you can—for example, filling in the right forms, or talking to someone such as a friend or the doctor—then resist the temptation to continue searching for something else to do. Try to accept that you have done what you can, and start thinking about yourself and your reactions to uncertainty instead. Stop and think now: *Have you done what you usefully can?*

THEN, DEAL WITH YOUR REACTIONS TO UNCERTAINTY

Some common reactions include worry, anxiety, disturbed sleep, feeling agitated and preoccupied, difficulty concentrating, and seeking reassurance. Everyone reacts differently, so your reactions will depend both on you and on the sort of situation that you are uncertain about.

Recognize the uncertainty for what it is. Uncertainty is an unpleasant and distressing feeling that can interfere with daily life. The difficulty is worth thinking about.

Limit the problem. Find some certainties to hang on to. A routine of going to work, or eating meals in the usual way, can provide the building blocks of basic certainty. Or you may turn to your most reliable sources of support, such as music or your friends.

Normalize your life. So far as possible, keep doing the things that you usually do, in the way that you usually do them. This is especially important if you are preoccupied or distressed about somebody else. If you run out of clean clothes, for example, because you were too worried to notice the washing mounting up, you will feel worse.

Be reasonably selfish. Treat yourself to something nice. Look after yourself well when you are going through a difficult time—just as you would look after someone else.

Do not withdraw from activities that you usually enjoy. Pleasures, relaxations, or recreations often feel like an effort when you are preoccupied with an uncertainty. You may feel too tired or too worried to bother. But withdrawing from these activities you used to enjoy can leave you brooding, unproductively, on your worries. Enjoyable activities will provide useful distraction, even if you enjoy them less than you usually would.

Talk to someone else about the problem. Most people feel worse if they isolate themselves with a worry. Try to find the balance between retreating silently into yourself and repeatedly seeking reassurance or talking about nothing other than your problems. Allowing your feelings to show helps you, and others, to understand them and to find ways of coping with them.

Do not cross too many bridges—keep the problem in perspective. It is only too easy to jump to the conclusion that the worst possible thing will happen. The more one thinks about the bad things that might happen, the more likely they seem, and the harder it is to see how to cope with them. So recognize that the worst has not yet happened. You notice a lump in your breast, or your groin, and immediately you imagine yourself dying from cancer. In your mind you have crossed too many bridges. Most lumps are not cancer; many cancers are curable. Take problems one at a time and keep your mind focused on the present.

Turn your mind to something else. Distraction is a very useful strategy, provided it is not the only one you use. If you always keep busy instead of facing your difficulties, you may find it hard to face them later. But if you have first considered carefully what constructive steps you can take, it is then extremely helpful to give yourself something to do, especially if it prevents you turning the problem over and over in your mind. Methods of distraction are described on page 252.

Take the pressure off. Living with uncertainty is tiring. It can deplete your resources. So this is not the time to take on an extra commitment, if you can help it. On the contrary, make sure that you are eating well, getting as much sleep as you can (see Chapter 24), and taking enough exercise to keep up your strength and stamina.

Ask: "What good might come of this in the end?" Uncertainty is unsettling, but old patterns of living may have become stale or sterile. Being swept along with the current of life can help people to adapt in creative ways, to develop new skills, or to overcome old anxieties. It is not always a bad thing to have one's foundations shaken up by uncertainties, even though the period of adjustment may be painful and difficult.

Turning to Others for Help

Other people can provide an enormously useful sounding board when you are feeling anxious or worried. They can ask the questions that help you work out what the worry is about, and they can keep you in touch with reality, so the fears do not get exaggerated. They can ask, just like Pooh, questions that challenge you to think about the situation from a different angle. Pooh took Piglet's fears seriously, and he helped Piglet to think again for himself.

Asking for reassurance, however, can become a bad habit, just like "getting a fix." It makes you feel better but the feeling does not last, and so the more you have the more you want. Reassurance becomes unhelpful when it subtracts from self-reliance. If you find yourself constantly or repeatedly asking for reassurance from others, use a *"questioning strategy"* instead: Ask yourself the question you want to ask someone else, and then try to answer it yourself. Work out if there is a problem that you might be able to solve some other way. Angela wanted to ask Andrew (repeatedly) "Do you think I'm really ill?" "Am I getting on your nerves?" You can imagine how he felt the third time she asked in one evening.

If someone is repeatedly asking you for reassurance, then take their fears and worries seriously and try to help them find ways of answering their own questions. Repeatedly reassuring someone is not helpful. Andrew repeatedly reassured Angela, both by his actions and his words, in an effort to help that proved to be counterproductive. He learned not to do this when Angela explained to him what else he could do instead.

Related Chapters in This Book

Very often anxiety and worry go hand in hand with a sense of vulnerability or lack of confidence, as if the ability to cope was precariously balanced between a sense of all the things that might go wrong and all the difficulties one would have in dealing with them. The specific strategies described in this chapter have helped many people deal with worry, but they are not the only ones available. The following chapters also contain helpful strategies.

Chapter 10   Building Self-Confidence and Self-Esteem. The skills and strategies described here fit well with those described in this chapter.

Chapter 8   Problem-Solving. This chapter will help you define problems, think of solutions to them and try them out in order to see which ones work for you.

Chapter 11   Learning to Relax. Physical tension is painful and exhausting. Physical relaxation is not something that happens automatically, but something that you can learn to do. Feeling more relaxed can help you in many ways: it reduces feelings of anxiety, gives you more energy, makes you feel calmer, and so on. Using meditation (a mental method of relaxation) is also helpful since it focuses your attention on the present moment, teaching you how to recognize the fears and worries, but allowing them to flow harmlessly by.

Chapters 25 and 23   Looking after Yourself Physically. The better you feel, the more confident you will become. Think about your diet, getting enough exercise, and the amount that you smoke or drink (especially alcohol and caffeine).

Chapter 7   Treating Yourself Right. When you have a problem, and worry about it, it can easily dominate how you feel, and makes you feel tired. There is less time or energy left for doing things that you normally enjoy, or that you are good at. Learning how to be kind to yourself when you have a problem helps to keep the problem itself in perspective.

Chapter 18   Stress: How to Live with the Right Amount of It. Anxiety, stress, and worry often go hand in hand. These chapters are a complement to each other.

Chapter 24   Overcoming Sleep Problems. Worry is exhausting and often interferes with sleep patterns. Give yourself a good night's rest and you will also feel less anxious and worried.

Chapter Summary

Worry makes you feel bad, but most of it is unnecessary. Worrying can be helpful if it prompts you to take action, so the first step is to work out what action you should take.

You can get rid of 90% of your worries by sifting out:

1. The unimportant
2. The unlikely
3. The unresolved

More persistent worries can be dealt with by

1. *Learning how to let them go.* Holding on to the worries keeps you feeling vulnerable. Life will feel calmer when you let them flow by.
2. *Learning how to look them in the face.* Exploring and examining the worries keeps them in proper perspective.

Living with uncertainty is especially worrying, but there are many things you can do to reduce the strain.

Other people can be a great help when you are feeling worried. Do not be reluctant to turn to them, but try not to fall into the habit of repeatedly asking for reassurance.

17

♦ ♦ ♦

Overcoming Fears and Phobias

About Phobias

Why some people have fears that seem, even to them, to be irrational is not known. Such irrational fears are known technically as *phobias.* Occasionally, a phobia has its origin in some specific experience: a child bitten by a terrier may grow up to be excessively wary of dogs, but often no such event can be recalled. Many people have a phobia of spiders even in countries such as Britain where no poisonous spiders exist. Perhaps this is an atavistic fear which goes back to a time in our evolution when dangerous spiders were common enough for those who feared them to survive better than those who did not.

None of this would matter if phobias did not interfere with the enjoyment of life. Elaine was frightened of spiders. She did not come across them often enough for that in itself to be a problem, but she was always anxious that she might. She cleaned her house obsessively to ensure that no spider could find in it a comfortable home. She stopped visiting friends because they were not so fastidious, and the fear interfered with her pleasures, her relationships, and her good mood.

Robert was terrified of dogs. He traveled everywhere by car, avoided walks in parks and the country, and had given up playing football. He was convinced that dogs could sense his fear and would come for him even when they might leave others in peace.

Pauline hated supermarkets. Crowds of any kind made her break out in a sweat. Even going to her local newsstand worried her, so she avoided doing any shopping at all. Gradually, she became almost completely housebound.

Some of these fears have a grounding in reality: dogs *can* be dangerous. But in all these examples the sufferers felt that their fear was excessive. They were embarrassed and felt stupid because their fear, and the way this fear interfered with their lives, was grossly in excess of any real danger. The attitude of their families and friends did not help. Pauline's husband was so considerate that he made it easy for her to place herself under house arrest by doing all the shopping. Elaine's husband could not believe her fear was real, and either teased her about it or became irritated. Robert's friends increasingly went their own way without him.

Phobias are the opposite of horror movies or suspense thrillers. The thriller frightens you, but deep down you know that you are safe. When the phobia frightens you, however irrational you know it is, deep down inside you feel unsafe.

THE FEAR IS REAL: THE DANGER IS NOT

The fear felt by Elaine, Robert, and Pauline was real. It was as distressing and frightening as a true danger. It affected their bodies, feelings, thoughts, and behavior, just as any other fear would. When Robert saw a dog, he would feel afraid and his heart would pound against his chest. His mind would be filled with worrying thoughts—for example, that the dog would suddenly break from its leash and go straight for his throat. He would walk rapidly away, down a side road if necessary, to get as far from the dog as possible.

Dogs are not this dangerous. What Robert needs to take seriously is the fear, not the dogs. Instead of berating himself and feeling ashamed, he needs to accept that *this is fear,* and that overcoming it requires *strategic planning.* Anyone trying to overcome fear is doing something courageous because it means facing a genuine fear. It is just as terrifying as it would be for most of us if we were asked to walk along a tightrope strung high up in a circus tent. The difference between facing a phobia and walking the tightrope lies not in the amount of fear, but in the amount of danger. Fortunately, with strategic planning and sensible training, you can learn to master your irrational fears and stop them from interfering with your life.

TYPES OF PHOBIA

One of the interesting things about phobias is that there are relatively few kinds of them. Perhaps the best known is the kind that Pauline had: the fear of being away from a safe place. This is called *agoraphobia*. The Greek *Agora* was the marketplace, and supermarkets seem to be the modern equivalent.

The Most Common Phobias

Fears of small animals
Spiders, snakes, mice, birds, moths, dogs

Fears of being away from a safe place
Driving
Leaving the house or going out alone
Going to crowed stores, or to open areas (supermarkets)
Traveling by bus, car, airplane, subway, or train

   This and the next type of phobia often go together:

Fears of being trapped or confined
Meetings, cinemas, or theatres, queues, escalators, elevators, showers

Social fears
Meeting new people, socializing
Doing things in front of others, like writing, speaking, eating, or using the telephone

Fears of illness or injury
Seeing blood, needles, vomiting, hospitals

Fears of natural phenomena
Thunder, lightening, or storms, water, heights, darkness

Vicious Circles Perpetuate the Problem

Fear usually dies away of its own accord, as if it had a natural life span. When it does not die away, it is usually because a vicious circle keeps it going. Robert avoided walking near parks and going to his friends' houses in case they had dogs. The more he avoided dogs, the more fearful he became. He thought of each successful expedition as a near miss or a lucky escape, and became increasingly preoccupied with how to protect himself from possible danger. These were some of the vicious circles that kept his problem going:

Robert's first circle. Robert's fear of dogs made him tremble and sweat. His immediate reaction was to avoid them. The more he avoided them, the more his fear grew. Avoidance made his fear grow stronger.

Robert's second circle. When Robert succeeded in avoiding a dog, he experienced an immediate sense of relief. He learned he could stop the fear by restricting his activities, and his avoidance increased as well as the fear.

Robert's third circle. As Robert's fear continued to grow and his activities became increasingly restricted, he felt more and more embarrassed about his difficulty and ashamed of being so fearful and "cowardly" that his confidence also began to dwindle. The less confident he felt, the more susceptible he was to increases in fear, and so on, round and round.

You can see from Figure 17.1 that Robert's reactions to his fear fed back into the vicious circles and kept his phobia going. *If you suffer from any phobias, try to draw your own vicious circles.*

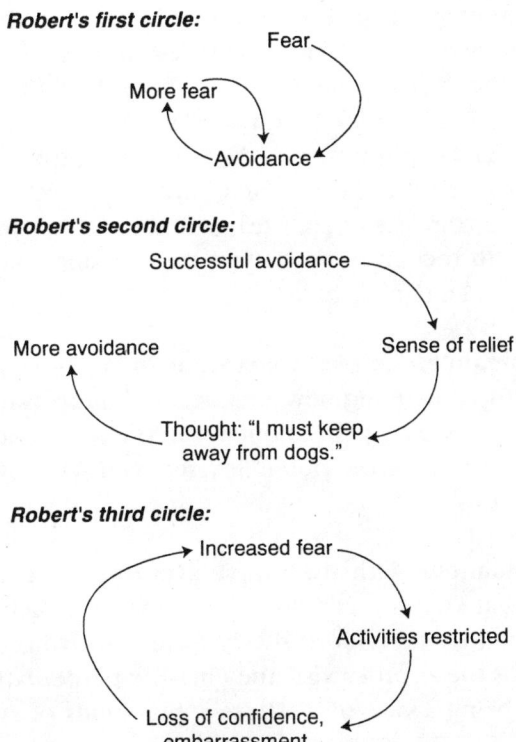

Figure 17.1 Robert's vicious circles.

Overcoming the Fear: Strategic Planning for Action

Strategic planning is needed to break the vicious circles that keep the problem going, so that the fear can die away of its own accord. The earlier you tackle the fear, the easier this will be. Each time you avoid something you fear, it becomes more likely that you will avoid it again at the next opportunity, like a river which cuts deeper and deeper into its bed. The best time to tackle your irrational fears, and to prevent them from becoming ingrained habits, is when you first notice that there is a problem. *If you can nip the fear in the bud, it may never grow into a full-blown phobia.* If the phobia you want to tackle is long-standing, however, it can still be overcome, but will take a little longer and may require more persistence. The strategic plan has three stages: (1) recognize your kinds of avoidance; (2) build yourself a ladder of increasing difficulty; (3) climb up the ladder and away from your fear.

1. RECOGNIZE YOUR KINDS OF AVOIDANCE

Avoidance is a natural reaction to fear and the biggest obstacle to overcome in most phobias. It is tempting because in the short run it makes you feel better. But if vicious circles are to be broken and fear is to be faced, the avoidance must be stopped. The first step is to learn to recognize it—which may be difficult because avoidance can take complex as well as simple forms. In both cases, the message is the same: if you can face the fear instead of avoiding it, you will be able to break the vicious circle and your fear will start to subside. It is important, therefore, to recognize when you are avoiding something either occasionally or on a regular basis.

1. Simple avoidance. Simple avoidance is the obvious kind: avoiding crowded places, or meeting new people, or cliff-top walks, or contact with dogs. There is no doubt about what you are avoiding, and it is relatively easy to reduce the possibility that you will come across the situation unawares.

2. Subtle avoidance. With the simple avoidance, you will not be in much doubt that you are avoiding the situations which you fear. But your avoidance may take more subtle forms, and you need to be on the look out for these; otherwise, they may be perpetuating your fears without your being aware of it. These subtle kinds of avoidance take many forms.

Putting things off. Robert put off making plans for his summer holiday. Somehow he always seemed too busy to think about it. He did not want to admit how much the phobia was interfering with his life.

Not accepting a challenge to do something a bit alarming. Elaine knew that her kitchen was spotlessly clean, but nevertheless waited until her husband came home to open the cupboard under the sink in case she found a spider.

Not talking about your feelings. Robert tried so hard to hide his fear from his friends that they could not understand what was happening and began to think he was avoiding them.

Keeping busy so you do not have to think about the problem. Pauline busied herself with housework, cooking, and knitting for all the family. She invited friends and neighbors in so often she had no time to go out.

Using others to hide behind, or as a kind of prop. Both Pauline and Elaine relied on their husbands to do things that made them feel nervous.

Doing something to keep yourself safe. Pauline bought herself a shopping basket on wheels to give her something to lean on if she felt shaky, and Robert went everywhere in his car.

In these subtle ways, they were able to do more things than they could otherwise have done. But at the same time, they relied on their props to keep them safe. Props can be useful when starting to tackle difficult and frightening situations, but it is not useful to become dependent on them. Then the fear of losing them, or of having suddenly to go somewhere without them, makes the phobia even more restricting.

- **All kinds of avoidance keep the phobia going: subtle as well as simple kinds, the things that you think as well as the things that you do.**

2. BUILD YOURSELF A LADDER OF INCREASING DIFFICULTY

The central strategy for overcoming your phobia involves constructing a ladder. This ladder makes it possible for you to tackle what you fear without becoming too frightened. The key is this: *Make inroads into your feared territory by degrees, tackling easier things before you face the harder ones.* The method, in effect, turns the vicious circles into benign ones as you gain ever-increasing levels of confidence. Throwing yourself in the deep end all at once may backfire, leaving you feeling both distressed and exhausted. By using a ladder, you can climb to a height that would be impossible in one step. With a ladder, no step is impossible. If you are on the fifth step, you can climb to the sixth. But to get to the sixth step from the first in one jump would not be possible.

It is this principle which underlies the step-by-step approach to overcoming your fears. Each step is small, but together they take you to new heights.

Make a list of the situations you avoid and that make you anxious, even if only mildly so. Then arrange these in order of difficulty.

Pauline had become so fearful of leaving her house that she no longer went out unless with her husband or a close friend. She felt anxious even at the thought of walking down the street. With her husband she could go to most places, but not to a supermarket or cinema. Her ladder of situations of increasing difficulty looked like this.

Pauline's Ladder of Increasing Difficulty	
Step	*Situation*
1	Walk alone to front gate.
2	Walk alone along street to first lamp post.
3	Walk alone along street and stand outside local store.
4	Go to cinema with husband.
5	Walk alone and go to newsstand without buying anything.
6	Go to supermarket with husband.
7	Go alone and buy something from local store.
8	Go alone to two of the local shops, and buy something.
9	With husband, go to supermarket entrance, but enter shop alone.
10	Go alone and buy something from supermarket.

Robert's ladder was quite different. It may look as if his progress must have been slow, but by starting at the *very beginning,* he was able to build his confidence faster.

Robert's Ladder of Increasing Difficulty

Step	Situation
1	Look at pictures of dogs in books, magazines, etc.
2	Talk to people about dogs; watch them on TV or video.
3	Watch real dogs out of the window or from the car.
4	Visit the pet shop where they have puppies.
5	Walk past the park; leave the car behind for small journeys.
6	Visit a friend who has a "safe" dog; tell him about the phobia.
7	Take friend's dog out into the garden.
8	Take this dog out on a leash, along the streets.
9	Go for a run in the park instead of using the exercise bike.
10	Take friend's dog to the park and let it run free.
11	Visit a local kennel.
12	Go to the pub where they have a German Shepherd dog.
13	Start football again (and plan a trip to the country).

Both Pauline and Robert had long-standing and deeply ingrained patterns of avoidance which is why they needed many steps in their ladders. If you are tackling a less severe phobia and tackling it earlier, you may need only a few steps, perhaps only one step if you can go straight to tackling your most feared situation. But however mild your phobia, if you want to overcome it, get clear in your mind what the steps are which you need to take.

3. CLIMB UP YOUR LADDER AND AWAY FROM FEAR

Having clearly identified the steps on the ladder, you can then go through each of the steps, only climbing to the next one when you have mastered the step you are on.

Here are seven keys to a successful climb:

1. The first step should be one that makes you slightly anxious but which does not frighten you so much that you can hardly tackle it.

2. If there is someone available, enlist their support. Ask them to read this chapter. Undertaking to report your progress to them will increase your ability to keep working at the program.
3. Plan treats for yourself so that you have something to look forward to each time you move up a step on your ladder (see Chapter 7).
4. Specify exactly what you are going to attempt, each time you try something new (e.g., Pauline decided she must touch the lamp post when that was her target).
5. Stay in the situation that you find difficult until you start to feel better, without being tempted to use subtle forms of avoidance.
6. Practice regularly and frequently: if possible every day.
7. Go on to the next step when your anxiety has decreased enough for you to feel ready.

THE COURSE OF PROGRESS

The optimum rate of progress is different for different people. It was a month before Robert felt more confident and six weeks before he was able to take a friend's dog for a walk. Pauline worked more slowly up her ladder, and needed to spend the best part of a month practicing shopping alone, while her husband waited nearby, before she felt sufficiently sure of herself to do the supermarket shopping entirely alone.

It does not matter how slowly you go. As long as you are practicing, you will keep progressing and will get there in the end. Concentrate on the step you are working on, rather than frightening yourself by thinking about the top of your ladder. It may take longer than you think to conquer your phobia, especially if you have had it for a long time and avoidance has become part of your life. Slow but sure wins the race.

Setbacks are a part of progress. Everybody has good days and bad days, whether they have a phobia or not. This means that sometimes it is hard to do today what you could easily do yesterday. Your confidence is bound to fluctuate, so apparent setbacks are a normal part of progress. They are disappointing and frustrating, but they are not a sign of failure. So do not be discouraged by them, but adapt your practice to the way you feel at the time. Make fewer demands on yourself when you are not feeling your best, and more when you feel better.

Sometimes it is hard to think of the right steps to take, or you get stuck at a particular step on the ladder and the next one seems too high up to reach. Think about how you could make the step easier for yourself. Robert found himself postponing walks past the park and made these easier by going first very early in the morning when it was almost deserted. He also found a friend to run with, and together they took "more adventurous" routes than he had been able to manage on his own. Pauline's anxiety in the supermarket never seemed to be far below the surface. She learned how to relax (see Chapter 11) and found this helped her to master the symptoms of fear.

Overcoming the Fear:
Strategic Planning to Control Thoughts

Fear fills the mind with horrors. Robert was convinced that if dogs "smelled his fear" they would set upon him; and the dire predictions he made increased his fear of dogs. In addition to a strategic plan for action, he was helped by a strategy for examining his thoughts. The strategy is a part of "cognitive therapy," which we have described in more detail in Chapter 9. In this chapter we will show how the strategy can be applied to help Robert examine his fearful, and counterproductive, thoughts.

The first step is to identify what the prediction is; the second step is to look for the evidence for and against it, keeping closely in touch with reality. Robert started some research. Do dogs spontaneously attack people? Of course, he read about pitbull terriers, and occasions when someone had been badly bitten. He knew that police dogs can be trained to attack and that postmen sometimes feel as if they are entering the lion's den when they open the garden gate and walk up to the front door. But he also found out that these were rare or special situations. Most dogs kept as pets are either kept under reasonable control or are harmless. The *probability* that he would be bitten was far lower than his fears had led him to believe. To check this out he asked a number of friends whether they had ever been bitten, and he was also interested in whether any of these friends were fearful of dogs. He wanted to find out whether dogs really do bite people who are frightened of them. Although most of his friends had not been bitten, a few of them had. However, nobody he knew had been spontaneously set upon or mauled, not even those who were themselves nervous of dogs. A few friends had been bitten, but those had been no more than nips received when playing with a dog or tripping over one. Robert thought he was unlikely to be involved in either of these situations against his will.

Robert had been doing what many people with phobias do: *overestimating the likelihood* that his fears would be realized and *overestimating how bad it would be* if they were. At the same time, he *underestimated* his ability to cope, to take action to improve the situation and get rid of the phobia. Reexamining his predictions brought him back in touch with reality, and helped him to feel more in control.

THE "EVER-READY" ATTITUDE

The unwritten message you give yourself when you avoid something, whether you do this in an obvious or in a subtle way, is "this is dangerous." Your attitude builds up an expectation that cannot easily be disconfirmed, because your avoidance prevents you from finding out that it is not really dangerous. The attitude of "approach" breaks this circle. The new message is: "When you feel like avoiding something, try to work out how you can approach it instead." Do not say to yourself, "I can't"; instead, ask yourself, "How could I . . . ?" This is the attitude which both helps you to nip fears in the bud, and to start the strategic planning that will make you feel better.

Adapting the Strategies to Different Types of Phobias

Fears that make it hard to practice. It is difficult to find practical ways of facing fears of flying, snakes, or thunderstorms on a regular daily basis. But you can practice in your imagination instead of in reality, and this is known to be remarkably effective. List the situations that you find difficult in exactly the same way as we have described earlier in this chapter; try to find a peaceful and relaxing place to practice; then imagine yourself in the situation that you fear, providing all the realistic detail you can muster to make yourself feel fearful. Allow yourself to get used to each situation in your imagination, and to feel calm about it, then give yourself a rest. Move up your list slowly, at your own pace.

Fears that induce fainting. Some people faint at the sight of blood, or when faced with things associated with illness or injury. If this is a problem for you, you should start by learning the method of "applied tension" to overcome the problem of fainting. Fainting is associated with a sudden drop in blood pressure, and this drop in pressure can be prevented by tensing up your muscles instead of trying to relax. Practice doing this at home first. The aim is to tighten all the major muscles in your arms, legs, and torso at once, and to hold this tension for about 5 seconds. Then, let it go briefly before tensing up again. You should practice doing this for 10 minutes twice a day, where you feel comfortable at home before you try to apply it in situations you find difficult. Learn to apply tension sitting down first, and then try it standing up. When you can do this, use the method as you climb your ladder of increasing difficulty—for example, as you look at pictures of things that make you feel faint or during situations that you find difficult, like having a blood sample taken. Many people who have practiced this method are able to become regular blood donors, and this commitment seems to help them maintain their newfound confidence.

Fears of social situations. One of the most common phobias is social phobia—fear of situations that involve meeting new people, going to a party, or a meeting at work, and speaking in front of a group of others. Since you cannot control what other people do, it can be difficult to adopt strategies for action; the precise situation may not be under your control. Furthermore, many of the things you might want to practice, like saying good morning or starting a conversation, cannot easily be repeated over and over again without making you feel foolish. Because of these difficulties, social phobias are often best tackled by focusing on strategic planning that can control your thoughts. One of the central thoughts which recurs for many people who suffer from social phobia is the idea that other people are continually evaluating their performance, and judging it to be inadequate or inappropriate. This thought can be examined and tested using the methods of cognitive therapy, just like any other problematic thought. If you suffer from social phobia, read Chapter 9 in order to help you to identify and tackle your problematic thoughts. In addition to this, *focus* on your thoughts, and think about how to increase your scope for planning strategies for action. For example, if you are fearful of meeting new people on your own, go along with a friend first. Watch what other people do and listen to what they say. Try talking to someone you do not find frightening and work up gradually to those who give you some anxiety.

You will find other useful ideas in Part 3, which focuses on relationships, particularly in Chapter 13. It can also be enormously helpful if you can tell one or two sympathetic friends about your anxieties, let them know what you are doing, and enlist their support: for instance, ask them to read this chapter, so that they have some understanding of your situation.

How to Help Someone Else Overcome a Phobia

It can be enormously helpful, in overcoming a phobia, to have the support of a husband or wife or other good friend. The purpose of this section of the chapter is to give guidance if you would like to help someone else in overcoming a phobia. It would be best if both of you read the whole of this chapter, and it is vital that the person with the phobia wants your help.

The fear is real. If you yourself have not experienced an irrational fear, you may find it difficult to be sympathetic with your partner's or friend's phobia. It is important that you realize that their fear is real, even though the danger is not. Do not trivialize this fear, and do not ridicule it. If you are having difficulty in understanding how they feel, think about times when you have been frightened.

One summer, many years ago, Josh was on holiday with two friends. They had lunch under the shade of a parasol in the garden of a pub on the North Coast of Devon. It was not long before a wasp came to investigate their food. It flew away, perhaps to tell its friends, for a few minutes later there were half a dozen wasps sipping their beer and feeding on the potatoes. Josh had never worried much about wasps, but his two friends were in a great state of anxiety. They thrashed uselessly in the air in an attempt to chase the wasps away. Josh laughed at these vain attempts and at their fear, bathed in the smugness of his own indifference. After this lunch the three friends continued their walk along the cliff. The path became narrower and narrower, and the cliff edge steeper and steeper. Although indifferent to wasps, Josh had a definite fear of heights. He came to a part of the path where he simply froze: ahead the path came close to a steep drop straight down to the sea, and as his courage evaporated, he could not face returning along the vertiginous path he had been walking along with increasing difficulty. His companions did not laugh at him. They saw how fearful he really was, and they helped him along until he came to a part of the path where he felt safe. For them the fear of the wasps around their food was like the fear of the steep cliff for Josh; he never trivialized their fear of wasps again.

Give support, but avoid becoming overprotective. The first way in which you can help people suffering from fears or phobias is to give your support; to show that you accept their fear and that you want to help them to overcome it. But the only way in which they will overcome this fear is if they *gradually* face it: if they embark on their ladder of increasing difficulty. They are going to need courage, and you can help to give them this courage, but you must not protect them from facing their difficulties. Such protection is "overprotection" because it will prevent them from doing the one thing that is vitally necessary for overcoming the phobia. This is what Pauline's husband did. He overprotected his wife by doing all the shopping so that, until he understood better how to help her, she never had to leave the home without him and consequently never faced her fear.

Clarify what role you are going to take. You will need to be clear what role you are going to take, and this must be agreed on with your friend: otherwise, your help may be resented. Your role in helping may cause friction between both of you if there has not been an agreement beforehand as to what exactly you should do.

Help to plan the strategy for action. A further way in which you may be able to help is in planning the strategy for action: in constructing the ladder of increasing difficulty. The mistake many people make is to choose "rungs" that are too far apart. In other words, people tend to overestimate the size of each step that they can take. The examples of Pauline's and Robert's ladders are given in order to show the kind of steps that are helpful. Another error is to make the steps too vague, so that there is room for wide interpretation of what exactly is to be done. You can help both in choosing the rungs and in defining each action. A third way in which you can help is to offer your support for some of the steps up the ladder. With many phobias it is enormously helpful if a close friend can give support particularly when facing some of the most feared situations. This is often a vital step on the way to facing these situations alone. In Pauline's ladder, for example, one of the rungs involves going to the cinema with her husband. If you offer to help in this way, you are committing yourself to giving some time to help and you must be sure that you want to give this time. It will be unhelpful if you offer to go with your friend to the supermarket on several occasions as part of the strategy of action and then cannot afford the time. It will also be unhelpful if your friend feels unable to rely on you to do what you said you would. It would be better if you had not made the offer in the first place and the ladder of increasing difficulty did not involve you. So do think carefully whether you can, realistically, make the commitment.

Helping to implement the strategy for action. Your support could help your friend to implement the strategy for action: for instance, you can be someone to whom to report. Your job is to receive the progress report while understanding just how much courage is involved in attempting to face things that provoke fear.

Helping to plan treats. Finally, you can help your friend by helping to plan treats. People with phobias often feel that they should not have the phobia in the first place, and so they do not feel they deserve treats as they make progress up their ladder of increasing difficulty. This is quite wrong. They need a great deal of courage to tackle their phobia, and climbing every rung of the ladder is an achievement. These achievements need to be recognized and marked by enjoying treats (Chapter 7).

Chapter Summary

Phobias are irrational fears that can interfere seriously with your life. The fear experienced by someone with a phobia is real, even though the danger is either imaginary or greatly exaggerated.

Overcoming phobias involves *strategic planning for action*

1. Learn to recognize the ways in which you avoid the things you fear.
2. Build yourself a ladder of increasing difficulty. This means working out for yourself which are the steps that you need to take.
3. Climb up the ladder and away from your fear using the seven keys to success (pp. 199–200).

Overcoming phobias also involves *strategic planning to control your thoughts*. People with phobias tend to overestimate the risks they face and to underestimate their ability to cope. If you learn to recognize, and then to change, these distorted ways of thinking, you will overcome your fear.

Progress will have its ups and downs: go at your own pace, and do not be discouraged by occasional setbacks.

18

◆ ◆ ◆

Stress: How to Live with the Right Amount of It

Some Facts about Stress

We are all experts on stress. Everyone of us has experienced it at some time, and few people manage to keep it under control all the time. The problem is so common that learning how to deal with stress should be part of the national curriculum! This chapter starts by looking at stress from several angles and then suggests ways of dealing with it.

THE UPSIDE AND THE DOWNSIDE

One of the difficulties about stress is that it can work for you or against you, just like a car tire. When the pressure in the tire is right, you can drive smoothly along the road: if it is too low, you feel all the bumps and the controls feel sluggish. If it is too high, you bounce over the potholes, and easily swing out of control.

The effects of stress are illustrated in Figure 18.1. This figure shows the results of different levels of stress on performance—for example, on the ability to understand instructions or to concentrate on what you are doing. For low levels of stress, for example at point A, increasing stress can improve performance. High levels of stress, however, impede performance. Susceptibility to stress varies from person to person, and in a

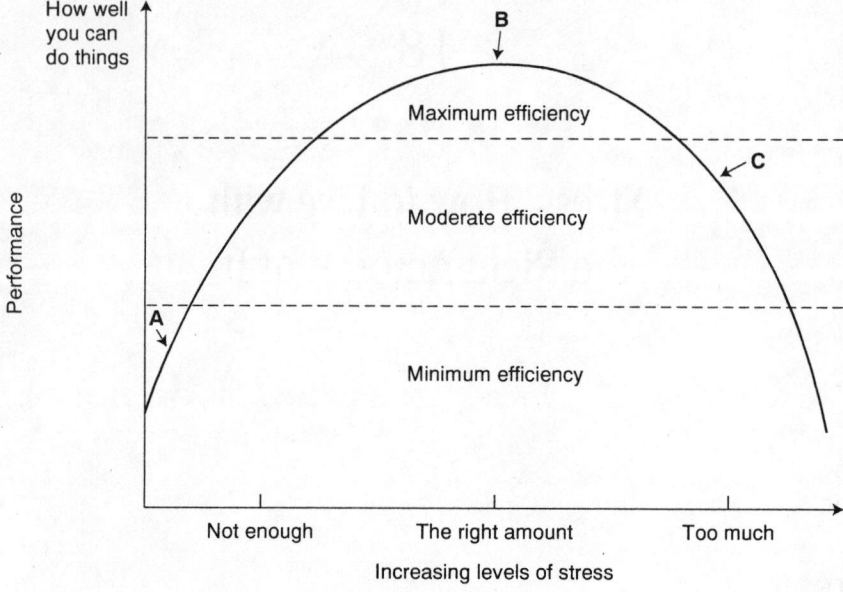

Figure 18.1   The effects of stress on performance.

single person it also varies from time to time. In general, as the stress increases beyond the level at B, performance gets worse. Once point C is reached, performance rapidly deteriorates with increasing stress. The difficulty is that many people, when they notice the strain, react by redoubling their efforts. What this tends to do is to increase stress at just the time when such an increase leads to a worsening performance. Then problems come thick and fast; it gets harder to think ahead and tempting to adopt the first solution that comes to mind: reaching for the bottle, asking for sleeping tablets, or hiding your head in the sand.

THE OUTSIDE AND THE INSIDE

Stress comes both from outside and from inside. Outside stresses reflect the pressure you are under or the burden you are carrying: your job, the demands your children or parents make on you, your mortgage and a myriad other things. Inside sources of stress reflect your reactions to these things. If the demands seem many and your resources seem few, you will feel stressed: "There's far too much to do." "There's no way I can cope." Internal sources of stress also include wants, feelings, and attitudes. Wanting to do your job well, to succeed, to be liked, or to make other people happy puts pressure on you. Feeling worried, angry, or jealous saps your energy. If you have the attitude that things should always be done quickly and efficiently, for example, you will feel more stressed than someone who is able to take a more "laid back" attitude. If you value the sense of being stimulated, interested, and useful, then you will find boredom stressful. None of these attitudes is, of itself, either better or worse than the others. But sometimes these internal sources combine with external sources to produce too much stress. When this is the case, stress can be reduced either by reducing the external stresses, or by reducing internal stresses (for example, by changing attitudes), or both.

Annie was able to cope with three children, a part-time job, most of the household chores, and worrying about her elderly mother. She fell apart one day when the washing machine broke down. Martin started his own business, was facing a shrinking economy, volunteered to help out at the local youth club, and was involved in a turbulent relationship. He exploded when his assistant was late for work.

THE PHYSICAL EFFECTS OF STRESS

The results of scientific research strongly suggest that stress can be bad for our health. Evidence comes from two types of study: the first is the investigation of physiological responses to stress in both people and animals; the second is the study of psychological factors associated with physical illness. The single most important effect of stress is that it, almost certainly, increases the chance of a heart attack. There is further evidence that psychological techniques that reduce the effects of stress in those who have had one heart attack reduce the chance of a second heart attack.

Stress can also cause bowel problems, notably diarrhea and tummy pain, as well as headaches; and it probably makes asthma attacks more frequent and severe in those already prone to asthma. Many people with chronic problems, ranging from skin rashes to arthritis to epilepsy, report that their problems are much worsened at times of stress.

Physiological research shows that stress can affect hormone levels, and the immune system (the system that helps fight against infection and some cancers), but whether these effects lead to disease is not known.

Are You Becoming Too Stressed?

One of the keys to managing stress is to recognize early when you are becoming too stressed. Go through the following *four* steps to help you decide whether this is happening to you.

STEP 1: LEARN TO RECOGNIZE YOUR OWN SIGNS

Everyone responds in their own way to increasing stress. Some people become progressively more frantic and impetuous, others drag their feet and avoid making decisions. In both cases, stress makes them less efficient. The important thing is to know how *you* react. The better you know your own signs, the better you will be able to cope with the problem. Learn about yourself by focusing on situations and times when you know you were stressed in the past. You can then learn to recognize your signs early in order, in future, to take action before the stresses get out of hand. The following questions will help you to recognize your reactions.

1. What does it feel like when you are stressed?
2. How does it show?
3. What thoughts run through your mind?
4. What do you do?
5. How does it affect others?
6. How do their reactions affect you?

In order to help you to detect stress in your life, we have listed some common changes in the following box. Read the list carefully, marking those which apply to you when you are stressed, and adding others as appropriate. Look for your personal signs of stress, and remember that the things on the list normally fluctuate as you negotiate everyday ups and downs.

The list is divided into four sections. Most people who suffer from stress find that it affects them in all four ways, so if you mark nothing in one of the sections, you should probably think again.

STEP 2: WEIGH THE SIZE OF THE LOAD

Take an objective look at the stresses you face, and write them down if you can. Stress is cumulative, so the small things (the chores) count as well as the big ones (your job, your finances, and friendships). Beware of discounting the load in the way that many people do, thinking, for example, "*everyone else* copes with at least as much," or "I *should* be able to manage. I could last year." A heavy load, carried for a long time, wears you down in the end, and different people find different things stressful. Discounting your load only adds internal stress to the external load and puts you under more pressure.

Changes that May Be Signs of Stress

Feelings

Irritability; you become short-tempered, or easily flare up
Anxiety or feelings of panic
Fear—e.g., of being out of control
Feeling worried—e.g., about your health, or anything else
Feeling miserable or tearful
Apathy or agitation
Lowered self-esteem

Thoughts

Forgetting things; making mistakes
Finding it hard to concentrate
Becoming indecisive
Getting muddled or confused
Procrastinating
Being unable to think far ahead
Worrying or ruminating rather than solving problems
Becoming rigid and inflexible, in an effort to keep control
Predicting the worst

Behaviors

Getting worse at managing your time
Getting worse at organizing yourself, and others
Rushing hither and thither
Finding it hard to delegate
Working longer and longer hours
Bringing work home; working on weekends
Avoiding tackling problems, or doing things you dislike
Cutting down on the things you do for pleasure
Losing touch with your friends
Blaming others for the problem,
Taking it out on others ("kicking the cat")
Finding there's no time to enjoy yourself
Needing a drink; turning to drugs
Needing tranquilizers or sleeping tablets

Sensations

Aches and pains, especially headaches or stomachaches
Tension—e.g., in your neck and shoulders
Frequent minor ailments
Disrupted sleep patterns
Appetite for food increased or decreased
Appetite for sex increased or decreased
Ulcers
Flare up of stress-related illness, such as asthma or psoriasis

STEP 3: THINK ABOUT RECENT CHANGES IN YOUR LIFE

Changes demand that you adapt, so all of them, even if they are for the better, contribute to your level of stress. The demand is obvious if the stress is an illness like arthritis or losing your job, and less obvious if it comes from being promoted or getting married. Changes that can lessen your load, like retirement or readjusting after your children leave home, can also be stressful. Changes of all kinds use up energy, leaving you less to spare until you have adjusted to the changes. Moving house is the most underestimated of major changes, and can take months to adapt to completely. Add to your list any changes that have happened to you in the last year. In the box opposite, you will find some examples of the types of change which research has shown commonly contribute to stress.

STEP 4: THINK ABOUT RECENT CHANGES IN YOURSELF

Having thought about how you respond to stress, the pressures on you, and recent events in your life, do you think that you are becoming too stressed now? Look again at the box on page 211, "Changes that may be signs of stress." Have you noticed any recent changes in yourself that might be due to excess stress?

Dealing with Stress

Most people who suffer from stress manage the problem sensibly themselves, and many succeed. If you catch the problem early, your own ways of dealing with it are likely to work, because you have probably developed effective strategies over the years. There are, however, two cautionary notes to bear in mind.

TWO NOTES OF CAUTION

1. *Make sure that the solutions you use will be helpful in the long term as well as in the short term.* As the demands upon him increased, Martin began to drink more. It helped him to relax, to find the energy for his extra commitments, and to deal more calmly with his difficult relationship. However, the stress continued and he found himself reaching for the bottle at ever-increasing intervals. As he drank more, he became more argumentative and slept less well. The more stressed he became the more he wanted to drink. This apparent solution became another of his problems.

Examples of Stressful Events

Major changes

Changing jobs
Getting married, separated, or divorced
Business readjustments
Pregnancy
Moving house
Leaving school, or changing schools
Outstanding achievement
Getting or losing a mortgage
Retirement

Losses

A friend or relative dies
People you are close to move away
Children leaving home
Stopping work
Giving up work to have children

Disruptions to routine

Vacations, Christmas, bank holidays
Someone new in the home (e.g., a friend or a new baby)
Stopping smoking or drinking
Dieting
No opportunity for exercise

Trouble and strife

Arguments, especially with a partner
Brushes with the law
Illness
Injury
Financial problems

Note: These are not in order of severity. That depends on you.

---

2. *Beware of caffeine.* Caffeine winds you up, and could undo the good work you are doing in other ways. Annie's efforts to fulfill all her commitments left her little time for herself. She forced herself to stop by making a drink of tea or coffee, by joining in the tea breaks at work, and by chatting to a friend over coffee while the children were at swimming classes. She started to suffer from tension headaches, felt more frantic rather than less, and had difficulty falling asleep. After

limiting the number of caffeine drinks she had in a day (including tea and cola as well as coffee) to about four, and cutting them out altogether after 6 P.M., she began to feel more in control.

When you are not able to get your stress under control, try these five steps.

STEP 1: TAKE STOCK OF THE SITUATION

The more you push yourself when you are stressed, the less you are likely to achieve, because trying harder increases the pressure—and also the inefficiency. Striving not to strive can also be counterproductive and add to the tension.

The first step is therefore the hardest of all: find a moment to stop and think. When stress builds to high levels, you need a breathing space. However pressured you feel, give yourself time to take stock. It is time well spent because it helps you put things in perspective and plan the next move. Have a brief rest if you can, and assess your level of stress in the ways already described. Think about the four main aspects of your life: work, play, health, and relationships (both family and friends). Are these equally important to you? Are some more important than others?

Ask yourself: to which do you devote most time and energy? Does the way you fill your time fit with what matters to you? Devoting all your time to one aspect of life—work or family, for instance—will create stress if you also value the others. Besides, if you put all your eggs in one basket, there is nothing to fall back on when things go badly awry.

STEP 2: START WITH THE END IN MIND

Stress makes it hard to give priority to the most important things. Indeed, the choice of what to do next often becomes so haphazard that you find yourself thoughtlessly taking up the first thing that comes along, and worrying about not having enough time for everything else. If you have clarified your major priorities, you will find it easier to interrupt this process, and make decisions that lead to a more balanced, and less stressful, life. Martin learned how to stop work in time to play squash or eat with friends; Annie learned how to share the family chores more fairly and joined an evening class with the idea of finding a more interesting job.

Use your priorities to guide small decisions, like how to spend the evening, as well as big ones like changing your job. If you know what is "vital" to you, it becomes easier to "cut your losses" when stress builds to high levels. You can then consider, for instance, whether someone else might like to take on a task that you could drop. The central importance of being guided by your priorities is explained in Chapter 5.

Putting your priorities into practice. The ideas discussed so far are easy to understand but hard to put into practice. Once you have thought about the basics, and about your priorities, start by dealing with the effects of stress. Here are some ideas about how to do this.

1. *Stress affects your memory and concentration.* Relieve yourself of this extra strain by writing things down—for example, in diaries, on wallcharts, or on lists.
2. *Stress makes planning and decisions difficult.* Give yourself planning time every day (first thing in the morning may be best).
3. *Stress makes you tired.* Give yourself proper breaks—for meals, refreshments, exercise, and on weekends.
4. *Stress slows down your speed of recovery, and lowers your resistance to illness.* Learn to stop before you are completely worn out. Take regular exercise, and eat a balanced diet.
5. *Stress makes you feel pressured.* Think about how to take the urgency out of your life (see Chapter 5).
6. *Stress tempts you to avoid difficulties or put off dealing with them, so that they do not get resolved.* Try to face them instead. It is often best to do your least favorite, or hardest, task first (see Chapter 6).
7. *Stress reduces your efficiency.* Find out how you use your time—for example, by thinking back or keeping a diary. Does the way you spend your time accord with your values and goals?

Keeping your values and priorities clearly in mind makes all of these easier.

STEP 3: REDUCE THE "OUTSIDE" LOAD: THE LESSON OF THE CAMEL'S BACK

Stress is cumulative. Deal, therefore, with small problems (the mess in your room, answering letters) particularly when there seems to be little you can do about the big ones (someone's illness, or the amount of traffic on the roads). Identify all the stresses on you; none is too small to consider. Which of these stresses can you reduce? Problem-solving strategies are explained in detail in Chapter 8.

STEP 4: REDUCE THE "INSIDE" LOAD: CHANGING ATTITUDES

Stress comes from the inside as well as from the outside. For each of us, it is determined partly by the way we see the world, or by our attitudes. Many of our attitudes originate in our childhood. Some, no doubt, are absorbed from authority figures, in particular from parents or parent substitutes and from teachers; others are derived from our experience, for example, from having grown up with a competitive brother or sister. Such early experiences probably determine to a great extent whether we are driven by a desire to please, or a wish to win, or whatever. And these different drives and desires affect what causes us stress (see also Chapter 14). Men who believe that success in life is measured by success at work are especially stressed by being unemployed. Women brought up to believe that they should devote the major part of their energies to their children are especially stressed by the demands of combining a career and a family. *Such attitudes are not in themselves right or wrong, but they can be more or less helpful.* Unhelpful attitudes of any kind make difficulties and increase your burden, while more helpful ones take the pressure off, so it is worth examining your attitudes and looking for alternatives that create less pressure. Some of the ways of doing this are explained in Chapter 9, and some common examples of attitudes that can contribute to feeling stressed are listed here, together with some more helpful alternatives.

Putting the pressure on	*Taking the pressure off*
I have to get this done.	I will do as much as I can in the allowed time.
I shouldn't ask for help.	Everyone asks for help sometimes. I would happily help someone else.
This is really important.	In five years this won't matter at all. When I'm on my deathbed, I won't be saying "I wish I'd spent more time in the office."
I must do things well.	I can only do my best.
Others cope far better than I.	Everyone is susceptible to stress. I am not alone in this.
There's nothing I can do.	Try solving the small problems first.
I'll crack up completely.	I need a break, so I'll take a break.
I can't let anyone see how I feel.	There's nothing to lose by talking to someone about my feelings.

STEP 5: LAY THE RIGHT FOUNDATION

Feeling stressed is a danger signal: a sign that you are reaching the limits of your resources. Stress is bad for your physical health as well as a cause of increasing inefficiency and worsening relationships. The danger is that when under stress you ignore your health, and put your relationships under increasing strain. This sets up a vicious cycle because poor health and poor relationships then add to the stress. It is important, therefore, to focus not only directly on the stresses but also to look after your health and your relationships.

Diet and exercise. Regularity is the key. You need regular meals and you need regular exercise—always, and not just when you are young and growing. If you feel stressed, now is the time to build up your stamina by keeping fit.

Martin regularly rushed out of the house without breakfast, skipped lunch or grabbed a sandwich on the way from one appointment to the next, and filled himself up with cookies, chocolate, and coffee when he noticed he was flagging. Annie tried to eat at regular times and to provide a varied and balanced diet for the family, but at mealtimes she constantly leapt up and down to fetch and carry for her children. Because she put her own needs last, her children learned to expect her to be constantly serving them. She hardly knew what it felt like to sit comfortably throughout a meal. Eating "properly" not only means eating the right things, but eating them in the right way. Eating properly would help both Annie and Martin cope better with their stressful lives, and encouraging Annie's children to look after their own needs, or to help at mealtimes, would be especially helpful to Annie.

The same idea applies to regular exercise. Even 10 minutes of daily exercise makes a difference. So does walking more and using the car less. Ideally, you should take at least an hour of exercise twice a week, building up the strenuousness gradually. It is time well spent, even if at first you feel too tired to change your clothes. Surprisingly perhaps, exercising when you are stressed is more invigorating than exhausting, and often leaves you with more energy than you started with. Of course, it improves your physical state, but it also marks an important shift in attitude, away from neglect and toward caring for yourself.

The 3 Rs: Rest, recreation, and relationships. Being stressed adds its own pressures. To prevent being caught up in the vicious cycle of stress, which leads to even higher levels of stress, you need: *rest*, to renew your energy; *recreation*, to provide you with pleasure and fulfillment; and *relationships*, as a source of support and perspective.

1. Rest. Stress is associated with tension and poor sleeping patterns. It makes it hard to switch off and to take advantage of opportunities to rest, especially brief ones. Good quality rest restores your good mood as well as your capacity to function well. So schedule regular rest periods, both brief ones and more substantial rest periods. Examples of brief periods of rest are: soaking in the bath; having a tea or coffee break with a friend; spending 30 minutes in formal relaxation. Examples of longer periods of rest are: a week's vacation; a day out with the family (unless the family is a source of stress); a weekend break. If you are sleeping badly, read Chapter 24. If you are unable to relax, read Chapter 11. If worry prevents you from getting rest, read Chapter 16.

Rest means not working. It does *not* mean doing your work sitting on the sofa while listening to music. Nor does it necessarily mean doing nothing. Almost everyone finds it hard to do nothing, except for rather short or rare periods, like when lying in the bath. It is even harder to do nothing when you feel stressed, when worries queue up ready to grab your attention whenever it is free.

2. Recreation. Recreation makes you feel better about yourself— more fulfilled, more satisfied, more interested, and more engaged in the world outside that of your own personal concerns. Recreations come in infinite varieties. They are often not restful in that they can be quite demanding and even exhausting (playing football or squash; cooking for friends), but they are a source of pleasure and satisfaction and a chance to extend your skills. If they are to be truly recreational, they should be markedly different from your work routine or from the source of your stress. If the stresses come mostly from your office, then cooking on the weekend could be recreational, but not if constantly providing for the family is itself a source of stress.

Hobbies are usually recreational. They give you an added interest and often bring you into contact with like-minded people (dog-breeders, gardeners, bridge players), and if they are to serve their purpose, they should be kept free from trouble and strife. Everybody needs recreations, which may be creative or contemplative, social or solitary.

3. Relationships. Relationships are a common source of stress. You may have problems with family members, colleagues, friends, or lovers. People who are stressed may also be irritable and argumentative with those to whom they are closest and to whom they would like to be able to turn for support and comfort. Stress easily affects relationships: disappointment, sadness, or anger about a relationship may add to your burden, but if it cuts you off from others, you will lose a major source of "restoration." The following box suggests ways you can gain support from your relationships.

Others Can Help When You Are Stressed

- Do not cut yourself off from other people.
- Talk to someone both about your difficulties and your feelings.
- Seek out companionship of the kind that you usually enjoy.
- Keep in touch with friends.
- Explain what is happening if you are irritable—others may take it personally when that was not what you intended.
- If you need time for yourself, say so.
- Think about how to help others when they, too, are stressed.

There is far more to be gained than lost from talking to others about how to cope with your stress, because although everyone reacts differently, the process is normal. Everyone would eventually suffer from it if their burden was continually increasing. Both Annie and Martin discovered that two heads were better than one when it came to looking for solutions although, perhaps because he is a man, Martin found it particularly difficult to talk about how he was feeling. Annie talked to her women friends and neighbors and heard about some volunteers able to visit and help with her mother. Martin's bout of anger with his assistant when he was late led, after some strong words had been said on both sides, to a discussion that surprised Martin. He discovered his assistant was bored and frustrated at not having more responsibilities. With a mixture of trepidation and relief, Martin shed some of the load he was carrying. Ways of sharing a load include delegating more of your tasks, unburdening yourself to a close friend, or asking someone to help you out.

Relationships with others are also an important source of pleasure. They are a resource when you feel stressed, but often an underused resource: because some of them contribute to the problem, because stress absorbs every ounce of energy, or because of a natural, but unhelpful, reticence and reluctance to talk about difficulties. Furthermore, when we are stressed we may inadvertently put a strain on our relationships, too, by "taking it out on others" or "passing on the bad news." In order to make constructive use of your close relationships, consider carefully who is likely to be able to give you support. This might be just one person, your special partner perhaps, or several people. Then think about whether you have explained clearly to this person, or persons, how you are feeling, and under how much stress you are. Have you been expecting them to make the first move? Finally, has your stress meant that you have been particularly irritable with those close to you? If you have, it may be helpful to apologize and explain that your irritability is not because of them, but because of the stresses you feel.

When tension runs high, most people need their relationships more, not less, and so it is in their own best interest to think about how to look after them. It may be important to let off steam in ways that do not run the risk of upsetting others and damaging relationships—for example, by going for a run, thumping a pillow, or expressing feelings of frustration and anger forcibly on paper. Ensuring that you continue to do things you enjoy with the people around you will both help you feel less stressed and keep the relationship in good working order. You will find many more ideas about how to foster good relationships in Part Three of this book.

Chapter Summary

1. Everyone gets stressed from time to time.
2. A moderate amount of stress can be helpful and make you function more efficiently. A lot of stress is not only unpleasant: it is counterproductive.
3. Try to recognize the signs of stress, as early as possible, by following these four steps:
    *   Tune in to the early signs of stress.
    *   Take an objective look at the pressures on you.
    *   Identify recent changes in your load at work and at home.
    *   Identify recent changes in how you feel.
4. Most problems with stress can be dealt with using a systematic approach.
    *   Make a little time to take stock of your situation.
    *   Review your values and goals: start with the end in mind.
    *   The camel's back: throw away some of the load.
    *   Restructure your attitudes: many pressures are stressful only because we make them stressful.
    *   Look after the basics: diet, exercise, and the 3 Rs of rest, recreation, and relationships.

19

♦ ♦ ♦

Dealing with Panic:
Controlling the Alarm System

When the Alarm Bell Rings

Liz was sitting at her desk, staring out of the window. By her side she had an empty coffee mug and a blank sheet of paper. The report was not due until next week and she was finding it hard to concentrate. She allowed her mind to wander among a familiar mixture of feelings, worries, and preoccupations, becoming increasingly irritated and frustrated with her inability to keep focused. The sun was shining directly onto the desk, and feeling hot she stood up to open the window. Suddenly she felt dizzy and light-headed. She felt apprehensive, just as if her internal alarm bell had started to ring. A confusing number of things then happened in quick succession. She grabbed the chair for fear of falling, started to tremble and sweat, noticed her heart was pounding, and wondered if something was seriously wrong. She felt a terrifying feeling of breathlessness and tried to gasp for more air. The papers on the desk seemed to recede to a great distance, and when she put out her hand to touch them, her fingers tingled even though they felt numb. By now she was seriously frightened, certain that something terrible was happening to her. She rushed to the bathroom and held onto the basin while she splashed some water onto her face. Then she sat down cradling her head in her hands. Slowly her body began to return to normal. The worst seemed to be over as the dizziness and heart-pounding gradually subsided. Still feeling frightened and shaky, she sat in a comfortable chair for half an hour before trying to get back to work again. The first thing she did when she reached her desk was telephone the doctor to make an appointment as soon as possible. She thought she might be ill, but was also puzzled about what sort of illness it could be, and she dreaded being labeled as yet another neurotic woman, unable to cope with both work and family life. Whatever the cause, the terrifying experience seemed to have come upon her with absolutely no warning: completely out of the blue. She no longer felt safe sitting at her desk.

Liz's terrifying experience was a panic attack—or as she came to call it, a "Satanic attack." Panic attacks are common. More than 10% of all people, men and women, experience at least one panic attack during their lifetime, and often the first one happens during early adulthood. They are more likely to occur at times of stress or strain, or after unpleasant or traumatic experiences, but they also occur at other times.

A panic attack is a terrifying experience. The physical sensations of fear escalate with amazing speed until it feels as if something catastrophic might happen, like collapsing, losing control, having a heart attack, or dying. The panic usually peaks within the first few minutes, and the sensations then subside, but more slowly than they started. It is not surprising, given how terrifying panic attacks can be, that once experienced, confidence can be greatly shaken. Some people live in dread of further attacks, searching for ways of ensuring they will not happen again. A panic attack is a version of the normal alarm reaction, except that it occurs in the absence of real danger. If you were threatened by a mugger, or slipped in front of a car as you crossed the road, you might react in a similar way, and the alarm reaction would die down soon after you were safe again. Panic attacks are harder to come to terms with, and their effects may persist, partly because it is hard to understand what precipitated them. Even people who can recognize the situations that make them susceptible to panic, such as queuing up in busy shops or speaking to a large group of people, are often at a loss to explain exactly what triggered a particular attack—It seemed to come out of the blue— and it is hard to believe that such a dramatic event could happen without there being something seriously wrong.

Dealing with panic involves understanding what happens during panic attacks, learning how to control them, and how to deal with their consequences. Recurrent panic attacks can now be treated successfully using psychological methods, and in the majority of cases people learn what to do quite quickly and can soon regain their confidence.

UNDERSTANDING PANIC

Panic affects all systems: sensations, actions, emotions, and thoughts. The main symptoms of panic are shown in the box on the following page. Read carefully through the list. If you have had even one panic attack, you may already have experienced a large number of these symptoms, and you may want to add some more of your own to the list. Not everyone reacts in exactly the same way.

Some people may find that reading through this list itself makes them feel quite panicky. If this should happen to you, think of it as a demonstration of the power of the mind. Thinking about the symptoms can be enough to trigger them off. Do not avoid reading through the list, but read the rest of the chapter first if you find it particularly difficult.

The bodily symptoms of panic are all part of the normal reaction to fear. They are useful, adaptive reactions for use in an emergency. They show that your body is preparing itself for action by, for example, pumping the blood faster or increasing the supply of oxygen to the muscles in case you need to take quick evading action. These reactions are protective in times of danger. They are normal and not harmful. Even when they occur in the absence of real danger, as in a panic attack, the symptoms themselves cannot harm you. They will do no physical damage, and they will not make you lose control or go mad. As soon as the danger is past, they will die down of their own accord. The heart beats faster during exercise (playing tennis, aerobics, climbing a mountain) than during a panic attack, so there is no danger of a heart attack.

Many people who have had panic attacks are particularly alarmed by the speed at which symptoms increase. They suppose that if the symptoms went on increasing at this rate "something dreadful would happen"—as if they might explode or burst. It is easy to assume that the symptoms would have gone on increasing if they had not taken action, such as sitting down, or running away. But they are wrong. The symptoms will reach a peak of their own accord and then start to decline. The fear reaction is designed to keep the body ready for action, and to protect it in case of need, not to blow a fuse at exactly the wrong moment.

TRIGGERING THE FEAR REACTION

The setting. It is, at first sight, strange that an extreme fear reaction, or panic, can be triggered in the absence of danger, but, like other kinds of alarm systems, the setting varies. If the setting is too low, it

Symptoms of Panic

Sensations

Palpitations: heart-thumping
Smothering or choking sensations
Feeling faint, dizzy, or unsteady
Sweating or hot flushes
Numbness or tingling—in the hands or feet
Breathlessness; shortness of breath; gulping for air
Trembling or shaking
Nausea
Feelings of unreality, as if things that are close at hand are at a distance
Tightness in the chest or chest pain

Actions

Shouting for help
Hanging on to furniture, or to people nearby
Running away; escaping from the situation
Sitting or lying down
Stopping ongoing activities
Seeking safety

Emotions

Apprehension
Dread
Fear
Terror
Panic

Thoughts

Something dreadful is happening.
I shall collapse.
This is a heart attack.
I can't breathe.
I'm going to die.
I might lose control.
I am going mad.
I'm trapped; I can't get out.

can scare you by producing false alarms, and if it is too high, the alarm may fail you in the hour of need. It is certainly possible that some people are naturally more sensitive than others, or react more quickly than others, and at times of stress or strain, when tension levels are already high, it is easier to trip the switch than at other times. But for everyone there is some level at which their alarm system will be triggered, and the ease with which this happens is changeable. For example, the more you dread having an attack, the more anxious you become and the more likely you are to trigger one off. As you learn to understand panic, and to control the processes involved, the easier it is to reset the system at a more comfortable level.

The triggers. It appears that thoughts, and in particular *misinterpretations of normal events,* play a crucial part in triggering false alarms. The first thing that Liz noticed when she stood up to open the window was feeling dizzy and light-headed. The panic reaction followed quickly after these sensations, which, understandably, made her feel apprehensive. Talking about it later she said that the speed of her reactions (the efficiency of her alarm system) made it hard to sort out what happened first. However, with help, she was able to disentangle the thoughts and the feelings and to pick out the elements of a chain reaction: first, she felt dizzy and thought she might faint. Then, she felt apprehensive, more unsteady (grabbed the chair), and thought something must be seriously wrong. This thought frightened her, and her heart started pounding. That suggested something was definitely going wrong. Even more alarmed, she gasped for breath, her fingers tingled, the papers before her receded, and she became convinced that something terrible was happening to her. At each stage, she interpreted the changes in her feelings as "danger signals." Each time she made such an interpretation, she boosted the fear reaction into the next gear until she suffered a full-blown panic. Although at the time her thoughts were not put into words, later Liz said that these were the things that were in her mind: "I might faint"; "Something must be seriously wrong"; "Something is definitely going wrong"; and "Something terrible is going to happen to me right now."

This illustrates the standard pattern of panic. The trigger is usually a harmless or normal occurrence, which sets off the alarm system because it is interpreted as dangerous. In Liz's case the trigger was an internal one: feeling dizzy. She may have been particularly vulnerable to feeling dizzy because she was hot, had been drinking coffee, and suddenly stood up after sitting at her desk for a while. Or it may have been an effect of the stage she had reached in her menstrual cycle. But she ignored these "harmless" explanations of the dizziness and thought instead that something must be wrong. The more alarming her thoughts, the worse she felt; and the worse she felt, the more she believed she really was in serious danger—of what kind she could not be sure.

The range of triggers. There is a vast range of potential triggers for fear reactions. Whenever something is interpreted as a danger signal, the fear may escalate into panic. Catastrophic misinterpretations of harmless events are the main triggers of panic, and the fact that they cannot be explained makes them even more distressing. Imagine you were walking home alone in the dark late at night when you heard footsteps close behind you. If you thought someone was creeping up on you, your alarm system might well "blow." The same thing might happen if you narrowly missed having a car crash. You might also feel highly anxious and "panicky" before an important, challenging, and demanding event such as an interview, examination, or golf match. The threshold of panic gets nearer in many such situations. However, the difference between these examples and Liz's experience is that the trigger can be understood.

When we can understand our fear and the sensations that accompany it, it is easier to accept what is happening. But when a panic attack comes "out of the blue," or in a situation which should not be stressful or dangerous, another dimension is added to the fear reaction: it feels unreasonable, inexcusable, or unacceptable. The feeling of panic is a profoundly disturbing and undermining experience when the fear is not associated with a real threat.

In searching for a cause, or trigger, people who have panic attacks often latch on to *internal* events. They may truly believe, at the time, that they are having a heart attack; or that they will suffocate or choke, collapse or die; or that they are losing control and going mad. The evidence for these beliefs comes from their feelings: the sense of panic feels *as if* one of these things might happen. Common internal triggers of panic include missed heart beats, changes in heart rate or breathing, temperature changes (particularly feeling hot), hunger and low blood sugar, visual anomalies such as occasional blurring, tension or chest pain, the effects of having a hangover or of taking strenuous exercise. Indeed, *any* physiological change in body state can be misinterpreted. It is the misinterpretation, the conviction that a normal, harmless event is potentially dangerous, that turns these events into panic triggers.

Changes in one's state of mind can also be misinterpreted and can therefore trigger panic attacks—for example, being unable to think clearly; having alarming images, thoughts, or memories; the mind racing or suddenly going blank. Particular situations like having an argument, being criticized, or being alone can trigger panic attacks because of the fear that these events might have personally or socially disastrous outcomes. Again, it is the interpretation—the meaning of the event—that can trigger the alarm.

Nocturnal panics. Waking suddenly in a state of panic can be very frightening, but is quite a common experience. During sleep the mind does not switch off completely—it can still produce alarming dreams—and it can also respond to normal bodily changes, for example, in breathing and heart rate, that can be misinterpreted as danger signals. So it it possible to wake in fear from a nightmare or to be frightened by unusual but harmless physical sensations caused, for example, by an episode of very slow breathing or by a missed heart beat, and to wake feeling terrified or gasping for air. The speed of the alarm reaction and its capacity to operate when you are asleep reflect its efficiency—not an impending disaster. Of course, panic triggers that occur during sleep can only be guessed at, so it is important to learn how to calm yourself down and not to add alarming thoughts to the fear.

Resetting the Alarm System

WORK ON THE THOUGHTS THAT FEED THE PANIC

A panic attack is analogous to a burglar alarm which goes off when the wind rattles the window panes. The key to overcoming panic, therefore, is to reset your alarm system so that it does not go off when there is no real danger. In order to reset your alarm you need to focus on four things: the thoughts that trigger the panic; your breathing; your responses to the attack; and your general level of anxiety. But even the best set burglar alarm can go off at the wrong moment, so you need also to learn some strategies for coping with the attack itself.

Clarify your thinking. If panic follows after the misinterpretation of harmless events, then the thoughts, the misinterpretations, will be your first targets for change. The best way to sort these out is to think in detail about a recent panic attack. Try to cue yourself in by remembering what was happening and how you were feeling before the panic began. Then tell someone, or write down, all the things that happened to you, moment by moment. Pay particular attention to the meaning of the events, to the way you reacted to what happened to you, as well as to the sensations of panic. See if you can disentangle a chain reaction of thoughts and feelings in the same way as we did with Liz. Separate the thoughts, including images, suppositions, beliefs, and assumptions, from all the rest. Try to put into words the thoughts that alarmed and frightened you. Ask yourself, *"What is the worst thing that could have happened?"*

The most common difficulty people have when they try to disentangle the panic reaction is missing the trigger. The panic grabs your attention in a way that the harmless trigger does not, and until you know, and believe, that ordinary, harmless events *can* trigger panic you will not know what to look out for. Remember that mild and completely ordinary sensations, such as those of hunger, or the after-effects of too much coffee, can be sufficient to start you off, and the process of panic, once started, gathers speed alarmingly quickly.

Pinpoint the misinterpretation. After the event you know that nothing dreadful happened. It might have been embarrassing or distressing, but you are still here to tell the tale, so you know that it must have been wrong to believe that something catastrophic was going to happen. Beware of being tempted into thinking that you just had a near miss—of thinking that if you had not sat down, or kept still, or kept completely silent you really would have suffered a disaster. Remember that the panic reaction is a self-limiting process. To be effective when you need it, it has to get off to a fast start, but it also reaches a peak and then slowly subsides.

So reexamine your understanding of what happened to you. Try and pick out what it was that alarmed or frightened you, and think about it again. Take another look at it and ask yourself now whether your alarm and fear were justified. Maybe the disaster you feared (e.g., having a heart attack) would actually feel different from the sensation that set off your panic. The most useful question to ask yourself is this: *Is what happened more like a real catastrophe, or is it more like being frightened and worried about that real catastrophe?* You will find more strategies for answering these questions, and more useful questions to ask yourself, on pages 76 to 87 (see Chapter 9, Keeping things in perspective: Help from cognitive therapy).

Some of the most common misinterpretations made by people who have panic attacks are shown in the following list.

Sensations	*Interpretations*
Heart-thumping or racing	This is a heart attack. I have serious heart disease.
	I will lose control.
Breathlessness	I can't breathe. I shall choke and die.
Dizziness	I will collapse or faint.
Confusion, lack of concentration	I am going mad. I'm losing my senses.

In a panic attack, blood pressure rises. When you faint, blood pressure falls. It is therefore most unlikely that you will faint during a panic attack.

CONTROLLING YOUR BREATHING

For some people overbreathing, or hyperventilation, contributes to their panic attacks. It is natural to breathe more quickly and more deeply when afraid because this prepares the body for appropriate action. However, hyperventilation is breathing in excess of what your body needs, and this produces mildly unpleasant sensations (associated with reduced levels of carbon dioxide). These new sensations are of course ripe for misinterpretation, and so they contribute to the chain reaction. One of the paradoxical sensations produced by hyperventilation is a sensation of breathlessness, as if one was short of air rather than *over*breathing, making the person who is panicking want to gasp or gulp to get more air. This only makes the sensations stronger.

Overbreathing and its effects can be controlled by learning how to breathe calmly. You should practice this many times when you are not anxious before using it to control the symptoms of panic. You may find that it takes much practice, and many attempts, before you are able to breathe calmly when you feel panicky, so it would be sensible to practice at least twice a day for a week before using the method during a real panic attack.

Calm breathing (see also p. 108). Breathe in through your nose and out through your mouth. Put a hand on your stomach while you do this, and see if it moves up and down when you breathe. You are aiming for diaphragmatic breathing, during which your stomach rather than your chest moves. Keep practicing even if you find it difficult to breathe naturally when focusing on your breathing. Just be patient, and repeat the exercise frequently until you can do it more easily. Once you are breathing in the right way, try to slow your breathing to a calm rate. It may help to count to yourself as you breathe ("one hundred, two hundred, three hundred"). Find out how much to count for each breath by doing it when you know you are breathing calmly and using this as your standard. Breathing out usually takes a little longer than breathing in.

Breathing into a paper bag. If you are troubled by hyperventilation during panic attacks, and you have not been able to overcome this through control of your breathing, you may be helped by using a paper bag. The idea is that you need to increase the level of carbon dioxide that has fallen because of the overbreathing, and that you can do this by rebreathing the air you have just breathed out. The technique, which you should use during the panic attack, involves holding an empty paper bag (*do not use a plastic bag*) tightly over your nose and mouth with both hands. Be sure there are no holes in the bag, and breathe in and out into it for a maximum of ten breaths; the unpleasant sensations caused by overbreathing should rapidly disappear.

DEALING WITH YOUR RESPONSES TO THE PANIC ATTACK

A panic is an alarming experience, and because of this it leads to a variety of responses that can maintain the problem and make you more susceptible to further panics.

1. Anticipatory anxiety. If you are expecting to panic, the expectation works like a self-fulfilling prophecy. Try to give yourself the benefit of the doubt. If you start to feel anxious, recognize consciously that this is *anxiety*, caused by misinterpretation of something harmless. Remind yourself that the feelings of anxiety are not due to physical illness, and are not signs of imminent collapse, insanity, or any other disaster— personal, physical, or social.

2. Avoidance. It is easy to avoid facing the situations that could provoke another attack. But the trouble is that if you do avoid these situations you will undermine your confidence and you will not learn that the situations in which the panic occurred, and the sensations it provoked, are in fact harmless. Of course, heart attacks do happen, airplanes crash, and elevators get stuck between floors. But these are relatively rare events which come to seem much more likely—even quite certain—when one is frightened. It is essential to face the situations or sensations associated with your panic. You should keep going to shops, traveling alone, running upstairs, or taking other forms of exercise even if this makes you apprehensive at first. Facing the difficulties gives you the opportunity to recognize your misinterpretations and to learn how to cope with them calmly once more. In Chapters 6 and 17 we deal with these issues in more detail.

3. Self-monitoring and hypervigilance. Because panic attacks are so unpleasant, you keep on the lookout for symptoms and sensations that could be "dangerous." Too much checking is counterproductive. If you sit perfectly still and think of nothing else but your heart for 5 minutes, you will become oversensitive to what it is doing. The normal beating will feel like thumping, and you will start to notice the small irregularities, missed heart beats, and changes in strength or speed that are quite normal. The more you focus on your sensations, the more changes you will notice, and the more opportunities you will have to misinterpret them and trigger another panic. A similar thing happens if you start to worry that the person sitting next to you has head lice; your scalp will start to tingle and itch and the desire to scratch becomes overwhelming. The imagination is a powerful instrument.

4. Fear of fear. The fear of the panic attack itself— the worry that the symptoms themselves could be harmful—helps to precipitate the next attack. This is why it is important to understand that a panic attack is not dangerous, and to tell yourself this whenever you start to worry.

LOWERING YOUR GENERAL LEVEL OF ANXIETY

Panic attacks are like mountain peaks that arise from the foothills. Most people who suffer from panic attacks tend to be more generally anxious. Reducing this general level of anxiety will reduce the chance of a panic attack. So the other chapters in this book which deal with general levels of anxiety will help in overcoming panic. The chapters which are likely to be particularly helpful are:

Chapter 16   Getting the Better of Anxiety and Worry

Chapter 11   Learning to Relax

Keeping yourself physically fit by exercising regularly, eating sensibly, getting a good night's sleep, and avoiding excess caffeine and alcohol will also help to reduce the chance of panic attacks.

COPING WITH THE ATTACK ITSELF

1. Try to learn more about the sorts of things that trigger your panic. It helps greatly to catch the panic early, before the chain reaction has gathered speed and the sensations and fears have escalated.

2. Try to stay where you are. If you run away, or sit or lie down, or take other evasive action, it makes it harder to learn that the panic will peak and then subside of its own accord. You do not need to do something to prevent a disaster occurring, as no disaster will occur.

3. Once you have sorted out the kinds of interpretations that frighten you, write down a reminder to yourself that shows how mistaken they were. Try to pinpoint the mistakes you tend to make, and to remember that panic attacks, although they seem frightening, are in fact harmless. When your heart thuds, or the train slows down in the tunnel, the cause of the problem is almost certainly benign. Write these on a small card to carry with you and read if you feel at risk.

4. Instead of focusing on what is happening to you, on the things that you fear, turn your attention to something else instead. Try to distract yourself. Keep busy, move about, talk to someone, or think of something else. Set yourself a mathematical problem to force yourself to concentrate on something else. Remember the birthdays of members of your family. Try to put something other than fearsome thoughts into your mind. The mind has a limited capacity. If you occupy it with something else, it will not be able to work overtime on alarming possibilities.

THE VALUE OF MEDICATION

A variety of drugs have been used to help people who suffer from panic attacks. Some of these are tranquilizers, which help relaxation in the short term but which become less effective over time and are addictive (p. 335). Others are antidepressants—which can help with panic even in the absence of depression. Addiction is not such a problem with antidepressants, but the symptoms of panic tend to return when the drugs are stopped.

Reminders for an Emergency

You could copy the following list, or photocopy it, to carry with you in case of need.

When you feel panicky, remind yourself:

1. The bodily sensations are normal, not harmful or dangerous.
2. There is no real danger. This is only a panic attack.
3. Do not run away. The fear will start to subside quite soon.
4. Practice breathing slowly.
5. Use distraction, and pay attention to something else.
6. What was the trigger? What was the first thing you noticed?
7. What made that happen then?
8. Make use of relaxation techniques.

Add to this list any ideas that you have found helpful. In the heat of the moment it is easy to forget the things that seem obvious later.

Chapter Summary

A panic attack is a terrifying experience during which it *feels as if* something dreadful, and probably catastrophic, is about to happen to you. The sensations of panic are normal reactions to danger, triggered by something harmless such as an odd sensation or change in heart rate. Interpreting the sensations as dangerous triggers your alarm system and can also produce more false alarms. At least one in ten people have had, or will have, a panic attack.

You can build your confidence again by resetting the alarm system. There are four main ways of doing this:

1. Deal with the thoughts that trigger the panic.
2. Learn how to control your breathing.
3. Keep your reactions to the panic under control, so that they do not keep the problem going.
4. Lower your general level of anxiety.

20

◆ ◆ ◆

Depression—
The Common Cold of the Mind

The distinguished psychologist Martin Seligman described depression as "the common cold" of psychiatry. About 12% of the population experience a depression severe enough to require treatment at some time in their lives, although the vast majority of episodes of depression end within 3 to 6 months even without treatment. This does not mean that there is nothing you need do when you feel depressed. There are things you can do to help yourself, things that friends and family can do, and ways in which professionals can help. We will show you how you can overcome your low moods more quickly, how you can recognize them early in order to nip them in the bud, and how to prevent a low mood from attacking you in the first place.

Nobody likes depression, either within themselves or in those around them. The result is that we often get little support when we are depressed. Friends and relations may tell us to pull ourselves together, if not directly then in subtle ways, or they may draw away from us to avoid the icy fingers of our low mood. This usually makes us feel even worse: on top of feeling depressed we are made to feel guilty and weak. When depression has us in its thrall, we can rarely throw it off with the ease that those around us would like. There are ways of gradually freeing yourself from depression, but these will not be like "pulling yourself together." It requires more kindness, more understanding, and in a way, more indulgence.

Many parts of this book are relevant to depression. Together with anxiety, it is the main enemy of "good mood." There is no single way of releasing everyone from their depression. It will be necessary to pick and choose from the ideas in this part and throughout the book, and to select those which seem relevant and helpful. Be wary of offers of a miraculous cure. There are many ways in which you can help yourself, some of which take time and persistence: but there are no quick and easy answers.

The Experience of Depression

We all know what it is like to be sad and miserable. It is normal for moods to go up and down from day to day, and the downward sweep of these fluctuations is usually not severe enough to make you depressed. However, if you can recognize problems before they become severe, then you can deal with them more easily and more effectively. So it is important to understand what depression is, and how to recognize when these bouts of low mood are slipping into depression.

Many people mark this difference by using the term "clinical depression" to describe the low mood that goes deeper than usual, or feels as if it has got stuck and gives you no respite. This is a useful term because it helps people to take the problem seriously, to think about how to get help, and to find out what they can do to help themselves feel better. Using the term also helps them to understand that it is not their fault that they feel depressed. Blaming yourself for feeling depressed only makes the problem worse. However, the term has no absolute and clear definition. There is no way of drawing a hard and fast line between low mood and "clinical depression" because the two shade into each other by degrees, just as shades of blue, as they darken, turn into black.

It is important to get to know more about the effects of depression and to think about what the early signs of depression are for you. If you observe yourself or ask those close to you what they first notice, then you will be able to learn what you can do when you start to slip. Make note of your early signs of low mood (a written note is better than a mental note), and read this and the following chapters again as soon as you feel you are getting depressed.

Effects of Depression on the Way You Function

You may be surprised by the effects of depression on your general functioning. Depression can take away your energy and interests. It can feel like you are wading through mud: everything becomes an effort. Things which you used to do easily are now impossible to face. Sexual interest often disappears relatively early, as the mind turns inward and focuses on the self. Disturbances of all of the body's daily rhythms can be expected: appetites, activity levels, and sleep patterns may all change. Sleep is often disrupted and no longer refreshing.

The feeling of depression normally varies to some extent over the course of the day. If the depression is closely related to daily problems, then it may get steadily worse during the day, and make it particularly difficult to fall asleep, as you are racked with worry, tossing and turning with all your problems crowding in on you. But often, if the depression pervades the whole of your being, the worst time is the early morning. Then the sufferer may wake much earlier than usual, feeling in the depths of despair. Gradually as the day wears on, these feelings may start to lift.

These changes in mood emphasize the episodic nature of depression: the periods of depression tend to have their own cycles that vary immensely, and within an episode of depression mood can vary considerably. Only in the deepest stages will there be no glimpse of the possibility of a lifting of the darkness.

Some of the main signs and symptoms of depression are given in the box opposite. These illustrate how depression affects thinking, feelings, behavior, and bodily functions. Read through the list looking for the signs that are yours, but remember at the same time that normal low mood shades gradually into depression, so if you have some of these signs and symptoms, you may not be "clinically" depressed.

Not everyone who is depressed has all of these symptoms, and for some people their depression will show in other ways. The list is given here to show the range of ways depression can affect you. When you have other symptoms as well as the depressed mood, it is important to recognize that this could be part and parcel of the same thing. It is not that there are many problems. There is one problem— and that is being depressed. There is no more point in blaming yourself, or others, if things like tiredness, irritability, and tension go with the depression than there would be for blaming yourself for feeling weak and lethargic when you have a fever.

Some of the Signs and Symptoms of Depression

Thinking

Inability to concentrate
Inability to make decisions
Loss of interest in the things going on around you, and in other people
Self-criticism: "I've made a mess of everything"
Self-blame: "It's all my fault"
Self-loathing: "I'm utterly useless"
Activities seem pointless
Pessimism: "This will never change," "there's nothing I can do"
Preoccupation with problems, failures, and bad feelings
Believing you deserve to be punished
Thinking about harming yourself

Feelings

Sadness, misery, unhappiness
Feeling overwhelmed by everyday demands, feeling burdened
Low confidence and poor self-esteem
Loss of pleasure, satisfaction, and enjoyment
Apathy, numbness
Feeling disappointed, discouraged, or hopeless
Feeling unattractive, or ugly
Helplessness
Irritability, tension, anxiety, and worry
Guilt

Behavior

Reduced activity levels: doing less than usual
Everything feels like an effort
Difficulty getting out of bed in the morning
Withdrawal—from people, work, relaxations, or pleasures
Bouts of restlessness
Sighing, groaning, crying

Bodily changes

Loss of appetite, or occasionally increased appetite
Disturbed sleep, especially waking early in the morning
Loss of interest in sex
Fatigue, lack of energy, or exhaustion
Inertia: Inability to get going, dragging oneself around

Understanding Depression

There is no single simple theory that explains and accounts for all aspects of depression. Some experts favor explanations that take into account fluctuations in the biochemistry of the brain: others account for depression in terms of early childhood experiences. Countless other theories have been proposed. Some of these theories are of academic interest only given the present state of knowledge. However, there are some ideas that might be helpful to you in overcoming your depression.

DEPRESSION AS LOSS

Sigmund Freud saw depression as a reaction to *loss.* The idea that anxiety is a reaction to *threat* and depression a reaction to *loss* is one that has proved to be useful over the years. Freud was led to the idea of depression as loss through observing the similarities between mourning—the normal reaction to the loss of someone close to you—and depression. But in the case of many people, when they are depressed, there is no obvious loss in their lives. This led Freud to consider other less obvious losses that people with depression might be suffering.

The usefulness of this idea is that it helps you to think about what losses might be important in causing and sustaining the depression. The losses are not necessarily bereavements; they may be losses of status or hope or self-image. Ken became depressed after he suffered a small heart attack at the age of 52 years. He had always prided himself on his fitness. His depression was "mourning" the loss of his self-image as 100% fit and healthy.

Simon was a 65-year-old man who retired from his job as managing director of a chemical company. Eighteen months later he came to the clinic suffering from depression. He had never before been seriously depressed. The root of his depression stemmed from his loss of status. His sense of self-worth had been closely connected with his high status within the organization, and without his job he lost sight of his self-worth.

DEPRESSION AS AGGRESSION TURNED AGAINST YOURSELF

Laura was a mild-mannered woman, 35 years old, who was regularly plagued by feelings of depression. She hated arguments. When her husband shouted at the children, she would become quiet and leave the room. She described herself as the snail who would withdraw into the inner security of her shell. When she became depressed, she would say how useless and valueless she was, and how wonderful everyone around her seemed. Her mind at these times was full of thoughts about how worthless and bad she felt, and everything that happened only seemed to confirm that she was right. It appeared as though she never had a negative thought about anyone but herself. Her friends saw her as the kindest and gentlest of people, but also as something of a doormat.

Her husband really did not do his share of caring for the children, and would go out for a drink with his friends when his wife could have done with some help at home. Surely she sometimes felt angry with her husband? The answer was that she did, but it took her months of being seen regularly in the clinic before she admitted even a single negative thought about him. One day she came to the clinic feeling more than usually depressed. Her husband had been out with his friends three evenings in a row. Her therapist commented to her that this seemed unreasonable of him, and suddenly the dam burst. She launched into a tirade against her husband. Her anger surprised both herself and her therapist, and it marked the beginning of her journey out of depression. Her depression had masked her anger with her husband, concentrating the bad feelings inward on herself.

DEPRESSION AS A DARK FILTER

Being depressed is like seeing everything through a glass darkly. Whether you are thinking about yourself, the world, or the future, everything appears in the same gloomy and depressing light. "Nothing ever goes right"; "I've been such a failure"; "I can't change anything, so there's no point in trying." People call "only out of a sense of obligation." When you make a mistake, or your mind wanders, it's "because I have lost the ability to do things properly"—and it seems to have gone for good. Thinking back, your memory is filled with a trail of failures, miseries, and losses and those things you once recognized as achievements or successes, your affections and friendships, seem to count for nothing at all. The memories are tinged with the color of depression.

Once the dark filter is there, you can no longer see anything in any other light. Negative thinking and depression go together: the low mood leads to negative thoughts and memories; the negative thoughts and memories lead to lower mood, and so on, in a cycle of sustained or worsening depression (see also Chapter 9).

DEPRESSION AS A BIOCHEMICAL CHANGE IN THE BRAIN

There is a danger that you will be too hard on yourself about getting depressed. This is a question of balance. To some extent you must take responsibility for your depression. There are many ways in which you can bring it under your control, and you may even be able to control some of its causes. You certainly can change, and if you really want to overcome the depression, you must change. But nevertheless, people differ in the extent to which they are prone to get depressed. Each of us has swings in mood, and it seems likely that this is partly due to differences between us in the precise biochemical makeup within our brains. Not all of this can be under voluntary control. It is sometimes helpful to treat your depression as if it were outside your control, and to treat yourself kindly just as you would if you had a bout of flu. Treating yourself kindly in this way can help you out of the depression and stop it from taking hold.

There has been a great deal of scientific work that attempts to understand the biochemical basis of depression. The evidence suggests that some kinds of depression can be caused by an abnormally low amount of two brain chemicals: noradrenaline and serotonin. These chemicals play an important part in the transmission of nerve impulses within the brain. The medication used to overcome depression ("antidepressants") helps to correct the abnormality by increasing these chemicals. Just as insulin is used to treat diabetes (which can be caused by a lack of insulin), so antidepressants *can* be used to treat severe depression.

SEASONAL AFFECTIVE DISORDER OR SAD

Some people feel depressed regularly during the winter months. It is possible, although by no means proven, that biochemical changes caused by the sun may contribute to mood. It has been suggested that exposure to bright light, or to specific types of rays, can help to improve the mood of people affected by SAD, but the evidence on this point is not yet conclusive.

Perhaps There Are Payoffs for Your Depression

It may seem inappropriate, perhaps even cruel, to suggest that you may be gaining something from your depression. But there are advantages to depression, and if you fail to recognize these, you may get stuck when, in fact, you are able to help yourself out of the prison. A clue to the fact that you are gaining something important from the depression is that you find yourself giving reasons for not adopting the suggestions which others make. This is what Dorothy Rowe in her book *The way out of your prison* calls the "yes but ..." response. Every time someone makes a suggestion about something you might do that could help you reply, "yes, but ...," and your doubts prevent you from trying. So what possible advantages could there be to depression?

One possible advantage is that it could get you out of facing some of the things you are frightened about. Being depressed can save you from facing responsibilities which frighten you; it can save you from carrying out duties which you find stressful; it can block your need to make important changes—for example, in a relationship or at work. Your depression becomes the reason for not doing things that, for one reason or another, you do not want to do.

Although this could be one advantage of depression, in the long term it causes more problems than it solves. Failing to face these problems and responsibilities gradually deepens the depression because it leaves these problems and responsibilities unresolved.

Underlying the resistance to helping yourself out of your depression there is likely to be a *fear of change.* This is especially likely if the depression is long-standing and if this low mood has come both to determine what you can and cannot do—in effect, suffusing your relationships. In these situations you may be holding the key to unlocking yourself from the prison of your depression. This key may be an understanding of the way in which your depression is helping you to avoid certain problems, and helping to hold you back from change. You may be less helpless, and the situation may be less hopeless, than it seems when you are under the influence of depression.

Kim was twenty-seven years old, and a low mood had become the rule rather than the exception for her. She had been married for three years and as yet had no children. When she got married, Kim gave up her job as a personal assistant, because she and her husband planned to have a baby. But when, after a year, there was no sign of a pregnancy she became depressed. They decided that they should stop trying for a baby until she felt better. After another year her husband, Howard, again wanted them to try for a baby, but Kim felt that she was still too depressed. The question arose as to whether she should get a job in the meantime to help with the mortgage payments. Howard suggested that it might help with the loneliness Kim felt during the day. "Yes, but ..."

the problem was that the kind of people she was likely to meet at work would not be the kind of people who would, she thought, supply her with the support and friendship she needed.

Kim had not worked for three years and the truth was that she was frightened that she could no longer be an effective secretary. And she was frightened of trying for children, because the first year of their marriage had been so stressful every time that her period proved yet again that she was not pregnant. She was frightened to go through all that again. She had vague but deep- seated worries that they might not be able to have a baby at all, and she was nervous of what would happen if she and her husband went to a doctor to ask for help.

So, the easiest thing was to go on being depressed and not to face the worries either about work or about having a baby. The key to unlock the prison of her depression was to confront at least one of these fears (see also Chapter 6).

The Time Course of Depression

When you are feeling depressed it is important to remember that moods swing up as well as down for psychological as well as for biological reasons. It is easy to lose sight of this fact when the walls of the prison press in, or when there seems to be no light at the end of the tunnel. The speed with which the upswings start is so variable that no two people are quite the same, and the same person may experience more than one kind of pattern at different times.

Before John found his feet in the building trade he spent ten years constantly changing jobs, feeling disillusioned about the choices he had made. Each spring he suffered a renewed bout of hopelessness, feeling that things would never improve. It was as if lost opportunities were accumulating and new beginnings were leaving him behind, and he began to dread the spring in anticipation of the start of the downward spiral. This expectation became almost self-fulfilling, but it completely changed when his career started to take off. Although he still had periods of low mood, these were no longer so regular, nor were they at their worst in the spring.

Helen's pattern was completely different. She had hardly known what the word depression meant, at least from the inside, until she was 47 and the children had all left home. Then suddenly her life seemed purposeless and empty. All the activities she used to become involved in now seemed pointless. The color of life was unremittingly gray, and occasional bursts of sunlight were so brief and unpredictable that sometimes she despaired of ever getting back to her old self. In her case the first episode of depression was the worst, like a dark and unfamiliar beast that she had no idea how to harness or tame. Gradually, helped by her family and by her doctor too, her mood lifted, and the darker periods grew shorter while the lighter ones grew longer.

So do not assume, when the roller coaster has taken you down once more, that each cycle will be like the last.

A Two-Part Strategy for Change

Whatever your pattern, there are two types of steps you can take to help yourself out of your depression: *long-term strategies* (p. 265) and *short-term strategies* (p. 246).

The long-term strategies involve thinking about how to make changes in a range of aspects of your life, which will make it less likely that you become depressed. These will put in place structures in your life that will help when you are depressed. The short-term strategies help you to dig yourself out of the slough of despond.

If, at the moment, you are in one of your deep depressions, then you will not be able to work on the longer term strategies. You need to do some of the digging out before you can get to grips with the long term. But if, at the moment, your mood is not profoundly depressed, then this is a good time to work on the long term.

Read both the following chapters, and reread the early sections of this book (Parts 1 and 2). Pick those suggestions that seem the most helpful to you. It is our experience that different people are helped by different things.

Chapter Summary

It is normal for moods to swing up and down, and most people experience relatively severe depression from time to time. There is no need to feel helpless in the face of depression. There is much you can do to help yourself out of a trough.

No single theory explains everything about depression. Four main ideas can be helpful:

1. Depression is a reaction to loss.
2. Depression results from aggression turned inward.

3. Depression is seeing everything through a dark filter.
4. Depression is linked with biochemical changes in the brain.

Sometimes depression has advantages, and overcoming it may involve facing fears or difficulties. There are ways of doing this, step by step.

The cycles of depression have many different patterns, even when they afflict the same person.

Short-term strategies for change will help you out of depression. Long-term strategies will reduce your chances of future depression.

21

◆ ◆ ◆

Digging Yourself Out of Depression

"It's not easy facing up when your whole world is black.
Paint It Black, The Rolling Stones

When you feel depressed, it can seem as if you will be stuck in the dark tunnel forever. Pessimism is the order of the day, and it colors your attempts to overcome the problem, just as it colors everything else. But this is an illusion wrought by the lens through which you see the world when you are depressed. We know that moods swing up as well as down, even though we lose sight of this fact when feeling at our worst, and there are many things you can do to speed the depression on its way. There are also things you can do to make it less likely that the depression will come back to plague you. So we have divided the ways of tackling depression into two sets of strategies: things that can be done immediately (described in this chapter) and things that are more helpful in the long term (described in the following chapter). Many of these suggestions are likely to be helpful to you, but probably not all. Each person's depression is to some extent individual, so pick and choose among these ideas, making use of those which help you most. Suggestions specifically for people who are feeling deeply depressed can be found on pages 261 to 262. Turn to these pages straight away if you think this applies to you, and then turn back to read the rest of this chapter.

Short-Term Strategies:
Dealing with Depressive Episodes

There are three areas on which to work to help pull yourself out of the pit: your *activities,* your *thoughts,* and your *support systems.* Depression will try and undermine you as you help yourself to get better, and you need to be on the lookout for this. When you plan to do something helpful, the depressive thinking will throw blocks in the way of change, filling your mind with bleak thoughts: "There's no point in trying"; "It won't make any difference"; "I'm feeling too bad even to try." This kind of thinking blocks you from using your own resources and gets in the way of change.

The best way of helping yourself out of your depression is to focus on small changes that take you in the right direction. Do not look at the distant horizon; look toward the next bend in the road. Aim to put down your burden. Aim to feel *better* than you feel now, but don't think you will feel well again all at once. If you concentrate on making small changes, you will find the rest will take care of itself. To start with, adopt one strategy at a time. Work on each for about a week, before adding another, and develop ways of using them that suit yourself.

Work on Your Activities

Depression makes us sluggish and takes away our energy. It can be just as potent as the flu in making us withdraw into inactivity, and this inactivity can get in the way of the healing process. The first way of helping yourself out of the slough of despond is to involve yourself once more in daily activities.

SET YOURSELF SIMPLE TASKS

Set yourself some simple tasks which, because of your depression, you are no longer doing. Do not worry if these tasks would normally seem simple, like writing a letter or making a telephone call, doing the shopping or ironing, fetching children from school or meeting with your colleagues. The fact that you are finding them difficult means that they are difficult for you at the moment, in just the same way that someone who has the flu may find it difficult to do things which would normally be straightforward. Be kind and realistic to yourself; acknowledge that you are depressed and that this makes a difference.

Those who are not much troubled by depression can adopt a rather unhelpful attitude: "Pull yourself together. Stop moaning and groaning, and get on with it." There is an element of value in this although the fundamental attitude is completely wrong. It is right to say that pushing yourself to do some of the things you dread or feel too tired to do will help to lift the depression. It is wrong to suggest that it is simple to do this, or that failing to do so is due to weakness of will. The attitude that is most helpful is to accept that you are suffering from depression, in rather the same way that you might accept that you are suffering from a bad cold, but then try and push yourself to doing a little more than you are doing at the moment.

Do not expect to find the activities you attempt to be enjoyable, even if you really like doing them when you are well. For example, because of your depression, you may have stopped meeting with friends over lunch, which is an activity you normally enjoy. When you are depressed it will probably feel somewhat pointless, you may not want people to see you feeling low, and you may tell yourself that you will be more of a liability than an asset. It is important to do it nonetheless, because it will be a first step in helping you out of your depression. As you re-engage in the activities you have given up, the grip that the depression has over you will weaken. But this *is* a gradual process and the depression will not lift overnight.

THE DIARY OF DAILY ACTIVITIES

Keeping a diary of daily activities is especially useful when you are feeling depressed because it helps you to focus on how you are spending your time. It can be used in a variety of ways to counteract the inactivity and loss of energy that accompany depression. This is a method that was invented by Dr. Aaron Beck in the 1970s and has been successfully used by thousands of people. There are four main steps in using the Diary of Daily Activities.

Step 1: Use the diary to find out how you spend your time. Divide up your diary so that you have a slot for each hour of the waking day, and for a few days fill in everything that you do. This is one way of counteracting the sabotaging effect of depressive thinking, which, when you look back over the day, tends to make you think that you did nothing much of anything. An example of such a Diary of Daily Activities is shown on the following page.

Diary of Daily Activities.   This is an example of an activity schedule which has been partly completed.

How do you spend your time?

	Friday, Oct 3	Saturday, Oct 4	Sunday, Oct 5
7–8 A.M.	Lying in bed awake	Made tea	
8–9	Get up late—no breakfast	Back to bed	
9–10	Bus to Work	Wash, had breakfast	
10–11	Short meeting	Breakfast	
11–12	Letters and phone calls	Shopping	
12–1 P.M.	Letters and phone calls	Shopping	
1–2	Lunch in canteen	Shopping	
2–3	Started monthly report, minutes from meeting,	Sandwich lunch	
3-4	sorting out desk		
4–5	Left work early		
5–6	Watched TV news, had a drink		
6–7	Brother telephoned, started supper		
7–8	Supper		
8–9	Watched video, had a cup of coffee		
9–10	Video		
10–11	Put clothes in washer, washed up, did assorted chores		
11–12	Detective story in bed		

Step 2: Rate your activities every day for *mastery* and *pleasure*. Go back over the diary at the end of each day and focus on two aspects. First, pick out those things you found particularly difficult to do, such as dragging yourself out of bed to get ready for work. If this was difficult and yet you did it, then you must give yourself credit, even if you got to work later than usual. Give yourself a *mastery* credit rating, using a 0 to 10 scale, to acknowledge that you overcame the difficulty. The rating should be a measure of how difficult the thing is for you to do *at the moment*, not how difficult it would be if you were not depressed. A rating of 8 to 10 is for very difficult things. A rating of 4 to 7 for moderately difficult things. Anything that was difficult needs a rating even if you rate it at 1 to 3. Ordinary activities are *much* harder when you are depressed. This is not your fault. It is a fact about depression.

When you have done this, go through the diary once more, picking out those activities or times when you were engaged in something that you found relatively enjoyable or pleasurable, and give these activities a rating for *pleasure*. Again, use a 0 to 10 scale. Even small amounts of pleasure should be rated. You might write P=4 beside watching an absorbing television program or P=6 for the time you escaped from the family and soaked in the bath. Looking back from the depressed perspective, it is easy to forget completely that anything remotely pleasurable happened. Do not agonize over the precise rating for *mastery* and *pleasure*. Put down the number that seems most appropriate.

Step 3: Troubleshoot. Think about how to increase the amount of mastery and pleasure in your day. The things that you find difficult and the things that you enjoy will be particular to you. Use the questions in the following box to help you think about how to increase these things for yourself.

Questions to ask yourself about mastery:

How do I feel if I make no effort to do the things that are difficult?
How do I feel if I do them, and give myself credit for doing them?
Which are the major trouble spots in my day?
What could I do to make it easier to master these difficult times?

Questions to ask yourself about pleasure:

What things are most enjoyable at the moment?
How could I do more of these things?
What could I do to increase the amount of pleasure I have each day?
What sorts of things used to give me pleasure?
Are there things I have stopped doing that I used to enjoy?

Copy these questions out, and keep them where you can find them when you need them.

Step 4: Plan. Use the diary of daily activities to help you plan ahead. Now you have the facts in front of you, you cannot be misled by the fantasies induced by feeling depressed. Use the facts to guide your future activities. Here are five ideas about how to do this:

1. Schedule more pleasant events: big ones such as an outing with a friend, and small ones such as taking a leisurely bath. If you find this difficult, turn to Chapter 7. Depressed people sometimes think they

do not deserve to enjoy themselves, or feel guilty about doing things they enjoy, especially after a day when they have found it difficult to do as much as they used to do. Use your diary to help you sidestep the guilt trap.

2. Schedule those activities that increase your energy level, like walking to the store, cutting the grass, or taking the dog out. The sense of fatigue that goes with depression can increase the less you do, and the more you withdraw. Becoming involved in daily activities can help to energize you, and so can regular exercise.

3. Look for activities that you find relatively absorbing. Being absorbed in something can bring much relief from a depressed mood. This is worth having, and building on, even if the relief is temporary at first. If concentration is hard for you, reading may not be absorbing, but looking at a magazine or watching a video might be.

4. Look at your diary and think about how you are using your time. Some people lose their sense of direction when they become depressed, and their activities become progressively more disorganized. If this happens to you, it could help to establish a daily routine for yourself. Other people become depressed when they feel completely stuck in a rut, and they can benefit from shaking up the routine a bit, even if this sounds somewhat alarming at first.

5. Think about the balance between duties and pleasures in your daily activities. Good moods are almost certain to ebb away if you live on a diet of pure duty without pleasure. This is counterproductive because depression interferes with your ability to carry out duties while feeling better makes it easier to do them better.

Work on Your Thoughts

Valerie was a twenty-year-old university student. Like most students she did some of her work assignments better than others. She came to the clinic because of depression. She had had several bouts of low mood over the previous two years, and these episodes were getting longer and worse. When her mood was low, she always had good reasons for being depressed. For example, she would say that her work was going badly, and would cite as proof a low mark which she had received for one of her assignments. Even the holiday times were bad: when she had arranged to meet a friend for a meal before going to a film, the friend had turned up so late that there was no time to eat; and the film had been dull anyway. The examples which she gave were accurate in themselves, but they were highly selected. The fact was that she had also done some work assignments which had gone well, and she had recently enjoyed a hiking holiday during which she had made a new friend.

The story of Valerie illustrates something you may well have noticed about yourself and that has been found, in research studies, again and again: that being depressed affects what we remember. And it affects memory in a way that maintains the depressed mood. When we are depressed, we tend to remember the bad things that have happened to us, and these memories confirm our depression.

It is not only memory that is affected in this way. Our judgments are colored by our mood too. We will blame ourselves out of all proportion for things we have done wrong: one depressed patient felt that she was a wicked person because she forgot to give her son his weekly pocket money.

These psychological facts have led to what is known as the *cognitive model of depression,* which was developed by Aaron Beck in 1985.[1] What this says is that there is a very close relationship between feelings and thoughts. When we are in a low mood, our thoughts and memories will be selectively bad. This will have the effect of making our mood even darker. Our thoughts get worse and our mood follows, and so we enter a downward spiral of increasing depression.

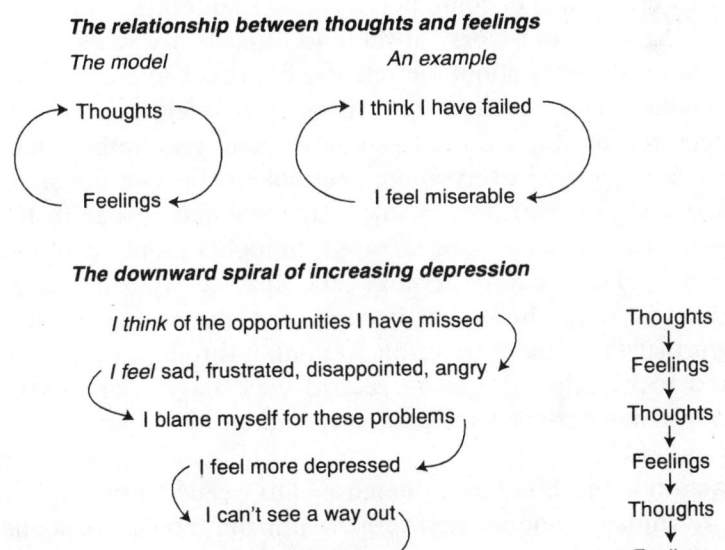

The relationship between thoughts and feelings

The model   An example

Thoughts   I think I have failed

Feelings   I feel miserable

The downward spiral of increasing depression

I think of the opportunities I have missed   Thoughts
                                                            ↓
I feel sad, frustrated, disappointed, angry   Feelings
                                                            ↓
I blame myself for these problems   Thoughts
                                                            ↓
I feel more depressed   Feelings
                                                            ↓
I can't see a way out   Thoughts
                                                            ↓
I feel hopeless   Feelings

This cognitive model leads to a particular kind of treatment called *cognitive therapy*. Essentially, this therapy concentrates on helping people to recognize and to reexamine their thoughts to get rid of the negative, depressive bias. The downward spiral is reversed by working to change the negative patterns of thinking. As thinking becomes more positive, the depression starts to lift, and produces more positive thoughts and feelings, until the downward spiral is converted into an upward spiral.

One of the most valuable aspects of cognitive therapy is that you can learn how to do it yourself. The techniques of cognitive therapy are useful in helping you to achieve a good mood whether you are climbing out of depression, trying to overcome anxiety, or dealing with a mixture of emotions. They provide some of the most useful skills for helping to develop and maintain a good mood. In Chapter 9 we explain how you can make use of the method of cognitive therapy to control your negative thinking patterns. If you want to use this method, you should read Chapter 9 after you have read this one. In this chapter we focus on its use for depression, but ideas in both these chapters will be helpful to you.

Applying Cognitive Therapy to Depression

BREAKING UP PATTERNS OF NEGATIVE THINKING

Ella's depression had become pervasive. She felt on the verge of tears most of the time, and worse at the end of each day when she sat at home, alone, thinking about the relationship that had gone wrong and all the failures and mistakes she had made at work that day. She had also been too tired to bother to shop, so there was nothing much to eat in her home, and everywhere she looked she saw the signs that she had lost her grip. The whole place seemed to her to be in a mess—just like her life. The unhappy thoughts churned round and round in her head, leaving her no peace. Ella was stuck in a stream of negative thinking. The longer it continued, the worse she felt. She thought that she "ought to be able to think it through," even though it seemed to her that the same record was playing endlessly, and painfully, inside her head and getting absolutely nowhere.

Distraction is the first line of defense. Ella needed a break from her negative thinking. She needed to interrupt the internal dialogue and to clear a small bit of mental space, and the easiest, quickest way to do this is to use distraction. Fill the mind with something else, and give yourself a rest from dwelling on unhappy thoughts. This will provide some respite from the ruminative pattern, and lift your mood just enough to allow you to start problem-solving instead.

Ella turned on the television. She made herself listen to a program for a short while and then she realized she was thirsty. She made a cup of tea and sat down to drink it. She looked around at all the papers in the room, and wondered how many there were: newspapers, cards, used envelopes, unanswered letters, a shopping list, magazines, and so on. She suddenly realized that she was no longer listening to the television, or to the thoughts about the things that were making her so depressed, but instead was wondering if she could find something to put all the rubbish in.

There are many ways of distracting yourself. Here are five ways that others have found useful:

1. *Try sensory awareness exercises.* What can you see, or hear, or feel, at the moment? Pay attention carefully to each of the senses in turn.
2. *Describe an object.* This is a way of forcing your attention onto the outside world. Pick an object you can see such as a window or a table. Imagine that your life depended on being able to describe it precisely, in every possible detail, to someone else. Test yourself in as many ways as you can think of (draw it, write down a description, memorize it, and so on).
3. *Involve yourself in an activity.* Choose something undemanding but as absorbing as you can manage. Reading may be too hard to concentrate on if you feel very depressed, so a physical activity like tidying up, knitting, or gardening may be easier. Stop and think: what activities might be the right ones for you?
4. *Recite a poem or sing a song to yourself.* Think of nursery rhymes, or poems you learned in school, or jingles from advertisements, or Christmas carols. Remember songs you enjoyed with friends or songs from a show you have seen. Concentrate on trying to remember the words.
5. *Play counting games.* Count things you can see, or count backwards, or add serial 7s, or say multiplication tables, or remember telephone numbers.

What happened to Ella when she first distracted herself by turning on the television reflects a common pattern. First, she tried to listen to what was being said, but could not concentrate very well. Nevertheless, the TV interrupted her thinking pattern just enough for other things to come to her attention: she noticed she was thirsty. This helped her into a more active mode: she made a cup of tea. Then, as she sat down with it, still not really concentrating on much, she found herself wondering about how to clear up the mess. She was starting to solve problems. Becoming aware of the way in which this process works helped Ella to use it more often, and more effectively.

SWATTING THE NATs

Negative Automatic Thoughts (or NATs) buzz around inside the head when you feel low: "It's pointless"; "I'm no good"; "Why bother?" The bites from these NATs can depress your mood even more. It's important to swat these NATs, and strategies for dealing with them are described in more detail on pages 74 to 87. An illustration is given here to show how they can be used when you are feeling depressed.

Step 1: Identifying problematic thoughts. Ella did not find this exercise easy. She was so immersed in her distress that she could not see things clearly. Besides, everything seemed so obviously bad to her that she could not see the point of trying to look for any other points of view. Nevertheless, she asked herself the *"Key Questions"* on page 78:

- What went through my mind at the time?
- How am I seeing things now?
- What is it about this that matters to me?
- What does this situation mean to me?
- Or what does it mean about me?

This is what she wrote on her Thought Record.

Situation: Coming into the flat after a day at work

Feelings: Hopeless and sad

Thoughts: It's all my fault. There's nothing I can do about it. My whole life is a mess.

Step 2: Looking for other perspectives. Ella decided she would try filling out an "Alternative Diary" form (p. 82), and wrote each thought down separately. She then asked herself, "Is there another way of seeing things?" She worked on the last thought first, as this seemed to her to be the central one. This is what she wrote:

Automatic thought: My whole life is a mess.

Alternative points of view: I've still got a job. It's only been like this since the relationship broke up, so I must have been able to hold things together before this. Maybe it's not surprising to feel sad right now, but that doesn't mean the feelings won't ever change. There's certainly a mess in the flat, and I'm not working well, and I've lost the person I cared about (the facts of the case), but I've still got friends and my music. This certainly is a rough patch, but everyone has rough patches from time to time. If I really take a look at my *whole* life I can see that I am probably exaggerating how bad this is.

When doing this exercise Ella had many doubts and queries. In particular, she found that for every new way of thinking she could also find some reasons for discounting it: that giveaway phrase "Yes, but ..." kept jumping into her mind. "Yes, but none of that really matters. What matters is how I feel right now." When this happens it is important not to get sidetracked. Write down the reservation, or "yes, but," and come back to it later in exactly the same way. After all, it is only another NAT, or automatic thought, and can be reexamined using the same strategy.

Learning how to reexamine *Negative Automatic Thoughts*— the NATs—when you are depressed is difficult. We recommend that you practice these skills using the two other thoughts that Ella identified: "It's all my fault" and "There's nothing I can do about it." It is often easier to work out where other people are going wrong than to see one's own mistakes and blind spots, so this is an especially useful exercise if you are feeling low.

The *key questions* to ask yourself are in the following box.

Key Questions

Questions about thoughts:

What other points of view are there? How would someone else think about this? How else could I think about it? How would I think about this if I were feeling better?

Questions about reality:

What are the facts of the case? How can I find out which way of thinking fits the facts best? What is the evidence?

Questions about crooked thinking:

Could I be making a mistake in the way I am thinking? Am I thinking straight? Am I using one of the thirteen kinds of crooked thinking (pp. 78–80)? Am I pressurizing myself? Or using the language of the extremist?

Questions about coping:

What is the worst that could happen? How bad is this going to get? What can I do when that happens? How can I get help?

Be specific. Depressed people tend to think in a rather vague and general way, as if the shaded, depressed view of the world obscured their detailed vision. It is therefore particularly helpful to focus on specific facts of the case when looking for alternative points of view. For example, instead of saying "I've still got friends", name the people with whom you are friendly, and think of specific things that you have done together in better times, or specific plans that you can make with them for the future.

If you write the key questions for identifying problematic thoughts (p. 78) and for reexamining NATs (p. 81) on opposite sides of a small card (or photocopy pp. 87–88 from Chapter 9), you can keep them at hand for whenever you need them. Answers to the key questions help you keep in touch with the facts, and to avoid some of the distorted perspectives of depressed thinking (see pp. 78–87). The most likely mistake that the depressed person is making is mistaking feelings for facts: supposing that because it feels this bad, everything really is this bad. Bit by bit, start to gather all the information together so that you can take a new look at it.

LOOKING AT BELIEFS AND ATTITUDES—THE HALL OF MIRRORS

Our attitudes to ourselves tend to be distorted, but the distortion is not all in one direction. When Brittany, age 6, went to the fair she visited the *Hall of Mirrors,* and she was fascinated by the different ways in which her body was distorted. In one mirror she looked tall and thin; in another short and fat. Other mirrors, however, distorted some parts of her body in one way and others in another way. Her head was made tall and thin; her chest long and wide; and her legs shrunk until her feet seemed almost to spring directly from her hips.

The distorted beliefs we have of ourselves can be very similar. Most of us operate in (at least) two ways: we can be extraordinarily critical of ourselves, or we can give ourselves outrageous leniency. We may do first one and then the other, even though they seem contradictory. We may put our own interests above those of others, and yet place our self-worth well beneath that of others. Indeed, perhaps one distorted view springs from the other. Because of the deep fear that we are inferior to others, we might try and boost our self-image through bragging and attempting to get the better of others.

At the root of depression there is usually a distorted view of oneself. To help you to see yourself more clearly, it may be helpful to think about what you would say about yourself if you were on the outside looking in: as if you could be another person and take a thoroughly objective look at yourself. When Ella did this, she uncovered one of her unwritten assumptions: "I can't be happy if I'm on my own—if I do not have a close relationship."

Here are some other common beliefs: "I must do well at everything I take on"; "Unless I am doing something useful my whole life is worthless"; "I'm no good unless people like me"; "If someone rejects me, it's because I'm not good enough." Beliefs such as these can be questioned and reexamined using the same methods as those used for examining automatic thoughts (pp. 80–87).

Even though it is difficult, it is important that you try to look at yourself with compassion and objectivity. Particularly when depressed, we are inclined to be excessively hard on ourselves. We whip ourselves, saying how useless and worthless we are. Take a *compassionate* view toward yourself, as you would towards someone else, and you will find it easier to develop a sense of ultimate trust in yourself.

THE BLACK DOG: TAMING THE BEAST BY GIVING IT A LABEL

Winston Churchill suffered from recurrent, short-lived depressions. He gave them a name: *the black dog,* a name that had been used by Samuel Johnson before him, and has been used by many others since. Labeling the depression helped him to cope with it and to accept it, knowing that in due course it would go away. Such labeling helps to domesticate the depression so that it becomes, if not a friend, at least an enemy you know and for which, perhaps, you even feel some affection.

When relatively short-lived, recurrent depressions attack you, it may be best to wall them off—to limit or contain them. Then they will take the shortest course. Say to yourself, "Ah, it's my depression again. It will pass away soon as it always does; I've just got to keep going." This is especially helpful for people who tend to get depressed about getting depressed, which is a very common problem and adds insult to injury.

A similar technique is used in the Buddhist method of mindful meditation. Such meditation encourages continual awareness of the present. Your moods and feelings are recognized, acknowledged, and accepted. In mindful meditation your feelings of depression would be quietly acknowledged. It would be as if you nodded acquaintance with your feelings, but your being would not be absorbed by the depression, or by regrets about the past or hopelessness about the future. Rather than being wholly dominated by depression, the aim is to become aware of depression but from a stance which is at one remove, and which helps to keep present feelings in perspective.

Use Your Support Systems

George Brown and Tirrel Harris[2] carried out an important study into the causes of depression in women. They studied almost 1,000 women and looked carefully at their mood and some of the factors which might affect it. A major finding was that a close confiding relationship was the single most effective protection against depression. This central finding probably applies as much to men as to women.

If there is someone with whom you can talk about how you are feeling, then do not shy away from letting them know. There are many things that make it difficult to tell someone else you feel depressed—such as feeling embarrassed or worried about bothering them; feeling guilty, as if being depressed was your fault and a sign of weakness; and living in a world in which talking about yourself, and especially about your feelings, is treated as if it were taboo. Nevertheless, "a friend in need is a friend indeed," and if you are depressed, you are in need. A friend can help you, in many ways, to overcome the depression. It is, first of all, very helpful just to have the support: to know that there is someone who realizes how you are feeling and who cares. Talking with a friend also gives you the chance to think about why you are depressed and about what problems in your life have got you down. The friend can help you to find ways of tackling these problems. A friend can also provide you with a different and, probably at the moment, a less distorted perspective, both on your problems and on your views of yourself. A friend can help to encourage you in carrying out the activities that you have chosen to do.

One of the ways which, as therapists, we help people who are depressed is not through any arcane skill but, by being essentially a friend—a professional rather than a personal friend—but nevertheless a friend. And the two things we do which are of particular value are to be a sounding board—to listen and reflect various perspectives—and to be someone to whom our client "reports back." Do not underestimate the power of this reporting back. When a patient decides, for example, to start meeting friends over lunch once more, something she stopped doing when she became depressed, the chance of her carrying this through is greatly enhanced if she knows that she will be reporting back to her therapist on how she got on.

Friends can fulfill this role as long as they know that you want them to help in this way. Choose one or two friends whom you think are in the best position to help you. This may include your special partner, if you have one, but sometimes a partner is too close to your problems, and perhaps too much a part of them, to be the ideal friend to help you out of your depression. When you have decided who can help you best, let them know that you are depressed and discuss how you feel, and how you see the problems, as freely as you feel able. It might be a good idea to ask them to read this chapter, including the section below (p. 262) "Supporting a friend who is depressed." But do respect your friend's position. While a good friend will want to help you, your depression may be a burden and the person you would like to have support from may not be able to give you as much support as you would like. If your friends make it clear that this is the case, then you need to respect the limits that they want to place on how much support they give you.

Thoughts of Harming Yourself

When depressed you may have thoughts of harming yourself. This is quite common. It does not mean that you are "going mad"; but you do need to take the thoughts seriously. *Tell someone else about your thoughts:* a friend, or your doctor. Do *not* be afraid of talking these thoughts over with someone else. Many people are reluctant to mention them for fear that others will disapprove, or fail to understand, or for fear that talking about them may actually make it easier to put them into effect. In fact, talking about thoughts of harming yourself usually brings some relief.

If you feel like putting these into effect, or making plans, then seek help at once, and promise yourself that at any time when you really do feel at risk of harming yourself, you will immediately talk to someone about how you feel.

If the thoughts are vaguer—more a feeling that life and its problems are too much for you at present—try to clarify them. The following three questions might help you to do this:

- What would prevent me from putting any plans into effect?
- What would I like to be able to do, supposing that the depression lifts?
- Which of my problems are so bad that no solution could ever be found?

You may find it helpful to discuss these questions with someone else. Throughout these low periods, hang on to the fact that it is your depression that is talking, and your depression will eventually lift.

When to See Your Doctor

Do not be shy of sharing your feelings with others whom you trust, and sometimes you will find it helpful to discuss these feelings with your doctor. If you feel you are seriously depressed, or have regular bouts of depression, and you would like to talk about how you are with your doctor, then do not hesitate to do so: you have nothing to lose and may gain a lot. To some extent this depends on how you feel, the other supports that you have, and the relationship you have with your doctor. But there are times when it is wise to see your doctor even if your first inclination is not to go. Professional help and medication can sometimes be of great benefit. Here are some guidelines that can help you decide whether it is time to see a doctor:

1. If you are so profoundly depressed that it is seriously interfering with your work or family life.

2. If those close to you think that you should see your doctor. It is a feature of depression that you cannot judge objectively how you are. If those around you are sufficiently worried to think that you might be helped by a professional, then they are more likely to be right than you are at the moment.

3. If you are consistently waking more than an hour earlier than usual and feeling particularly miserable at that time. Disturbances in physiological functioning (e.g., sleep and appetite) are good indications that medication might help you.

4. See a doctor if you are having some bizarre experiences, such as hearing voices when there is no one there.

5. If you are seriously considering harming yourself or doing away with yourself, see a doctor immediately.

6. If your mood swings both up and down, so that in addition to becoming very depressed you sometimes become very "high," doing things which others consider excessively extravagant, and which when your mood is normal you realize were excessive, it is important to see a doctor. This is called "manic-depressive" illness, or "bipolar depression," because it has two poles: a depressed, underactive pole and a manic, overactive pole. Medications can be particularly useful in helping to prevent both the deep depression and the excessive highs.

Your doctor may prescribe antidepressant medication for you, and this is very likely to be helpful. It is also useful to think of yourself as working at the problem from two angles: the biochemical one, which is helped by taking medication, and the psychological one, which is helped by working on your activities, your thoughts, and your support systems. The two approaches go well hand in hand. You should not think that, because you have approached the problem in one way, the other way will not also be helpful. Combined methods of treatment for depression can be very effective.

Deep Depression

If you are currently suffering a deep depression, you may not be able to make use of all of the techniques described. They may be too complex for you at the moment. The purpose of this section is to help you focus on the essentials. When you are a little better, read or reread this chapter and make use of the more complex techniques. It is a part of depression to feel hopeless about the future. That means that severely depressed people feel that they will never get better. If this is how you feel at the moment, then *hold onto the fact that your depression will eventually lift.* If you are in one of the troughs, you will in time come out of it. We do not want to trivialize the depression in any way, and we do not underestimate the utter despair that you may feel. Glib reassurance is banal; but time is a healer.

If you are currently imprisoned within a deep depression, there are several things you can do to help yourself.

- *Seek professional help.* Trying to defeat the depression on your own may be taking on too much. Medication and professional therapy are likely to be of immense value.
- *Do simple things and give yourself credit.* If you are severely depressed, nothing that you do at the moment will be pleasurable. Indeed, you are probably finding it a struggle to do almost anything. Even the simple chores of everyday life—preparing meals, getting washed and dressed, getting up in the morning— can seem like hard work. This is all part of the depression. Do not blame yourself for these feelings. Instead, *set yourself simple tasks and give yourself credit when you do them.* This is the stage to start using a diary of daily activities (p. 247).
- *Reduce tasks to manageable proportions.* If you approach the things you have set yourself to do with the same standards that you would use when feeling good, you will run the risk of failing at your set task, and blame yourself for not being able to function in the way that you usually would. But would you blame some-

one with bronchitis for not being able to sing a song? When very depressed, it can feel as if you are shouldering all the burdens of the world. Everything is an effort. Everything takes more time and an amount of energy far greater than seems available. No wonder you think: "I won't be able to do this"—and are tempted to give up trying. Set yourself much smaller tasks instead. What matters is that you do *something,* rather than nothing. Set your objectives low enough to be sure you can succeed.

- *Do not try to do too much.* To some extent you must let yourself, as it were, be carried along by the depression and float along with it until you reach shallower waters. If you try too hard to defeat it, you will become dismayed and will blame yourself for what you will then see as your failure. This will only make you feel worse about yourself and deepen the depression. Deep depression is like quicksand: if you struggle too much, you will only dig yourself in further.

Supporting a Friend Who Is Depressed

If a close friend is suffering with depression, then your support, if given in the right way, can be particularly helpful. If that friend is very close, your partner for example, you may be finding it especially difficult. Living close to a depressed person engenders ambiguous and complex feelings. Part of you will feel sympathy and a desire to help; part of you is likely to feel frustrated and irritated. You may make what seem perfectly sensible and straightforward suggestions which are resisted on what seem to be totally inadequate grounds, and you may get your head bitten off for trying to be helpful. Yet despite this, you can see that your friend is deeply unhappy and needs help and support.

When helping someone else, you may yourself need some support: someone with whom you can talk. But make sure that you do not break any confidences. Depressed people who open up to others will need to know that they can talk about things that they would not like anyone else to know.

One of the most difficult things in trying to help is that it is easy to become increasingly unsympathetic. Depressed friends and relatives may seem alternately pathetic and unreasonably irritable. They may be quite hard to be with, different from their normal selves and even quite unlikeable. It is because of this that it is vitally important to understand the effects of depression, and the differences in personality that seem to accompany it. Hang onto the fact that, underneath the mask of depression, people you have known and liked remain unchanged. Sooner or later, the depression will pass and they will once again return to their former selves.

You may have been trying to help but finding that all your help appears to be rejected. What, you may be wondering, is the point of giving support? This is when it is important to know just how valuable is the fact that you are there, that despite the apparent rejection of all your attempts to help, you have not, emotionally, run away. It may not be obvious now, but in the long run the support you are giving by simply tolerating the person when depressed is providing the framework within which recovery can grow. Try not to overestimate the speed of recovery, even when you can see clearly that it has started. There will be intermittent breaks in the clouds and black patches to go through before the sky clears again.

Encourage your friend to read this and the previous chapter, if they have not already done so, and possibly the books recommended in Further Reading at the end of the book. This will help you both to clarify your role, and will give your friend some ideas about what action to take. The two main ways in which you can help, in addition to simply being there and not rejecting your friend, are: to act as a sounding board; and to act as a listener to whom your friend can report.

You cannot expect to be an expert counselor, but you can use some of the well-known principles of counseling. We have used the words "sounding board" to emphasize one of the important points: your role is not to solve other people's problems for them; not, on the whole, to give advice. Your role is to listen, and to reflect honestly on what you have understood. It is to help clarify what has been said, to help establish the various options. Try and help people when they are depressed to decide what specific activities they want to set themselves and then act as someone to whom they can bring a progress report. Give encouragement to carry out these activities. However, it is not your role to use persuasion. Often when trying to help someone who is depressed, one feels helpless because one cannot solve the problems. But solving problems is *their* responsibility. Your role is to act as a sounding board. Do not think that you are failing because you are not solving problems. Indeed, if you imposed your solutions, it would not work in the long term.

Do not try and force people to talk to you. Everyone has a right to privacy and a right not to tell, just as you too have the right not to be used as a support. If you are finding that trying to give support is too painful, or if you are not able to give it, for whatever reason, then you have the right to say so.

Related Chapters in This Book

Chapter 9   Keeping Things in Perspective. It is important to read this as well if you are working on your thoughts.

Chapter 10   Building Self-Confidence and Self-Esteem. Many people who are depressed think badly about themselves and can be helped by learning how to build up their confidence and self-esteem.

Chapter 16   Getting the Better of Anxiety and Worry. Sometimes anxiety and depression go together, and sometimes when depression lifts, it leaves you feeling worried about how to take up the reigns again, so this chapter may also be helpful.

Chapter Summary

When you feel depressed, hold onto the idea that moods swing up as well as down, and focus on the short-term strategies that can make you feel better:

1. *Work on your activities.* Keeping active is helpful, even though it is harder to do when you are depressed.
2. *Work on your thoughts.* Depressed thinking keeps you stuck. Learning how to look at things differently helps you to get moving again.
3. *Work on your support systems.* Try not to be reluctant to ask others for help and support. Depression is so common that many of them will understand.

If you feel seriously depressed, start working on your activities first. The chapter also contains important guidelines concerning:

1. Thoughts of harming yourself
2. When to see your doctor
3. Deep depression
4. Supporting a friend who is depressed

22

♦ ♦ ♦

How to Become Less Vulnerable
to Depression

*The Fundamental Importance
of Long-Term Strategies*

It is normal and natural to miss people when they are not there, or occasionally to feel melancholy or sad. Experiencing the full range of emotions is a normal part of life. People often use the word "depression" to describe these sad episodes, but serious depression, as we explain in Chapter 20, is different. It weighs you down and diverts you from the mainstream of life. The aims of this chapter are to help you to reduce the depth of your depressive swings, and to help to protect you from serious depression. If at the moment you are in a seriously depressive phase, then you need to focus on helping to restore yourself to normal (Chapter 21). But it is unwise to ignore your depression during the good periods because this is precisely when you can work most effectively on those things that make you vulnerable to further episodes.

Low mood has both *physical* and *psychological* causes, and for most people there will be several contributory causes of each type. These can add up, so tackle any which can be affected, even those which you do not think are of major importance. As with stress, it can be the straw that breaks the camel's back. There are *five strategies* that help to prevent future depression.

Strategy 1: Attend to the Basics of Sleep, Diet, and Exercise

Do not ignore the fundamental physiological factors that can contribute to low mood. If you sleep badly, fail to eat well, and allow yourself to fall into poor shape physically, you become more susceptible to low mood because daily activities drain away your resources and more quickly get you down. Poor *sleep* is a common consequence of low mood, but it can also contribute to making you vulnerable. During periods of depression there may be little that you can do about poor sleep directly: you may need to focus instead on overcoming the depression. But at times when your mood is relatively good, make sure that you develop sensible sleeping habits. In Chapter 24 we describe many ways in which you can improve your sleep.

Be careful, too, about *alcohol*. This can be a particular problem for those who are prone to depression. In the short term alcohol can help to hide problems and worries. The relaxation and warm glow of confidence which alcohol can activate are, however, skin deep. Below the surface the problems lie, developing and growing in the dark. Eventually they burst forth, bringing with them a depression that is deeper and more intractable than it would otherwise have been. If alcohol could be a problem for you, turn to Chapter 26.

Excessive *dieting* can make you irritable, depressed, tired, and weak. It is common, in our culture, for women to feel better about themselves when they feel happy about their weight and shape, and are able to control what they eat. For some, however, self-esteem can become much too closely bound up with physical appearance and with diet. If this is the case for you, then read Chapter 25.

Exercise protects against episodes of depression and can help to build up physical stamina and energy. It can also temporarily lift your mood and provide a brief respite from depression.

Strategy 2: Clarify Your Values and Goals

If you are prone to depression, then you need to look at your goals and values and at how you spend your time. One of the major reasons for recurrent low mood is that there is a mismatch between what you really value and what you do. Instead of this mismatch making itself obvious, it becomes manifest as general depression.

Derek was apparently very successful. He had done well in his university studies, and after his degree he trained as an investment advisor, working in the City of London. He earned a great deal of money, but still he suffered from recurrent depression. He sought professional help. During the therapy it became clear that he did not value the kind of success he had attained. He castigated himself for being selfish and wanted to feel that his work was more directly of benefit to others. That is what he valued. He started to look for other jobs. A position was advertised which would make use of his financial skills working for a housing association. Although the salary was very much less than he was making in the City, he applied for the job because he was convinced that happiness in his work depended on doing work which he valued. He got the job, and two years later, although his moods continued to go up and down, he did not experience anything like the depth of depression that had previously been his frequent experience.

You might think that Derek was lucky, and also that he had many advantages that others do not have, which, of course, is true. But thinking about your values if you are stuck and feeling depressed is not just a luxury. Janet was working as an office cleaner when she found herself in a similar situation. What she valued in her work was the opportunity to meet people and to talk to them, but arriving as others left, to work on her own made her feel like a drudge at work as well as at home. She found a new job at a local bakery which suited her much better, and as her depression lifted her confidence and self-esteem grew.

If you have not yet written out your own personal statement of values and goals (described on p. 34 in Chapter 5), we recommend that you do this. It will help you to evaluate whether what you are doing in your work and in your personal life is in tune with your values, and if it is not, then it may help you to work out which sorts of changes are likely to help you move away from depression.

Strategy 3: Put Pleasures into Life

Depression goes hand in hand with low self-esteem and even self-loathing. People prone to depression are often kind, thoughtful, and altruistic but yet do not value themselves highly, and they frequently downgrade themselves by denying themselves pleasures. Even when their mood is normal, they often feel that they do not deserve to do enjoyable things. They are not worth it, and other people's needs always come first.

Some parents can be like this. They put their children's needs so much above their own that they give themselves no personal time and space. Ron and Miriam used to enjoy going out once a week dancing and meeting with a couple of friends for a drink. Then they had a baby girl. For three years they never had an evening out together. They could have arranged babysitting, at least occasionally. Ron went out to work so he, at least, had some space for himself away from his family. But Miriam felt that it would be wrong to go out and enjoy herself in case her daughter woke up while she was out and "needed" her. She became increasingly miserable and irritable, and her relationship with Ron became strained. At this point Miriam saw her doctor. He made time to talk with them both and to discuss their situation. It rapidly became clear to them all that Ron and Miriam had lost the time alone with each other that they used to enjoy before their daughter was born. They agreed to go out together once a month, and the space that this gave them greatly improved both her mood and their relationship. This small change in their routine had enormous impact on the lives of the whole family.

Even if at the moment you do not think that you deserve to enjoy yourself, make sure that you do things that you like doing. However busy you are, you need to make some time to indulge yourself: a little of what you fancy does you good. Present pleasure will help to protect you from future depression. Indeed, putting pleasures into life is one of the basic strategies for good mood (Chapter 7).

Strategy 4: Do Not Put All Your Eggs in One Basket

Nothing goes well all the time. Everyone experiences occasions when work, or some aspect of work, is going badly—when there are difficulties with close relationships, when a hobby ceases to be fulfilling, or when life seems to be full of problems. If all our self-esteem, therefore, is bound up in just one aspect of our lives there will be times when we become very vulnerable. Think about your own depression. Is it closely bound up with how things are going in just one aspect of your life? Is it, for example, when your work seems to be going badly that your mood becomes low? If the pattern of your depression suggests a close connection with just one part of your life, then it is likely that you have too many eggs in this one basket.

In order to protect yourself from such dependency, it is wise to have several parts to your life: friends, family, work, hobbies and interests, both inside and outside the home, both social and solitary. Each part contributes to your self-esteem. At those times when one part of your life does not seem to be going well, you can gain comfort and support from other parts.

Strategy 5: Build Up Supportive Relationships

Being able to confide in someone else, whether a relative, partner, or friend, is one of the most important forms of protection from becoming depressed when something bad happens. If you do not have a close supporting relationship, or if your friends do not provide you with the kind of emotional support which helps to protect you from depression, then it will be useful to look at how you could begin to build up such supports.

Building up supportive relationships takes time and effort. It does not happen overnight, and when it seems difficult, it helps to remember it can be done at any stage of life and there are always many steps on the way. Here are some examples of how you can get started.

Step 1: Meeting new people. Seek out places where you will come across people with similar interests or hobbies. Make contact with neighbors. Get involved with local political or voluntary groups. Join a club.

Step 2: Building a friendship. Friendships flourish on shared experience, especially shared activities and shared pleasures. Think of things you can do together with new friends.

Step 3: Consolidating a friendship. Keep in touch. Regular contact helps, and so does remembering about other people's concerns and becoming a good listener as well as a good talker (see Chapter 13).

Step 4: Keeping your friendships in good working order. Look for ways of showing you care—in good times as well as bad. Do what you can when others are in trouble. Tolerate their moments of bad temper or silence.

Step 4: Using your friendships for support. Do not run away from people when you are depressed. Try to keep in contact even if you feel less outgoing than at other times or embarrassed about imposing yourself on them. Low moments are so common that many other people will know how you feel. Many different kinds of relationships, not just intimate ones, can be supportive.

A supportive relationship must not be a smothering one. We need our own space, our own independence and autonomy, as well as support. Think about your key relationships. Are any "too supportive," giving you too little of your own independent time? If so, you need to negotiate a change (Chapter 15) in order to find the best balance between support and independence. A lack of independence can be a particular problem for elderly people, especially when they are unwell and forced to depend on others. In these circumstances, retrieving as much independence and autonomy as possible may be the best protection against future depression. If you are trying to help a close friend in this situation, be careful not to do too much, and not to take over. Listen and try to understand, but continue to foster a sense of autonomy and a feeling of being in control.

Work on these five strategies and you will protect yourself from future depression.

Chapter Summary

If you deal with some of the contributory causes of depression *in between bouts of low mood,* you can do much to help prevent future depressions.

1. Attend to the basics of sleep, diet, and exercise. Do not ignore your body just because the problem is with your mood. The two are inextricably entwined.
2. Clarify your values and goals. Think about the direction your life is taking overall.
3. Put pleasures into life. Everyone deserves pleasures—in fact, no one can function well without them.
4. Do not put all your eggs in one basket. This leaves you vulnerable when something (inevitably) goes wrong.
5. Build up supportive relationships. They provide both a protection and a support.

PART FIVE

◆ ◆ ◆

Mind and Body

How the mind and body work together is a question to which no one has found a complete answer, but one thing is clear: the mind affects the body and the body affects the mind. In order to keep fit mentally, therefore, you need to attend to your body. The purpose of this section is to help you to overcome problems that affect your body, such as difficulties with sleeping, eating, drinking, smoking, or relying on tranquilizers. Many of these problems involve bad habits, so the first chapter on breaking habits is a key to the others. Here are the main themes that recur throughout these chapters:

1. *Make a definite decision to change.*
2. *Be systematic in the way you go about it.*
3. *Tackle other problems as well.*
   If your bad habit makes you feel (temporarily) better, it is easy to lose sight of how short-lived these feelings are. There are longer lasting solutions to problems such as worry, shyness, loneliness, and unhappiness.

General Strategy

Read the chapter on breaking habits first, then choose which chapter you want to work on. Read it through once, then go back to the beginning and start to take STEPs.

S: Select an idea and work out how it applies to you.

T: Try it out.

E: Evaluate how it went (keep a diary in your notebook).

P: Persist until you feel better.

Work at your own pace, without hurrying. The right pace is the one that works for you. Buy yourself a notebook in which to keep track.

If you have not already done so, read Part Two of the book (*The seven basic skills*). Several of the skills will help you deal with physical problems—provided you do not try to work on too many things at once.

23

♦ ♦ ♦

Breaking Habits and Stopping Smoking

Habits are automatic routines of behavior that are repeated regularly, without thinking, and most of them are very useful. Without them you would not be able to do things nearly so efficiently. If you had consciously to direct and control every action each time you dressed in the morning, or drove a car, it would take as much effort as it did when you learned to do these things in the first place. Most complex skills—for example, writing or playing a musical instrument—require the development of well-learned habits. Once you can rely on your fingers to play the tune, you can turn your attention to more important things, like what the conductor is doing, and the sounds coming from the rest of the orchestra. The more you can do automatically, the more attention you will have left over for other more important and interesting things. Habits, therefore, are very useful to you. However, most of us also develop *bad* habits—habits which can be harmful or unpleasant, like scratching or nail biting; habits which irritate others, like criticizing or nagging, or habits which get in the way of other things we want to do, like losing things. The purpose of this chapter is to explain how to break the habits which you want to get rid of.

The Varieties of Habits

There are many different kinds of habit which you may want to break or change.

SO-CALLED "BAD" HABITS

These include bad physical habits such as nail biting, thumb sucking, pulling or plucking out hair, scratching, and so on, which have the potential for doing harm to the person who has them. They also include bad interpersonal, social, and emotional habits like interrupting, "comfort" eating, leaving your shoes where others fall over them, saying "no" without thinking to the demands of the children, crying when criticized, or hitting out before you get hit. These habits can potentially damage your relationships.

ROUTINES OF DAILY LIVING

Do you put your clothes on a chair when you take them off? Or do they land on the floor and stay there? How do you make sure that you do not lose your keys? Each of us carries out regular routines in a standard way, but these routines do not always work well for us. You may wish to replace some of these routine habits with other more helpful or less irritating ones.

CHARACTERISTICS

Many aspects of what we think of as essential characteristics of a person are routines or habits—untidiness, for example, or reaching for the cookies when you feel upset. Others might reach for the telephone or the box of tissues instead. "Characteristic habits" can be changed in just the same way as other habits.

INTERPERSONAL ROLES

People living close to each other usually divide up their responsibilities in ways which suit them—and then develop habits which go with those responsibilities. Some of these habits, however, can become a cause for irritation. For example, if one person takes total responsibility for cleaning the kitchen, others may develop messy kitchen habits. Or habits may clash. One person may use the telephone pad to write down shopping lists, while another may doodle over the shopping list making it unreadable. Such clashes of habit are trivial, even funny, but over time they can wreak havoc in a relationship.

ADDICTIONS

Some habits are addictive—for example, smoking (see this chapter), drinking excessive amounts of alcohol (see Chapter 26), and becoming dependent on tranquilizers (Chapter 27) or dangerous drugs. The ideas in the first part of this chapter will also be useful when trying to break addictive habits.

How to Break a Habit

We learn our habits, and therefore we can unlearn them. The point about habits is that we have learned them so well that we have to take active steps to break them. Just as a stream will cut deeper and deeper into the rock, so the repeated performance of our habits results in their becoming more and more entrenched. If a stream is diverted, temporarily, into a shallow channel, it will readily revert to its old course. But if it is repeatedly diverted, it will cut out a new path and, in time, naturally flow this way. So it is with habits. Each time you perform your old habit, it is strengthened; each time you replace the old habit with a new way of behaving, the old habit is weakened and the new one strengthened. The way to break habits is to replace the habitual way of behaving with the desired way of behaving. When this is done repeatedly, new channels of behavior are created, and then the new way becomes automatic.

Do not be beguiled by those who say that breaking a habit is easy. It can be done, but it involves adopting a structured, step by step, approach and it involves persistence. In order to travel from Oxford to London by train, you have to go through Didcot and Reading. In order to break your habits, you have to go through the steps explained below; if you skip some of the stages, you may not reach your destination.

WHY DO YOU WANT TO BREAK THE HABIT?

You will only break the habit if you are motivated to do so, and this means becoming absolutely clear about whether you really do want to change. You will need to be motivated not only to break the habit, but in order to be able to persist. Think carefully about the following questions, and then decide: Do you really want to put in the effort needed to break the habit? What do you stand to gain?

1. Is the habit harmful to me? Am I likely to hurt myself if I go on doing it—by, for example, scratching myself raw or chewing my nails down to the quick?
2. Is the habit dangerous, either to myself or to others? For example, forgetting to turn off the iron or the cooker, smoking in bed, or not using the rear-view mirror when driving.
3. Is the habit embarrassing, irritating, or upsetting to me? For example, sniffing, or sucking my teeth; pulling out patches of hair or an eyebrow; crying or losing my temper easily; talking with my mouth full.
4. Is the habit my problem, or someone else's problem? Is it a problem about how I live or work together with others round me? If so, it may also help to learn more about negotiating change (see Chapter 15).
5. If I persist with the habit, what are the three worst possible consequences?
6. If I break the habit, what are the three most important gains?

Six Steps for Breaking Habits

Step 1: Decide to change.

Step 2: Use awareness training.

Step 3: Devise strategies to help in stopping the habit.

Step 4: Replace the habit with an alternative behavior.

Step 5: Persist by being consistent and keeping track of progress.

Step 6: Learn to manage lapses.

STEP 1: DECIDE TO CHANGE

The most usual reason for failing to break a habit is going about it half-heartedly. You must be certain that you want to change. *To increase your resolve, think about the disadvantages of the habit* and about the advantages if you break it.

Imagine the habit clearly, then ask yourself "What's wrong with doing this?" What are the disadvantages, both immediately (the pain, making your fingers bleed), and in the longer term (losing your job as a hairdresser). Or imagine someone else doing what you do (complaining; giggling), and think what the disadvantages might be for them. Do they apply to you too? What are the worst possible consequences of going on with the habit? Describe them to yourself in detail and face up to them squarely. Finally, ask yourself "Why should I bother to stop?" *Make a list of reasons for stopping the habit* and put it where you will read it often (use it as a bookmark, or stick it in your wallet or handbag). It may help to take a photograph (if the effects of your habit are visible) to demonstrate to yourself the reasons why you want to break the habit.

We have labored the importance of getting clear why you want to break the habit because it is *the single most important step.* Without it you will fail. By itself it may well be sufficient to break the habit that you want to break. Gary came to the clinic because he was getting into the habit of checking everything he did. As soon as he stepped out of the house in the morning, he would go back inside to check that he had switched the grill off. As soon as he got to work, he would return to his car to check that he had locked it. He was starting to develop obsessional habits, and his doctor referred him immediately to a specialist. We asked him to answer the six questions we posed above and to come to a clear decision. He needed no more help. It was enough, for him, to get clear that he did not want to become enslaved by repeated checking. He nipped his bad habit in the bud.

STEP 2: USE AWARENESS TRAINING

Because the habit is automatic, you may not be aware of when you do it, or of exactly what it is that you do, so you need to become aware of it in order to stop it. If this is the case, the next step involves studying the habit. You will need to do two things: first, to *describe* it; and then to *monitor* it.

Describing the habit. You need to know the details, from the first move to the last. If you bite your nails, find out whether you bite all of them and whether you bite your fingers as well. What makes you move your hands up to your mouth? Which teeth do you use? What happens to the bits you bite off? On which side of the nail do you start? You may find it helpful to enlist someone's help at this stage.

Monitoring the habit. The only effective way of monitoring the habit is to keep a record. An example of a self- monitoring sheet is shown on page 279. The precise form of the record depends on you and on the habit. Use the monitoring sheet to answer *three* questions:

1. How *often* does the habit occur over a particular time, such as a week, day, or hour? If you cannot carry your monitoring sheet with you, keep count by using a knitting or golf counter or by moving small objects (e.g. paper clips) from one pocket to another.

2. *When* does the habit occur? Note the time of day on the monitoring sheet.

3. *What* is going on when you start doing it, and *where* are you at the time? For example, do you pull out your hair, absentmindedly, when on the telephone, or only at work? Do you criticize others when you feel attacked? Or cry when you feel undervalued? The situations in which you tend to perform the habit are known as the *setting conditions.*

Study your habit record. Self-monitoring, or keeping a habit record, helps you to detect relevant patterns and influences. So examine your record carefully after about a week, and work out how often you performed the habit, at what times, and in what situations. When are you most at risk? What triggers the habit? You may find it happens after meals, or when you are bored, embarrassed, or upset. For you it may be a sign that you are under stress (see Chapter 11), or tired.

A note of caution. Self-monitoring often changes the habit you are trying to record. This is largely because it makes you more aware of what you were previously doing unawares, and so gives you a chance to interrupt it before it starts. If so, then remember that your record will underestimate how bad the habit really is. Do not be tempted to stop there: if you do, you will forget all about the habit once again and it will come back precisely because it *is* automatic.

Example of a monitoring record for studying a nail-biting habit. The person with this habit used the form as a brief diary to remind herself of things that she thought might be relevant. She did not keep a record of how long she went on biting her nails each time, because either she stopped as soon as she noticed, or she did not notice when she started, so could only guess.

Nail-Biting Record

When?	How often?	Situation	Feelings
Aug 12			
7:30 A.M.	3	Waiting for kettle	Nothing—sleepy?
8:45	1	Caught in traffic	Worried and late, also angry with myself
10:30	2	Coffee break, alone	Bored
2:15	5 or 6	Waiting to see boss	Afraid she noticed I was late
4:25	1	Learning new job	Interested; concentrating hard
6:00	5	Watching TV	Nothing much
9:00–11.00	12+	In pub: met Jeff	Embarrassed; couldn't think of anything to say

Note: There may have been more than this. Probably did not notice every time I did it.

STEP 3: DEVISE STRATEGIES FOR STOPPING THE HABIT

You are now in a position to bring Steps 1 and 2 to bear in breaking the habit.

Prepare yourself. To make the effort, you will need repeatedly to remind yourself why you want to break the habit (Step 1). Keep a list of the reasons so that you can look at them at least every day—more frequently if need be.

Develop an early-warning system. To catch the habit before it starts, learn to be on your guard at the times when you are most likely to carry it out. You can then make a special effort at these times. The "warning lights" should go on when you are in those situations in which the habit commonly occurs (the *setting conditions* for the habit); and when you find yourself performing an early part of the habit, think about what you are doing. For example, suppose that you tend to pull your hair out, with your left hand, when speaking on the telephone. Your warning bells should ring both when you are on the telephone and when your left hand goes up to your head. If you raise your voice and start shouting as soon as your ideas are questioned, you should be on your guard whenever faced with a possible questioner.

Develop a STOP **strategy.** If you catch yourself carrying out the habit, it is not too late to do anything. Stop doing it straight away. You could say "STOP" to yourself, out loud at first and later under your breath. Or write "STOP" in big colored letters on a card that you can look at, or imagine a "STOP" barrier coming down in front of you. Some people find it helpful to have a "stop routine." This might include: looking at your list of reasons for stopping the habit; or shocking yourself out of the habit by wearing a *loose* elastic band round your wrist and snapping it hard whenever you catch yourself doing it.

Enlist the support of others. Other people can be extremely helpful when you are trying to break a habit. They can help you notice when the automatic behavior has come back, and they can encourage you when the going gets tough. Showing your monitoring sheets to someone else can help you persist. Of course, it does not help to be nagged, so if you want someone else's help, you should tell them exactly what you need them to do, and possibly ask them to read this chapter.

Monitor. Continue to fill in your monitoring sheets so that you are keeping a record of how frequently you are carrying out the automatic behavior.

Reward yourself for success. Set yourself targets for reducing the frequency of the habit, and reward yourself when you reach these targets. A celebration with someone else at each target point can be particularly effective (see also Chapter 7).

A second note of caution. Sometimes when people try to break a habit, it seems to get worse before it gets better. This may be because trying to keep track of something you tend to do automatically reminds you of doing it. Or it can be because the effort to stop makes you more tense and your habit is triggered by feelings of tension. This stage is usually short-lived, so do not get discouraged and give up trying.

STEP 4: REPLACE THE HABIT WITH AN ALTERNATIVE BEHAVIOR

Most people experience urges when trying to break a habit and these can be hard to resist unless you find something else to do instead, and best of all, something that uses the same part of the body—even the same muscles. If the habit involves your hands, as when pulling out hair, then try to occupy them in some other way. Playing with a toy or Play-doh might be the answer. Or you could clench your fists for a couple of minutes. People who pull out their hair could use a comb instead, or put on gloves. The habit of scratching can be replaced with rubbing in some lotion or patting with the palm of the hand. Nail biting can be replaced with using handcream or a manicure set. One 35-year-old woman who used to rub her eyes with the heel of her hand until they became sore and often infected found it helpful to put on makeup when she was tempted to rub.

If the habit is triggered by upsetting feelings such as tension, worry, or boredom, then it may be necessary to resolve these feelings. What is making you feel tense, worried, or bored? What could you do to make yourself feel better? (See Chapter 16.)

Untidiness is best tackled by developing a "habit of organization." Relatively simple measures, like buying a set of coat-hangers for your shirts or picking up a ring-binder for your statements from the bank, can dramatically reduce the amount of hassle caused by losing these things. This alternative behavior can then become the focus for self-monitoring to ensure that you carry it out regularly.

Interrupting people can be stopped by developing better listening skills (p. 136), and many of the habits that affect relationships (arguing, making excuses, telling fibs) can be changed by learning how to be fair both to yourself and to others (Chapter 13), and by learning negotiation skills (pp. 161–166).

STEP 5: PERSIST BY BEING CONSISTENT AND KEEPING TRACK OF PROGRESS

It is important to be consistent when working to break a habit. Trying hard one week but giving yourself a holiday from trying the next will change nothing, and could be counterproductive. You could, for example, bite one nail and immediately feel better without doing yourself much harm because the urge has gone. So you might be tempted to conclude that biting your nails just once makes no difference. This is the "beginning of the end." Once leads to twice, and before you know where you are, the habit is reestablished in full force.

In order to be consistent you will also have to persist. It is not easy to break a habit. There will be times when you want to give up altogether and times when you feel discouraged despite making a big effort. You may also get tired of trying. You have made an enormous effort to be tidier, but still the place looks a mess, and you keep losing things. This is the time to think of the *advantages of stopping your habit* (as opposed to the disadvantages of going on with it). Keep the list you made earlier and read it regularly. Think about the gains you have made so far, even if they seem ridiculously small.

At this stage make sure that you reward yourself for the effort you are making. Rewards are a better way of helping yourself than punishment. The carrot is better than the stick, and you deserve to be rewarded for your progress in breaking the habit (see Chapter 7).

Finally, make sure you continue to keep your habit record. Write down, as close to the time as you can, each time you catch yourself "in the act." It may help, once the habit has diminished, to keep a record of the urges to perform the habit and to rate their strength. Make your record form simple, and fill it in at the same time every day. At the end of each week look back over the 7 days and work out how you are changing.

STEP 6: LEARN TO MANAGE LAPSES

The problem with habits is that they are automatic, which means that until they are fully broken they can easily come back. It can be disheartening to have made progress in breaking a habit and then to find that it is back, possibly in full force. It is easy to think that you are back to square one even though you are not. If you have made progress once, you can make progress again, and the second time it will be easier because you have trodden the path before. It is helpful to think about why the lapse occurred so that you can learn from this, but the most important thing is to repeat the steps that helped to reduce the habit before. The key to success is to see the present setback as a *lapse* not a *relapse*. The lapse is like falling off your bike: if you pick yourself up and dust yourself off, you can continue cycling along.

How to Stop Smoking

Smoking is both a habit and an addiction, and it is the habit that is the harder to break. The methods for stopping smoking are the same as for breaking any other habit; and the key to stopping is motivation. *If you really want to stop, you can.* Most people who are diagnosed as having lung cancer stop smoking immediately, however much they smoked before. They simply stop because they feel highly motivated. It is a great pity that they did not feel so highly motivated earlier.

The Key Facts about Smoking

WHY STOP SMOKING?

The reasons for stopping smoking, in two words, are *health* and *wealth*. The connection between smoking and serious ill health is stronger than any other environmental cause of disease, and it is not lung cancer which is the biggest killer. If you smoke 20 or more cigarettes a day, you are five times more likely to suffer a stroke than if you do not smoke, and three times more likely to have a heart attack. This is because smoking accelerates the formation of atherosclerosis—the narrowing of arteries. This narrowing leads to poor blood flow. Poor blood flow to the brain can cause stroke; poor blood flow to heart muscle can cause a heart attack. Look at the list of major diseases in the following box which are strongly associated with smoking.

Major Health Problems Caused by Smoking

Stroke

Heart attack

Severe chronic bronchitis

Poor circulation leading to leg amputation

Lung cancer

Stomach cancer

Cervical cancer

Miscarriages

Low birth weight babies

Secondary effects of smoking on your children: increase in chest problems— for example, asthma, pneumonia, bronchitis—and increase in infant mortality.

Heavy smokers, of pipes as well as cigarettes, are twice as likely to die in middle age than nonsmokers. In broad terms, your chance of dying, if you are a heavy smoker, is the same as that of a nonsmoker ten years older than you.

All these dangers and risks of smoking are proportional to how much you smoke. The more the worse, but any amount of smoking is harmful, and so-called mild, or low tar, cigarettes are also harmful—there is no such thing as a safe cigarette. All these problems become less likely once you have stopped smoking, and dramatically so. The chance of heart attack, for example, has halved a year after stopping smoking, and after 5 years it is almost the same as if you had you never smoked.

THE BENEFITS OF GIVING UP SMOKING

It is helpful to turn the question around and to focus not only on the dangers of carrying on with smoking but the benefits of giving up smoking. The main benefits are listed in the following box. Think about how these benefits will affect your life in specific ways. Stopping smoking will improve your health not only in the sense of lowering the risk of death and serious disease, but also in improving your everyday health and fitness: increasing the amount of energy you have and your ability to get things done efficiently. Work out just how much money you will save over a year if you stopped smoking. What else could you do with this money?

Some Benefits of Stopping Smoking

A longer life

Improved physical fitness

Better skin (fewer wrinkles)

Better appearance (no nicotine stains)

Smell better to others

Taste food better

More money

ARE THERE DISADVANTAGES TO STOPPING SMOKING?

Not really, except for the unpleasantness just after stopping. Some people are worried that they will put on weight if they stop, often because this has happened when they have tried stopping before. The most common reason you gain weight is because you replace cigarettes with high-calorie foods, such as snacks, potato chips, and sweets. But whatever the reason for the weight gain, it is a problem that is easy to deal with: first by eating a sensible diet and increasing your intake of fruit and vegetables; and second by increasing your exercise (see also Chapter 25). Some people, especially those with chronic bronchitis, find that immediately after stopping smoking their chest feels "tighter," and they conclude that the smoking is good for their chest because it helps them cough up the phlegm. This is a very dangerous and a false conclusion. It is the smoking that has caused, and is causing the chest problem, and continuing smoking will cause gradual but steady worsening of the chest problem. Immediately after stopping smoking, there may be a short-lived change in the way in which secretions are cleared from the chest; but the important fact is that your chest will get *better* if you stop smoking and *worse* if you continue to smoke.

How to Stop Smoking

EIGHT STEPS TO STOPPING SMOKING

1. Be clear in your mind about why you want to stop. Motivation: that is the key, so be sure you are quite clear about why you want to stop and what the advantages of stopping will be. Write down these advantages and keep the list at hand.

2. Assess your smoking (study your habit). As with breaking any habit, it is most helpful to have a clear idea of exactly what you are doing. A "smoking diary" will show you not only how much you smoke, but in what circumstances, when, and with whom. This is invaluable information when planning to make it as easy as possible for you to stop.

Assess also why you smoke. In the box on the following page there are listed seven major reasons why people smoke. What are your reasons? You may think of one which is not on the list. If you understand which reasons are important for you—and there may be more than one reason for your smoking—you will be better able to plan how to stop.

3. Develop your personal strategy. You can stop all at once, or you can cut down and stop over five or so days. It doesn't much matter which you do as long as you do two things: decide exactly which day you are going to stop (or start the process of cutting down); and do exactly what you planned. If you choose to stop over several days,

---

Some Reasons for Smoking

It helps you to relax.

Handling cigarettes feels good.

You like the taste.

It gives you confidence, particularly in company.

You think it helps you to concentrate, and gives you energy.

You just automatically light one up.

You are addicted, and feel ill if you don't have a cigarette.

---

the best plan is to smoke fewer cigarettes each day. For example, if you currently smoke 20 cigarettes a day, plan to decrease each day by four, so that on the fifth day you have stopped smoking. The easiest way of doing that might be to have the first cigarette of the day later and later.

4. Find something else to do instead. Go back to your smoking diary and think about what the dangerous situations are for you. How are you going to reduce the temptation to smoke? How can you make it easier to give up? One important way is to make sure that there are no cigarettes around. But there are also other ways. For example, you may tend to smoke when in the car, in which case this will be a situation in which you should take special care not to have cigarettes available, and in which you should find a substitute for smoking (chew gum, or listen to music). Or you may tend to smoke after meals, especially if you also have coffee, in which case consider leaving out the coffee as well and occupying yourself in some other way at this time. The craving for the cigarette will pass once you are out of the situation which normally prompts you to smoke, and once you are well passed the time at which you habitually lit up.

Think too about your reasons for smoking and use this insight to help you. If you like the feel of the cigarette in your mouth then what else could you put in your mouth? A pencil when at work? Sticks of carrot when cooking or waiting for a meal? Or if you are a pipe smoker, an empty pipe. If you smoke to help relax, look for less harmful ways of relaxing (see Chapter 11). If you smoke to boost confidence, read Chapters 10 and 13. If smoking makes you less anxious, read Chapter 16.

5. Enlist support. To keep the momentum going, enlist support from friends and family. Other people can help, and if they do not know that you have given up smoking, they may offer you cigarettes and thus tempt you. So let key people know that you no longer smoke, and discuss ways in which they can help you. If you know other people who also want to give up smoking, it can be helpful to everyone to form a group to help each other quit. Plan together, and use the group to report on progress. Some groups plan treats as a way of marking successes, and they may also use "punishments" or demand a "forfeit" for continued smoking. Each member of one successful group put a "deposit" into a kitty. If someone smoked, the deposit would be paid to that person's *least* favorite charity (a hated political party, for example) as punishment.

6. Start a "Ciggy bank." When you stop smoking, you will have more money. It is easy for this money to be "hidden" in your day-to-day living expenses. In order to see just how much you are saving, put the money you would have spent on cigarettes into a "ciggy bank." You can then use this money for something special.

7. Freshen up. Ask your dentist to clean all the stains off your teeth, and air your clothes and your house. Throw away all ashtrays. You will soon dislike the stale smell of smoke and this dislike will help you to keep off cigarettes. Taking up exercise will also help because you will feel and enjoy the fitness which smoking otherwise takes away.

8. Be assertive. You will be offered cigarettes, particularly by those who know you as a smoker and do not know that you have given up. Simply say: "*No thanks, I don't smoke.*" If they say that you did smoke, reply: "*I did smoke, but now I don't.*" Practice saying these phrases until they feel right. There is no need for further explanation (see Chapter 13).

WHEN YOU FEEL A GREAT DESIRE TO SMOKE

The feeling of craving will pass shortly. So when it comes over you, remind yourself that it will pass. Take a few slow deep breaths; do something to distract yourself; and take a drink of water to occupy both you and your mouth.

If Addiction Is a Problem

If you have smoked heavily for a long time, you are likely to be addicted. The addiction will show in cravings for a cigarette, and in some withdrawal symptoms on occasions when you have not had a cigarette for several hours. If, on the other hand, you regularly go 12 hours without a cigarette, then you are unlikely to have a significant physical addiction. The following box lists typical withdrawal symptoms which indicate addiction.

Common Symptoms of Withdrawal

Becoming irritable and snappy

Gasping for a drag

Feeling jittery and clammy

Feeling dizzy

Tingling feeling

Headache

Feeling nauseated

These withdrawal symptoms are worst in the early days when you have just stopped and may last a few weeks if you have been a very heavy smoker. Although they can be unpleasant, they are not dangerous or overwhelming. You have a lot to gain if you can persist and beat the habit, and this is the hardest time.

NICOTINE CHEWING GUM, OR NICOTINE SKIN PATCHES

You can separate the problems of physical addiction from the difficulties in breaking the habit by replacing the nicotine using either patches, which stick on your skin and from which the nicotine is slowly absorbed, or by chewing nicotine gum. If you replace the nicotine in this way, then you will not experience the withdrawal problems, and so you will not have to deal with these while coping with the difficulties of breaking the habit. Two or three months after stopping, you can wean yourself off the nicotine by using a lower dose patch, or chewing less gum (your pharmacist can advise you). *Do not smoke on the same day as you take nicotine* if you make use of one of these methods. If you do, you will have a *nicotine overdose* which may give you severe stomach pains.

Obtaining Help

It helps to get support. If you cannot form your own support group and are finding it hard to stop smoking on your own, contact your doctor and find out if your local hospital has a chest clinic which organizes support groups. In the United Kingdom, call the help line *quitline* (0171 487 3000); or find your nearest *withdrawal clinic* (the local library of the Citizen's Advice Bureau should know the number); or contact *ASH* (Action on Smoking and Health: 0171 935 3519) which publishes self-help guides to help you stop smoking.

In the United States, contact your local chapter of the American Lung Association, or call toll-free, 800-448-54864, or call your local Smokenders (toll-free: 800-823-1126) or Smokenders International (800-828-4354). You are not alone, and if you really want to stop, then take whatever measures are needed.

Chapter Summary

Habits are hard to change because they have become automatic. Nevertheless they can be changed by following these six steps:

1. Make a positive decision to change; do not be half-hearted about it.
2. Study the habit until you are aware of exactly what you do.
3. Develop a personal strategy for stopping.
4. Find something else to do instead.
5. Once you have started, keep the momentum going.
6. "If you don't at first succeed, try and try again".

These steps can be used to break any habit—from smoking to nail biting.

24

◆ ◆ ◆

Overcoming Sleep Problems

Why we need sleep remains a mystery. Yet about one in five people think they have a sleep problem and sleeping badly can make you feel miserable, irritable, and unable to cope. There are three main kinds of problem: difficulty falling asleep, wakefulness during the night, and waking too early in the morning. In each case there seems to be a shortage of sleep: however, it is notoriously difficult to estimate how much sleep you really get. For many people the problem is not that they sleep too little, but rather that they *think* they are not getting enough sleep. If this becomes a worry, then the problem tends to get worse. Worrying both interferes with sleep and leaves you feeling exhausted the next day.

Two key questions can help you decide if you have a sleep problem:

1. *Do you regularly feel tired throughout the day?*
2. *Does sleepiness interfere with your daily activities?*

If the answer to one or both of these question is *yes,* then you may have a sleep problem. Luckily, for nine out of ten people the problem is easily solved.

SOLVING THE SLEEP PROBLEM

It is always helpful to know your enemy. The first step is to learn some facts about sleep, so you can settle your worries about not getting enough. The next step is to learn four simple but effective solutions:

1. *Tackle physical problems.*
2. *Establish regular routines.*
3. *Control your thoughts.*
4. *Use sophisticated sheep counting.*

We recommend that you read the whole chapter first, and then work through the solutions in order, because most people are likely to need only the first two. However, it is always worth experimenting, to build on these methods in your own way, and to find out whether the other ones may also be helpful.

Some Facts about Sleep

1. On average, adults sleep 7½ hours each night. Two- thirds of the population sleep between 6½ and 8½ hours. A few people feel fine on 4 hours a night and a few need as much as 10 hours.
2. The amount of sleep a person needs may well be inherited, and determined in the same way as their height. So you are not lazy if you need more than average, as Albert Einstein did, nor virtuous if you need less than average, as did Winston Churchill.
3. You need less sleep as you grow older.
4. The depth of your sleep varies throughout the night, and cycles of deep and light sleep are continuously repeated in waves. It is normal occasionally to wake at the "top" of one of these cycles, when you are in the lightest phase of sleep, and to fall into deeper sleep quite soon as the cycle continues.
5. A number of rather "odd" experiences may occur as you are falling asleep or as you are waking. For example, your muscles may twitch, or you may feel as if you are falling, or paralyzed and unable to move. You may also think you hear voices, such as people calling your name. These experiences are all normal.
6. One hour of sleep before midnight is worth just one hour of sleep—neither more nor less. Maybe this old wives' tale was designed to persuade people to get to bed earlier!
7. Experiments on sleep deprivation show that the occasional night of poor sleep may make you feel tired the next day, but has little effect on your performance. Two hours of sleep, as long as this occurs on occasional nights only, seems adequate to prevent noticeable effects on thinking tasks. So there is no need to worry about sleeping badly the night before an exam. However, you cannot make a drastic cut in your sleep on a regular basis

(e.g., from 8 to 2 hours a night) without suffering bad effects. A reduction of one hour may not be harmful, but reducing by more than this may have a bad effect on your mood, concentration, memory, and on the more creative aspects of your thinking. Experiments also show that everybody has dreams, but some people do not remember them. If you deprive someone of their dream sleep, they automatically make it up. In fact, it is very hard to prevent people from dreaming.

8. Sleep is affected by many things: exercise, food, medications, alcohol, illness, mood, stresses, worries, among other things. You may be able to solve your sleep problem by changing any of these.

9. Sleep patterns tend to change slowly. It usually takes a few weeks to establish a new pattern.

SOME FACTS ABOUT SLEEPING PILLS

Sleeping pills are addictive, and may also make you feel drowsy during the day. If you are not already taking them, then do not let yourself develop a new habit. An occasional sleeping pill, taken on your doctor's advice, might be useful in the short term, but you should not take them regularly and frequently, and should not let yourself rely on them.

If you regularly take sleeping pills, then read pages 332 to 339 and discuss the alternatives with your doctor.

Four Solutions to Your Sleep Problem

1. TACKLE PHYSICAL PROBLEMS

Pain. Ensure that physical problems such as arthritis are adequately treated. Tell your doctor if pain interferes with your sleep—there will usually be a solution, and your doctor may not have realized your difficulty.

Breathlessness. If you regularly wake short of breath— needing to sit up or even get up, see your doctor. This could be caused by an accumulation of fluid in the lungs, or by narrowing of the airways (asthma). In either case, you may benefit from medication.

Waking to pass urine. The need to urinate often disturbs sleep, particularly for older men and pregnant women. If this disturbs you, the suggestions about how to change your drinking habits in the following box might help. We are not recommending that you drink less fluid overall, only that you redistribute the timing of when you drink. If you suffer from *diabetes* and have problems waking to pass urine, see your doctor. Since dehydration (lack of fluid) is a danger with diabetes, it is important that, in your attempt to solve the sleep problem, you do not drink too little fluid.

How to Reduce the Frequency of Waking to Pass Urine

1. Redistribute your drinking. Keep your overall drinking to between 2 and 3 liters or U.S. quarts a day, and limit yourself to half a pint after 4 P.M. Drink the rest before then. It will help to calculate how much you drink in an average day before making changes.
2. Drink nothing for two hours before going to bed.
3. Urinate just before retiring.
4. If you normally take diuretic medication ("water tablets"):
   a. Check with your doctor that you still need them.
   b. Do not take them in the evening—discuss when to take them with your doctor.
5. Drink no alcohol or coffee within 3 hours of going to bed. These are both diuretics—that is, they make you urinate more than the amount of liquid they contain.

Alcohol. Alcoholic drinks interfere with sleep in two ways. First, they are diuretics (see box above). If you drink alcohol in the evening, you may wake several times in the night to pass urine or because you feel thirsty. Second, it is a sedative drug. It will send you to sleep at first, but tends to wake you as the effect wears off. For those who regularly drink more alcohol than is healthy, a poor night's sleep can be the normal state of affairs, and often reflects a vicious cycle. The poor sleep makes it hard to cope, which makes reliance on alcohol more attractive. But alcohol makes the sleep problem worse. In this case the reliance on alcohol should be tackled (see Chapter 26).

Your bed. Is your bed lumpy, or does it sag? If it is uncomfortable, then think of buying a new one. You will spend so much time in it that it is worth getting the best you can afford, and it is important to choose the kind of bed that makes you feel comfortable and not be unduly influenced by sales talk or labels. Calling a bed "orthopedic" or extolling the virtues of waterbeds is not enough to make those beds good for you, or to make them comfortable for both you and your partner together, particularly if you are very different sizes and shapes or if one of you is more restless and easily disturbed than the other.

Ask to lie on a bed before you decide to buy, and refuse to be hurried. Take your partner with you if possible. Remember that if you both lie quite still, flat on your backs staring up at the ceiling, you will certainly have no way of telling what will happen to one of you when the other stretches out or turns over suddenly.

Also, ask yourself whether you are too hot in bed. It is surprising how many people complain they wake up hot and sweating in the night only because their bedclothes are too warm. Opening the window or turning the heat down might help.

Cut out stimulants. Coffee, tea and tobacco are the main culprits, although chocolate, cocoa, and cola drinks also contain caffeine. Different people are affected differently, so you may have to experiment to find out whether they affect you and try out alternatives like herbal tea, camomile, or dandelion coffee. If you sleep badly, then consider all caffeine drinks guilty until proved innocent. People vary as to how close to bedtime they can take caffeine. For some people even a cup of coffee after lunch can interfere with sleep.

Many stimulants are hard to stop taking because they are addictive. If you are addicted, you may go through a phase of feeling worse before you feel better after stopping them. Once you have got through this "withdrawal" phase, however, your sleep should improve.

When your partner snores. Snoring is likely to cause sleeplessness not for those who snore, but for their partners. The noise of snoring can be extremely irritating, and it is difficult not to get upset or angry if repeatedly woken just as one is falling to sleep. It is usually caused by vibration of the soft palate—the upper, back part of the mouth, and happens most often when people breathe through the mouth or if they have an unusually floppy soft palate.

Some people snore when they have a blocked nose. This can be caused by colds and allergies—for example, to house dust mites. These mites are present in all houses and common in pillows and mattresses, as they flourish in warm conditions. Allergic responses to dust mites are therefore likely to be worse at night and to be present all the year round. Your doctor may be able to advise you on how to deal with the allergy.

Others snore only in some positions. Sleeping propped up may help, but pillows may not work as it is easy to slip off them. A bolster is better, or you could consider raising the head of the bed. If your partner snores only when lying on his back, it may help gently to persuade him to turn over, or to sew a ping pong ball into the back of his pajamas or to prompt him to turn over of his own accord whenever he moves onto his back.

Some people snore only at some stages of the sleep cycle—for instance, they might snore for a while as they are falling asleep but become quiet as they settle into deeper sleep. If you can be patient the snoring may stop, but if you wake these people up as they start to snore you will only have to go through the process all over again.

Sedatives (including sleeping pills) tend to make the soft palate more floppy and to increase the chance of snoring, and the most common sedative is alcohol. Try cutting out all alcohol, both during the day and in the evenings, for *at least a week* to find out if this is the cause of the problem. A one-day trial is not enough.

For reasons which are not clear, obesity is associated with snoring, in which case it is worth considering losing some weight— without being too quick or ambitious about it (see Chapter 25). Pregnancy, too, can bring on snoring which usually disappears after the pregnancy is over.

If the snoring continues to disturb you, it might be worth buying earplugs, or talking to your partner about sleeping in separate rooms (if you have the space)—occasionally, for part of the night, or regularly. Sleeping well may be better for the relationship than *sleeping* together. The decision to sleep apart because one person snores need have no profound repercussions on a relationship if both of you understand what you are doing and why.

Finally, if snoring is a major problem, and the measures already discussed fail, see your doctor. Some people have a particularly floppy soft palate, or polyps at the back of the nose, for which surgery is effective.

2. ESTABLISH REGULAR ROUTINES

If you have dealt with the physical problems and still sleep badly, then try to establish regular routines.

An evening routine. A relaxing bedtime routine gives your mind time to settle for the night, and helps you leave behind all the worries and excitements of the day. Your last meal should not be too large nor too late, and we recommend that you start the evening routine 1½ hours before you aim to be asleep. You can shorten the routine later if you want to.

Here is an example: from 9:30 to 10:15 do something calm and enjoyable, like knitting, watching TV, playing with the computer, or reading. At 10.15 have a bath and get ready for bed. Make a warm drink to take to bed with you (warm milky drinks reduce the chances of waking once you are asleep, or you could try herbal tea), and read for 15 minutes before you settle down at 11.

If you have chores to do in the evenings, like making packed lunches or sorting out clothes, then do them before you start the routine (or make them the first step in the routine). You will only worry if they are not done. The routine should be a way of closing the old day, not a way of getting ahead on the new one.

Give your routine a high priority, even though you will not always be able to stick to it. Explain what you are doing to others so that they understand and respect it, and remember how much better you will feel if you can overcome the irritability, weariness, and other problems caused by sleeping badly. You may have to unplug the telephone or ask people not to call you after 9:30.

A morning routine. Sometimes a sleep problem continues even after you have established an evening routine. This is the stage to think about what you do in the mornings as well. No amount of will power will send you to sleep at the right time, but you can force yourself to get up in the morning. We suggest that you give yourself a *short sharp shock* to make sure that you are tired in the evenings and to find out more about how much sleep you really need.

Here is an example. If you normally start the day around 7:30 A.M., then for one week set your alarm earlier than this—for instance, at 7 A.M. Get up immediately. Do not even wait until 7:05. Make yourself a getting up routine that you can go through without thinking—washing, making tea, dressing—and only think about the day ahead when the routine is done. Do *not* snooze during the day or in front of the TV at night, and for the moment do not allow yourself to sleep late on weekends.

After one week (or perhaps two) you should notice yourself becoming sleepy in the evenings, and find it easier to fall asleep. If you are getting sleepy around 11 P.M. and getting up at 7 A.M. then you need about 8 hours sleep. You may then want to shift back to your normal wake up time, but remember to shift bedtime correspondingly.

3. CONTROL YOUR THOUGHTS

If you have dealt adequately with physical problems and established regular routines but still lie awake worrying, then you need to consider those two great enemies of good mood: *anxiety* and *depression* (see Part 4 of this book).

Lying awake worrying: Sheep in wolves' clothing. Are you kept awake by your worries? Or do they simply fill the time you are awake? Lying awake worrying may be a bad habit that can be broken by establishing a firm rule with yourself. When you catch yourself worrying say to yourself: *this is not the time.* Once you have settled down it is time to sleep, not to think about problems. You have probably noticed that at 3 A.M. problems loom large, and worry spreads rapidly from topic to topic. The problems seem overwhelming or insoluble, and get alarmingly out of proportion. They are far better tackled during the day rather than when you should be sleeping. So tell yourself *this is not the time* and think them through properly later. You could use the techniques of problem-solving (pp. 62–68), or learn the decision-tree technique for dealing with worry (p. 181).

You may worry that by the morning you will have forgotten something important. Two simple methods can help. First, spend five minutes, before you settle down, making a note of the things that you think you might worry about. Get them out of your head and onto the paper, ready to deal with later. Second, keep a notepad by the bed and jot down anything that seems important whenever it occurs to you. Then if you start worrying instead of sleeping, you can say *this is not the time,* feeling safe that these things will not be forgotten.

Some couples make a habit of discussing important issues at bedtime, such as work, the children, or troubles between themselves—no wonder they sleep badly. Such discussions should be vetoed. *This is not the time* should be sufficient for one partner to veto the discussion. Make a time to discuss the issue properly—and not within 1½ hours of bedtime!

Waking early if you are depressed. Waking *at least* an hour before your usual time without being able to get back to sleep, *and* feeling very miserable—worse than at any other time—can be a sign of severe depression. If this describes you, then read Chapters 20 to 22 on depression and think about whether this is a time to consult your doctor.

4. USE SOPHISTICATED SHEEP COUNTING

The fourth solution combines relaxation techniques with counting "games." This is the solution to try last. It is not a substitute for the others, but a supplement.

Relaxation. Learn how to relax, then you can use the method to help you sleep. Instructions are given in Chapter 11. When lying in bed, it may be easiest to use the "relax only" method rather than tensing muscles up before you let them go, but try anything that you think might be helpful.

You could relax first, and then start the counting games. When you are as relaxed as you can get, focus your attention on your breathing. Keep your attention entirely in the present, thinking about exactly how it feels as you breathe in and out.

Counting games. Three games are described here, and you could probably invent some more of your own. You could even try counting the proverbial sheep. If so, it helps greatly to imagine them passing through a gate or walking single file along a path. In other words, fix your attention on one spot and visualize the sheep moving endlessly past it. Counting is helpful because it is monotonous and takes little effort. Just like a boring television program, it holds your attention sufficiently to prevent you from thinking of other things. Of course, as you get sleepier, your attention wanders; you will lose count, and may then start worrying again. When this happens, calmly return to the counting game, starting wherever you like and trying to focus only on that.

Counting backwards. Count steadily backwards from a high number like 400, or 232. Count backwards slowly, lying comfortably with your eyes closed if possible. Continue counting down, one number at a time, roughly for each full breath. See how far you can get. Reset yourself calmly when you lose count, or go on from wherever you next choose. It is the monotony of counting, and not the actual numbers, that matters.

Counting breaths. Count each full breath. Breathe in, count one. Breathe out steadily. Breathe in, count two. Continue up to six, hold your breath and count six of your heart beats then breathe out. Allow yourself to take, naturally, a deep breath in, then as you breathe out pass into an even deeper state of relaxation. Breathe naturally for a few minutes.

The count down. For this you need to imagine a place of "serene tranquillity," or somewhere you have been calm and relaxed, like sitting in your favorite armchair, lying in the sun, or sitting by a stream. Think of somewhere you have been and try to imagine it clearly. You will visit this place by descending to it down a soft staircase of ten steps. In your imagination stand at the top of your staircase. On each count down, you will take one step and sink slightly into the softness of the stair. Count down about one step a second, and as you say the last one, "zero," imagine arriving in your calm and tranquil place. Feel all the sensations that go with it. Stay there and enjoy it. Don't worry if it fades, and don't try to will yourself to sleep. Just stay in your place.

A note of caution. Exercise during the day can make you tired enough to sleep at night, but exercise late in the evening can keep you awake because it is stimulating and arousing mentally, even if it tires you out physically.

Waking in the middle of the night. If you wake during the night and toss and turn restlessly, settle yourself down as you did when you first went to bed:

1. Try not to worry. Losing some sleep is not harmful.
2. *This is not the time to worry.*
3. Think about your physical state. Are you thirsty? Or too hot? Or too cold? Is the room stuffy?
4. Do something to break the pattern, and to trigger off the next stage of your sleep cycle. You could read for a bit, or go to the bathroom and have sip of water, then settle down again as if for the first time.
5. Relax and use counting games.
6. If all else fails, get up and do something simple and undemanding. This usually feels better than tossing and turning with worry and frustration all night.

NIGHTMARES AND DREAMS

Nightmares are more common in children than in adults and also when people are upset, worried, or distressed. They can be especially alarming or distressing following severe stresses or traumatic events, such as a car accident or assault. Often they disappear of their own accord, as if the mind had completed its natural reprocessing of daily happenings, made sense of what happened, and been able to lay the matter to rest. When they persist, it can be helpful to talk to a sympathetic listener about the nightmares, and especially about the feelings they arouse in you. Some people find that nightmares become much less frequent if they make a habit of thinking in the early evening about anything that might have troubled or upset them during the day and try to deal with the problem, or talk about it calmly, before starting their bedtime routine.

Some of the images in nightmares and bad dreams may well have symbolic meaning. For example, at a choice point in life you may dream of crossing a river, or of leaving someone or something important behind. Your sense of being powerless to help someone you love may appear in a nightmare scene of watching them sink into quicksand. Dreaming that you are being chased and are unable to run away may reflect your feelings of being trapped or threatened in some way.

But symbolic elements of nightmares and dreams may also combine with some completely random and unrelated elements, as if (as some psychologists suggest) brain cells need to keep firing just for them to keep functioning well, and different ones will do so at different times. Images associated with recent events, and their meanings, may also be reprocessed during sleep and only some of them break through to consciousness, producing bizarre and incomprehensible associations that we then try to make sense of when we wake.

When frightening dreams or nightmares happen repeatedly, their frequency may increase if going to bed makes you anxious about having them. Then, just as when overcoming a phobia (see Chapter 17), it is helpful to face the fear: to relate the dream, or write it down, several times, describing *all* of its alarming and disturbing aspects, and reminding yourself repeatedly that it is "only a dream" and not really harmful.

Chapter Summary

Almost everyone with a sleep problem can overcome it by taking simple steps. There are four simple but effective solutions.

1. Tackle physical problems first. Make sure you can get comfortable; avoid diuretics and too much alcohol in the evening; and cut down on stimulants such as coffee, tea, hot chocolate, and tobacco.
2. Establish regular routines for the evening, and possibly for the morning as well.
3. Control your thoughts. *This is not the time* to think about problems.
4. Relax and use counting games to help you switch off.

25

♦ ♦ ♦

Good Eating Habits

Habits That Last a Lifetime

Eating should be a source of health and of pleasure, but for many, it is a source of neither. A bad diet can cause heart disease, obesity, tooth decay, ulcers, and other disorders of the digestive system, and excessive concerns about shape and weight engendered in modern society can turn eating from a pleasure into a burden. Dieting has become a way of life for a very large number of people, especially women; and in its wake follow bulimia and anorexia.

There are two basic elements of good eating, and of the habits that can last a lifetime: *what* to eat, and *how* to eat.

WHAT TO EAT: FIVE PRINCIPLES FOR A HEALTHY DIET

Over the last twenty years, a great deal of scientific research has been carried out on the relationship between diet and disease. National committees have been set up to assess this research and to pinpoint the practical lessons to be learned. One such committee, the U.K. *Committee on medical aspects of food policy,* published its report in 1991. The practical lessons can be summarized as *five* principles.

1. There are no good or bad foods, only good or bad diets. No single food is "evil." A crème brûlée contains a great deal of fat including cholesterol. But the occasional crème brûlée is not harmful. The important issue is how much fat there is in the total diet, not in individual foods. The first principle, therefore, is to think in terms of your whole diet. Whatever your favorite foods are, you can eat them, at least occasionally.

2. Reduce fats. In Western society we eat too much fat, and in particular too many saturated fats. The practical ways of reducing the intake of saturated fats are summarized in the accompanying table.

Ways of Reducing Intake of Saturated Fats
Grill rather than fry.
Use lean meats—and cut off excess fat.
Eat fish, beans, legumes, or nuts.
Choose low-fat cheeses.
Use unsaturated oils for cooking: olive, rape-seed, or sunflower oils.
Avoid large quantities of high-fat foods: e.g., pastries, cakes, biscuits, chips, chocolate.
Eat no more than four eggs a week.
Eat oily fish: e.g., mackerel, herring, salmon, and tuna.

3. Reduce total sugar. Use fruit rather than sugar to add sweetness. Choose low sugar drinks and avoid adding sugar to drinks and cereals.

4. Increase dietary fiber. The word "fiber" is going out of fashion to be replaced by *non-starch polysaccharides* or *(NSP),* but the principle is the same. A good diet contains a lot of NSP which is to be found in fresh fruit, preferably with skins, lightly cooked vegetables, wholemeal bread, potatoes (with skins), pasta, rice, porridge oats, and high-fiber breakfast cereals.

5. Reduce salt. Use spices (and herbs) to add variety to life.

HOW TO EAT

The main problem about eating is the *way* we eat, and the culprit is the extreme views which our culture engenders about shape and weight, especially in women. These views can lead to extreme ideas about diets which may result in either a cycle of binge-eating followed by starvation (bulimia) or to extreme losses in weight (anorexia).

If the way you eat or your concerns about your shape and weight are a problem for you, then read the rest of this chapter.

BODY AND MIND

Recent research has found that about 80% of American women and almost 50% of men have tried to diet at some time in their lives. This is despite the fact that less than 20% of the population are over-weight—in the sense of being at a weight associated with an increased risk of ill health. Indeed, if you look at an active group of men and women in sports, such as tennis players or footballers, they will be of quite widely differing shapes and weights, many of which do not conform to the fashionable norm.

Dieting seems to be rather like a cultural disease, or even an epidemic. Fashion dictates, and fashion at the moment favors slimness—for men as well as for women, but especially for women. Therefore to look good it is important to be slim, and if you are not slim, you will be pressured by the media, by the diet industry, and by the people around you to do something about it. Regardless of whether nature intended you to be that way, regardless of the number of curves or muscles you were born to develop, it is hard to resist the many influences on you to slim down.

IMPLICATIONS FOR SELF-ESTEEM AND SELF-CONFIDENCE

The message beamed at us in Western societies is that we should be slim; and that if we do the right things we will be slim. This has little to do with health and a lot to do with commercial interests.

When this cultural message is swallowed hook, line, and sinker, it has wide-ranging effects on the way that people feel about themselves, particularly on their self-esteem and self-confidence. As dieters are only too aware, losing weight is supposed to be a way of making you feel good about yourself. It is as if losing weight is a way of solving all of life's problems at once. In this cultural climate it can feel devastating to be the "wrong" shape.

Six Determinants of Weight and Shape

There are two things wrong with this cultural message. The first is that slimness, to the degree envisaged, is *not* especially healthy. The second is that, contrary to the impression given, it is not easy to lose weight. And this is because weight and shape are not determined only by what we eat: many other factors make their contribution as well.

1. Genetics. There is a strong genetic influence on body shape, size, and weight. In an interesting research study carried out in Denmark, a large group of adults who had been adopted, as young children, were weighed. Their weights were compared with the weights of both their natural (biological) parents and their adoptive parents. The result showed that their weight was similar to that of their biological parents, but not to their adoptive parents. It seems that what we inherit goes a long way to determining our shape and weight: we are likely to look like our parents and grandparents.

2. The set point and metabolism. The body acts, possibly for genetic reasons but also according to your age and activity levels, as if it was seeking its own weight level. It seems as though each of us has a weight "set point"—which works rather like the thermostat in a house. If we try to lose weight so as to fall below our set point, physiological forces act to try and prevent the loss in weight. Our body makes better use of the food we eat. In other words the way that our bodies use food is not fixed and static. It changes according to how we treat it, and tends to protect itself from the effects of dieting.

3. Age. Young adults, both women and men, continue to change in weight and shape, or to "fill out," after they have gained their full height. Older people in general are heavier than they were when they were younger, and many women gain weight rather suddenly around the time of the menopause. However, elderly people may lose both weight and height toward the end of their lives.

4. Exercise, fitness, and posture. Certain types of exercise build up certain muscle groups, so swimmers develop big, strong shoulders and runners develop their calf and thigh muscles. People may look different when fit because their posture changes and they move more flexibly. At the same time exercise uses up energy. Although regular exercise increases appetite, its overall effect tends to be a reduction in weight.

5. Drinking habits. Alcohol, because it is high in calories, is not only fattening, it also fills you up without providing you with the nourishment you need.

6. Eating patterns and habits. Eating a large quantity of fatty foods, despite the genetic and physiological factors described above, will lead to weight gain. If you gain weight when you eat a small amount of fatty food, then you may be trying to hold your weight below that demanded by your genetic constitution and your "set point."

The Dangers of Diets

Dieting is deprivation. It is going without. The body is a well-adapted mechanism designed to help you survive, and it resists attempts at severe dieting with physiological means. The more often you have tried to diet, the more efficient these means become and the less effective your diet will be. Your body will find ways of compensating for the way you treat it, so the weight you lose by dieting will not be equivalent to the energy reduction you make. You will be fighting a never ending or losing battle. At the same time, dieting poses some serious dangers.

- *Cycles of starving and overeating.* The more you deprive yourself of food, the more you will crave it. The stronger the cravings, the more likely you will give in. Once you give in it is tempting to overeat: "I've blown it now; I might as well give up, and start again tomorrow." Because you gave in, you then try to impose greater control and the cycle begins again. Many people on diets swing between the extremes of restricting and overeating. The net result is not a loss of weight, but a feeling of being out of control.
- *Upsetting the appetite controls.* Frequent dieting can upset the natural feelings of hunger and fullness. The hunger is never satisfied, and therefore it never leaves you, but at the same time, you get used to it and cease to notice it. When the diet is stopped, this appetite control system no longer functions adequately: it becomes hard to recognize whether you are "really" hungry, even when you are full. The natural control system can be reestablished by eating regular meals over a period of a few weeks.
- *Preoccupation with food.* The natural reaction to deprivation, to severe dieting, is to think more about food. Food can become a serious preoccupation, and ruminating about it starts to interfere with other activities. The preoccupation is counterproductive because it makes the diet harder to bear and binging more likely.

- *Pseudo-success.* It can be tempting to confuse successful dieting with other kinds of success. Dieting can feel good because it helps to achieve a socially desired goal. It takes effort, and so demonstrates a certain kind of strength. These successes make people feel better about themselves, as if being slightly smaller made them better people. It is easy to forget that you are the same person, with the same personality, strengths, and weaknesses whatever size you happen to be.

- *Mood swings.* Happiness may go with a successful dieting plan and misery with an unsuccessful one. Self-esteem can be higher when you are able to restrict your food, but lower (sometimes extremely low) when you overeat. Mood swings start to feel out of control, and dieters may learn to control their moods by eating. Eating improves mood, but only temporarily. It brings relief from hunger and from preoccupations with food, and after eating, while the food is being digested, other bad feelings are dampened down. Eating is often followed by a period of relative calmness. In the long run this has two undesirable consequences: food intake is controlled by mood rather than by physiological requirements; and both mood and eating swing violently. It becomes progressively harder to stick to a diet, and easier to blame oneself for failing to stick to it. The result is more unhappiness, not less.

- *Fatigue, stress, and strain.* This is a direct consequence of deprivation, and can be exacerbated by the emotional roller coaster that goes with dieting.

Eating Disorders Associated with Dieting

The two problems associated with dieting and with excessive concern with weight and shape are anorexia and bulimia nervosa. These are both potentially serious and dangerous conditions that usually start in adolescence and affect many more women than men. For the vast majority of cases, these problems begin following attempts to control weight by dieting. It is important to seek professional help for either of these conditions, even if they are at an early stage.

ANOREXIA NERVOSA

Anorexia involves excessive dieting and loss of weight that can sometimes be so extreme that it threatens life. People with anorexia will go to enormous lengths to lose weight, often eating tiny, calorie-controlled meals in secret, and exercising excessively. Some take large quantities of laxatives after eating, with the mistaken idea that this will prevent them from gaining weight. They may overestimate their body size, even when emaciated, and remain convinced that they are too fat. Being "fat" is associated, in the minds of people with anorexia, with being bad, and putting on weight feels terrifying. Most people with anorexia stop menstruating, feel exhausted, and find it hard to keep warm. They also lose contact with their contemporaries and suffer from low self-esteem and lack of confidence.

BULIMIA NERVOSA

Bulimia is also associated with a fear of gaining weight, with fears of losing control, and with low self-esteem. People who suffer from bulimia, however, are usually of normal weight. They are subject to an extreme eating cycle and alternate between complete starvation and enormous binges, usually carried out in secret. In an effort to control possible weight gain after binging, they may also induce vomiting or take laxatives. They often feel that their eating is out of control. Those with bulimia may eat carefully controlled, reduced-calorie foods between binges and binge on large quantities of "banned" foods, such as chocolate, cakes, pies, bread, and soft drinks. They usually feel distressed and upset by the binge eating and less upset if they succeed in following a strict diet. Binge eating, like anorexia, may disturb menstruation.

DANGEROUS BEHAVIOR

Some of the things that anorexics and bulimics do are dangerous, and can cause serious harm. These are listed in the box on the next page.

Sensible Weight Control

Because of the dangers of anorexia and bulimia, it is important if you want to diet to do this in a safe and sensible way. It is certainly possible to diet while using habits that can last a lifetime, and this is the safest way to work at it, provided that you are absolutely certain that you both want, and need, to lose weight.

First, set yourself a broad, not a narrow, target. Consider the determinants of weight already discussed and think about what is likely to be a healthy, natural weight for you at your age. This is like asking you to decide what your "set point" is at the moment—something that

---

The Dangers of Anorexia and Bulimia

The dangers of low weight

Biochemical abnormalities in blood (especially low potassium) leading to dangerous heart arrhythmias and seizures
Low blood glucose leading to loss of consciousness and death
Heart failure
Dangerously low blood pressure
Weak bones leading to fractures
Dehydration

The dangers of using laxatives

Laxatives do not help to overcome the fattening effects of food. Loss of weight following laxative use is due to loss of fluid. This is dangerous. It leads to bio-chemical abnormalities in blood—including low potassium—which may cause dangerous heart arrhythmias.

The dangers of self-induced vomiting

Dental erosion and caries
Biochemical abnormalities in blood (including low potassium) leading to dangerous heart arrhythmias

---

you will only be able to guess. Then, define a weight to aim at, within for example, a range of 4 to 6 pounds (2 or 3 pounds either side of a precise target). The reason for this is that weight is always subject to minor variations, depending on factors such as water retention, so you will never be able to keep yourself exactly at one weight.

Next, set up a routine that can help you establish a lifetime habit. Plan regular eating times. The traditional pattern of three meals a day is a good one, but it does not suit all people. It is important, however, that you do not try to go for long periods during the day without food—if you do you are in danger of pushing yourself into a binging-starvation cycle. Small snacks between meals and right before bed-time help to prevent hunger-induced binges. Having established regular eating *times,* the next question is what, and how much, to eat. The key to safe dieting is to eat a well-balanced diet but slightly less of it, and since the aim is to establish eating patterns to last a lifetime, there is no hurry. So, at this stage, having decided on a pattern of eating times, simply keep to these times and eat a balanced diet. Do not ban any foods (this might be counterproductive because you might develop cravings for them), and do not restrict what you eat (this might trap you into thinking more about food). At this stage you are trying to find out how much to eat in order to keep your weight stable: neither gaining nor losing, but remaining within your chosen range. You are also ensuring that your appetite control system is in good working order: telling you when you are hungry, but leaving you alone in between meal times. This stage should last at least three weeks (a month if you can manage it).

If you have eaten in this way for at least three weeks, and your weight is above your target range, make a *small* reduction in the overall amount you eat, but retain a balanced diet and regular meal times. The best way is slightly to reduce your intake at each meal. Fatty foods contain more calories than other foods, so reducing the amount of fat is particularly effective. It is essential to make small changes only. Your body will react dramatically to dramatic changes, and will undergo physiological alterations that resist weight reduction. Alcohol contains many calories. One good way of reducing overall intake is to reduce alcohol.

One "trick" to help you reduce food intake is to eat slowly. The feeling of being satisfied comes partly from the level of sugar in your blood, and this rises with a short delay when you eat a normal meal. If you eat slowly, you will be less likely to go on eating beyond the point of satisfaction.

Losing weight cannot be done both quickly and safely. There are real dangers involved, and it is far better for your health and well-being to adapt a sensible, lifetime habit through making small changes so that you lose weight steadily but slowly.

Do not weigh yourself too often, or you could get discouraged and misled by normal day-to-day fluctuations or become increasingly preoccupied with your weight. We recommend weighing yourself no more than once each week. Your size, weight, and shape are reflections of only one, relatively unimportant, aspect of yourself. To keep them in perspective, think also about the many other aspects: your work and daily occupation, family and relationships, pleasures and relaxations, skills and talents, and about your involvement in activities of all kinds, physical, social, and political. You are not your weight.

Establishing Good Eating Habits

Experiments done with golden hamsters showed that these animals naturally controlled the types of food they ate. The precise way in which they did it remained mysterious, but the effect was to provide them with a balanced diet containing all the elements that they needed. If they were deprived for some time of one kind of food, they appeared not to suffer, but when it was offered they then chose to eat it in preference to other things.

Children are obviously not like golden hamsters. But the principle may still be important. If a child is being offered a varied and nutritionally healthy diet, then there is no need to worry about which of the foods offered will be eaten. Too much of one thing will eventually give way to something else. It is far more important, once out of babyhood, to establish regular meal times. Children will have likes and dislikes, and parents may feel it is important to encourage them to try new things, but the child itself is likely to be the best judge of how much it wants to eat. If it is important to you that a child finishes up what it is given, then give it very little to start with, and as the child gets older, allow it to help itself on condition that it eats what it takes. It takes quite a long time to learn how to make this judgment, so the sooner you start the better. Nobody can learn to get it right without making literally hundreds of mistakes on the way.

The message is that small children can control their eating very well, and they will do so better if their appetite controls are set by regular meal times, if they are offered a well-balanced variety of foods, and if they are allowed to make their own choices. Eating then becomes a pleasure rather than a pain.

One of the difficulties of establishing lifelong eating habits in the family is that food is so readily available. Walk into the kitchen or open the fridge, and you can find it any time. So another useful strategy, both for families and for people trying to lose weight slowly by sensible methods, is to use "stimulus control" procedures.

STIMULUS CONTROL

Being controlled by a stimulus means that whenever you see it you react to it. Whenever you see food you eat some. If this is a problem for you, if you tend to nibble at, or binge on, food which is lying around, then the solution is to control the stimulus. There are three steps to stimulus control. The first is to make sure that food is out of sight and out of reach except at meal times. The second is to develop the habit of eating only when you are sitting down to a meal at a table. And the third is to concentrate on eating and enjoying your food whenever you do eat. That means not swallowing it down as you read the paper or spooning it in automatically in front of the TV. In brief, outlaw the casual consumption of food. You can use the method of stimulus control in other ways too. For example, avoid walking past the bakery just as the bread comes out of the oven. Shop from a list, and at a time when you are not ravenously hungry. Buy foods that need preparation, so that you cannot nibble whenever you feel tempted. Limit the amount of food you store at home. Drink water or eat some carrots rather than dipping your finger into the cakemix if you have to cook when you are unbearably hungry.

It is precisely because food is good, because it gives pleasure, that it is so tempting to eat too much, and at the wrong time. But if it were not so enjoyable, our ancestors might not have bothered to search for it and might not have survived. This "searching" behavior dies hard. New and tempting foods and recipes are constantly set before us. Once the lifetime habits are securely in place, there is nothing to be lost from enjoying eating in all sorts of ways, including meals with friends, visits to restaurants, and the occasional feast.

MISUSES OF EATING

Because food is such a potent source of pleasure, it can be used as a substitute for something else. Using food to show love can lead to bad habits: for example, eating for comfort or when feeling sad; eating to control mood; and eating as a cure for boredom or loneliness. Eating is not a way of solving other problems. The danger of using it in this way is that it will become a problem in itself, leading to obesity, bulimia, or anorexia.

People with anorexia and bulimia suffer from an extreme form of the problem that also besets dieters: they feel good about themselves when they succeed in restricting their eating, and bad about themselves when they fail. In many cases self-esteem is based entirely on their opinion about their shape and weight. If you are suffering from anorexia or bulimia, then we recommend that you read one of the books mentioned at the end of the book and also seek medical or psychological help. If, in attempting to diet, you are starting to lose control of your eating—by sometimes binging, or being tempted to use laxatives, or making yourself vomit, read this chapter carefully (and also Chapter 10) and start by focusing on regular meals with snacks: breakfast, snack, lunch, snack, evening meal, bedtime snack. The snacks can be as little as one small apple. The meals need not be large, but should be well balanced. By carefully planning three meals and three snacks each day, you will find it easier to regain control of your eating.

HELPING SOMEONE WITH AN EATING PROBLEM

It can be very difficult if someone close to you is suffering with anorexia or bulimia. People with these difficulties often reject help. They may be secretive, easily upset and angry, and often do not tell others honestly what they are doing. This can be because they feel bad both about their behavior (which may include such things as lying and stealing) and about hurting people they love. Or they might be terrified of trying to change because they feel they will not be able to control the weight gain. For some people their entire sense of self-esteem depends on their success in controlling their eating and weight. For them, being encouraged to change is especially frightening. It may seem to threaten what has become an essential support system. They can become angry when others try to help.

One of the most difficult things for those close to people with eating disorders is to find a way of showing that they care, without either becoming overanxious and overinvolved, or angry and overdetached. The middle road is best, although difficult to maintain. It is helpful if close friends acknowledge openly that there is a problem. But it is usually more fruitful to try and help sufferers to develop as independent people than to try and solve the eating problem for them. The aim for friends and family is to remain emotionally close—available when needed—without becoming intrusive. These eating problems are common in teenage girls and young women. It is at a time when relationships within the family are changing. It is likely to be a time of turbulence and distress. The best way of helping may be to remain the stable point within an unstable world.

Chapter Summary

Good eating habits ensure that eating remains a source of health and of pleasure. They involve limiting, rather than banning, those foods that are fattening or unhealthy, and developing a regular eating pattern: *what you eat* and *how you eat* are both important.

Cultural pressures to diet can spoil the pleasure and undermine self-esteem rather than make you feel good about yourself, because the amount you eat is not the only thing that determines your weight and shape.

Dieting can lead to serious problems:

- Cycles of starving and overeating
- Upsetting the appetite controls

- Preoccupation with food
- Pseudo-success
- Mood swings
- Fatigue, stress, and strain

Two disorders associated with dieting—anorexia and bulimia— have dangerous consequences.

It is possible to control your weight both safely and sensibly by establishing regular meal times and avoiding cycles of either undereating or overeating. Keeping food out of sight (and out of mind) in between meal times—stimulus control—is helpful, and it is important not to use eating as an (ineffective) way of solving other problems, such as feeling lonely or bored.

26

♦ ♦ ♦

Averting Problems with Alcohol

Alcohol can give great pleasure. We use it to mark celebrations, like weddings and birthdays, and other important occasions like homecomings, departures, or funerals. Alcohol is available at most social gatherings, and it would be flying in the face of reality to deny that having a drink has its uses. It can oil the wheels of communication or dampen down fears and sorrows. But it can only do this when used in moderation—in a controlled way—because alcohol is a dangerous, addictive, and depressant drug. In large quantities, or when not carefully controlled, it can also destroy life. The passage from pleasure to destruction is so insidious that a person can have been dependent on alcohol for years before realizing that there is even a problem. The purpose of this chapter is to help you to drink alcohol with safety and pleasure, and to give you some guidelines if you already have a problem. The first part of the chapter explains how to assess your drinking, and the second part explains how to manage your drinking.

1. Assessing Your Drinking

THE ASSESSMENT TREE

There are three questions to ask yourself, which can be illustrated as shown in the tree diagram on the facing page.

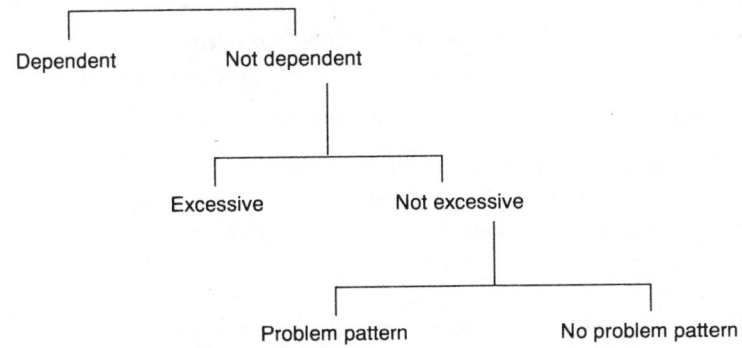

Assessment tree for deciding whether your drinking could be problematic.

1. *Are you dependent on alcohol?* If you are, then the dependence needs to be tackled whether it is physical or psychological. If you are not dependent,
2. *Are you drinking too much alcohol?* Even if you are not dependent, you could be drinking enough to cause you serious health problems in the future. If you are not drinking excessive amounts, then
3. *Is your drinking pattern potentially dangerous?* Some patterns of drinking are likely to lead to problems with alcohol even if you are neither dependent nor drinking excessive amounts.

Question 1. Are you dependent on alcohol?

If you are dependent on alcohol, you may find it difficult to be honest, even with yourself, about your drinking. You may, at some level of thinking, have a sense that all is not well with your drinking but resist confronting yourself with exactly what this sense of unease is about. If so, you have a great deal to gain from being straight with yourself. You may not want to be honest with anyone else, but if you are fooling yourself, you are certainly on a dangerous path.

In order to assess whether you are dependent on alcohol, answer the questions in the box on the next page. Think carefully about each, and answer each honestly. If you cannot be honest with yourself, this itself will tell you that you do have a problem with alcohol.

If you have answered *yes* to four or more of these questions, you are probably dependent on alcohol. Even a single answer of *yes* should cause you to think carefully about the level of your control over drinking and the harm it might be storing up for you.

The Dependence Questionnaire

Answer yes or no to each of the following questions:

- Does one drink tend not to satisfy you?
- Do you almost prefer to drink alone?
- Do you tend to have a drink at night to help you sleep?
- Do you tend to drink in such a way that others are not aware of how much you drink?
- When expecting to drink, would you have something you do not normally like, if that was all that was available?
- Would it feel strange to leave half a glassful of drink?
- Do you have an absolute rule not to drink before a certain time of day?
- Do you often drink significantly more than you intend?
- Have you committed two or more driving offenses?
- Have you ever lost a job because of drinking?
- Has anyone else ever been seriously concerned about your drinking?
- Are you worried about your drinking?

Source: Adapted from B. Colcough, *Tomorrow Will Be Different* (London: Viking, 1993).

THE DANGERS OF DEPENDENCE ON ALCOHOL

Dependence on alcohol has two aspects: physical dependence and psychological dependence.

The key point about *physical dependence* is that if you stop drinking you may experience *physical withdrawal*. This is a potentially dangerous condition which usually starts from a few hours to a few days after the last drink. The first signs of withdrawal are "the shakes," followed by a feeling of acute anxiety and restlessness. As the withdrawal progresses, there may be disorientation (not knowing the time or place where one is); hallucinations (either seeing things or hearing voices which are not really there); and delirium tremens (the DTs), in which the person feels completely terrified with vivid hallucinations and marked shaking. Occasionally, if not treated under proper medical supervision, withdrawal can lead to seizures, coma, and death. There is no absolute rule about who will experience withdrawal symptoms, but it generally takes several years of heavy drinking—fifty units (see p. 320) a week or more. If you get "the shakes" in the morning, needing a drink to steady you, then you are physically dependent—the shakes are the beginning of the withdrawal. If this happens, then you *should seek medical help.* Your drinking is likely to seriously damage your health, but it is also *dangerous to cease drinking without medical supervision* because this could precipitate a full-blown withdrawal.

The key point about *psychological dependence* is that alcohol comes to feel as if it is essential. You need it, and rely on it, and feel bad without it even though you do not suffer the effects of physical withdrawal when you do not have a drink. Many people who are psychologically dependent drink as a way of coping with problems, and they may do this because they cannot find, or do not know, a more effective way of managing them. There is no doubt that alcohol, which is a *depressant* drug, can dull psychological as well as physical pain.

Although psychological dependence on alcohol can start at any stage of life, people are especially vulnerable at moments of stress and difficulty—for example, when coping with a baby who cries a lot at night; when feeling anxious or lonely in a new place; when stressed or overworked; when the children have all left home or when life seems empty; when facing apparently insoluble housing, financial, or employment problems. People who spend a lot of time with other people who drink heavily, and to whom having a good time means having a lot to drink are also more vulnerable than others.

People who have seen their families, friends, or colleagues use alcohol to help them cope with problems may also be more at risk than others of becoming psychologically dependent. They have firsthand evidence that this is an acceptable way of behaving *in the short term,* and they may not have learned many other ways of behaving that are likely to be more effective—as well as being a lot less dangerous—*in the long term.*

Both physical and psychological dependence are dangerous and are likely to cause, not solve, serious problems. Heavy drinkers are three times more likely than others to die in a car crash and six times more likely to commit suicide. The number of arguments and fights they have with their families and close friends is enormously increased. They frequently have problems at work sufficient to disrupt their careers and are often troubled by unhappy relationships.

Question 2. Are You Drinking Too Much Alcohol?

Even if you are not dependent on alcohol, you may be drinking an excessive amount: that is, an amount that will cause problems for you in the future if it continues. In the long run this might cause you serious health problems, and it will also increase the chance that you will become dependent (physically and psychologically) on alcohol.

THE DANGERS OF ALCOHOL TO HEALTH

Medical students are taught always to think of the possibility of alcohol as a cause of a patient's health problems. This is because alcohol can cause a very wide number of problems. The following box summarizes some of the more common ones seen by doctors.

Some of the Physical Dangers of Alcohol

- Irritation of the stomach, leading to bleeding and stomach ulcers
- Liver damage, leading to liver failure or dangerous internal bleeding
- Brain damage, leading to very poor memory
- Heart failure
- High blood pressure
- Impotence
- Poor sleep
- Peripheral nerve damage
- Pancreatitis
- Diabetes
- Anemia
- Injury from falls and poor driving

Alcohol is also a common cause of problems in daily living because it affects your mind, your feelings, your actions, and the workings of your body, as shown in the next box. As you read through this box, ask yourself whether any of these problems have happened to you as a result of drinking. Add on any other problems you have noticed.

HOW MUCH ALCOHOL IS SAFE?

There is no clear-cut answer to this question because people differ markedly in how much alcohol is needed to damage their health, and it is very difficult to collect the research evidence to pinpoint just what problems are caused by just how much drinking. The simple, but not very helpful, answer is that any amount of alcohol *could* cause a problem. One drink might cause someone to fall, or crash the car, and a single binge on alcohol could cause dangerous bleeding from the stomach. Most of us, however, enjoy having a drink, and either deny there is any risk at all, or think that it is worth taking such a small risk.

Common Problems Caused by Alcohol

Effects on your mind

Poor concentration
Forgetfulness
Permanent, severe damage to memory following very heavy drinking
Slow reaction times
Muddled thinking

Effects on your feelings

Unhappiness
Depression
Frustration
Irritability
Hostility
Hopelessness
Despair

Effects on your actions

Disagreements and arguments
Difficulty doing your work, inside or outside the home
Carelessness, leading to more frequent accidents or mistakes
Difficulty getting up and going to work
Secretive behaviors, and suspicious behaviors
Telling lies, to yourself as well as to others

Effects on your body

Loss of appetite
Feeling thirsty for some hours afterward
Disturbed sleep in the later part of the night, having initially slept quite well
Loss of interest in sex and inability to get sexually aroused (this is a problem
for both men and women)
Headaches
Nausea (and vomiting)
Reduced motor coordination; clumsiness
Blurred vision
Dizziness
Feeling shaky or wobbly

This lack of clarity is reflected in the conflicting advice being given by various authorities over the years. However, a guideline is useful, and we suggest the one provided by The Royal Colleges of Psychiatrists, Physicians, and General Practitioners and by the Health Education Council. This says that each week *men should drink no more than 21 units* and *women should drink no more than 14 units*. The different recommendations reflect differences in metabolism. If you drink less than these recommended amounts, there is little danger of causing yourself physical harm or of becoming psychologically dependent. Many people may be able safely to drink more than these quantities, but the risks of harm increase if they do.

HOW MUCH ARE YOU DRINKING?

The standard way of measuring how much alcohol you drink is in terms of *units (or "drinks") per week*. One unit represents 8–10 grams of pure alcohol. The following box gives the unit equivalents of various drinks.

Number of Alcohol Units in Various Drinks

- One pint of beer   2 units
  (many bottled beers are much stronger)
- One small glass of wine   1 unit
- One bottle table wine   8 units
- One bottle of sherry   12 units
- One measure of spirits
  (whisky, gin, vodka)   1 unit
- One double measure   2 units
- One bottle of spirits   30 units

Note: Drinks poured at home are nearly always much bigger than standard measures.

A DRINKING DIARY

The best way to work out how much alcohol you drink is to keep a drinking diary. This should be filled in using a diary, cards, or small notebook which you can carry around with you throughout the week. In order to calculate your intake, you need to write down every single drink you have (including "refills"), giving the type of drink and the quantity. Work out the number of units using the information in the box. It is important to fill in the diary very close to the time you drink, and if you have several drinks in an evening, you should make a note of each one. Trying to guess how much you had later that night or in the morning is not likely to be accurate. If you want to keep the diary private, you might be able to go off to the lavatory to fill it in, or you might be able to find another way of keeping a tally—for example, by putting one coin, or match, or bit of paper in whichever pocket you have empty for each unit of alcohol you drink.

A drinking diary can also be used to find out about other factors that affect your drinking, like where you were, who you were with and what else you were doing at the time. This is very helpful if you want to cut down. In order to keep a *full drinking diary,* write down the headings as shown in the following example, and always fill the diary in whenever you drink, or it will inevitably be inaccurate.

Example of a drinking diary

Questions	Answers	
	6:00 P.M.	8:30 P.M.
Where?	Home	Home
With whom?	Alone	With Ben
What?	Sherry after work	Wine
How much?	2 large glasses	2 glasses
Units?	3	2
With food?	No	Yes
Why?	Tired and strained	Usually do

You are now in a position to answer the question about whether you are drinking too much. The recommended guideline for men (21 units a week) works out to an *average* of three units a day, or one and a half pints or three glasses of wine: in a week, this would add up to 10½ pints or 2½ bottles of wine. The recommended maximum for women (14 units a week) works out to 2 glasses of wine or 1½ glasses of sherry a day. The message is that *if you drink almost every day, you do not need to drink very much for it to add up to more than the recommended amount.* If you are drinking more than these guidelines, then you should seriously consider whether to cut down. Your long-term health might be at risk.

Question 3. Is Your Drinking Pattern Potentially Dangerous?

Even if you are drinking less, at the moment, than the recommended maximum, your pattern of drinking may be potentially dangerous because it may lead to serious problems in the future. There are two danger signs to look out for. The first is turning to alcohol when you are stressed, when you feel as though you *must* have a drink. The danger is that the more stressed you are, the more you will drink, and the more dependent you will become. Try to break the habit now, before it becomes deeply entrenched, by dealing with the stress instead. Read Chapter 18. The second danger sign is if you are getting into a habit of drinking unthinkingly, on a regular basis. If someone at age 20 drinks one vodka every evening when getting home from work, there is a danger that that will creep up to two vodkas, because once the habit has been established, most people become tolerant of alcohol and need more to achieve the same effect. This will gradually extend until the quantity drunk is likely to do physical harm in the long run. Of course, many people regularly enjoy one or two drinks a day for most of their lives. You do not *have* to decline into the danger zone, but you do need to be constantly on the lookout: in order to be able to enjoy the pleasure that alcohol can give, it is important to know that there is always potential danger, and to know how to calculate how dangerous your level of drinking really is.

2. Managing Your Drinking

CHANGING DRINKING PATTERNS

If you are concerned that you might be at risk because of the pattern of your drinking, there are four points to bear in mind.

1. Break any regular patterns, like having a drink every day after work. Find out how it feels to have at least one alcohol-free day each week.
2. Keep below the recommended maximum, using a drinking diary to assess accurately how much you really are having. It cannot be emphasized too much how easy it is to underestimate how much you drink, especially if you drink at home.
3. Make sure that you do not use alcohol as a "crutch" when you have other problems, such as feeling depressed, stressed, lonely, or anxious. There are other solutions to these problems. Drink-

ing may dull your feelings about them in the short term but in the long term it only compounds them.

4. Learn to be able to say *no* when you are offered a drink. It is easy to start drinking too much if you often go to social gatherings in which alcohol is not only freely available but almost pushed upon you. Fortunately, it is more socially acceptable to refuse an alcoholic drink now than it was a few years ago. Increased awareness of the dangers of driving after drinking has had a great effect. But whether it is socially acceptable or not, we each have the right to say *no* if we want to (see also pp. 142–143). If you find it difficult to refuse a drink, then practice doing so until you are making the decisions that you want to make.

REDUCING THE AMOUNT YOU DRINK

The physical harm that alcohol can cause depends on the amount you drink, not on whether you are dependent. The more you drink, above the recommended maximum, the more likely you are to suffer one or more of the physical dangers of alcohol. If you are not dependent, cutting down will not be too difficult. It will be rather like breaking any other habit (see Chapter 23). In this chapter we show how the six steps described in Chapter 23 can be adapted for cutting down the amount you drink.

Step 1: Preparation: Making a positive decision to change. As with changing any habit, the most important step is the first: getting it clear in your mind that you want to change. Unless you really want to cut down, you will not succeed in doing so. Start by thinking about what is good about drinking for you. *What do you gain from it?* Take time to think about this, and ask yourself whether you really gain what you hope to gain (for example, peace of mind, a good night's sleep, a feeling of friendship, better communication). If you do, then before cutting down, you should think about how else you could get these things. Ask yourself how other people get them. Read those chapters in this book that deal with the things that concern you.

Go on to think about what makes you want to cut down. *What problems does drinking cause for you? Or for others around you?* Think about a whole range of problems like putting on weight, sleeping badly, sexual difficulties, hangovers, arguments, poor concentration, worry, loss of trust or self-respect, the expense, and so on. Think about problems that it *might* cause as well as problems that it *already has* caused. Alert yourself to as many risks as you can.

Your next task is to weigh up the balance between the two lists and to decide whether you really want to cut down. It can be very helpful to talk to someone else at this stage, since many of the advantages of drinking are immediate and relatively easy to remember, while the disadvantages are often delayed and not so easy to keep in mind. If you make a positive decision to cut down, summarize your reasons for doing so. Keep your summary and read it frequently while you are changing your drinking habits.

Step 2: Keep track of how much you drink. Assess your current drinking carefully before you make any changes. Keep a detailed drinking diary for at least a week (maybe two), even though your pattern of drinking may be regular. Remember to count more for the (larger) drinks poured at home, and for refills. Examine your diary to see if there are any times or situations when you tend to drink more than you want—or risky situations for you. These are the times for which you need special preparation so as to be forearmed and on your guard. Continue to keep an accurate diary while you make the effort to change, and at the end of each week, work out how well you have done.

Step 3: Devise your personal strategy. Plan your week ahead in detail in order keep within the recommended number of units. Decide exactly how much you are going to drink and when. If you are uncertain what you will be doing, then make out a simple plan for yourself, like drinking only on three days, and drinking not more than four units on any one day. If you drink at home, it may help to remove the alcohol, or put it out of sight, and to explain what you want to do to others. If you go out with friends on Thursdays and drink a great deal, losing track of how much you have, devise a strategy to help yourself keep within limits. You could have one drink only and then switch to soft drinks, or you could alternate soft drinks and alcoholic ones. And you could drink slowly. But if you find it difficult to refuse a drink, then read Chapter 13 on assertiveness. If you cannot readily say *no,* then either you have difficulty asserting yourself, or you have a problem with alcohol dependency which should be tackled if you are not to damage your health.

Step 4: Think about what you could do instead. If you replace the drinking with another activity, your task will be much easier—especially if going without leaves a void to fill. It is even helpful to *combine* drinking with another activity, such as eating a meal, talking to friends, or playing a game of darts. The other activities divert your attention from the drink and help you to drink less. If having a drink has become a way of not thinking about problems—of sweeping them under the carpet—the problems may well re-emerge to trouble you when you go without. Problems rarely go away when you look the other way. It would be more useful to face them instead (see Chapter 6) and to revise your problem-solving skills (Chapter 8).

Step 5: Persistence and tracking your progress. At regular intervals, a week is probably best, use your diary to work out whether what you actually did matched with your plan. There are two possibilities: either you did well or you drank more than you planned. If you did well, you should reward yourself before going on to plan the next week. You are trying to break a habit and that always takes persistence. If you drank more than you planned, you need to look carefully at why before you make a plan for the next week. If things did not go according to plan, remember that the carrot works better than the stick. Think again about what you want to gain by drinking less. Think about any gains you have already made, however small. If you keep trying, you will be able to make the changes you wish to make.

Step 6: Managing lapses. Do not be hard on yourself when you break your resolve and have a lapse—just try not to let the lapse turn into a relapse. If you have failed, it may reveal that you are more dependent on alcohol, physically or psychologically, than you realized, and that is very useful to know. This does not mean that you will not be able to overcome the problem, but it does mean that there is a significant problem that you need to solve. At least you have discovered the size of the problem and have had the courage to face it; the next section describes strategies you can use to help you overcome the problem of physical dependence on alcohol.

Overcoming Dependence on Alcohol

Many people who have a problem with dependence on alcohol do not acknowledge this even to themselves, and therefore they cannot work to overcome it. If you have a dependency problem, and have acknowledged this to yourself, you are halfway there.

It is very easy to chastise yourself, even to despise yourself. Dependency on alcohol can make you do things which you do not really approve of, like breaking promises, or causing hurt and pain to those you love. Other people might be suffering because of the time you spend drinking and away from home; because you are irritable and unable to show affection when you feel it; because you are violent; because your marked changes in mood make it difficult for those around you to know where they stand; or because you are unreliable. Alcohol is expensive, so that the money you spend may be causing problems for you and others also. Alcohol dependence may cause problems at work, although some people who are dependent are able to carry on effectively at work without others even suspecting there is a problem. It may be your family rather than your work that suffers.

It is important, therefore, clearly to distinguish the "real" you from the things that you sometimes do, and from the way you behave because of the alcohol. You may be doing things you do not approve of. Instead of using this as a stick to beat yourself with, recognize that it means that the "real" you does have standards and ideals, and that is why you can recognize the difference between what you are doing and what you would like to be doing. It is important to recognize the self within, whom you respect, because if you cannot find this inner self-respect, it will be much harder to overcome the dependence. Overcoming dependence requires you to value yourself (Chapter 3) and enables you to see yourself beyond the alcohol dependence.

SEEK MEDICAL HELP

If you are dependent on alcohol, we advise you to see your doctor and to discuss the problems. Your doctor will know what help and support is available, and there is no doubt that overcoming your problem will be much easier with support. But there is also another important reason for seeing your doctor, and that is the question of withdrawal. If you have been drinking quite heavily for a long time, you might get withdrawal symptoms when you stop drinking, and these are potentially dangerous. You may need your doctor's help through this withdrawal phase, which may need to be done in a hospital or clinic.

DO YOU REALLY WANT TO OVERCOME YOUR DEPENDENCE?

Unless you are sure that you want to overcome your dependence, you will not be able to do so. The first step is the same one described on page 323: think through all the advantages and disadvantages of overcoming it. Are you happy with the way things are at the moment—with your family or other close relationships? With your work? If you are not, then think what you have to gain by overcoming your dependence. There are tremendous rewards for giving up alcohol: two things that you will have more of will be time and money; and all your positive features, all those parts of your personality which you like, will still be there. One of the myths that those dependent on alcohol often believe is that they will be less fun, or less amusing, without drinking—or less able to cope. But quite the opposite is true. If you decide that you want to overcome your dependence, then list all the things which you have to gain and keep the list in a place where you can frequently look at it.

REDUCED DRINKING OR ABSTINENCE?

If you have a problem with alcohol, should you reduce your drinking or give it up entirely? The traditional answer to this question used to be that you should aim for abstinence, not simply reduce the amount you drink. Then in the 1960s and 1970s there were a number of reports which suggested that some people formerly dependent on alcohol were able successfully to return to "social drinking." However, later evidence suggests that the majority of those who return to social drinking relapse, and start to drink too much again. It appears that so few people dependent on alcohol are able to return to social drinking without relapsing that the only good advice is to *become abstinent*. If your aim is simply to cut down, it is unlikely to work.

HELPING YOURSELF TO BECOME ABSTINENT

If you really want to give up alcohol, you can; but you must give yourself as much help as possible because it is going to be difficult. Think as often as you can, daily if possible, about what you have to gain in the way of a better life. As Beauchamp Colclough has written, from both his personal experience and his large experience of helping others: "Your worst day recovering is not as bad as when you were drinking."

Get help. It is going to be much easier if you have help and support from people who understand your situation. There are several sources of help and it is worth approaching them all. First, there is *Alcoholics Anonymous,* or "AA." There are branches in almost every locality, and the number and address should be in the telephone directory, and available from your library, or your doctor. AA runs "self-help" groups where you will meet others in the same situation. Their work has a distinct religious aspect which some do not like, but the main focus is on helping each other to remain abstinent from alcohol. There are also many medical services now available for dealing with substance abuse. Your doctor can put you in touch with special services to help you abstain from alcohol, some of which are hospital based and some community based. The advantage of these services is that people who know the position you are in will be able to help and support you through the most difficult times.

Exercise. Spending less time drinking gives you more time for other things. Use some of this to get physically fitter. This will help you to feel good about your body and make it easier to abstain.

Look after your appearance. If you have let your appearance slip, and have extra money available because you are not spending it on alcohol, you could buy new clothes. As with exercise, this will help you to feel good about yourself. The better you feel, the easier it is to abstain.

Take one day at a time. Do not look far into the distance, but concentrate on remaining abstinent for today. There are two aspects to this injunction. The first is not to be too ambitious, not to say to yourself: "I won't ever drink again." Focus just on today. The second aspect is that you need constantly, every day, to renew your resolve not to drink. Once you have been dependent on alcohol, you are always at risk of drinking excessively again. Even when you have been abstinent for ten years, you cannot take for granted that you will not start drinking to excess again. You should renew your vow not to drink every single day.

Recognize the voice of the tempter. There will be times, frequent at first, less frequent later on, but never gone forever, when you are tempted to have a drink. The voice inside you will make it sound so plausible and attractive: "One drink can't do any harm." But it can—it will take you straight back to excess. "Everybody has the occasional drink; don't be such a fool." Not everybody has a problem with alcohol dependence—and that makes all the difference; but many of those who have an occasional drink have a great deal more than the occasional drink, and are doing themselves a great deal of harm. "No one will know." How is that relevant? You are returning to the way of life which you know you want to leave behind. "Don't believe that silly book you read— really, how can one drink harm anyone?" Do not believe this voice. There is no end to its thirst for alcohol.

This time is different. You may have tried to give up alcohol before and failed, so why, you may be thinking, should this time be different? The answer is that this time can be different if you are better prepared, have taken more precautions, have thought it through more, and have found yourself more help.

Do not be hard on yourself. You need all the positive encouragement you can get, and you particularly need it from yourself. You cannot afford to undermine yourself. Be prepared to forgive yourself for what you have done because of the dependence on alcohol. Value yourself and be positive about yourself.

Avoid drinking companions. Look back at your drinking diary. What were the situations in which the drinking occurred? Think about this carefully and then do all you can to avoid those situations which were particularly dangerous, or try to change them. One of the most dangerous for many people is being with others who drink. The voices of your companions add to your own inner voice: "Go on, have a drink." This is not the time to test your assertiveness skills to their full. It is better to avoid these situations instead. If you can only see these friends when they are drinking, it is better not to see them. Good friends will be prepared to see you on other occasions too. Surround yourself, as far as possible, with people who support your abstinence, not with people who undermine your resolve.

Understand that those close to you may be skeptical. Those close to you, your family, for example—may be skeptical that this time you will abstain. "I'll believe it when I see it" may be their attitude. Their attitude may well be reasonable in the light of past experience. How are they to know that this time will be different? Do not be angry with them. It will take some time to regain their trust in you. Accept this fact and you will not waste your energy fighting against their beliefs.

If you relapse. Take stock. Why did it happen? Go through the steps you took carefully. Did you miss out some of the ways of helping yourself? Did you prepare yourself fully? Did you try doing it on your own without any help or support? Prepare yourself again, only this time with more care, and if you find that there are other problems in your life that tempt you into drinking, like social anxiety, boredom, loneliness, depression, or lack of confidence, think about how to tackle these problems as well. There are many ideas in this book, and your doctor will also be able to tell you what other help is available.

Chapter Summary

Alcohol is a source of pleasure in life, but it can be dangerous.
Assess your drinking using the assessment tree:

- Are you dependent on alcohol?
- Are you drinking too much?
- Is your drinking pattern potentially dangerous?

A drinking diary will help you work out how much alcohol you drink.
You can change your drinking pattern using six steps.

1. Make a positive decision to change.
2. Keep track of how much you drink.
3. Devise your personal strategy.
4. Think about what you could do instead.
5. Persist.
6. Manage lapses.

Be honest with yourself about your drinking: you can overcome problems although you may need a helping hand.

27

◆ ◆ ◆

Tranquilizers and How to Stop Taking Them

Tranquilizers are used to relieve the symptoms of anxiety, stress, and tension, and to induce a "good mood." When they were first introduced, they were thought to be completely harmless, trouble-free drugs that people could take for as long as they liked, even for years at a stretch. Not very long ago, if you had visited your GP because your problems were really upsetting you, you might have been prescribed a tranquilizer. Your distress could have been caused by stress at work, a physical illness, poor housing, difficulties in your marriage, a recent bereavement, worry about finances, poor sleep, tension headaches, or almost anything else. Tranquilizers were offered because they would make you feel better.

This way of using tranquilizers has since been questioned. Although no one denies that taking a tranquilizer can quickly calm you down, taking them regularly, for long periods, is no longer recommended. This chapter gives you information about tranquilizers, and explains how you can stop taking them.

Some Facts and Figures

Tranquilizers are anti-anxiety drugs that may have a sedative or sleep-inducing effect. They are often called "minor tranquilizers," to distinguish them from the "Major Tranquilizers" used in the treatment of more serious disorders. Most of the minor tranquilizers commonly prescribed belong to the benzodiazepine family of drugs (see box on facing page). Both major tranquilizers and antidepressants can also have a calming effect and are prescribed by some doctors in low doses to treat anxiety. There is another, and quite different, group of drugs that is sometimes prescribed for anxiety, called "beta-blockers." Their main use is in the treatment of high blood pressure and of some kinds of irregular heart beat. They also reduce physical symptoms of anxiety, such as shaking (tremor) and fast heart rate. Some musicians, for example, take them just before giving a concert. This chapter is about minor tranquilizers.

The use of minor tranquilizers rocketed in the 1960s and 1970s. About 10 years ago, it was calculated that about one in fifty of the adult population took tranquilizers every day and night of the year. People over 75 and middle-aged women were then, and still are, the most frequent users. Overall, women receive twice as many prescriptions for tranquilizers as men, partly because more women than men visit their GPs and talk about their anxieties and worries.

Tranquilizers are not only used to treat stress and tension. They have a strong muscle-relaxing effect and so may be used after injury; they are often used by anesthetists before giving a general anesthetic, and as anticonvulsants because they make seizures less likely. They can have unwanted effects or "side effects" too. These include dizziness, drowsiness, poor memory and concentration, blurred vision, headaches, and feeling sick. Elderly people are more likely to have side effects and can become quite confused even on small doses. Loss of alertness is sufficiently common to affect performance at work, and it may be advisable not to drive or operate machinery while taking the drugs. Mixing tranquilizers and alcohol can be dangerous because the two substances interact, increasing the effects of both of them.

FOUR PROBLEMS ARISING FROM LONG-TERM USE OF TRANQUILIZERS

There are four main reasons why tranquilizers should not, normally, be taken for more than a few weeks.

1. Tranquilizers can prevent you from finding more lasting solutions to your problems. If you were especially stressed at work and sleeping badly, a tranquilizer might help you sleep, and enable you to rejoin the fray feeling calmer, but it would not have taught you how to manage

Some Tranquilizers and Sleeping Pills

Benzodiazepines

Long acting

Diazepam (Valium)

Nitrazepam (Mogadon)

Chlordiazepoxide (Librium)

Flunitrazepam (Rohypnol)

Flurazepam (Dalmane)

Alprazolam (Xanax)

Bromazepam (Lexotan)

Clobazam

Clorazepate (Tranxene)

Medazepam (Nobrium)

Short acting

Temazepam (Restoril)

Oxazepam (Serax)

Lorazepam (Ativan)

Lormetazepam

Loprazolam

Minor tranquilizers that are not benzodiazepines

Chloral hydrate (Welldorm; Noctec; Somnos)

Triclofos

Chlormethiazole (Heminevrin)

Promethazine

Zopiclone (Zimovane)

Buspirone (Buspar)

Chlormezanone (Trancopal)

Amobarbital (Amytal)

Pentobarbital (Nembutal)

Butabarbital (Butisol)

Secobarbital (Seconal)

Meprobamate (Equanil; Miltown; Equagesic)

Some antidepressants that may be prescribed as tranquilizers

Amitriptyline

Imipramine

Clomipramine (Anafranil)

Nortriptyline (Aventyl; Allegron)

Mianserin (Bolvidon; Norval)

Desipramine (Pertofran)

Lofepramine (Gamanil)

Dothiepin (Prothiaden)

Trimipramine (Surmontil)

Trazodone (Molipaxin)

Some major tranquilizers that may be used for mild sedation

Chlorpromazine (Largactil)

Thioridazine (Melleril)

Some Beta-blocking drugs

Propranolol (Inderal)

Labetalol (Trandate)

Atenolol (Tenormin)

Metoprolol (Lopressor, Betaloc)

Note: The generic name is given first, and some brand names are given in parentheses.

your work demands and stress levels more effectively. Many women feel they have to cope not only for themselves but also for other people in the family. If they do this without adequate emotional support, they may turn to their doctors for help and be offered a prescription for tranquilizers. But this does not provide the support they need even if it reduces distress. Although tranquilizers can make you feel better in the short term, they may actually help to keep the problem going. You may get caught up in either the *tranquilizer spiral* or *tranquilizer dependence*.

The tranquilizer spiral

Have too much to do

Feel stressed and unable to cope

Take a tranquilizer

Calm down

Cope better for a few days

The pressure builds up again

Reach for another tablet

Tranquilizer dependence

Something shakes your confidence

You feel worried and apprehensive

You avoid difficult situations

You take a tranquilizer

You can face the world again

You learn: "I can't cope without tranquilizers"

2. Tranquilizers can dull your feelings. Tranquilizers dampen down feelings—the good ones as well as the bad ones—until, in the words of one of our patients, "It is as if something comes between you and your natural reaction to things." Barnie had been taking Valium tablets three times a day for 4 years when his daughter came in to tell him she was pregnant and that his first grandchild would be born in about 6 months' time. At some level he was delighted; he knew he was really happy for her, and for the whole family. But inside he felt much the same as usual, which both worried and saddened him. He feared it was a sign that he was now getting depressed as well as anxious. Because they interfere with your spontaneity by ironing out the ups as well as the downs, tranquilizers could even prevent you noticing a change for the better. Usually problems come and go, and anxiety, stress, and tension come and go with them. If you regularly take tranquilizers, these changes become blurred. Furthermore, some problems need to be dealt with by "working through" feelings about them—for example, sadness when a relationship breaks up. Taking pills *on a long-term basis* does not help you get over this sadness.

3. You can come to depend on tranquilizers psychologically. Tranquilizers, taken regularly, can create the need they satisfy. It is easy to become psychologically dependent on them and, for example, to carry them with you wherever you go "just in case," or make sure you never let them run out. The problem with this kind of dependence is that it gradually whittles away at your confidence. It can make you feel there is something wrong with *you,* rather than with *what's happening in your life.* Paula had lost her job three years ago, and being unable to keep up the mortgage payments on her house, she had moved with her children into a small apartment. At the same time, her mother became ill, and then died, and her eldest child was taking important exams. She was under enormous stress and started to take tranquilizers. With them she found she was able to sleep better, and to stop worrying, but whenever she tried a night without them, she felt worse again. Any demand she placed on herself made her feel so bad that she kept on taking the tablets. In the end she no longer believed she could go into town without them, and the thought of being interviewed for a job only made her think how incompetent she now was compared with her former self.

As this sort of thing goes on, it is easy to start doubting yourself, and feeling helpless when the next problem arises. Then it is tempting to go on managing the problem by taking a pill, rather than by learning new coping skills. Finding your own way of coping is more likely to build your confidence up again.

4. You can become addicted to tranquilizers physiologically. Contrary to what was originally believed, tranquilizers are now known to be addictive. This means that as your body gets used to them you may have to take more to achieve the same effect, and if you suddenly stop taking them regularly, you may suffer from withdrawal.

WITHDRAWAL SYMPTOMS

If you suddenly stop taking tranquilizers, particularly if you have been on them for a long time, you may experience unpleasant feelings which are called "withdrawal symptoms." It may be because of these withdrawal symptoms that you have not been able to stop the tranquilizers before now. Withdrawal symptoms are unpleasant, but worse than that, they are confusing. Although they vary enormously from person to person, many of the more common ones are very similar to the symptoms of anxiety. For example, they include sweating, shaking, panicky feelings, being aware of your heart thumping or speeding up, disturbed sleep, pins and needles, and difficulty concentrating. The problem is that you may mistake these withdrawal symptoms for anxiety and believe that you still need the tranquilizers. One withdrawal symptom that is not usually associated with the original problem is an enhanced sensory sensitivity: lights may seem especially bright, noises unexpectedly loud, and so on. If you restart the tablets when this happens, the symptoms will quickly disappear. But this could just as easily show that they are withdrawal symptoms as symptoms of anxiety.

HOW LONG CAN YOU TAKE TRANQUILIZERS SAFELY?

Tranquilizers should be limited to occasional use—for example, to times when someone is extremely anxious about something they cannot avoid doing, or when they urgently need, and have been unable to get, a good night's sleep. If anxiety or other distress is acute, then intense drug therapy should be limited to about four weeks and should be combined with additional support, self-help, therapy, or counseling.

The long-term use of tranquilizers should normally be avoided. However, for some elderly people and for those rare people who suffer from severe and persistent anxiety, long-term drug therapy may, nevertheless, be the best option, possibly using one of the newer types of drugs now on the market.

- **Reminder: all anti-anxiety drugs suppress symptoms without necessarily removing the cause of the problem.**

Coming Off Tranquilizers

About 50% of people who have been taking tranquilizers for more than a few weeks (and that includes those who have been taking them for many years) can stop them with no difficulty. Most of the others have *some* withdrawal problems, but *very few indeed* have serious difficulty.

We recommend a two-pronged attack on the problem:

1. Gradually reduce the tablets until you can cut them out altogether.
2. Learn how to manage the problems another way.

You should work on both prongs at once, but first you need to make the decision to stop.

DECIDING TO STOP

Think about the answers to these questions:

1. Are you dependent on the tablets? Do you automatically reach for them at the same time every day? Do you count the time between tablets? Do you worry about what would happen if you did *not* take one?

2. Are they still helping? Or have you sometimes forgotten to take one, and only noticed later on? Are you using them more as a prop than anything else?

3. What might you gain by stopping? List the advantages of stopping. Then list the disadvantages. Most often the advantages are long term and seem out of reach (feeling more confident), while the disadvantages are short term and seem to be immediate (worrying so that you sleep badly). Look at your lists and see if this fits for you. Then try to balance one against the other. Are you convinced you want to stop? You need to be sure about what you hope to gain, as being half-hearted or unclear is a sure way of making the task harder for yourself.

4. Who could help you? Talking to someone else helps, and others often find it easier to keep the reasons for you to stop in mind when the doubts creep in. *If you decide you want to stop, discuss the decision with your doctor first.*

Many doctors know of local tranquilizer withdrawal groups that could be helpful to you, and of course, only your doctor knows both you and the particular tranquilizer you have been taking.

If you are taking a short-acting drug, it may be best to change to an equivalent dose of a long-acting drug and then gradually reduce the dose (see the box on p. 333). This is because most people find it easier to stop taking a long-acting drug than a short-acting one. You will need to discuss this with your doctor.

A STEP-BY-STEP GUIDE TO STOPPING TRANQUILIZERS

Step 1. Stabilize your dose by taking your tablets at (roughly) the same time every day.

Step 2. Plan to reduce your tablets gradually. Work out what you think would suit you best, without comparing yourself with others. Everyone is different, and your program should be made for you. These are some of the questions to consider:

- How big should the first cut be? Answer: As small as you wish.
- Which tablet should I cut out first? Answer: The one you need least.
- When should I start? Answer: Not when you are "in crisis." Choose a relatively stable time if you can.

If you think it might help to have weaker doses at some stage (e.g., 2 milligrams rather than 5), discuss this with your doctor.

Step 3. Make the first cut. This takes courage, and you may feel unconfident, hesitant, and apprehensive. Try not to confuse your natural fears about managing without the pills with a return of your original problem. When Paula made the first cut, she found herself doubting her ability to cope with even the simplest demands. By taking them one at a time, she gradually learned that she managed them fine. She came to recognize the difference between having too much to do and worrying about having too much to do.

Once you have made a cut, do not go back on it. If you keep lowering and then raising your dose, you are likely to have more difficulty withdrawing than if you make a smooth and slow reduction.

Step 4. Settle down at the new level. Stay at each level for at least three days, until you feel you can make another cut. The pace of reduction will be influenced by many things: the type of tranquilizer, the length of time you have been taking it, the problems you face, the support you have, your ability to cope with difficulties, your ability to understand, recognize, and tolerate withdrawal symptoms, and your ability to learn new ways of solving problems. There are probably other factors too, some of which will be peculiar to you, so you should take charge of your own withdrawal plan. Most people need time to adjust psychologically and to build up alternative ways of coping.

Step 5. Repeat Steps 3 and 4 until you have given up tranquilizers. Many people would rather "get it over with quickly," but if you go too fast, you may trigger withdrawal symptoms. You should aim to strike a balance between dragging your feet and trying to run before you can walk. As a general guide, it should take between three weeks and three months to come off tranquilizers. When it comes to the last stages, it can help to cut the tablets in half, or even in quarters, using a sharp knife. If the drug comes in syrup form, you could dilute it, or if it comes in capsules, you could ask a pharmacist for some empty ones and make two half doses out of one. You may find that the most difficult step is stopping the final dose. This is quite normal, but beware of prolonging the agony by drawing the last stage out too long. If you are coping already with only a half tablet, you will also be able to cope without any tablets.

ADJUSTING TO FLYING SOLO

Most people have a few bad moments when coming off tranquilizers, and at first find these difficult to manage. But bad moments are normal. Everyone has them, just as everyone has good days and bad days, and you may notice the fluctuations more if your reactions have recently been dampened by drugs. Your mind and your body will need to readjust once you are no longer taking tranquilizers. The time this takes varies enormously, from a few days to a few months, so you should work at developing new problem-solving and coping strategies right from the start.

COPING STRATEGIES

The coping strategies you need to develop will depend on the problems that need to be tackled. We suggest that:

1. You write down the main problem that you hoped tranquilizers would solve, or that coming off tranquilizers will leave you with.
2. Read through the list of alternatives to tranquilizers in the box on the following page.
3. Select *one* of these to start with.
4. Learn about this strategy, then practice using it regularly, even if at first it does not work for you, before taking on a second one.

In the end, you can use as many strategies as you like, but you should focus on learning one at a time.

Chapter Summary

Tranquilizers are helpful because they calm you down, but they do not remove the cause of the problem. Taking them regularly for long periods is not helpful because they may discourage your search for

---

Alternatives to Tranquilizers

Learning to relax: Chapter 11

Dealing with stress and tension: Chapter 18

Dealing with anxiety and worry: Chapter 16

Building self-confidence and self-esteem: Chapter 10

Becoming more assertive: Chapter 13

Managing yourself and your time: Chapter 5

Setting limits on work and family demands: Chapter 13

Facing things that you fear: Chapters 6 and 17

Overcoming sleep problems: Chapter 24

Difficulties in your relationships: Part Three, all four chapters

Keeping things in perspective: Chapter 9

---

long-term solutions, they dampen down good as well as bad feelings, it is easy to rely on them, and they are addictive.

Coming off tranquilizers is easier than it sounds. First, make a positive decision to change. Then, reduce your dose gradually— allowing yourself to settle down at each new level and learning how to manage your difficulties in other ways.

P A R T   S I X

◆ ◆ ◆

The Working Mind

This final part of the book is about your mind as a tool for thinking. Just as a degree of physical fitness contributes to pleasure from physical activity, so a degree of "mental fitness" enables you to gain pleasure from the use of your mind.

The first two chapters in this part on study are not for students only. They are for anyone who wishes to learn or to develop a hobby or interest.

Our memories often let us down. We devote two chapters to showing how you can make sure that your memory works for you.

The last two chapters, on making decisions and thinking straight, bring together many of the themes of this book, and take them a step further.

Your mind is a powerful tool. "The Working Mind" shows how you can use it to enjoy your life to the fullest.

28

♦ ♦ ♦

The Fundamentals of Effective Study

The Pleasures of Study

Study is not only for students: good study methods are useful to us all. A little regular study is analogous to a little regular exercise: it strengthens habits and develops skills that are useful for a lifetime. The principles explained in this chapter are appropriate to a wide range of situations: to school or university students studying full-time; to part-time students, attending evening classes or studying alone; to people who wish to improve their vocational qualifications; and to people who want to pursue a hobby or learn some Spanish. This chapter is relevant whether you want to study a topic, learn a musical instrument, or write a novel, because the ideas in it can be applied to any task which requires you to make use of your mind in a systematic way.

A little regular study can provide you with one of the great pleasures in life; your learning will accumulate and you will enjoy knowing more about the things that interest you. Such knowledge will also build your confidence and help you to feel proud of your achievements. If you are a student, then studying efficiently will be a bonus, giving you more free time as well as better results. Good study techniques are not difficult to master, and it is surprising how few students make use of them. Do not be put off by their apparent simplicity; often the simple and straightforward methods are the most effective.

The Law of Mass Effect

There is one central law about study: the law of mass effect. This states that the amount of work you do (the amount you learn; the amount you write; or whatever) is strongly correlated with the amount of time you spend doing it. Certainly, many students study in an inefficient way, so that long hours of hard work achieve much less than they could. But it is important not to believe the myth that by studying incredibly efficiently you can achieve a lot by doing remarkably little. What you can do is achieve a great deal by combining work and recreation in moderate amounts. Any worthwhile study will therefore take some time. The main reason why people who study often achieve less than they want to is that they do not put in the hours. Therefore, if you want to study, you need to set aside time to work. So why not make it easy to start, and fun to do?

Making It Easy to Start

Most people find it difficult to get down to work. You might promise yourself that you will sit down and write for an hour at eight o'clock in the evening. At eight o'clock you think it would be nice to have a cup of tea. At a quarter past eight you make a quick phone call. At half past eight there is a program on the radio or TV. At nine o'clock you listen to the news. At twenty past nine a friend phones. At half past nine .... .

All this is common experience and there must be few people who do not waste time in this way. But the single most important difference between good and bad students is in the ability to get down to work.

The problem with not getting down to work is twofold: first, it results in too little work being done; and second, it results in an unsatisfactory use of the time when you are trying to get down to work, because so much of the time not working is spent in a kind of no man's land, which is neither work nor recreation but being about to work, worrying about work, not quite relaxing but not quite working either.

In order to get down to work, you need to make it as easy for yourself as possible. Just as it takes time for an engine, starting from cold, to run smoothly, so it is with ourselves. Sometimes we need a kick-start to get going; but once in the swing of it, it is usually much easier to keep going and can be a real pleasure too.

FOUR WAYS OF HELPING YOURSELF TO GET DOWN TO WORK

1. Create a good work environment. There is nothing more dispiriting than looking at the place where you are going to study and finding that it fills you with gloom. Try and keep a particular place, a room or part of a room, for work. Make this place attractive in your own particular way. Decorate it with pictures, or flowers, or whatever it is that you enjoy. Make yourself an inviting table top, for example, by getting rid of unnecessary clutter.

2. List the tasks beforehand. We tend to use any excuse not to get down to work, and one is uncertainty over where to begin: "Shall I do this, or that?" And the uncertainty becomes an excuse for doing something else. Plan in advance what it is you are going to work on. The simple expedient of writing a list of the various things to do and the order in which you are going to do them can save hours of wasted time. Do not be too ambitious: set yourself specific targets that you can certainly manage in the time available, and then do something extra if there is still time.

3. Keep the benefits of study clearly in mind. However easy you make it for yourself to start the work, there will still be a small hump to get over. You need to keep before you the benefits to be gained from doing the work. With large tasks this is particularly important; otherwise, an initial enthusiasm might wane and you may never find the energy to start. Write down all the things you could gain from doing the work, and read the list when you are due to start, to give yourself a boost. This is particularly useful if you are going through one of those phases when you feel discouraged, or have lost heart.

4. Leave your work environment inviting for the next time. Most people tidy up, and find the things they need in order to get started, at the beginning of the study session. When they stop the session, they leave everything in a disorganized mess. The problem with this is that the mess becomes a barrier to starting the next work session. The solution is simple. Spend the last few minutes of the study period tidying up and getting ready for the next session so that it will be easy to start. This is also one of the best times to plan in advance what to do next.

Making It Fun to Do

MAKE USE OF YOUR BEST TIME OF DAY

You may have little choice when to study, or it may not matter for you anyway. But some people work better, or more easily, at some times of day than at others. Some people are morning workers; others work best in the evenings. If you have preferences, try and accommodate them.

STUDY IN SHORT PERIODS

Many people fail to study because they believe that once they get down to it they should keep at it for hours. This is so daunting that they do nothing at all. It is much better to have more modest goals and actually do the work. We recommend that you work in fairly short, "bite-sized pieces," the size of the bite depending to some extent on you and to some extent on the subject matter. If you are studying in the evenings, after work, then we recommend keeping the bites small; otherwise, you are likely to turn on the TV instead.

VARIETY—THE CHOCOLATE BOX APPROACH

An enormous slab of chocolate would be difficult to eat all at once, but in a box of assorted chocolates each chocolate is small, and there is a great deal of variety. Whatever it is you want to study, break up the study into short periods with frequent breaks, and give yourself variety. If you do this you will find it much easier to "eat" your way through the box, and you will find that you have completed a great deal of work.

A student came to us for help because he was finding it very difficult to carry on with his studies. Each morning he faced several hours of sitting in the library "studying," feeling bored and tired. We asked him to tell us about his study. "It's just the same each day. I go to the library and read." "Do you never write anything?" "Of course, I have to write essays." We carried on asking him exactly what he did. It turned out that what he saw as the one task of "studying" was a myriad of different tasks. He would order books from the librarian; some he would read as reference books, selecting material and taking notes. Sometimes he would read novels, as part of his study, reading all the way through. Before writing an essay he would return to his notes, and condense them. He would plan his essay and play around with some of the ideas. Then he would write, and then edit what he had written. At any stage he might talk to other students or discuss topics with a tutor.

In fact, he was not just doing the same task all the time but doing a wide variety of tasks. We suggested that he plan out his next morning's study, identifying the different tasks and ensuring that he only did each one for a relatively short period—for example, about forty-five minutes at a time. We also asked him to schedule in breaks. The plan for his next morning looked like a chocolate box. It was made up of a variety of small, more or less, appetizing chunks. A week later he was a transformed student: keen on his work and satisfied that he was studying better than before.

This transformation had been achieved by the simple process of breaking the study period up into a variety of tasks, and showing him that what he had seen as one boring activity was in reality a number of different activities, any of which might become boring if you did them for too long. When study becomes boring and repetitive, like an assembly line, it loses its variety and hence its attractiveness.

Planning and Organization

STUDY WITH A PURPOSE IN MIND

Why do you want to study? Whatever the reason, keep it in mind. Keep it in mind in order to: decide what information you want, decide on your priorities, and choose what to do with the information you collect. You do not have to have a very erudite or scholarly purpose; you could just be curious.

Suppose you want to learn Portuguese because you want to be able to speak a little when you go to Portugal on holiday. The words and phrases that you learn—the tapes and books which you might use to learn from—all these should be chosen bearing in mind that it is for a holiday that you wish to use the language. If you were learning Portuguese for business purposes, then you would need a different vocabulary. Your purpose helps you decide what and how to learn. Perhaps you want to learn Portuguese in order to read business reports but do not need to speak the language. So your purpose also helps you to decide what to practice. If you want to learn the language in order principally to read it, then practice reading it. If you want to learn it principally to speak, then practice speaking it. If you want to be able to understand, then practice listening to it. The purpose helps you to decide how much you need to do. Your aim, in learning Portuguese, might be to be able to order a meal and ask directions. You may not need to be fluent.

Most people read books from cover to cover in a linear fashion even though, for most study purposes, this is not the best thing to do (p. 351). It is unfocused, and wastes a lot of time. When studying, think more of the way in which you might read a newspaper—browsing, selecting, reading some articles right through, dipping into some and ignoring others altogether. Select what you read and select how much you read. In making the selection keep the purpose in mind. What are you aiming to get from this bit of reading, this bit of study?

The same is true when taking notes (p. 353). Keep the purpose in mind. Do you want these notes to replace having to read the book again? Or to remind you what is in the book and where to find it? Do you want to remember the contents in detail, or to bring away some main ideas? Is the material such that once you have remembered the main headings you can remember the rest, or does it demand that you remember a great deal of specific information? It is not only the ultimate purpose (ordering a Portuguese meal) that you need to bear in mind, but also the more immediate one. Reasons for note-taking can vary from improving concentration to making you feel productive; notes can provide a memory aid or a sense of achievement. Exactly what form your notes will take depends on what you are making them for.

SALAMI—CUTTING BIG PROJECTS INTO SLICES

Big projects often pose particular difficulties. They can be daunting at the beginning because they are so big. And they can be dispiriting in the middle when the initial blush of enthusiasm has paled and the end is still out of sight.

No project is too large, or large projects would never get done, but large ones do need to be tackled systematically—for example, by using the *salami* principle: cut big projects into slices. If you "eat" the slices one by one, you will eventually consume the whole "salami." In other words, set yourself small manageable tasks so that by progressing through them you will eventually accomplish the large task. Most people grossly underestimate how long it takes them to do something they have set for themselves, and often have to double their original estimates. Focusing on the demands made by each "slice" makes these estimates much more accurate, as well as making each slice more appetizing.

AN ATTITUDE OF PROJECT COMPLETION

The *salami* approach can enable you to organize and begin a large project, but there may be other, new projects you are keen to get on with as well, and this is where the danger lies. It can be tempting to abandon the current project and start a new, more exciting one instead, so that over the years you accumulate a number of half-finished projects. If you want to complete them, you need to adopt the kind of attitude that helps to ensure that starting new projects does not prevent you from finishing old ones. Be prepared to delay the onset of new projects. Keep them in the planning stage until the old ones have been completed.

Finishing the Study Period

FILE YOUR WORK FOR EASY ACCESS

At the end of your study period, sort and file your materials. "I know I've made some notes on this somewhere . . ." The best notes in the world are of little help if you cannot find them at the right time. When studying, one of the things you need not be wasting your time doing is looking for information, looking for notes you put somewhere, or looking for the right file. You need a simple and effective system for filing your notes and materials. The system does not need to be elaborate. It can make use of shoe boxes or those well-tried methods which efficient offices find effective: envelopes, files, storage boxes, filing cabinets, or a series of notebooks. If you do not know how to file your notes, then it may be sufficient simply to file them in the order in which you write them. We tend to be good at remembering roughly when we did things and which things we did before others. If you use a loose-leafed file, and take a separate piece of paper for each new learning time, then you can always re-sort later if you want to.

The other key to not wasting time trying to find things is to have a specific place in which you keep your notes. When you finish a piece of work, always put it back in its place. Do not leave it out where it might get mixed up with other things, or incorporated into the newspapers or your children's play.

REWARD YOURSELF FOR EACH STUDY PERIOD

Animal trainers know the importance of reward. The principle is simple: you will enjoy doing things more if they are rewarding and then you will be more likely to want to do them again. In order to boost your chance of studying, you can build in extra and immediate rewards. For example, you might decide that if you spend three hours studying on Saturday afternoon you will then go out to the cinema. If you are studying in smaller chunks, then you may need to use a token system. For example, for each hour of study you might give yourself a token. You can then "spend" the tokens on "luxuries"—things that you would not allow yourself to do or buy without the tokens, but that you very much enjoy (make yourself some pancakes; soak in the bath; buy a plant or new pen). In this way studying becomes associated with pleasures that you can think of if you are finding it difficult to get down to work. The key to success is to keep the rewards simple and fairly immediate. Giving yourself something good to look forward to helps you to work, whereas giving yourself the pleasure before you work makes working that much harder.

Chapter Summary

1. Regular study can be fun and rewarding.
2. The principles of effective study are simple, but often ignored even by experienced students.
3. The *law of mass effect* is central to study: even if you study efficiently, you still need to put in the hours.
4. *Four ways of making it easy to start study:*
   • Make yourself an inviting work environment.
   • List the tasks to do beforehand.
   • Keep the benefits of study clearly in mind.
   • Leave your desk inviting for the next time.
5. *Make study fun:*
   • Use your best time of day.
   • Use the *chocolate box approach* by keeping study periods to bite-sized chunks, and by giving yourself variety.
   6. *Study with your main purpose in mind.*
7. Supply the *salami* principle: regular small slices of study will add up to big achievements.
8. *Complete* your projects.
9. *File and tidy up* at the end of your study periods.
10. *Reward yourself* for each completed study period.

29

♦ ♦ ♦

Key Study Skills: Reading, Taking Notes, and Using the Material

Reading

One of the most valuable skills students need to master is the ability to learn from reading. The method most people use is to read from cover to cover—the method most of us learned in childhood. This is an excellent method for some purposes—for example, if you are reading a novel or a biography, or if you want to follow an author's train of thought through an interesting or complex field. It may also satisfy curiosity, and be a relaxing way of reading, but nevertheless it is not the only method, nor is it the best method for some purposes. You would not read the Sunday papers in that way (or you would do nothing else all Sunday), nor is it the best way to get the most out of reading for study purposes. The four-pronged approach which follows provides you with another option.

THE FIRST PRONG: PREPARATION

Read to extend your knowledge, not for learning. The kernel of truth that lies in this remark is that we learn better if we can relate what we read to what we already know, and if we can fit what we read into categories that are meaningful to us. Using a period of preparation enables you to prepare your mind for the new knowledge. First, spend three minutes thinking about what you already know about the subject. Then browse through the book or chapter. *Browsing* is a skill which many people have but which has often been knocked out of them by attitudes to reading picked up at school. When you go into a bookstore looking for something to read, such as a guide to your next holiday destination or a novel, you probably browse through a few books to help to decide which to choose. Such browsing, far from being an inferior kind of reading, is a key reading skill, and it is useful not only in bookstores and libraries. It is an excellent preparation for serious study. It gives you an overview of the material and helps to prepare your mind which, subconsciously, is laying down the structure that will help you to learn.

When you browse you let your attention be caught by whatever attracts it: think of the way you glance through a newspaper or magazine. Do not read a great deal of continuous text. You may go through the book or chapter backwards, or forwards, or skipping around. Browsing should feel more like play than hard work. It will set your subconscious mind to work. You will be learning about the organization of the text; you will be taking in its use of diagrams, footnotes, and headings. You will be seeing what topics it covers and getting an idea about the style. You will also be relating the new information to what you already know.

THE SECOND PRONG: OVERVIEW

Having quickly browsed through the chapter or book, concentrate next on obtaining an overview. Read any summaries. Look through the headings and the index. Read the conclusion. Go back through the material, and for each main section, look at any diagrams or tables. Then skim through the sections looking for the main points: these are often presented at the beginning and ends of sections.

By the end of the overview you will know what the chapter or book is about and have taken in its main messages. For many purposes you will have done as much reading as you require. But if you need to study the material in detail, you may need to carry out a closer reading. Try this method out on the other chapters in this book.

THE THIRD PRONG: THE CLOSER READING

Even for this closer reading you should not, normally, read the chapter or book through, word by word, from beginning to end; nor should you reread those parts which you have already read. After the overview you will be in a position to decide which parts you already know and do not need to study, which parts you do not wish to study, and which parts you do not already know, and therefore wish to study. Only those parts which are of this third kind should be studied in detail.

Understanding difficult passages. Everyone when reading comes across parts they do not understand. This may be because the material is inherently difficult, or it may be because the author has not written clearly. Do not spend hours trying to understand a difficult passage before reading beyond it for two reasons: first, if you leave the difficulty on one side, your subconscious will set to work on it; and second, what comes after the difficult passage may help you to understand it.

THE FOURTH PRONG: REVIEW

An early review of what you have read and learned is a key step both in organizing the material and in remembering it in the long term. The 35-minute study period (p. 376) incorporates this early review within its structure.

This four-pronged approach, far from taking longer than the normal method of reading from cover to cover, will take much less time and will also help you to learn and remember the material. It takes less time because for most material you only need to read a portion of what has been written. Reading all parts of the chapter, regardless of whether you already know the material and regardless of whether you want to know it, wastes time and can also be boring and discouraging.

Taking Notes

Most people try to make use of notes. Notes are a way of recording information, but they are not passive recording. Note-taking involves actively organizing the material and putting your own stamp on it. There is no one right way of doing it: that depends on your preferences, on the purpose for which you are taking notes, and on the material. When you are taking notes you are writing for yourself. As long as you can understand your notes when you reread them, they will have achieved their purpose.

Notes can take many forms. You can rewrite notes and condense them (see below), and each rewriting will help you with remembering and processing the information. Notes might take the form of pictures as well as words.

WHY ARE YOU TAKING NOTES?

When considering whether and how to take notes, think first of how you wish to use them. For example, if you are taking notes from a book, do you intend never to look at the book again? In this case the notes may need to be fairly detailed. Or are they intended to serve as a summary or reminder only?

What are you studying for? Whatever the reason, tailor your notes to this purpose. Do not spend a lot of time making detailed notes when this is not appropriate—for example, when you can refer back to the book for the details.

At different times in your study you might use notes for different purposes. Notes can help in understanding; they can be used as an external memory; or they can be used in helping to prepare an essay or other piece of writing. Note-taking while reading (or listening) can also help you to concentrate.

NOTE-TAKING AS AN ACTIVE PROCESS

Working with the material you read, rather than just absorbing it, makes it easier to remember. It puts a stamp on it, and makes it yours. So your notes should be your way of organizing the material, and not just a brief copy of what you are reading. Try to pick out what you think are the key points, and organize the material in your own way. Your organization may reflect the structure of what you are reading, but it need not do so. In making notes you are choosing what you consider important in the light of your understanding of the material, your interests, your purposes, and what you already know. It is always easier to remember material that you have worked with than material that you have just allowed to sink in.

TYPES OF NOTES

If you own the book you are reading, you might underline or highlight key points, make comments in the margins, and put a query by those passages you find puzzling or with which you disagree. If you read with a pencil in your hand and not too reverent an attitude in your mind, then you will be reading actively— processing the information as you read it. Your pencil marks can form the basis for your notes.

The most common form of notes are those written in a linear, but *hierarchical* fashion. The hierarchy is provided by headings and sub-headings. The summary to this chapter is an example of such a structure. In deciding how much to write under each subheading, the guiding principle should be the least that will ensure that you can recall what you want to recall when you make use of your notes later.

Spider diagrams. Spider diagrams are another form in which notes can be made, and an example is given in Figure 29.1. The hierarchical structure is readily represented. One advantage of such notes over linear ones is that relationships between elements which are not in the form of a hierarchy can be more readily indicated by drawing lines that connect the elements. Another advantage is that it is easier to add elements.

There are two situations in which spider diagrams are particularly valuable. One is in condensing notes. For detailed initial notes an ordinary linear set may be best—but just before taking an exam, for example, it can be very helpful to condense all the relevant points onto a spider diagram drawn on a single sheet of paper. The visual memory of this sheet of paper can work as a cue for remembering more details and help in organizing answers to questions. Their second main value is in making notes prior to writing something. Tony Buzan

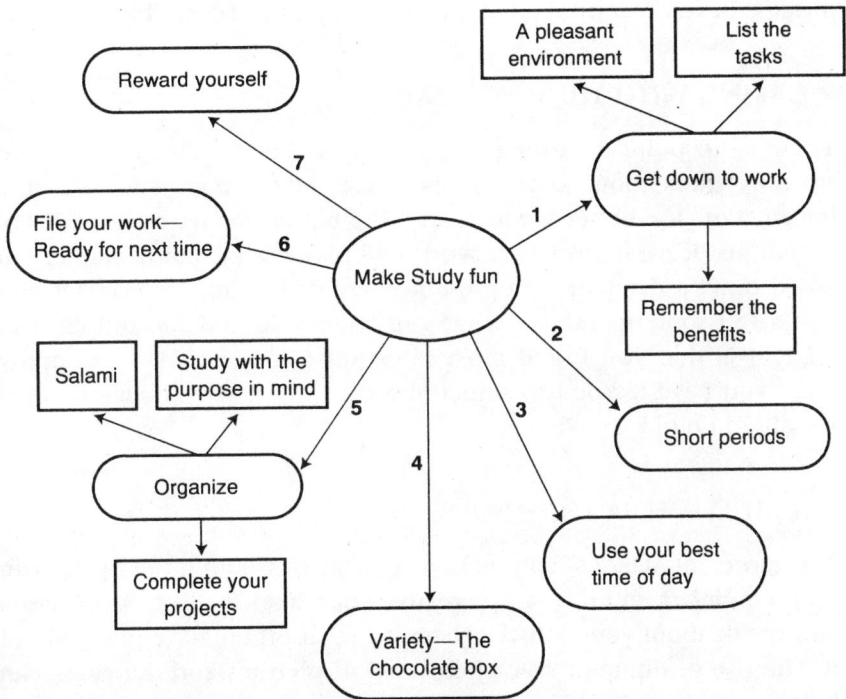

Figure 29.1 The Spider Diagram.

is an enthusiast for spider diagrams; he calls them "mind maps," and further details are given in his book; *Use your head.*

Using the Material

CONDENSING THE NOTES

One technique which many people find useful when working toward exams is that of condensing notes. The process is like that of making a stronger and stronger liqueur: the notes are boiled down until only the essence is left, the vital part. At each time of revising, a new set of notes is made—notes of notes. In making the notes of notes, you will do some reorganization—as you notice similarities between what were disparate elements. In reducing the notes, you also make use of your increasing understanding—what you once needed full notes to remember you can now remember using only one or two key words, and these key words can cue you in to all the rest. The *process* of condensing also involves using the material and working with it, which makes it easier to recall when you need it. It helps you to rehearse the process of retrieving it, and makes it more readily accessible.

WORKING WITH THE INFORMATION

There is no point in storing information if it is not useful. The more ways we think about something new, and the more ways we use new information, the better we learn and the better use we make of it. So, do not just learn information; work, and play, with it. For example, you could draw a diagram to represent some of the information. Or you could tell someone about what you have read and try and explain what it is that you found most interesting. You could try to apply what you have learned to something else you know about—to shed new light on old knowledge.

THE MULTIMEDIA TECHNIQUE

The more "modalities" you make use of in your study, the better you will remember and the more creative your work will be. Write, read, and speak about your subject. Listen to what others have to say about it. The use of different color pens, and of pictures and drawings, can help in making notes. They can serve as useful aids to memory; they can force you to clarify the relationships between the different elements of your notes, and they can help in processing and manipulating information. An attitude of playfulness in making notes stimulates creativity. If you are bored with your notes, you will be bored and uncreative with the material. Think of ways of making your study *fun*. Are there audiotapes of your subject, or video recordings? You could dictate audiotapes of your notes and listen to them in the car, or in the evenings at home. In this way you are not only making use of different *modalities* for learning but also using time which would otherwise not be used for such learning.

BOOSTING

In Chapter 31 we stress the value of "a little and often." (p. 379) If the kind of studying which you are doing involves a significant amount of learning, it will be helpful to boost your learning with short periods of revision. This might be done by carrying a notebook which you can read at odd moments—when waiting for a friend to show up or when traveling on a bus. Portable and car cassette machines can be valuable aids to learning. You can record on cassette the facts you need to learn, and play back when you are driving. You can also make use of odd times in the day to run through what you have learned in your head.

A Revision Strategy for Exams

If you are studying for exams, then it is best to plan your revision well in advance (see also pp. 375–379). Do not panic, however, if your exam is already looming and you have only just picked up this book. There are still some things you can do to help.

First, we will consider the situation in which the exam is still some way off and you can plan a revision strategy. The elements of such a strategy are as follows:

1. Start with an overview: What are your strong points? Where are your gaps in knowledge? Where should you devote your energies? It is never possible to know everything. Think more about how to make use of what you do know than about how to learn a large number of new things.
2. When learning, use the rehearsal method outlined on page 375.
3. Plan a timetable for your revision. Do not be too ambitious. Make the amount of time you can spend revising realistic, and don't expect to revise too much in any given time.

4. Plan a revision of the revision. In other words, plan to cover your material in revision once, and then to revise everything again in about a quarter the time it originally took to revise. You might even revise a third time—in an even shorter time.

5. You will always cover less in a given time than you originally estimated. Make sure that there is some slack in your timetable. End your revision some time before the exam (as much as two weeks before if possible) so that there is time to readjust when you fall behind schedule (this happens to everyone). If one part of the revision is taking a lot longer than you thought it would, cut your losses and move on to the next topic. Use the "slack" in your timetable to return to the problematic topic.

6. Condense your notes at each revision so that you end up with brief notes you can revise just before each examination.

7. If possible practice answering examination questions, and under conditions as close to those of the exam as you can devise. For multiple-choice examinations, practice answering relevant multiple-choice questions. For essay papers, practice writing and giving yourself the same time allowed during the exam.

Every exam is to some extent a game, and you will improve by practicing playing the game. Once you have a basic knowledge of the subject, then how well you do in the exam will depend more on your examination technique than on your extra knowledge. Indeed, too much knowledge causes its own problems because extra knowledge may enable you to see complexities in the questions which the examiners do not intend. If your teachers cannot provide opportunities to practice then form a group with your fellow students, or do it on your own. Answer some questions under examination conditions, and then discuss your answers with others if you are part of a group. This provides examination practice as well as extra learning and revision.

If the exam is imminent and you have not previously planned a revision strategy, the key is to use your remaining revision time well. The danger is that you will feel so anxious about the exam that you will waste the time you do have. Work out the number of hours you still have for revision. Decide on the best use of these. Would it be best to use the time practicing exam questions, or revising your notes? Do you have time to browse through your notes? Or to highlight important bits? Could you write a series of condensed notes, perhaps using spider diagrams? Do not forget the fundamentals of good study (see Chapter 28), such as getting down to work and rewarding yourself, and, however the exam goes, give yourself a treat after it.

Examination Nerves

It is normal to worry before an exam—the problem is how to manage the worry so that it works for you rather than against you; so that it helps you to focus your attention rather than allowing it to wander over alarming possibilities; to keep your nose to the grindstone rather than escape into endless distractions; to think quickly and coherently rather than become muddled and confused. Anxiety, even in quite high degrees, can be extremely useful both when you are preparing for an exam and during the exam itself, so anxiety in itself is nothing to worry about. Thinking of it as "arousal" instead of anxiety may make it more understandable and acceptable, and learning how to keep it within the "effective" range for you may well be useful (see also Chapter 18). This is something that can be learned, and that improves with practice.

First, it helps to know what to expect. Anxiety may make it hard to sleep, filling your mind with thoughts about all the things that could go wrong (none of the topics you studied come up; your mind goes blank; you answer the wrong questions; you misunderstand what the examiners want of you; you forget everything you ever knew). Thinking these things does not make them true—they are just reflections of the pressure you are putting yourself under to do well, so do not be tempted to believe that they are likely to happen just because they are in your mind. Thinking you are stupid does not make you stupid—it makes you miserable or angry. For more on how to deal with upsetting, or catastrophic, thoughts, see Chapter 9.

Anxiety about exams also increases the chances of making unrealistic predictions: that you will fail completely, that your career will be ruined, that your family will never forgive and forget. Research studies have shown that these unrealistic predictions increase the nearer the exam comes and decrease dramatically the moment the examination is over. Just before an exam, it is common to predict not only that the exam will go wrong for you, but that everything else in life will also go wrong: your relationships, your finances, your health, and even events in the outside world—airplanes seem more likely to crash, earthquakes more likely to happen, and so on. One reason for this is that the heightened level of anxiety produced by the impending exam has "primed" other information in your mind concerning things that could go wrong, as if they were all stored in the same box, and facing the examination has taken the lid off. The most important message you can give yourself is this: these predictions are exaggerated and unrealistic. They are another sign of anxiety, and you do not need to believe them but rather should ignore them.

Anxiety about exams also tends to polarize the difference between students and their teachers, sometimes to the extent that it feels like a battle between the two—as if *they,* the examiners, are against *us,* the students. Teachers once they have turned into examiners are suddenly supposed to be on the lookout for your mistakes and errors, to be lying in wait to catch you out, to have an eye only for your shortcomings and not for your strengths. This is another "distorted" way of thinking that is common when anxiety is high, and it ignores the important fact that teachers and examiners are basically pleased and proud when their students do well. The better the students do, the better it reflects on their teaching. They actually remain on the same side as the student throughout, and can probably also remember just how it felt to be taking exams, and how easy it is to suppose that such an assessment reflects one's qualities *as a person* and not just one's performance in an exam on a particular subject.

Some of the strategies for dealing with exam nerves are outlined in the box opposite.

The post-examination blues. Some people can bask in relief the moment the exam is over, but others feel let down and rudderless. An exam is rather like a hurdle that you cannot see beyond, as if life stopped at that point, which is of course absurd. But the purposefulness provided by preparing for an exam can feel good. So losing it can leave you feeling purposeless and lost. At the same time the result of the exam is unknown, leaving you in limbo, in a state of uncertainty. The more exclusively your life before the exam is focused round the exam, the worse the post-examination blues are likely to be. One solution is to make sure that you keep time beforehand for the pleasures you usually enjoy: talking with friends, going to the cinema, listening to music, and so on. Then these pleasures will remain with you afterwards. If they feel somewhat blunted, then do not withdraw from them, but recognize that you may be tired—even exhausted—and that until you have had some rest, and some recreation, they may not be so enjoyable as once they were. You will find more ideas on how to deal with uncertainty in Chapter 16 (pp. 186–189).

Finally: What if you fail the exam? This is where it helps to apply the 100-year rule (p. 177). Who will remember in 100 years? Or even in 2 years? What do other people do who fail exams? What other sources of pleasure and success do you have? Seeing the exam as a hurdle does not mean that you are running a race after which those who do not get a prize are chucked. Are people who always pass

Some Strategies for Keeping Exam Nerves under Control

Overall strategy: The long-term view

Answer these questions:

- Which topics do you know?
- What is essential or optional?
- Where are the gaps for me?

Make a detailed plan for what to do when. Write it down.

Daily technique: The short-term view

Close your eyes to the longer term, and:

- Take one topic at a time.
- Stop when your time is up, and move on to the next one.
- Take frequent, but brief, breaks (e.g., every 1½ hours).
- Do *not* stay up all night, or overdose on coffee.
- Eat, sleep, and take exercise regularly.
- Do *not* revise your plan daily but, for example, weekly.
- Take a whole day off each week.
- Rehearse your exam technique (writing to time, etc.).
- Condense your notes and ideas at each stage.

On the day

Prepare yourself in advance: your clothes, how to travel, etc.

- Look at your condensed notes, not at new material.
- Arrive in good time.
- Do not listen to scaremongering from others.
- Give yourself time to settle down.
- Read the instructions on the paper first.
- Read the questions carefully.
- Plan your timing, and write it down.
- Adapt what you know to the questions if they seem hard.
- If stuck, start to write notes. You will find that one thing leads to another and you will trigger your memory quite easily. You have not really "forgotten," so much as lost the way in.
- Do not try to write everything you know. Answering the question is enough.
- Do not try to be a genius, just answers the questions.

Note: Given the brief time, your answers may have to be superficial. They can still be good, and well put together.

exams any happier than those who do not? These are the questions to ask yourself, in order to see the failure for what it is: a temporary set-back but not a judgment on you as a person.

Chapter Summary

1. Reading is a key study skill. Use the four pronged approach:

   Preparation (browsing)

   Overview

   The closer reading

   Review

2. Make notes. These are personal and should be as short as is needed by you for your purpose.

   Why are you making notes?

   Note-making is an active process

   There are several types of notes:

   > Underlining and highlighting of text in the book

   > Linear and hierarchical lists (like this summary)

   > Spider diagrams

3. Many find it helpful to condense notes at repeated revisions.
4. Work with the information.

   Practice skills (such as drawing, doing calculations, or speaking German).

   Draw a diagram to represent the information.

   Explain your subject to someone else.

   Relate what you have learned to other things you know.

5. The multimedia approach: make use of several "modalities."

   Write.

   Speak.

   Dictate audio tapes.

   Listen to tapes or radio.

   Watch video or TV.

   Use color in your diagrams.

6. Give yourself a boost: a little and often.

Carry a notebook and look at it at odd moments.

Listen to a cassette in your car.

7. Use a revision strategy if studying for an exam:

Rehearsal

Timetable

   Include a revision of the revision

   Build in slack

Practice

Reward yourself after the exam

8. Examination nerves are normal.

Learn how to manage them.

Prepare yourself for whatever the future brings.

30

♦ ♦ ♦

How to Improve Your Memory

Part 1: The Palest Ink and Other External Memory Aids

Since Greek times, people have been fascinated by memory. Before the widespread availability of portable writing materials, a good memory was vital for many activities. A politician in ancient Athens could not rely on the projected text, which for television newscasters and U.S. Presidents has become routine. Carefully prepared speeches had to be memorized. The memory methods developed to help in such circumstances provide the basis for modern techniques used by entertainers and described in many books on memory. However, such methods play a relatively minor role in improving memory. Pencil and paper were not invented for nothing, and are still our most valuable external memory aids.

In order to improve your memory, you should consider making use of both external and internal memory aids. Internal aids are strategies for improving your mind's ability to retain the material you want. They are dealt with in the next chapter. External aids are techniques to relieve your mind of the need to remember. They are the subject of this chapter.

Your Mind Is Not a Computer

The computer on which this sentence is being typed has a magnificent memory, but a poor mind. You have only to write a sentence once, and it has remembered it, word perfect, forever more. You could give it a meaningless jumble of letters—wlklkk geio gui—and it still remembers accurately.

It is a mistake to believe that our memory works like a computer. How many times have you thought: "I'm bound to remember that," and then forgotten it the very next day? We can rarely write on our minds just once and expect to remember the information forever.

Developing Your Memory Is about Using Appropriate Strategies

Memory techniques will enormously improve your memory, but using them will not be like changing your mind into a computer. Change will come through learning *strategies* which make the best use of your mind as it is. It is probably just as well that we do not remember most of what we experience. The Argentinean writer, Jorge Luis Borges, tells the fictional story of a man who remembered in the minutest detail almost everything which he had ever experienced.[1] But this ability was not a blessing. He could scarcely think because his mind was completely clogged up with disorganized memories. Twenty years after Borges wrote his story, the Russian psychologist, Luria, wrote about a real man who possessed an extraordinary memory, and again this ability interfered with his thinking.[2] In contrast, the techniques and strategies we describe here will enhance *thinking* as well as memory.

Eight Reasons Why You Might Want to Improve Your Memory

In order to make best use of this and the subsequent chapter, decide why it is that you want to improve your memory. In what circumstances does your memory let you down? Read both chapters and then focus on learning those strategies which seem best suited to your particular situation.

Here are eight reasons why you might want to improve your memory:

1. To remember future events: appointments, meetings with friends, invitations, etc.
2. Because you keep losing things—your eyeglasses, for example.
3. To remember your bank pin number, or important phone numbers.
4. Because you keep forgetting to do things.

5. To remember people's names.
6. To help you to learn a new subject at school or in evening classes more efficiently.
7. To enable you to pursue a hobby more thoroughly.
8. To remember how to do something you need occasionally to do, like putting the roof-rack on the car; or changing the Hoover bags; or using "mail-merge" on your computer.

Even the Palest Ink Is More Reliable Than the Strongest Memory

Why do you need a good memory? In order to have access to the right information at the right time. This goal of having access at the right time is often better met by writing the information down in the right place than it is by searching your memory. A pocket diary is a good example of a written memory aid. An address book is another commonly used memory aid: common because effective. These aids sometimes fail in their desired use because they are not available at the right time (or because you forget to use them, or forget where you put them). The key to using written information effectively is to choose a few specific places in which to write your notes; and a few specific places in which to keep them.

Three Rules for Making Your Diary Effective

A reputation for poor memory is often made by forgetting appointments, or forgetting to do things which were promised. The solution lies in keeping an effective diary. There are three "rules" for making your diary effective:

Rule 1: Write *all* future engagements in the diary.

Rule 2: Look at the diary frequently, and at least every day.

Rule 3: Have only one master diary.

All three rules are easy to follow if the master diary is readily available. A small diary that you can keep in a pocket or handbag is best. Never make a firm appointment without checking your master diary or without writing it into the diary. If these guidelines are followed, then the master diary will be a faithful record of your plans and engagements. Rule 1, by itself, is not sufficient, because if you fail to look at your diary you may miss an appointment. To prevent this, look through the day's appointments at the beginning of the day, and at the next day's appointments at the end of the day. It is also wise to look a week ahead once a day to ensure that you adequately prepare for each appointment. Rules 1 and 2 are not sufficient if you use more than one diary because you may look in the wrong one, and end up with two clashing appointments.

USING THE DIARY FOR FORWARD PLANNING

A diary is a valuable tool not only for appointments but also for forward planning. For example, you may be going on holiday in July. Perhaps three weeks before this, you need to order your traveler's checks; and the week before, you should arrange to cancel the milk or newspaper deliveries or for someone to feed the cat. These things are easy to forget, or to leave until they are inconveniently late. The diary can be used to put these instructions to yourself on the appropriate days.

Alarms

Simple alarm devices can solve some memory problems. Suppose that you need to remember to put the casserole in the oven at 10:30, or to phone a friend at 11:00. It is easy to forget these things, but an alarm, such as is readily available on electronic wrist-watches or on kitchen timers, solves the problem.

A Portable Notebook

Our memories often let us down because we do not jot down a note at the right time. Either we do not have a notebook and pen handy at the right time, or we tell ourselves the old lie: "I can't forget that." Buy yourself a portable notebook. Then if you come across any information that you wish to remember, you can write it down at once—or as soon as convenient. At the end of the week, go through your notebook; transfer any notes which need to be placed in a more permanent place; and get rid of the others so that your notebook does not become cluttered.

A portable notebook is one good way of helping with that almost universal problem of forgetting people's names, but in this case it is also extremely useful to combine external with internal memory aids, which are described in detail in the next chapter. Suppose that you are at a party and meet several people whose names you wish to remember. First, make sure that you take in what their names are. Then, use their names in a natural way when talking to them; and say good-bye to them by name when you leave: "See you next week, Barry." As soon as you possibly can after meeting them, write down their names together with a reminder, such as a one-sentence note about each of them. Back at home you could also describe them to someone else, and you can transfer your notes to a permanent place so that you can record the people's names before going to an event where you are likely to meet them again. If you want to be in a position to remember them at the drop of a hat, then it will help to notice any striking characteristics and to associate them with the name (Barry was the one with red-rimmed spectacles). You will also need to revise your notes often, and could use the revision strategy given on pages 375–379.

Remembering Vital Pieces of Information, Like Your PIN Number

Because of the reliability of even the palest ink, the best thing to do with vital information is to write it down. But two problems arise: you may not have the information on you when you need it; and others may be able to read your secret information. The best solution to the first problem is always to have something on you in which you can store such information, such as your wallet or purse. If you have no such thing, then it may be worth buying a very small notebook and keeping it with you. The problem with secret information is that it is harder to deal with. One way to ensure that others cannot read it or use it is to "hide" the information. For example, your PIN number might be "hidden" in a list of telephone numbers as a phoney phone number. The use of "internal" memory devices for remembering long and rarely used numbers is explained on page 380. This has the advantages both of secrecy, and of the information being with you in your head. The disadvantage is that you need to practice such devices, and to use them regularly, if they are to be reliable.

How to Put on Your Roof-Rack

Even quite simple tasks, if we only do them occasionally, can be difficult to remember. The temptation is to put off doing the task because you know that you are going to waste a lot of time trying to relearn it. The root of the problem, again, is that old myth: when you first learn the task, you think, "I will never forget how to do this." The solution is therefore simple: write down instructions for yourself when you first learn the task, and keep these instructions in a convenient place. The best place might be with the relevant object—for example, the instructions for putting on the roof-rack could be placed in an envelope and stuck to the roof-rack with tape. Alternatively, you could file all such instructions in one place.

The Knot in the Handkerchief

The proverbial knot in the handkerchief reminds you that there is something you should remember, and it works well provided that you can remember what that is. One simple way of eliminating most of those irritating things we forget to do is to place an object or note to yourself in the right place. Suppose that you have written a letter and want to post it in the morning. Place it where you will see it as you leave the house. Perhaps you need to check your tire pressures before leaving for work. Put the reminder on your car's steering-wheel so that you cannot miss it. The two keys to success are: think carefully about the best place to put the reminder; and put the reminder there *now*—that is, when you are thinking about it. It also helps to have a standard place where you look for notes and messages—for instance, by the telephone, or on the kitchen table—and always to keep pencil and paper in those places. Then all the miscellaneous things you need to remember—to get some coffee, to go to the bank, to return the garden hose you borrowed, to give someone a message—will naturally draw themselves to your attention. Remember to throw away outdated reminders.

Where Did I Put My Keys?

Are there any things you often misplace—your keys or eyeglasses, for example? If there are, then the solution lies in creating a habit. Car keys are a good example. If there is no one routine place to put them, they get left on any convenient flat surface: the top of the fridge or by the phone, and later you have no idea where they are. This problem is solved by creating a routine place, such as a hook on the wall near the front door, and then establishing the routine of putting them on the hook immediately on coming into the house. The more automatic routines you can devise for yourself, like automatically putting the bottle opener in the left hand drawer, the less time you will waste hunting for things that are lost.

Beware of Safe Places

One way of avoiding misplacing objects is to have a "place for everything." Obviously, you need to remember where that place is. A final warning before we leave the subject of external memory aids: whenever you find yourself thinking, "This is important; I will put it in a safe place," think again. The problem with safe places is that they are likely to be out of sight and out of mind too. If you forget where the "safe place" is, you are unlikely to find the object until months after you need it, and wherever you do put important things, tell someone else, so that if you forget there is at least one other person who might remember.

Chapter Summary

1. Your mind is not a computer: you are likely to forget things which you learn only once.
2. Many of your memory problems can be solved by making good use of pencil and paper.
3. Develop habits that work to your advantage.

31

♦ ♦ ♦

How to Improve Your Memory

Part 2: Internal Memory Aids

In the last chapter we stressed the use of external memory aids because they are simple and effective for many purposes, and often ignored in books on memory. But they are only half the picture. The other half of the picture is provided by using your mind efficiently, by using internal memory aids.

The law of mass effect (p. 344) is as important to remembering as it is to studying. It states that the amount you remember is strongly correlated with the amount of time you spend learning, and the strategies described in this chapter will enable you to make good use of the time you spend learning. Just as with studying, you cannot expect to learn and remember unless you put in time. The use of efficient strategies makes the time you spend learning both more effective and more fun.

The amount you remember is also affected by your mood, and in particular by your level of anxiety. If your head is full of worries, it is very difficult to learn. In order to learn most efficiently you need to be able to concentrate but without being anxious: *attention without tension* is what you need.

Organization

Four aspects of organization can help you to improve your memory: *chunking, using cues, relating,* and *making sense*.

CHUNKING

In order to remember a great deal of information, it is best to break it into mind-sized chunks of about *seven items*. You probably already use *chunking* when doing the weekly shopping. Suppose that you have fifty items to buy. It would be very difficult reliably to remember a list of fifty items, but the items are automatically classified into smaller chunks by the type of shop or section of the supermarket in which they are found: fruit, vegetables, meat, fish, dairy products, household items, drinks, toiletries, etc. This method of chunking used by supermarkets as well as by shoppers can be applied to a wide range of situations, such as preparing for the new school year or for reorganizing the accounts department.

USING CUES

The weekly shopping also demonstrates the value of using cues. We look around the shop, at the different kinds of fruit, for example, using them as cues to remind us what we want to buy. We can provide internal cues for ourselves as well. If we know that we want five things for packed lunches and we have only bought four, we must look around for the fifth. Remembering that there should be *five* things serves as a cue.

RELATING

Relate new bits of information to other things you already know, or to each other. In this way you can structure the material to be learned in a way that will make it easier to remember later. For example, you might remember that the Spanish word for cheese is like the English word, but not like the French one; or that Romanesque arches are like the ones at Exfield Church; or that Patricia is the person who came to the party with Tom. What you already know can be used as a basis, or structure, to build on. The more you know, the more building blocks you have on which you can add new knowledge, and the more rapidly you will learn. As you consolidate what you learn, you are setting up an exciting learning spiral which will increase more and more rapidly.

MAKING SENSE

It is much easier to learn and to remember something that is meaningful than it is to learn something that makes little sense to you. Meaning can be given in many ways: for example, by relating what is to be learned to your previous experience and knowledge— "The gear shift is the same except that reverse is up not down"; "Setting the timer overrides the on-off button"—and by understanding the relationships between the different elements of what you are learning—"You have to open up the valve before you switch on the gas"; "Saving the work you have done onto the old file makes a new copy, so the old one is lost."

THE CASE OF ITALIAN WINES— AN EXAMPLE OF ORGANIZATION

Let us see how these methods of organization can work in practice. Suppose that you want to learn about *Italian wines* and you have bought a relevant book. In the section on *taking notes* (p. 354) we discuss the value of thinking about the subject matter before you start to read, to start the process of organizing. You might draw these initial thoughts in the form of a *spider diagram* (p. 355). Figure 31.1 shows what such a spider diagram could look like.

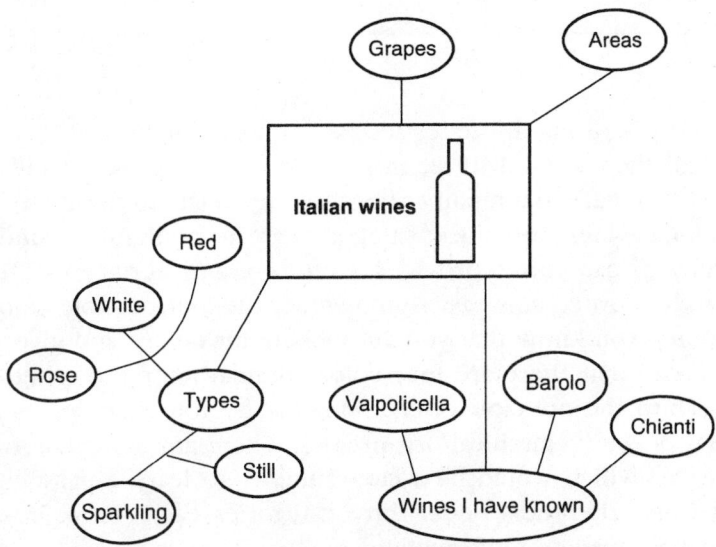

Figure 31.1   A spider diagram for learning about Italian wines.

You are now ready to look quickly through the wine book to get an *overview* of the subject (p. 352). This overview will enable you to improve on your initial organization. For example, after browsing through the book, you might restructure the category types, as shown in the following box.

Types of Italian Wines

Color

Red
White
Rose
Amber

Sugar

Sweet
Semi-sweet
Dry

Fizz

Sparkling
Frizzante (lightly bubbly)
Still

This restructuring illustrates several features that aid your learning. First of all, there are only three main categories (color, sugar, and fizz), and these are easy to remember because they relate to the experience of drinking wine. Thus these categories are meaningful. Second, the hierarchy of categories provides a *relationship* between different items to be learned. It is easy to remember the four possible colors of wine when you know that you are looking for colors, and give yourself the *cue* that there are four colors. Similarly for the other categories. Third, the principle of chunking has been used: it comes naturally out of the hierarchical organization. There are ten categories of wine listed which would be a large number to learn as one chunk. But by organizing them under three categories, each *chunk* has only three or four pieces of information.

A Revision Strategy

Unlike a computer, we rarely remember something we have learned just once. We tend to forget what we have just learned (as illustrated in the graph in Figure 31.2) unless we rehearse and use the material or revise our learning. Adopting an efficient revision strategy is one of the best ways of improving your memory. Revision shortly before exams is discussed on page 357.

WHAT IS AN EFFICIENT REVISION STRATEGY?

It turns out that the most efficient revision strategy is to *revise very soon after the original learning and then to space out additional revision periods further and further apart.* This applies whether you are a student or whether you are learning bus routes in a new town, a complicated recipe, or how to set the video recorder. In plain language, if you recite to yourself, or go over in your mind's eye, something you want to remember, as soon as possible after learning it, you will find it easier to remember later, and the more often you rehearse something, the better it will withstand the test of time. Your rehearsals can then be spaced at ever-increasing intervals. An efficient

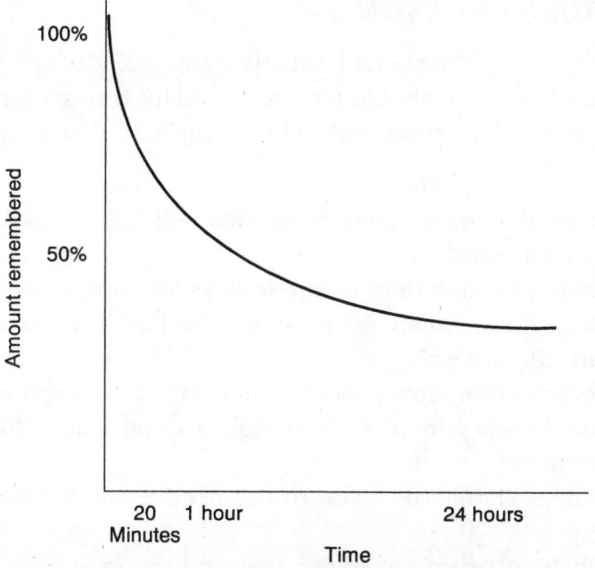

Figure 31.2 Graph of how quickly we forget material we have just read.

revision strategy for everyone is one which leads to your remembering most after spending the least possible amount of time learning. Although the theory behind a good revision strategy is somewhat complicated, the practice is simple, and can be illustrated using the *day-week- month* strategy that applies most obviously to students.

THE DAY-WEEK-MONTH (DWM) REVISION STRATEGY

The *DWM* system is simple. We will explain it in some detail so that you can see how to design an efficient revision strategy. But do feel free to design your own strategy to suit your own needs. Some flexibility is needed because few of us can keep to a rigid timetable

Suppose that you wish to learn some Portuguese before going on holiday to the Algarve. You learn 20 words today. The *first revision* could take place at the end of the session in which you first learn the words. The *35-minute study period* explained on the next page is one way of doing this. Your *second revision* could be one *day* later; your *third revision* could be one *week* after the second revision; and the *fourth revision* could be one *month* after the third revision. Each revision will take only a fraction of the original learning time. If it takes 20 minutes to learn in the first place, each revision will take about 2 minutes.

VARYING THE DWM SYSTEM

The *DWM* system is simple and effective. Like most of the skills presented in this book, you should feel free to adapt it to your needs. But there are a number of principles which will help you to make your own adaptations.

1. If you do not revise, your memories will fade away like a line drawn in the sand.
2. The most effective time to revise is as you are about to forget, but can just remember. Revise when the line on the sand is faint but can still be seen.
3. You forget more slowly (and remember for longer) after each revision. This is why revision periods can be spaced further and further apart.
4. Two things should alert you to the need to adapt your revision strategy:
   • If when you come to revise, you find that you have forgotten most of what you learned. In this case you need to revise sooner than you are doing.

- If when you come to revise, you find that you remember it all clearly. In this case you are revising sooner than you need to and may be wasting time.

To take, again, the example of learning Portuguese. Suppose that you learn 20 new words. If when you revise them a day later, you can only remember 10 words, and these with difficulty, you need to revise sooner. If, on the other hand, you can remember 19 words without much trouble, you can probably shift your revision to two days after the first learning.

MICROREVISION

One of the keys to good memory is *revision*. A structured revision process ensures that you learn *effectively* and *efficiently*. This is the purpose of the DWM method. Structured revision can usefully be enhanced by unstructured revision. Even brief periods of revision can have a very powerful effect on memory. Revise for a few minutes whenever you can: while waiting for a bus or for a friend to show up. The effect is like polishing silver. *A little and often* will keep your memory shining. Remember revising is not just reciting, but making the material yours in some way, so you need to work with it, to remold it, and to use it during revision in as many ways as you can think of.

Going through things in your head is extremely helpful. It makes you more sure of the things you can remember and also pinpoints the gaps. These tell you where to focus your energies next time. If you can use your notebook at the same time, you will be even better able to take advantage of opportunities for microrevision.

THE 35-MINUTE STUDY PERIOD—
AN EFFICIENT LEARNING TOOL

The 35-minute daily study period is an efficient way of learning a new subject. This is an ideal strategy if you wish to learn or study and can only devote a small amount of daily time to it. For example, you may wish to learn a new language, or study a new subject, such as history or botany. The 35-minute study period is relevant if the principle task is learning—acquiring knowledge or information. It makes use of three central principles of learning and memory:

1. The length of time we can maintain high-quality concentration
2. The optimum revision strategy
3. A little and often

The great value of the 35-minute study plan is that it is a very efficient way of working and it has, built into it, an effective revision strategy, so your learning accumulates. The problem with the way in which most people learn is that they do not think about revision until the last minute, and unless you revise as you go, you forget most of what you learn.

The 35-minute study period is a flexible learning unit. You can use it once a day or less; or if you are a student, you can divide your daily learning into a number of 35-minute units. Think of this period as a building block.

Why 35 minutes? This is a period for which most people can concentrate well. If you study without a break for as long as an hour, the last 20 to 30 minutes is likely to be less efficient, your concentration less good than in the first 35 minutes, and it is also much easier to get down to work knowing that it is for a 35-minute stretch than it is if you have set aside an hour or more.

The general principle of the study period is that you spend about 60% of the time in new learning. The rest of the time is for revising— revising things you learned recently, and things you learned a month ago. Figure 31.3 illustrates one efficient way of using the 35 minutes. Use this as a guide for your own study.

The first 20 minutes are spent in new learning. A short break allows your subconscious to consolidate this new learning. You can then spend a couple of minutes revising what you learned new in *yesterday's* 35-minute study period; a couple of minutes revising what you learned new in the study period *one week ago;* and a couple of minutes revising what you learned new in the study period *one month ago.*

In the last 5 minutes, revise what you learned in the first 20 minutes of the study period. Thus the first revision occurs about 10 minutes after the end of the learning period. This is *not* too soon to revise. On the contrary, it will prevent that first rapid phase of forgetting.

We wish to emphasize that only about 60% of the study period is spent in new learning. The rest of the time is used for structured revi-

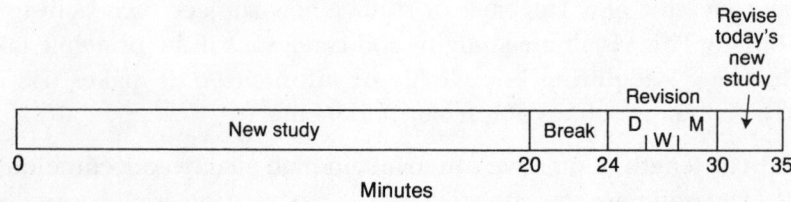

Figure 31.3 A 35-minute study guide.

sion—including a consolidating rest period. Most people are tempted to use up all the time on new learning. Indeed, it can feel silly to stop the new learning almost as soon as you have started. But this is just the ineffective method which most people use. At first it seems fine, but then it becomes clear that you are forgetting most of what you have previously learned and getting progressively more muddled. You will end up, at the end of the year, having wasted most of the study time. These frequent but short revision periods work, both because they reinforce the memory and because they help you to consolidate what you have learned. This prepares you for absorbing what you next want to learn.

Practicing a Skill—A Little and Often

What is the most efficient way of learning a skill—learning to type, for example? *The answer is to practice frequently for short periods.* This has been elegantly shown by Alan Baddeley and his colleagues. To reach the same standard in typing, they found that it took, on average, 80 hours for those who practiced 4 hours each day, and only 55 hours for those who practiced 1 hour each day. Furthermore, those who practiced 1 hour a day retained their skills better than those who practiced for 4 hours a day. Of course, if you want to learn how to type in as few *days* as possible, it is better to practice for many hours each day. Those practicing for 4 hours each day took 20 days to reach the standard that those practicing for 1 hour a day reached in 55 days. But such concentrated practice is inefficient in terms of the total number of hours spent learning to type.

Recall—The Sherlock Holmes Approach

This is a common experience: you have lost your watch, or a bunch of keys, or a letter. You had them the day before yesterday but cannot find them now. You have looked in the obvious places. The temptation is to go on looking. The solution, however, is to *think*—the Sherlock Holmes approach. When Sherlock Holmes was puzzled by a problem, he would take to his armchair. A really difficult problem was "a three-pipe problem." Four times out of five you will find the object by thinking, if you think hard and persist. When can you last remember seeing the item? What were you wearing then? What were you carrying? Who was with you? What did you do then? Go through the time since you last saw the object in meticulous detail. If you are lucky, you will suddenly realize where it must be. If you are less lucky, you will have narrowed down the possibilities: there can only be two or three places where you could have lost it. Of course, you might realize that one explanation is that you left it in the train and that it has gone for good. The method of recall cannot magically restore all items, but it will usually result in your finding it if it can still be found, or realizing what must have happened if it cannot, without wasting a lot of time.

This method of recalling in detail has other uses. You may have been introduced to someone and cannot now remember his name, or you know somebody asked you to do something, but you have no idea what it was. Think back to the situation in which you learned the name or the time when the request was made. Think about the details of the conversation. Who else was present? What did they say? If the conversation was not too long ago, you may remember something that happened or was said which can trigger the memory you need, or you could just think about the person who asked you to do something and allow your mind to wander around aspects of this person, and things associated with her. What sorts of things has she asked of you before? Is it to do with work or something else? Did it feel urgent? Or not very important? Give your mind a chance to "come at it sideways" by opening up all the relevant boxes in which the lost information might be stored.

Mnemonics

"Roy of York gained battles in vain" is a mnemonic device which many of us learned as children to remember the order of the colors of the rainbow (*red, orange, yellow, green, blue, indigo, violet*). Similar devices, some too rude to print, are used in medical schools to help in learning human anatomy. Although they are no substitute for revision and organization, they can be particularly useful in helping to memorize lists or sequences of things. The method of connecting two visual images can help when learning foreign languages. Using them can also be entertaining, and with some persistence you could master a technique for memorizing the order of a pack of cards, but this would not help you to do much else.

The most frequently used mnemonic devices are simple rhymes, such as "thirty days hath September ...," and sentences such as "Roy of York ...." However, we also know that it is much easier to remember information that might not otherwise hang together if we apply the rules that we already know. It is much easier to remember how to say "supercalifragilisticexpialidocius"—especially after hearing it sung, which gives it both a tune and a rhythm—than it is to remember Aunt Susan's address if she lives in Llanfairynghornwy. Not only do few of us know the rules of Welsh pronunciation, we also do not know how to understand the parts from which the word is made up. Nonsense can be memorable if it takes a form that we can make sense of.

And this is a rule we can make use of as a memory aid. If something you have to remember seems like nonsense to you, or comes in a string of disconnected bits, like a list of facts, names, or numbers, the best thing to do is to try and turn it into sense any way you can: sing it, make up rhymes, apply grammatical rules, transform the material into visual images, or use it to tell yourself a story, and it will instantaneously become more memorable.

Putting It All Together

We all depend on our memories all the time, whether we are students or not, and memory can let us down when we are tired, stressed, or distressed. That is when we are likely to rush out of the house leaving the keys behind, wander into another room only to wonder why we are there, or put the frozen peas in the bread bin and the bread in the freezer. Memory is both robust and also vulnerable. It is robust in the sense that most information which we find useful remains in our memory. It is vulnerable in the sense that sometimes it is hard to retrieve or recall it. Marthe, whose first language was French, but who spoke only English from the age of 18, reverted to speaking in French when she was 82 (and still in England), although until then, she had to search her memory for French words whenever she needed them. So we need as many strategies as we can devise, both to lay down the traces for the future and to help us get on the right tracks when we want to.

FOUR GENERAL STRATEGIES FOR LAYING DOWN THE TRACES

1. Important things are easier to remember than unimportant ones. Things that stand out in some way (your first kiss, the time you stood on a sea urchin or the time you said something acutely embarrassing) will stick in your memory. Unimportant things can become more memorable if we attach to them some of the "signs" of importance—for example, by making them more *vivid* or by giving them a personal *meaning*. The bright yellow folder will be harder to leave behind than the beige one, and writing your name on the outside of it will be more likely to draw it to your attention than writing something of no personal importance to you— like "memos" or "minutes."

2. It is important to forget things as well as to remember them. Although our memories seem to have an almost unlimited capacity, there is a bottleneck on the way in. Things can get lost in transit. So when you are in a confusing situation (meeting lots of new people, starting a new job, finding your way around a new place), *tell yourself what to forget.* You will remember best those things you pay attention to, but if everything grabs your attention, your memory will be overloaded. You can reduce the load by concentrating on what is most important to you (the job your boss wants done first, how to find your way home again), and try not to get distracted by too many other things.

3. You need time for digestion. The memory traces are not laid down, in permanent form, all at once. So if you cram in too much, or try to learn too many new Portuguese words without giving yourself some revision time, you will feel as if your brain is full. Notice when you get to the stage of diminishing returns— when it no longer feels as if you can take in any more, both when learning how to use a new computer or when walking around an exhibition. Ideally, you should stop before this point. Continuing beyond it will not help you to lay down good traces, while stopping may enable you to observe a rather peculiar phenomenon. At first, when suffering this form of mental indigestion, you may feel confused or muddled. However, after a pause and a rest, you may be able to make *more,* not *less,* sense, and remember some of the material better. This is most obvious when learning a physical skill or a skill that involves coordinating mind and body, like typing or playing a new computer game. If you push yourself too far at one go, after an initial period of improvement you will start to make mistakes and your performance will deteriorate. If you stop practicing at this stage, instead of pushing on in an effort to overcome the problem, you will find that your performance improves apparently of its own accord—as you can see if you try again after an interval. It is as if your mind continues laying down the traces after you have stopped practicing.

4. Ideas are sometimes more useful than facts. Facts may not hang together, and will therefore be hard to remember. Ideas, and meanings, may help the facts to hang together, or give you a set of pigeon holes in which to file the facts. It is sometimes worth thinking of yourself as a filing system, and working out how to label the separate storage places so that you know what to find in them—in personal as well as in other ways. For example, use labels such as "Things I did with Marion" and "Feeling the way I felt in my first job," as well as "Letters to be answered" and "things to tell so and so."

FOUR GENERAL STRATEGIES FOR IMPROVING YOUR MEMORY

1. The more you make use of information, the more readily available it becomes. If you are finding it hard to remember something you normally remember well, think of things associated with it, or "prime the related categories." Imagine you have a thousand and one things to do at work, and at the same time are trying to plan a talk for the next day. If you give yourself some of the main headings or topics for your talk early on, you will prime the right categories in your mind, which may almost literally continue ticking, warming up the machinery for the bits that you need to use, so that when you do get time to think about the talk, you will more readily remember the things you need. This works even better if you write down the title for the talk and jot down briefly any ideas that come to you whenever you can.

2. Give your mind space to work in. A similar phenomenon occurs when one is focusing on a major project, whether that is working out how to decorate the kitchen and continue to use it, or how to put together an entirely new sales policy. First, immerse yourself in the project totally so that your mind can set to work on it, and then focus on particular aspects of it, but remember that the closer in you get, the harder it is to see the whole picture. At this point your memory can surprise you, and enable you to see entirely new possibilities: after working hard on one part of the project you drop it to do something else, or collapse because you are tired, and then at an unexpected moment— for example, lying in bed, shopping or in the shower the next morning—you have a new idea. It is as if you were only able to put the information in your memory together in a new way after standing back from the front line. In order to make the most of your memory, you need to give your mind space to work in—give yourself both focused work on a project and time away from it.

3. It is easier to recognize things than to recall them. Even if you cannot tell someone else the way to Aunt Susan's house, you may be able to find it quite easily if you have been there before. If you cannot remember which brand of pasta was the good one, a glance at the supermarket shelves may do the trick. If you cannot recall what was in the document being discussed, a brief glance at it will tell you whether you have read it, and that can start you moving along the right track until you find the information associated with it in your memory.

4. Association works wonders. It is not just that one thing leads to another, so that you can eventually find the word you want by thinking of others related to it, but also that the circumstances surrounding an event provide a wealth of information to cue you in. Deep-sea divers can remember the things they learned at the bottom of the sea better during their next dive than they can on dry land. This (partly) explains why so many people forget, once they reach the office, to do things related to their home lives, and remember them again as soon as they get back home. One of the added advantages of going away for a holiday is that it helps you forget the concerns associated with home. There is no need to worry that you will lose the thread completely on holiday, because the associations aroused by coming home again will trigger your memory efficiently on your return—and the new perspective provided by getting away may also lay some unnecessary concerns to rest.

In summary, for your memory to work well, you need to be able to forget things as well as remember them. The art of remembering well lies first in *selecting* what it is that you need to remember for your purposes, and then *deciding* what needs to "be in your head" or what can more usefully be stored in an "external" memory, in a diary, for example.

Chapter Summary

You can improve your memory through developing good strategies rather than through mental muscle-building exercises.

The law of mass effect: The amount you remember is strongly correlated with the amount of time you spend learning.

To learn most efficiently, you need to concentrate without being anxious: *attention without tension*.

Organize your thinking using four methods:

- *chunking* to break the information into chunks of a maximum of seven items

- *using cues* to remind you of what you want to remember
- *relating* the new information to what you already know
- *making sense* of the new information

Use an efficient *revision strategy.* Revise soon after the original learning, and then space out additional revision periods further and further apart.

32

♦ ♦ ♦

Making Decisions

In both our domestic life and at work, we need to make decisions, and in order to make good decisions, we need to be able to think clearly and weigh up evidence effectively. In the long term the decisions we make greatly affect our lives, so it is important to be able to make good decisions as often as possible. This chapter highlights the pitfalls in decision-making and provides a strategy for helping to make decisions that feel right.

Myths about Decisions

There are many myths about decision-making. One of them is that everything hangs on making the right choice. Open the right door and you will find yourself in the enchanted garden, open the wrong one and you will fall into the dungeon from which there is no escape. A second myth is that people are either decisive or indecisive. The decisive prince is determined, resolute in the face of uncertainty, knows at a glance what is right, and his good judgment is rewarded with lasting peace and prosperity (and possibly a princess). The hesitant fool wavers and deliberates, seeks advice which he ignores or forgets, selects inconclusive solutions to irrelevant problems, and suffers the agonies of indecision apparently in perpetuity. He who hesitates is lost.

Most people fall between these extremes, and can sometimes make up their minds quite easily and at other times are paralyzed: stuck on the horns of a dilemma. We seem to be able to play the part both of the prince and of the fool, for the most part, without attaining mythical levels of perfection or suffering, but also without knowing how to take control of the process.

These myths have interesting parallels today. Successful and hard-working people in many walks of life appear to make complex, quick, well-informed, and accurate decisions at a speed that defies the less experienced. When something goes wrong, then we hear how the weight of unremitting choice and responsibility leads to exhaustion, ulcers, disagreements, and loss of good judgment.

The general health and well-being of elderly people who are cared for by others show substantial improvement if they are encouraged to continue to make decisions, even about small things, such as which clothes to wear and when to have their tea. People working in emergency settings and those involved in the aftermath of distressing events of many kinds have lesser degrees of subsequent suffering if they were involved in making decisions at the time (for example, by directing the traffic around the crash, or comforting those in distress). The opportunity to make decisions, whether in daily life or in unusual, difficult situations, appears to protect people from suffering. Decision-making seems to be good for you.

But the demands can be too great. The responsibility of having too many, too weighty decisions to make quickly provokes high degrees of stress (see Chapter 18). It can produce quite uncharacteristic changes in someone's ability to function, leading to poor physical health, stomach ulcers, irritability, increased used of alcohol or caffeine, and eventually to "burnout." When the decision-making processes are overloaded, or impaired as they can be by fatigue, illness, worry, or other forms of distress, they become inefficient.

This was demonstrated in a simulated experiment made during attempts to develop safe and reliable systems for air traffic controllers. Air traffic controllers (at the time) used many different channels of communication. They watched movements on a video screen, listened to and provided information over earphones, received and sent messages using computer terminals and a note pad, and sat in a room surrounded by other noisy people doing the same thing. The methods they were using worked efficiently and safely— if one chan-

nel were to become faulty another was ready to back it up—provided
the level of air traffic was within reasonable limits and everyone was
functioning well. When these limits were surpassed, for whatever reason, communication and decision-making first slowed down and then,
if the disruptive conditions persisted, fell apart. Some surprising
things happened. Controllers shouted messages to each other and
thumped the table. They stood up, gesticulating and pointing, while
trying to communicate with pilots thousands of feet up in the sky.
Under these conditions they were able to understand the problem,
but no longer able to make effective decisions. The demands made by
unremitting decision-making can stretch people to their limits.

Six Strategies to Help You in Making Decisions

It is rarely possible to make the "perfect decision." Every course of
action will lead to more choices and will throw up some unexpected
difficulties. The following strategies should help you in making difficult decisions, but if you become too worried in the pursuit of the perfect decision, you will be more likely to become painfully indecisive.

1. THE BALANCE SHEET

Use a balance sheet to apply the "problem-solving method" (Chapter
8), to weigh up the advantages and the disadvantages of different
choices. Divide a large sheet of paper down the middle into two sections, one for advantages and the other for disadvantages. Write the
specific question you are thinking about at the top: Shall I expand the
business now? Shall I book a summer holiday? Shall I take the com-
puting course next term? Then fill in the columns, considering the
decision from all its aspects: how it affects others as well as yourself,
including its implications and consequences. Think of factors that are
important in the long term as well as in the short term. This exercise
is best done on paper since it is difficult to hold all the ideas in one's
mind at once. Now look through the list and weigh up the balance.
Some items will count much more than others. It can be helpful to
give points out of 100 to each advantage and disadvantage, according
to how important they are, and then to add the columns separately:
67 "for" and 38 "against." Or it might help, if there are many advantages and disadvantages, to decide on the two most significant in each
column, and weigh them against each other without being distracted
by relatively unimportant considerations.

2. TRIAL RUNS AND TIME PROJECTION

If you are having difficulty in making a choice—whether or not to move house, for example—pretend that you have made one choice (to move) and then imagine, as fully as possible, what it would be like had that choice been made. Does it feel right? With important decisions which are not urgent, imagine "living" that choice for several days, and then imagine the other choice. This exercise gives you the opportunity to take yourself through a trial run and to make contact with your "gut reaction." You may then know what to do, but if not, you can go back to your balance sheet and think whether other points need adding.

Another way of doing this is to make use of "time projection." This is a simple strategy that involves imagining yourself at some future date, 6 months, 5 years, 10 years ahead (see also Chapter 9, p. 86) having made the decision that you are now finding difficult. From your new vantage point, look back at the present, and at the decision you are trying to make. You may immediately find it easier to make up your mind, or you may wish to imagine taking different options in turn until you find the one that you like best.

You could also test out your reactions by tossing a coin, or thinking about what would happen if you made no decision at all.

3. A SOUNDING BOARD

Other people can provide a useful sounding board, and may reflect back to you their understanding of your problem and of your inclinations. Consulting too many people, however, can be a mistake because you may end up with too many opinions. "Ask three people whom you trust, and then make up your mind" is a useful guiding principle to prevent endless rumination. It is tempting to consult only those people with whom you expect to agree, but this will narrow down the possibilities. If you are searching for a completely new line of thinking, it may be more sensible to choose someone with a rather different, or more objective, opinion, such as the accountant rather than the sales manager, or the teacher who understands your talents and strengths rather than the parent who desperately wants you to become a doctor. If you were deciding whether or not to convert your house to make room for your elderly in-laws, you would probably talk it over with your partner and with other involved members of the family. It may also be sensible to consult a specialist in the care of the elderly, or to search in the library for other relevant information.

4. INFORMATION GATHERING, AND SIFTING

Information is critical to making many decisions. If you are choosing a car, and safety is an important consideration, you need information about the safety features of the different cars. Before making such decisions, it is important to clarify those factors which are significant to you, but about which you need more information. Once you know what these factors are you can think about how to find the necessary information.

It also helps to learn how to evaluate the accuracy and reliability of the information available to you. Research tells us that decision-making improves with practice. It is a skill that can be acquired through experience, and more skilled decision-makers are less likely to forget important factors or misinterpret ambiguous information than inexperienced ones. In order to make effective decisions in some business settings, for example, inexperienced people need both to be trained in the use of relevant information systems, and given practice in making decisions. Otherwise, they will be more likely to make mistakes.

5. DEALING WITH CHAIN REACTIONS

Often decisions hang together. Larry wanted a new job, but his wife Emily was happy in the one she had. They discussed the options first, and made the decision that Larry would try to get a new job nearby, but that if he failed, then Emily would think about making changes herself. As things transpired, Larry found an exciting new opportunity, but it was a 4-hour drive away—an impossible commute. A chain reaction of decisions was then set in motion. Major decisions were demanded of them thick and fast. They concentrated on making these decisions in the most sensible order for them. First, they discussed whether to work in different places, and decided they wanted to continue living together. Then, Emily decided to look for a new job. She was uncertain how to proceed, so she consulted a colleague, and with her advice in mind, spoke to her boss before starting the search for new jobs. She found a choice of jobs. One, less interesting to her, started immediately; the other could not begin for 6 months. Together she and Larry now had to decide when to sell their house, and when and where to look for another one. Every possible option seemed to involve them in financial strain (renting temporary accommodation in one place or two, storing their belongings, etc.), and every decision seemed important. For each aspect of the problem they could specify, they balanced up the relative advantages. They then made the best decisions they could. Having first given their attention to the series of big changes in their lives, they were then able to tackle the host of minor ones that followed—whether to sell the old sofa, how to transport their belongings, and so on.

6. KEEPING UP THE ENERGY RESERVE

Theoretically, you should spend more time and energy on big decisions than on little ones. Deliberating whether to wear the brown socks or the green ones, or whether to buy the giant size pack of soap powder, or which traffic line to join makes little sense. However, this is harder in practice than in theory. The first interfering factor is fatigue. Being tired can make it difficult to make even the simplest of decisions.

Preoccupation is the second interfering factor. People whose energies are necessarily devoted to important and worrying decisions, like whether to close the business or to have major surgery or to get divorced, frequently find the smaller decisions especially difficult and intrusive, as if their reserves are already depleted, and they have little attention for anything else. It helps then to ask yourself, "How much does this really matter?" Next, turn as many small decisions into routines as you possibly can, and leave the less important ones for later or for others.

False Dictators and Unsettling Gremlins

Many pitfalls beset the decision-maker, so it is important to know how to recognize them, and where to look out for these false dictators and unsettling gremlins that can put one off one's stride.

1. Biased thinking (for more on this see Chapter 33). The opinion of the last person you spoke to often seems the most convincing. Or the more weighty the authority behind a pronouncement that affects your decision, the more likely it is to influence you. Our decisions are easily swayed by minor or irrelevant factors, like whether the person you are interviewing for a job arrives soaking wet, having been caught in a storm.

2. Categorical thinking. This is the error of supposing that there is only one right choice. Completely "right," or indeed completely "wrong," choices are extremely rare. One might even go so far as to say that there is no such thing as a right choice. It is, therefore, more important to ask yourself how you could live with the choice you have made, what adaptations it will demand of you, whether it is a permanent choice, and whether it could be changed if things work out differently from the way you expected, than to bother about whether you have got it right. How could you ever know?

3. Not thinking beyond the decision. It is a mistake to assume that your decision will fix things for good, as if the process of change will stop as soon as the decision is made. Change never stops, and it constantly demands adaptation from us. It is an illusion to think any decision will fix a particular state of affairs in a static grip.

4. Conservatism. We have a tendency to think that whatever happened last time is bound to happen next time. It is easier to decide to do the same thing this time as you did last time, but that way you may miss new discoveries. Keep an eye open for new choices.

5. Confusing problem-solving with worrying. Some people, especially those of whom many decisions are demanded on a regular basis, expect themselves to be able to make decisions quickly. They may then find it worrying when a decision takes longer than usual. They may accuse themselves of worrying and fail to recognize that sometimes the process of problem-solving is difficult and takes time. Recognize that some decisions are more difficult to make than others and allow them more time.

6. Information tangles. Forgetting and misinterpreting information are two of the most misleading gremlins. Control them by keeping a notebook, using information sources efficiently, and asking others to keep you up to date. Most decisions can wait until you have the information you need.

7. Expecting the feeling to come first, and the decision to follow. Waiting until you feel "right," or feel "strong enough," to make a difficult decision may keep you waiting forever. The more difficult the decision the more tempting, and disrupting, this can be. You may have to decide whether to fire someone, or how to allocate redundancy payments, or tell an employee clearly that his carping criticisms are having a counterproductive effect on the whole department. In these cases you will be more likely to feel better *after,* than *before,* the decision is made (and the action taken).

8. Fears and worries. Fears and worries of all sorts can interfere with the process of making decisions. The decision may plunge you into a situation that you find frightening (accepting a promotion that involves speaking in front of large groups of people), or it may give pain to others (breaking up a relationship, telling relatives about your homosexuality). Remember that the harder the decision the more likely it is that two heads will be better than one. Find someone to share the problem with if you can, and think through the consequences of making your decision.

9. Other "bad" feelings. Almost any kind of distress interferes with the ability to make decisions, including fatigue, stress, depression, illness, and problems with relationships. One definition of the process of deciding explains that it involves "giving overt expression to one aspect of behavior while others are temporarily suppressed." Expressed in the language of a dictionary, this sounds like jargon. Expressed in other words, it means that making a decision occupies a fair amount of your attention, so other things have to be ignored or "put on hold" while you do it. Even experienced and speedy decision-makers have to think about the decisions they make, although they may hardly notice that they do so. If you are preoccupied, or your attention is demanded by other things, including distressing feelings, then this will be much harder to do. Decision-making then becomes unexpectedly burdensome. There are many solutions. You could allow yourself to take longer, and decide things more slowly. You could deal with the distressing feelings first, and then return to the decisions. If the decisions keep pressing, you could fall back on "conservatism" (less adventurous, but also less risky), delegate, or ask others to share some of the responsibility for the time being. Or you could plan a well-timed holiday and give yourself a break.

SOME DIFFERENT DECISION-MAKING STYLES

People vary in the way they make decisions and in the speed at which they make them. But our decision-making patterns are not fixed: they are more like tendencies that can be more or less influential depending on how they are used. Each style of decision-making has advantages as well as disadvantages, and different styles are useful in different situations.

Risk takers may tolerate a high degree of uncertainty with equanimity or they may enjoy the brush with excitement and danger. Their decisions may seriously alarm their more cautious friends if the costs of failure are high, but they may also earn our respect. They may need to learn to count the costs of their mistakes with accuracy. They need steady nerves.

Impulsive people tend to jump from one decision to another without due consideration. Their decisions can feel intuitively right (giving a compliment at exactly the right moment), but they can also be ill-considered and regretted later. If they focus on delaying the decision, and on weighing up advantages and disadvantages, they may feel happier with the choices they make.

Cautious people can provide a valuable check to risk takers, and often enjoy working in settings where safety is an important consideration. Overcautious people may hesitate before crossing the road, signing the insurance policy, or agreeing to take on an additional task at work. It may be helpful for them to practice making small decisions quickly, to tune in to what fits with their ultimate goals and values, and to cut down on the deliberation.

Clashing styles. Brendan made decisions quickly, and once the decision was made, he would say "So that's settled," putting any doubts and deliberations out of his mind and getting on with the next thing. His wife Claire wanted to talk things through thoroughly, and in doing so she wanted to tune in to how it would feel to jump one way or another. This kind of clash can easily turn into an argument, but one thing it is pointless to argue about is which decision-making style is the best one. People go through different processes before they feel settled about a decision. Rather than accusing each other of jumping to premature conclusions or of wanting to rake over old ground, it would be more helpful to recognize the different styles and use negotiating skills (see pp. 162–166) to settle the difference.

Age differences in decision-making styles. Decision-making styles, generally speaking, change over the life span. When involved in the decisions of others, or asked for advice, it can be helpful to bear in mind these differences and to adapt accordingly. Younger people are more influenced by immediate and short-term considerations, pay little attention to longer term consequences, and worry relatively little about making mistakes. Elderly people find adaptation to changes harder to cope with, and each adjustment a little more unsettling than the last. They may need longer to make decisions, and find decision-making about major issues progressively harder.

A rest from taking decisions. For many people, one of the pleasures of being on holiday is having to decide nothing more important than what to eat or where to swim. Like anything else that is effortful, having an occasional rest from decision-making is beneficial. It is sometimes even essential—for example, when someone is ill. Then hearing someone say, "Leave that to me. I'll take care of that until you are well again," can bring great relief. Being unable to drop the reins temporarily when one is ill can also delay the process of recovery.

And to console those of you who are indecisive, let us quote Coleridge, who wrote to a friend in 1837: "Indecisiveness of character ... is almost always associated with benevolence."

Related Chapters in This Book

Chapter 8   Problem-solving: A strategy for change

Chapter 5   Managing yourself and your time

Chapter 33   Thinking straight

Chapter Summary

Decision-making is a skill that improves with practice.
Six strategies that help when making decisions:

- The balance sheet
- Trial runs and time projection
- A sounding board
- Information gathering, and sifting
- Dealing with chain reactions
- Keeping up the energy reserve

Nine pitfalls to avoid:

- Biased thinking
- Categorical thinking
- Not thinking beyond the decision
- Conservatism
- Confusing problem-solving with worrying
- Information tangles

- Expecting the feeling to come first, and the decision to follow
- Fears and worries
- Other "bad" feelings

There may be no such thing as the "right" decision, and there is certainly no one decision-making style that fits all people and all circumstances.

33

◆ ◆ ◆

Thinking Straight

A central theme running through this book is that psychology is useful. If you understand the psychological aspects of everyday life, you will be better able to face problems, to treat yourself right, to keep things in perspective, and to build up self-confidence (Part 2). You will be able to do this when dealing with difficulties in relationships, and when dealing with anxiety and depression (Parts 3 and 4). Knowing a little psychology can also be essential when tackling problems that affect sleeping, eating, and drinking (Part 5). Furthermore, knowing how the mind works will help you develop your ability in learning, remembering, and making decisions (Part 6).

In Chapter 1, we wrote about the "two book shelves," one devoted to psychology and the other to management skills. Deeply ingrained in our culture is this false dichotomy between the skills needed for work and the skills needed for home. Many of the same skills are needed in both places: for example, the three keys of good relationships are just as important to the manager as they are to the parent, and time management is an organizational skill that is as important in running a home as it is in running a business. This book is about the organizational and psychological skills that will enable you to make changes in your life—in all aspects of your life—to make improvements both for yourself and for those around you. In this final chapter, we bring together some of the themes of this book by focusing on straight thinking.

Thinking straight is not always easy: it is harder to think logically, and to avoid being led astray by illogical pitfalls, than it would seem. Even those of us who pride ourselves on our rational approach to life still make judgments on the basis of inadequate information—for example, when we jump to conclusions and think "I'll never get out of this mess," or try mind-reading and conclude "They think I'm stupid." Far more frequently than we realize we use thinking strategies that are based only loosely on fact, or we make one of a number of the standard mistakes studied and analyzed by psychologists. In Chapter 9 we explained how thoughts and feelings are related, and how it helps, when you feel bad, to look for another way of seeing things. This chapter describes some of the standard mistakes that bias our thinking, and explains how we can try to avoid making them in order to make better use of our minds for solving the problems and dealing with the impediments which we face.

Four Common Mistakes in Thinking

1. BEING MISLED BY THEORIES, BELIEFS, AND ASSUMPTIONS

We need theories of all kinds. They enable us to operate efficiently in a constantly changing world, and define for us those things we can take for granted: for example, that aspirin will relieve headaches, that friends will listen when we talk to them, and that suntan lotion is harmless. But opinions once formed are remarkably resistant to change, even in the face of contradictory evidence. As Francis Bacon once said, "The human understanding when it has once adopted an opinion draws all things else to support and agree with it."[1]".

Opinions can easily slip into prejudices. Prejudices, such as beliefs about ethnic characteristics or about the differences between the sexes, are good examples of theories that may bias our judgments and be hard to change, and by looking at them in more detail we can unravel some of the ways in which beliefs are maintained in the face of disconfirming evidence. Imagine believing that children who take a long time to learn to read are less intelligent than others. Many processes combine to make it hard to change this belief. These can be demonstrated by illustrating what happens when you come across information that does not fit, such as hearing that your exceptionally clever friend, Max, was a slow reader.

First, information that does not fit is *discounted*. You decide your clever but slow-to-read friend is the "exception that proves the rule." One clever person who was a slow reader just does not count. Evidence about him impinges not at all on the belief: it is not even worth noticing.

Second, information that does not fit is *distorted*. You might argue that Max misremembers how long he took to learn to read. It felt hard because everything else came easy to him, or because his class was full of exceptionally able children and he was one of the slower ones. It is as if your mind argues like this: slow readers are not very intelligent; Max is intelligent; therefore he cannot have been a slow reader. In other words, we select facts that fit with our beliefs, theories, and assumptions and forget or dismiss the rest. We also confuse preferences with facts: it may be preferable to think that the criticism one receives from others is unwarranted, and a product of someone else's short temper, than to accept that it is justified or well deserved. It feels better to attribute the failure to achieve a target at work, such as an increase in turnover or greater client satisfaction, to the economic climate or to the behavior of one's competitors than to one's own mistakes and failings.

Third, information that does not fit is *deflected*. You recognize the challenge to the belief, but pay no attention to it, and forget it so it does not get stored. It is just as if the mind had no "pigeon hole" ready to accept discrepant information about clever people who were slow to learn to read. When you try to recall such information later, none comes to mind, because none has been committed to memory. Maybe you remember that Max is one of the cleverest people you know and assume that his cleverness must have been apparent from the start, whatever he says about it now.

What we see, notice, attend to, and remember is in many ways determined by the beliefs, frameworks, and theories that we already have, rather than the other way round. Our daily observations hardly ever change our preconceptions. This is relevant because distressing beliefs—such as "I'm not as good as others," or "Everyone else copes better than I do," or "The world is a dangerous place"—will be just as resistant to change, and just as likely to be inaccurate, as other sorts of beliefs. They are prejudices about yourself, about other people, or about the world. One of the reasons why these "prejudices" are hard to change is because we also *discount, distort,* and *deflect* information that does not fit with them (see also Chapter 10, pp. 97–101).

Insuring against the bias

1. Look for evidence that could disconfirm your belief rather than for evidence that confirms it. If you believe that all swans are

white, then your belief can only change, and fit with reality, if you look out for swans that are not white. Finding more white swans only endorses the belief you already have without helping you to verify it. Looking for non-white swans (or for clever people who learned to read slowly instead of quickly) can tell you when an old belief needs changing.

2. When you come across instances that do not fit with your preconceptions, make sure you think about them, remember them, and ask yourself whether old beliefs need modifying (do not discount or deflect your successes or the compliments you receive).

3. Keep your preferences and inclinations out of it. This means both knowing what they are, and becoming aware of how they might bias your powers of reasoning. If you know what you "want to think" then it is easier to check out whether the facts really fit the case, or whether you are just shaping them up that way.

4. Do not worry about modifying beliefs as you go along. It can feel unsettling to have to change your mind—for example, about the benevolence of a certain teacher in your children's school, or the belief that hard work will ultimately be rewarded and recognized. Beliefs, theories, and assumptions can shift gradually over time, or change suddenly. In both cases the ability to adapt and change with circumstances is more likely to keep you thinking rationally and clearly than hanging onto the safe but unsupported beliefs.

2. BEING MISLED BY WHAT SPRINGS TO MIND

The information that most readily comes to mind has a disproportionate effect on opinions and reasoning in general. In 1946, Solomon Asch demonstrated this point in an experiment in which people were asked to form an opinion about a person who was described as "intelligent-industrious-impulsive-critical-stubborn-envious." If the adjectives were presented in that order, the opinions were more positive than if they were presented in the reverse order (starting with "envious-stubborn-critical . . ."). The adjectives presented first created a favorable or an unfavorable impression, and these first impressions then influenced the final judgment. All of us tend to give undue weight to things that spring to mind. The trouble is that what springs to mind at a particular time is often determined by extraneous factors like the order in which things were said during a work appraisal, or by whether you were feeling anxious or depressed.

There are many sources of this particular bias. The more recent an event, the more likely it is to influence your judgment. If you have a "near miss" when driving a car you will tend to be more careful the more recent this event. Unfortunately, in this case, the effect of recency soon wears off, and you quickly revert to your usual, less careful, behavior. But this may not happen if a recent argument has biased your view of someone you love and makes it hard to make peace once more.

Vivid, or emotionally salient, events also have undue influence on the way we think. This is a fact exploited by advertising, and it also affects our daily lives. Feeling good about something you did will make you think it is worth doing again; feeling bad about it will put you off. In summary, if something is important to you, arouses strong feelings, happened recently, or attracts your attention in an unusual way (for instance, because it is a novelty or rarity), then you are more likely to remember it and doing so is more likely to influence, and to bias, your judgment.

Ensuring against the bias

1. Take your time when thinking something through. Snap judgments are more likely to be unduly influenced by irrelevancies than considered ones.
2. Try to stand back from the heat. If your feelings are strongly engaged, your thinking may change when the feelings change. It helps to label your feelings, to identify the thoughts that go with them, and to check out whether these make sense and fit with reality (see Chapter 9).
3. Check out your thoughts on others. See how they react. Because everyone's experience and interests are different, using two minds rather than one is a good way of reducing this form of bias.

3. BEING MISLED BY THE INFLUENCE OF OTHERS

Thinking straight is often easier, and more likely to be logical and helpful, if you can use others as a sounding board. But there are nevertheless some pitfalls to avoid when listening to the opinions of others.

The halo effect. We tend to believe people we admire, even when their opinions may not be especially well informed. Sportsmen and popstars are asked to endorse brands of soap powder or to give their opinions on world affairs, regardless of their expertise, because their fame alone carries a weight that influences our judgment. If you love French food, you may be more inclined to think that all things French are wonderful.

When people are influenced by the weight of authority, they run the risk of being misled by the halo effect. For example, people may listen to their doctor's pronouncements about career decisions, and to what their lawyers have to say about personal relationships. Or they may borrow authority to lend weight to an argument of their own: "Mr. Stein, a leading researcher and university professor, says that he has found a new method of weight control that really works." Or they quote from articles they have read in newspapers or journals as if the printing of the word lent it immediate credibility.

The presentation effect. If a salesclerk holds your interest by speaking well, by making you laugh, and by using apt illustrations, you will be more likely to believe what he or she says. The same is true at work, at home, and in social settings. The more boringly someone talks, irrespective of what they say, the less influence they will have. If you learn to express yourself assertively (Chapter 13), you will be more likely to be listened to.

Scientific reality. We live in times which set great store by the objectivity and "reality" of scientific observations. These are indeed responsible for much of the progress from which we benefit daily. The opposite side of the coin is that appealing to the scientific evidence, regardless of whether this is justified, is an unduly persuasive form of argument. As most of us are not experts, we are easily led astray. We may buy a new type of tire for our car, or stop buying cholesterol-rich foods, without knowing whether these decisions are really reasonable. Perhaps the best we can do is to keep an open mind, learn more about how to evaluate the information with which we are presented, and guard against false prophets.

Most branches of science develop their own technical language, or jargon. Jargon, or obscurantism, can easily mislead, especially if it is being used to impress or lend weight to a particular point of view. Asking people to explain in language you can understand is an excellent protection. Explanations may be hard to make, and understanding them may involve learning some new terms (the meaning of the word "software" is now understood by many more people than it would have been 15 years ago), but it is nearly always possible, and if it is not possible, then you may be justified in suspending judgment for the time being. This is not to say that you need to understand how the fax machine works in order to be able to use it, but that you would be justified in asking for a clear, intelligible explanation of the advantages of the new model if you were considering replacing your old one. The same goes for evaluating the psychological advice you are given.

The fundamental attribution error. Dick is a social worker. He enjoys the contact with clients most of all, and is a committed, hard-working member of the local childcare team. His colleagues think of him as reliable, communicative, level-headed, calm, and responsible. Dick is 29 years old, married to Clara, who works part time in a residential home for elderly people, and they have two young children. Dick comes home from work exhausted and his marriage is suffering. Clara describes him to a friend as silent, detached from the family, forgetful when it comes to the chores, irritable, and irresponsible in that he leaves the vast majority of the parenting to her. The two views of Dick are almost diametrically opposed, and both of them are expressed as if they described his personality: in terms of stable or fundamental characteristics likely to endure. This is the fundamental attribution error: behavior is attributed to enduring qualities of people rather than to the situations, circumstances, and events that surround them.

In fact, people vary enormously in different situations. They adapt according to the demands made, and change as circumstances (and times) change. So we should beware of labeling others, or ourselves, as if our reactions and behaviors were fixed. The potential for change can be increased by changing circumstances rather than trying to change people. It is not that you cannot "teach an old dog new tricks," but rather that "all work and no play makes Jack a dull boy." In other words, changing the situation is extremely likely to change the person. The disaffected, lazy employee can become motivated and energetic if circumstances change.

4. BEING MISLED BY ASSOCIATIONS

Jim has a bad cold which has left him with a headache. He meets someone who complains of a headache and they start talking about the kind of cold they both have, about how to fend off its worst effects, and about how much it interferes with the ability to think straight. They are both making a fundamental thinking error which involves being misled by similarities. Because their problems are associated—they both have headaches—they assume the problems have the same cause. But the friend may be suffering from a totally different ailment—an allergy, sinusitis, an infection from a different source, and so on. The same argument would apply if they had been stressed, anxious, or had a tendency to drink too much.

You see a politician being interviewed on television. He has been caught unawares, wearing a crumpled shirt with his hair unbrushed. His appearance is more like that of an absent-minded professor than of a reputable politician, and your judgment about him follows suit. You will be likely to judge him as forgetful, a theoretician, with his head in the air rather than his feet on the ground. No wonder politicians take such pains to polish their appearance—and to get their hair cut at the right time.

A smart middle-aged man in a suit, carrying a briefcase, comes to your door and offers you his business card. He says he is opening an antique shop nearby, is interested in buying antiques from local people, and is offering free valuations to those who are interested. He is very polite, apologizes for interrupting if you are busy, and offers to come back at a more convenient time if you wish. You invite him in, make a cup of coffee, fetch your grandmother's picture to ask him about, and when he leaves you find your purse has gone with him. His behavior was similar to someone more respectable, and he has capitalized on the general tendency to think that superficial similarities tell you about underlying ones.

Insuring against the bias

1. When you notice that two things are similar, ask yourself also how they differ. See if you can find out whether they have different causes. My depression, or eating problem, might or might not have the same cause as yours.
2. Check out your expectations. Ask what you are basing them on, and whether that makes good sense. Are appearances a good indicator of the facts? They usually are, and this is why people can exploit them to their advantage, but they can also mislead. Taking them at face value, especially if the circumstances are unusual, may be misleading.

Four Statistical Rules

Statistics, the science of numerical facts and data, is complex and technical, but the ordinary thinker need not be a statistician in order to think rationally. A number of common errors in thinking can be reduced by knowing about basic statistical rules.

1. THE LAW OF LARGE NUMBERS

The larger the sample the more likely it is to reflect the characteristics of the population from which it is drawn. You may hear from a friend that the type of car you are thinking of buying is wonderful—entirely reliable, easy to park, and comfortable to ride in. You could check out its comfort and the ease with which it can be parked by taking it out for a test drive. But experience of just one car can tell you little about the reliability of the model. In order to judge whether this type of car is reliable, you need information from many cars. Arguing from other people's experience, or from your own, is often unsound. The larger the numbers on which the information is based, and the more random the sampling involved, the more valid your judgment is likely to be. Some features of the problems or difficulties you have will be like those of other people, but others will be unique to you. The same applies to the solutions you find. Using this book as a source of ideas that others have found helpful should not put you off trying out others for yourself.

2. COMPARISON, OR CONTROL, GROUPS

It is easy to be impressed with statistics such as the large number of people killed on the roads, or the small percentage of babies who die within the first year of life. In the absence both of comparison groups and of a knowledge of the total population at risk (the total number of car drivers, or of babies), most of these figures are of limited value. They may shock us, but they do not provide an adequate basis for value judgments or for decision-making, unless they are put into the context of comparison groups. Do the figures represent an improvement on previous years? How do they compare with other similar countries? What is the rate of change? Most statistics need to be placed in the context of comparison or control groups if they are to be meaningfully interpreted.

3. MAKING PREDICTIONS

It has been argued that boys are better at math than girls. Indeed, a difference between the mathematical skills of boys and girls has been found in various studies and at various stages of development. But this does not make it possible to predict how easily any individual boy or girl will learn mathematical skills. This is for two reasons. First, the behavior of the group does not tell us anything about the actual behavior of an individual. Second, the overlap between the groups may be far greater than the differences between them. In the case of mathematical abilities, there is an enormous range of ability present in both boys and girls. The similarities between boys and girls in mathematical abilities are far greater than the differences between them—and the similarities between people who have problems and difficulties in their lives also are far greater than the differences between them, as the vast majority of people experience difficulties at some stage in their lives.

4. CORRELATION AND CAUSE

It is often mistakenly assumed that because two things go together that the one causes the other. People with red hair often have pale skin, but the one does not cause the other. To take a different kind of example, Matthew gradually became more confident and more skilled as he settled down in his new job. During the same period his manager met briefly with him weekly to check out how he was getting on. The two events are correlated, because they happened over the same time period. But gradual change is far more likely to be independent of particular, intermittent events than to be caused by them. Taking an aspirin or two as you recover from the flu may make you feel temporarily better but is most unlikely to influence your rate of recovery.

It is harder to be certain about causes when thinking about social issues than about scientific ones. We are more certain that an icy wind in spring will wither the daffodils in its path, and less certain that family disruption will "cause" delinquent behavior in adolescents. We tend to assume that the one variable that we have identified (family disruption in this case) is the only relevant one, and to ignore the people from disrupted homes who never became delinquent. Indeed, these are so easy to ignore, especially when counting troublemakers, that in most societies we do not even know how many of them there are. Maybe this is like ignoring the things that go right in your life, or that you have done well, when you have a problem or things are going badly. Then it is easy to assume that the things you did wrong are the cause of the problem—which they may not be.

Persuasion, Manipulation, and Group Pressure

The pressure to conform to the group is surprisingly strong. If no one adopts a policy for dealing with harassment in the workplace (racial or sexual), then those who suffer from harassment may find little support. But as soon as most people have such a policy, then the group pressure to conform and adopt appropriate policies in the workplace increases. Groups can influence decision-making and individual thinking in many ways, but they can be wrong as well as right. So it may take strength of mind, and assertiveness, to maintain your opinion when everyone else disagrees with you.

Parting Words

Becoming aware of the sources of error in thinking is the main resource we can draw upon to improve our thinking. The clearer we think, the better we will be at making decisions, at problem-solving, and also at keeping things in perspective: (see pp. 78–80 for some more examples of crooked thinking).

Related Chapters in This Book

Chapter　6　*Facing the problem*

Chapter　9　*Keeping things in perspective: Help from cognitive therapy*

Chapter 32　*Making decisions*

Chapter Summary

The skills described in this book, whether they are drawn from the field of management or of psychology, are equally relevant to your work life and to your home life. They will help you to make the changes that you wish to make in any aspect of your life.

Many of these skills can be seen as various ways of thinking straight.

There are *four common mistakes* in thinking:

- Being misled by false assumptions
- Being misled by what springs to mind
- Being misled by others
- Being misled by false associations

Many common errors in thinking can be avoided by knowing four statistical rules:

- The law of large numbers tells us that anecdotes are unreliable.
- Comparison groups are needed to provide a context for new information.
- Individual predictions may be impossible from group generalizations.
- Two things may go together without either being the cause of the other.

Pressure to conform to the group is surprisingly strong. Use all of your skills and strategies to resist when you need to. If you keep thinking straight, you will be better able to keep things in perspective, to make decisions, and to solve the problems that come your way.

Notes

Chapter 1   What to Expect from This Guide

1. L. P. Hartley, in the prologue to *The Go-Between* (Harmondsworth, England: Penguin, 1990).

Chapter 6   Facing the Problem

1. Konrad Lorenz, *Man Meets Dog* (Harmondsworth, England: Penguin, 1964).

Chapter 7   Treating Yourself Right

1. Charles Dickens, *The Life and Adventures of Nicholas Nickleby* (Oxford: Oxford University Press, 1987), p. 93.

Chapter 9   Keeping Things in Perspective

1. Several books by Albert Ellis and Aaron Beck are available (see "Further Reading").

2. Viktor E. Frankl, *Man's Search for Meaning* (London: Hodder and Stoughton, 1964). (First published in German in 1946.)

3. D. M. Clark and J. D. Teasdale, (1985). Constraints on the Effects of Mood on Memory, *Journal of Personality and Social Psychology, 48,* 1595–1608.

4. D. M. Clark, P. M. Salkovskis, M. Gelder, C. Koehler, M. Martin, P. Anastasiades, A. Hackmann, H. Middleton and A. Jeavons, Tests of a Cognitive Theory of Panic, in I. Hand and H. U. Wittchen (Eds.), *Panic and Phobias 2* (Berlin: Springer-Verlag, 1988).

Chapter 10   Building Self-Confidence and Self-Esteem

1. Alice Walker, *The Color Purple* (New York: The Women's Press, 1983).

Chapter 14   The Second Key to Good Relationships

1. Amy and Thomas Harris, *Staying OK* (London: Pan Books Ltd., 1986).

Chapter 16   Getting the Better of Anxiety and Worry

1. A. A. Milne, *The House at Pooh Corner* (London: Methuen, 1928), Chapter 8.

2. Philip Wakeham, "Living Target," in R. Hope (Ed.), *Seamen and the Sea* (London: George Harrap & Co. Ltd., 1965).

3. Letter to Madame de Grignan, 26 April 1671. In *Madame de Sévigné, Selected Letters,* translated by Leonard Tancock (Harmondsworth, England: Penguin Books, 1982).

Chapter 21   Digging Yourself Out of Depression

1. A. T. Beck, A. J. Rush, B. F. Shaw, and G. Emery, *Cognitive Therapy of Depression* (New York: Guilford Press, 1985).

2. G. W. Brown and T. W. Harris. *Social Origins of Depression: A Study of Psychiatric Disorder in Women* (London: Tavistock Publications, 1978).

Chapter 30   How to Improve Your Memory: Part 1

1. J. L. Borges, *Funes the Memorious* (in *Fictions* by J. L. Borges, London: Calder, 1965, pp. 97–105).

2. A. R. Luria, *The Mind of the Mnemonist* (Cambridge, MA: Harvard University Press, 1987).

Chapter 33   Thinking Straight

1. Francis Bacon, *The New Organon and Related Writings* (New York; Liberal Arts Press, 1960). Originally published in 1620.

Further Reading

In this section we have provided a list of books which you may find of further help. We have grouped the books according to their relevance to each Part of this book. For a comprehensive guide to self-help books see:

John W. Santrock, Ann M. Minnett, and Barbara D. Campbell, *The Authoritative Guide to Self-Help Books* (New York; Guilford Press, 1994).

Introduction

R. Atkinson, R. Atkinson, E. Smith, and D. Bern, *Introduction to Psychology,* 11th ed. (Orlando, FL: Harcourt Brace, 1993).

Part One   Two Principles Underlying Mental Fitness

Viktor K. Frankl, *Man's Search for Meaning* (Boston: Beacon Press, 1962; London: Hodder and Stoughton, 1964. Fifth impression, 1992).
  Dr. Frankl used his experiences in four different concentration camps to find ways of healing sickness of mind and spirit. "He who has a why *to live can bear with almost any* how."

Anne Morrow Lindbergh, *Gift from the Sea* (New York: Vintage Books, a Division of Random House, 1978. (Twentieth Anniversary Edition)
  A brief, eloquent, thoughtful account of one woman's examination of her roles in life and her struggles to balance a life of work and relationships.

David G. Meyers, *The Pursuit of Happiness* (New York: William Morrow, 1992).

This book discusses four main characteristics of happy people: self-esteem, optimism, extroversion, and personal control. It looks at the influence of beliefs and perceptions in determining our state of happiness, and conclusions are based on research rather than on clinical observation.

Carol S. Pearson, *The Hero Within,* rev. ed. (San Francisco: Harper, 1989).

An interesting and useful book about the course that psychological development can take, with stages represented by common archetypes that most of us know.

Part Two   The Seven Basic Skills

A separate list of books focusing on cognitive therapy is to be found on page 413. These books are useful in many different situations. They are especially relevant for keeping things in perspective, building self-confidence and self-esteem, and dealing with anxiety and depression and with difficulties in relationships

Herbert Benson, *The Relaxation Response* (New York: William Morrow, 1975).

From this book readers learn how to achieve a relaxed response so as to deal effectively with the negative effects of stress.

Herbert Benson, *Beyond the Relaxation Response* (New York: Times Books, 1984).

Benson combines an awareness of spirituality and faith with the relaxation response and looks at how our beliefs as well as the mental strategies we use can help us with our physical health.

Stephen R. Covey, *The Seven Habits of Highly Effective People* (New York: Simon & Schuster, 1989).

This is one of the best accounts of the principles of time management. It is a very well-structured book, and although aimed at the business management world it contains many useful ideas relevant to everyone.

Mihaly Csikszentmihalyi, *Flow: The Psychology of Optimal Experience* (New York: Harper & Row, 1990).

About actively giving meaning to our life's experiences through setting challenges for ourselves, and mastering something worthwhile.

Martha Davis, Elizabeth Robbins Eshelman, and Matthew McKay, *The Relaxation and Stress Workbook,* 4th ed. (Oakland, CA: New Harbinger, 1995).

Loaded with sound advice and strategies for coping with stress, this book focuses on applied relaxation, exercise, nutrition, time management, meditation, visualization, thought-stopping, job-stress management, and more.

Wayne Dyer, *Your Erroneous Zones* (London: Sphere Books, 1977).

Many ways to recognize and overcome the self-defeating behavior

that keeps opportunities for change at bay. Written in an accessible and light-hearted way.

Albert Ellis and Robert Harper, *A New Guide to Rational Living* (Englewood Cliffs, NJ: Prentice Hall, 1975).
An excellent source for the ideas and suggestions that come from Rational Emotive Therapy.

Sheila Ernst and Lucy Goodison, *In Our Own Hands: A Book of Self-Help Therapy* (London: The Women's Press, 1988).
Many different kinds of therapy are described, and 140 exercises and self-help strategies are presented with sensitivity and clarity.

Harold Kushner, *When All You Ever Wanted Isn't Enough* (New York: Summit Books, 1986).
Harold Kushner, a rabbi, discusses the many questions we have about the purpose of our lives and how to find answers through meaning, love, and integrity.

Joanna McGrath and Alister McGrath, *The Dilemma of Self-Esteem* (Wheaton, IL: Crossway Books, a Division of Good News Publishers, 1992).
A clinical psychologist and a Christian theology teacher write about the ways in which low self-esteem can hinder people from achieving their potential and sabotage relationships and careers. Their ideas help to develop a sense of self-worth and acceptance.

Matthew McKay and Patrick Fanning, *Self-Esteem,* 2nd ed. (Oakland, CA.: New Harbinger, 1993).
The focus is on dealing with self-criticism, using the techniques of cognitive therapy.

Penelope Russianoff, *When Am I Going to Be Happy?* (New York: Bantam Books, 1988, London: Cedar Books, 1989).
This book provides well-thought-out strategies to help you recognize and break your emotional bad habits.

Books Focusing on Cognitive Therapy

Aaron T. Beck, *Cognitive Therapy and the Emotional Disorders* (New York: International Universities Press, 1987; reprinted by Penguin, 1989).
This book was written primarily for the professional mental health community, but ideas are presented in a clear and accessible way.

Aaron T. Beck, Gary Emery, and Ruth Greenberg, *Anxiety Disorders and Phobias* (New York: Basic Books, 1985).
Excellent description of the cognitive view of anxiety; clear and readable but not a self-help book.

Aaron T. Beck, *Love Is Never Enough* (London and New York: Penguin Books, 1989).

Concrete help and advice about how to unravel the problems that can lead to breakdown in relationships, from a leader in the field of cognitive therapy.

David Burns, *Feeling Good: The New Mood Therapy* (New York: William Morrow, 1980).
The essential components of cognitive therapy for depression are lucidly presented in a readily usable self-help format.

David Burns, *The Feeling Good Handbook: Using the New Mood Therapy in Everyday Life* (New York: Harper & Row, 1989; Penguin Ewing, Plume Book, 1990).
This more detailed cognitive therapy, self-help book provides suggestions for people who doubt their self-worth, are subject to anxiety or depression, desperately strive to be perfect, or just feel bad without knowing why.

Dennis Greenberger and Christine Padesky, *Mind Over Mood: A Cognitive Therapy Treatment Manual for Clients* (New York: Guilford Press, 1995).
This book teaches step-by-step cognitive therapy skills that have been shown to help people recover from depression, anxiety, and relationship problems. It contains lots of specific exercises and worksheets to identify and change thinking patterns and behavior.

Martin Seligman, *Learned Optimism: The Skill to Conquer Life's Obstacles, Large and Small* (New York: Pocket Books, 1990).
Talks about how the way we see the world is not fixed at birth. People can learn how to develop a more optimistic style, which Seligman documents is associated with better mental and physical health.

Shelley Taylor, *Positive Illusions: Creative Self-Discipline and the Healthy Mind* (New York: Basic Books, 1989).
Quite academic in places, but contains a wealth of documentation of the positive distortions that are associated with mental and physical well-being.

Part Three   How to Improve Your Relationships

Robert Alberti and Michael Emmons, *Your Perfect Right: A Guide to Assertive Living* (New York: Penguin Books, 1981).
Discusses the importance of assertive behavior and how it differs from nonassertive and aggressive behavior. Teaches readers how to look for mutual gains and how not to allow themselves to be taken advantage of.

Robert Bolton, *People Skills* (New York: Touchstone Books, 1979).
A good general introduction to a wide range of communication skills applied to many different situations. The book focuses on five important skills: listening, assertiveness, conflict resolution, collaborative problem-solving, and skill selection.

Sharon Bower and Gordon H. Bower, *Asserting Yourself: A Practical Guide for Positive Change* (Reading, MA: Addison-Wesley, 1976).
Helps to construct a personal program for becoming more assertive and for developing friendships; describes a proven technique for handling most interpersonal conflicts.

Michael Broder, *The Art of Living Single* (New York: Avon Books, 1988).
Lots of practical advice for adults living alone. This book contains sections on social strategies, loneliness, romantic strategies, nurturing a relationship, sexual relationships, and survival strategies.

David Burns, *Intimate Connections: The New Clinically Tested Program for Overcoming Loneliness* (New York: William Morrow, 1985).
Learning to like oneself, how to make social connections, and how to improve one's sexual life. Full worksheets, checklists, mood logs, etc.

H. Cornelius and F. Shoshana, *Everyone Can Win: How to Resolve Conflict.* (Simon & Schuster Australia, 1989).
A clear account of the application of win-win negotiation techniques to personal relationships.

Anne Dickson, *A Woman in Your Own Right* (London: Quartet Books, 1982).
Explores the unhappiness and frustration that can arise from compliance with traditional ideas about a woman's role and provides practical advice about how to change behavior patterns and make the choices you wish to make. Useful for men as well as women.

Roger Fisher and William Ury, *Getting to Yes: Negotiating Agreement Without Giving Up* (New York: Penguin, 1981).
Covers a wide range of conflict situations, interpersonal and international, and helps people look for mutual gains and protect themselves from being browbeaten.

Amy Harris and Thomas Harris, *Staying OK* (London: Pan Books, 1985).
The sequel to I'm OK—You're OK, written by the same authors in 1973, this gives a good summary of transactional analysis and some further uses of its techniques.

Harriet Goldhor-Lerner, *The Dance of Anger* (New York: Harper & Row, 1990; London: Pandora Press, 1992).
Focusing largely on the family, this book provides the reader with the insights and practical skills to stop behaving in old predictable ways; offers guidelines for people to make constructive changes to their family relationships.

Harriet Goldhor-Lerner, *The Dance of Intimacy* (New York: Harper & Row, 1989).
The author outlines the steps to take to strengthen good relationships and improve difficult ones. This book, and the preceding one, are written primarily for women, but the ideas in them are useful for everyone.

John Gray, *Men are from Mars, Women are from Venus* (New York: Harper-Collins, 1992).
The different communication styles of men and women are described in an illuminating way. This book provides the kind of understanding that can be used as a practical guide.

Gael Lindenfield, *Assert Yourself: How to Reprogramme Your Mind for Positive Action* (Wellingborough, Northamptonshire, UK: Thorsons, 1987).
How not to blame yourself for feeling inadequate. A self-help course that helps you remove feelings of guilt and inferiority.

Matthew McKay, Martha Davis, and Patrick Fanning, *Messages: The Communication Skills Workbook* (Oakland, CA: New Harbinger, 1983).
Covers a wide variety of specific skills and approaches, including listening, self-disclosure, self-expression, body language, assertiveness, negotiation, making contact with strangers, sexual communication, parent effectiveness, and small-group pressures.

Matthew McKay, Peter D. Rogers, and Judith McKay, *When Anger Hurts* (Oakland, CA: New Harbinger, 1989).
A practical, down-to-earth book full of readily applicable techniques, written in a friendly, constructive tone.

Manuel J. Smith, *When I Say No I Feel Guilty* (New York: Bantam Books, 1975).
This book helps you to say no without feeling guilty and to get what you want without offending or upsetting others.

Anthony Storr: *Solitude* (London: HarperCollins, 1994).
Storr, a psychotherapist, argues that solitude is different from loneliness and has many positive effects. He is particularly interested in the connections between solitude and creativity.

Deborah Tannen, *You Just Don't Understand: Women and Men in Conversation* (New York: Ballantine Books, 1990).
This book explains how we can get along better by increasing our understanding of the conversational styles of the opposite gender. Instead of blaming others when communication goes wrong, we should learn about the different styles of communicating used by men and women.

Carol Tavris, *Anger: The Misunderstood Emotion* (New York: Touchstone Books, 1989).
This book draws on research findings to challenge many myths about anger and takes a calm and reasoned approach to a volatile subject.

Judith Viorst, *Necessary Losses* (New York: Simon & Schuster, 1986).
A positive tone pervades this account of how we can achieve fuller wisdom and maturity in our lives as a result of experiences with inevitable losses, including separation and giving up our personal power.

Jeffrey E. Young and Janet S. Klosko, *Reinventing Your Life* (New York: Dutton, 1993; Plume, Penguin Books, 1994).
How to free yourself from those destructive patterns or longstanding "life traps" that repeatedly make for difficulties, especially in relationships.

Philip Zimbardo, *Shyness* (Reading, MA: Addison-Wesley, 1987).
Contributing factors to shyness, such as negative evaluations, low self-esteem, and weak social skills, are explored, and specific ways of overcoming them are discussed.

Part Four   The Twin Enemies of Good Mood

Anxiety

Edmund J. Bourne, *The Anxiety and Phobia Workbook* (Oakland, CA: New Harbinger, 1990).
This self-help guide offers step-by-step strategies for overcoming panic and other anxiety problems. It covers breathing and relaxation skills, coping, underlying belief systems, uses of medication, exercise, nutrition, expression of feelings, self-esteem, and existential-spiritual perspectives.

E.A. Charlesworth and A.G. Nathan, *Stress Management: A Comprehensive Guide to Your Wellbeing* (London: Corgi Books, 1984).
A useful and practical book, with many good ideas. Encouraging to read.

David Fontana, *Managing Stress* (London: BPS Books and Routledge, 1989).
Identifying exactly what stresses you, both in the external world and inside yourself, helps you to focus on how to increase resistance to stress and how to enhance efficiency.

Ros and Jeremy Holmes, *The Good Mood Guide* (London: JM Dent, 1993).
This is a self-help book for dealing with a wide range of moods (for example, shame, boredom, and frustration as well as depression and anxiety) using techniques derived from both psychotherapy and meditation.

C. Ingham, *Panic Attacks: What They Are, Why They Happen, and What You Can Do about Them* (London: Thorsons [Harper Collins], 1993).
A practical guide to overcoming panic attacks.

Isaac M. Marks, *Living with Fear: Understanding and Coping with Anxiety* (New York: McGraw-Hill, 1978).
One of the first self-help books in this area, written from a behavioral point of view, and still useful.

Dorothy Rowe, *Beyond Fear* (London: Fontana Paperbacks, 1987).
Learning to admit to fear is the starting point for overcoming it.

Gail Steketee and Kerrin White, *When Once Is Not Enough: Help for Obsessive Compulsives* (Oakland, CA: New Harbinger, 1990).
An excellent self-help book that teaches a behavioral approach and includes how to recognize and confront fears, response-prevention exercises, coping strategies, and dealing with relapse.

Depression

R. Abrams, *When Parents Die* (London: Letts, 1993).
This is a sensitive self-help book based on the author's own loss; aimed at young people whose parents have died.

Melba Colgrove, Harold Bloomfield, and Peter McWilliams, *How to Survive the Loss of Love*, 2nd ed. (Los Angeles, CA: Prelude Press, 1991).
About a variety of losses, the book provides help in understanding loss, surviving it, healing, and growing.

K. Hill, *The Long Sleep: Young People and Suicide* (London: Virago Press, 1995).
This book was written specifically for persons who have been bereaved through suicide.

Therese Random, *How to Go On Living When Someone You Love Dies* (New York: Bantam Books, 1991).
Looks at the many different ways we grieve and the best strategies for coping with them. Very practical and easy to understand.

Dorothy Rowe, *Depression: The Way Out of Your Prison* (London: Routledge & Kegan Paul, 1983).
An award-winning book about how to become free from depression and remove the isolation that goes with it.

Averil Stedeford, *Facing Death: Parents, Family and Professionals* (London: Heinemann Medical Books, 1984).
Shows how a caring approach to the dying can be enhanced by an understanding of psychology and how the stresses can be alleviated.

William Styron, *Darkness Visible* (London: Jonathon Cape, 1993).
A personal and sensitive account of the experience of depression, written by a distinguished writer and novelist.

B. Ward, *Healing Grief: A Guide to Loss and Recovery* (London: Vermilion, 1993).
A good book to give support to those who have been bereaved.

Part Five   Mind and Body

Sleep

Jacob Empson, *Sleep and Dreaming* (London: Faber and Faber, 1989).
A clear and entertaining account of the results of research on sleep.

Michael van Straten, *Don't Just Lie There* (London: Kyle Cathie Ltd, 1990).
A sensible and well-written "how to do it" guide to getting a good night's sleep.

Eating

P. J. Cooper, *Bulimia Nervosa: A Guide to Recovery* (London: Robinson Publishing, 1993).
A practical and detailed self-help manual specifically for persons suffering from bulimia nervosa.

Christopher Fairburn, *Overcoming Binge Eating* (New York: Guilford Press, 1995).
This book provides both a review of the facts and a self-help program for overcoming binge eating.

J. Moorey, *Living with Anorexia and Bulimia* (Manchester: Manchester University Press, UK, 1992).
A useful book for parents, friends, and relatives of individuals who suffer from these eating disorders.

Geneen Roth, *When Food Is Love* (London: Judy Piatkus Publishers, Ltd., 1992).
Using her own experience as well as that of others, Geneen Roth helps others to understand and to overcome cycles of obsessive binging and dieting.

Terence J. Sandbek, *The Deadly Diet* (Oakland, CA: New Harbinger, 1993).
Specific tools and techniques from cognitive-behavior therapy for overcoming eating disorders.

Roberta Trattner Sherman and Ron A Thompson, *Bulimia: A Guide for Family and Friends* (Lexington, MA, and Toronto: Lexington Books, 1990).
Written by two psychologists, this book discusses the development of bulimia nervosa as well as its treatment.

Ulrike Schmidt and Janet Treasure, *Getting Better Bit(e) by Bit(e): A Survival Kit for Sufferers of Bulimia Nervosa and Binge Eating Disorder* (Hove, Sussex, UK: Laurence Erlbaum, 1993).
A book that concentrates on those key behavior changes needed to achieve a happier life as well as greater control over eating.

Alcohol

Beauchamp Colclough: *Tomorrow I'll Be Different: The Effective Way to Stop Drinking* (London: Viking, 1993).
A good self-help book by someone who has been abstinent for ten years.

Albert Ellis and Emmett Velton, *When AA Doesn't Work for You* (Fort Lee, NJ: Barricade Books, 1992).
An alternative view to the disease model of addiction that does not require a spiritual commitment. Emphasizes self-control and personal responsibility and provides specific self-help strategies.

Neil Kessel and Henry Walton, *Alcoholism: A Reappraisal—Its Causes, Problems and Treatment,* 2nd ed. (London: Penguin Books, 1989).
Not so much a self-help book as a good, clear source of information and an account of the evidence on which treatments are based.

So You Want to Cut Down Your Drinking? A Self-Help Guide to Sensible Drinking. The Health Education Board for Scotland, Woodburn House, Canaan Lane, Edinburgh EH10 4SG.
Sound advice, in a compact, illustrated form.

Tranquilizers

C. Haddon, *Women and Tranquillisers* (London: Sheldon Press, 1984).
Provides information about tranquilizers and the dangers of taking them for prolonged periods. Also provides information about how to devise a proper withdrawal plan.

Peter Tyrer, *How to Stop Taking Tranquillisers* (London: Sheldon Press, 1986).
How to recognize tranquilizer dependence and overcome it. Clear and easy to read.

S. Trickett, *Coming Off Tranquillisers* (Wellingborough, UK; New York: Thorsons Publishing Group, 1986).
A step-by-step guide to gradual withdrawal from tranquilizers.

Miscellaneous

Ellen Bass and Laura Davis, *The Courage to Heal,* rev. ed. (New York: Harper Perennial, 1992).
Especially for women who were abused as children, this book outlines stages of recovery and takes the reader step by step through the healing process.

Herbert Benson and Eileen Stuart, *The Wellness Book* (New York: Birch Lane Press, 1992).
Full of specific, sound advice on preventing disease and improving health; contains helpful exercises.

Annabel Broome and Helen Jellicoe, *A Self-Help Guide to Managing Pain* (London: British Psychological Society in association with Methuen, 1987).
About understanding different sorts of pain and using relaxation and stress-reduction techniques to reduce pain level.

Eliana Gil, *Outgrowing the Pain* (New York: Dell Publishing, 1983).
A brief, clear, and simple introduction to the process of recovering from being abused. Short and well illustrated.

Lenore Walker, *The Battered Woman* (New York: Harper & Row, 1979).
Very helpful in understanding the cycle of abuse that battered women experience. Contains useful self-help strategies.

Part Six The Working Mind

Alan Baddeley, *Your Memory: A User's Guide* (Harmondsworth, UK: Penguin Books, 1983).
A well-illustrated and entertaining guide both to the scientific background and practical aspects of memory.

Tony Buzan, *Use Your Head* (London: BBC Books, 1974).
A clear study and memory guide particularly good on reading skills, on the use of "mind maps" (spider diagrams) for both note taking and writing, and on a rehearsal (revision) strategy. This is a good practical guide to study methods; includes valuable advice on memory.

Andrew Northedge, *The Good Study Guide* (The Open University, Book Trade Department, Walton Hall, Milton Keynes, MK7 6AA, UK, 1990).
Aimed at individuals taking Open University courses, this practical book will be useful for anyone studying at home. It has good sections on writing essays, working with numbers, learning from radio and TV broadcasts, and techniques for taking examinations.

Richard Paul, *Critical Thinking,* 3rd ed. (Santa Rosa, CA: Foundation for Critical Thinking, 1993).
This book explains how to deal with the present-day flood of information and propaganda so as to make sense of the world and become intellectually fit.

R.H. Thouless, *Straight and Crooked Thinking: Thirty-Eight Dishonest Tricks of Debate* (London: Pan Books, 1974).
A revealing guide to the many common mistakes in thinking, which helps one recognize them in oneself and in others.

Seeking Further Information

New Harbinger Publications specialize in self-help books covering a wide variety of topics. Their emphasis is on understanding and skill building, and they convey a strong belief in the possibility of change. In order to obtain a catalog, contact them at 5674 Shattuck Avenue, Oakland, CA 94609, USA. (Fax: 510.652.5472. Telephone: 800.748.6273).

Compendium Books, 234 Camden High Street, London, Telephone: 0171 485 8944, has an excellent collection of self-help books.

Index